A-Level Year 1 & AS

Chemistry

Revising for Chemistry exams is stressful, that's for sure — even just getting your notes sorted out can leave you needing a lie down. But help is at hand...

This brilliant CGP book explains **everything you'll need to learn**, all in a straightforward style that's easy to get your head around. We've also included **exam questions** to test how ready you are for the real thing.

There's even a free Online Edition you can read on your computer or tablet!

How to get your free Online Edition

Go to **cgpbooks.co.uk/extras** and enter this code...

2817 4751 9327 0336

This code only works for one person. If somebody else has used this book before you, they might have already claimed the Online Edition.

A-Level revision? It has to be CGP!

Contents

Topic 9 — Alkanes and Halogenoalkanes

Topic 10 — Alkenes and Alcohols

Topic 11 — Organic Analysis

Topic 12 — Organic Synthesis

Published by CGP

Editors:
Katherine Faudemer, Emily Howe and Sophie Scott

Contributors:
Mike Bossart, Vikki Cunningham, Ian Davis, John Duffy, Max Fishel, Paddy Gannon, Emma Grimwood, Richard Harwood, Lucy Muncaster, Derek Swain and Chris Workman.

ISBN: 978 1 78294 289 4

With thanks to Katie Braid and Mary Falkner for the proofreading.
With thanks to Jan Greenway for the copyright research.

With thanks to Chris Priest / Science Photo Library for permission to reproduce the photograph used on page 94.

With thanks to NASA / Goddard Space Flight Center / Science Photo Library for permission to reproduce the photograph used on page 128.

Cover Photo **Laguna Design**/Science Photo Library

Clipart from Corel®
Printed by Elanders Ltd, Newcastle upon Tyne.

Based on the classic CGP style created by Richard Parsons.

The Scientific Process

'How Science Works' is all about the scientific process — how we develop and test scientific ideas. It's what scientists do all day, every day (well except at coffee time — never come between scientists and their coffee).

Scientists Come Up with **Theories** — Then **Test Them**...

Science tries to explain **how** and **why** things happen. It's all about seeking and gaining **knowledge** about the world around us. Scientists do this by **asking** questions and **suggesting** answers and then **testing** them, to see if they're correct — this is the **scientific process**.

1) **Ask** a question — make an **observation** and ask **why or how** whatever you've observed happens.
   E.g. Why does sodium chloride dissolve in water?
2) **Suggest** an answer, or part of an answer, by forming a **theory** or a **model** (a possible **explanation** of the observations or a description of what you think is happening actually happening).
   E.g. Sodium chloride is made up of charged particles which are pulled apart by the polar water molecules.
3) Make a **prediction** or **hypothesis** — a **specific testable statement**, based on the theory, about what will happen in a test situation.
   E.g. A solution of sodium chloride will conduct electricity much better than water does.
4) Carry out **tests** — to provide **evidence** that will support the prediction or refute it.
   E.g. Measure the conductivity of water and of sodium chloride solution.

A theory is only scientific if it can be tested.

...Then They **Tell** Everyone About Their **Results**...

The results are **published** — scientists need to let others know about their work. Scientists publish their results in **scientific journals**. These are just like normal magazines, only they contain **scientific reports** (called papers) instead of the latest celebrity gossip.

1) Scientific reports are similar to the **lab write-ups** you do in school. And just as a lab write-up is **reviewed** (marked) by your teacher, reports in scientific journals undergo **peer review** before they're published.

   Scientists use standard terminology when writing their reports. This way they know that other scientists will understand them. For instance, there are internationally agreed rules for naming organic compounds, so that scientists across the world will know exactly what substance is being referred to. See page 111.
2) The report is sent out to **peers** — other scientists who are experts in the **same area**. They go through it bit by bit, examining the methods and data, and checking it's all clear and logical. When the report is approved, it's **published**. This makes sure that work published in scientific journals is of a **good standard**.
3) But peer review **can't guarantee** the science is **correct** — other scientists still need to **reproduce** it.
4) Sometimes **mistakes** are made and bad work is published. Peer review **isn't perfect** but it's probably the best way for scientists to self-regulate their work and to publish **quality reports**.

...Then **Other Scientists** Will **Test** the Theory Too

1) Other scientists read the published theories and results, and try to **test the theory** themselves. This involves:
   - Repeating the **exact same experiments**.
   - Using the theory to make **new predictions** and then testing them with **new experiments**.
2) If all the experiments in the world provide evidence to back it up, the theory is thought of as **scientific 'fact'**.
3) If **new evidence** comes to light that **conflicts** with the current evidence the theory is questioned all over again. More rounds of **testing** will be carried out to try to find out where the theory **falls down**.

This is how the **scientific process works** — **evidence** supports a theory, loads of other scientists read it and test it for themselves, eventually all the scientists in the world **agree** with it and then bingo, you get to **learn** it.

This is how scientists arrived at the structure of the atom (see p.16-17) — and how they came to the conclusion that electrons are arranged in shells and orbitals. As is often the case, it took years and years for these models to be developed and accepted.

The Scientific Process

If the **Evidence** Supports a Theory, It's **Accepted — for Now**

Our currently accepted theories have survived this **'trial by evidence'**. They've been tested **over and over again** and each time the results have backed them up. **BUT**, and this is a big but (teehee), they never become totally indisputable fact. Scientific **breakthroughs** or **advances** could provide new ways to question and test the theory, which could lead to **changes and challenges** to it. Then the testing starts all over again...

And this, my friend, is the **tentative nature of scientific knowledge** — it's always **changing** and **evolving**.

For example, when CFCs were first used in fridges in the 1930s, scientists thought they were problem-free — there was no evidence to say otherwise. It was decades before anyone found out that CFCs were actually making a massive hole in the ozone layer (see p.128).

Evidence Comes From **Lab Experiments**...

1) Results from **controlled experiments** in **laboratories** are **great**.
2) A lab is the easiest place to **control variables** so that they're all **kept constant** (except for the one you're investigating).
3) This means you can draw meaningful **conclusions**.

For example, if you're investigating how temperature affects the rate of a reaction, you need to keep everything but the temperature constant, e.g. the pH of the solution, the concentration of the solution, etc.

...But You **Can't** Always do a Lab Experiment

There are things you **can't** study in a lab. And outside the lab controlling the variables is tricky, if not impossible.

- *Are increasing CO_2 emissions causing climate change?*
  There are other variables which may have an effect, such as changes in solar activity. You can't easily rule out every possibility. Also, climate change is a very **gradual process**. Scientists won't be able to tell if their predictions are correct for donkey's years.
- *Does drinking chlorinated tap water increase the risk of developing certain cancers?*
  There are always differences between groups of people. The best you can do is to have a **well-designed study** using **matched groups — choose two groups** of people (those who drink tap water and those who don't) which are **as similar as possible** (same mix of ages, same mix of diets etc). But you still can't rule out every possibility. Taking new-born identical twins and treating them identically, except for making one drink gallons of tap water and the other only pure water, might be a fairer test, but it would present huge **ethical problems**.

Samantha thought her study was very well designed — especially the fitted bookshelf.

Science Helps to Inform **Decision-Making**

Lots of scientific work eventually leads to **important discoveries** that **could** benefit humankind — but there are often **risks** attached (and almost always **financial costs**). **Society** (that's you, me and everyone else) must weigh up the information in order to **make decisions** — about the way we live, what we eat, what we drive, and so on. Information is also be used by **politicians** to devise policies and laws.

- **Chlorine** is added to water in **small quantities** to disinfect it. Some studies link drinking chlorinated water with certain types of cancer (see page 99). But the risks from drinking water contaminated by nasty bacteria are far, far greater. There are other ways to get rid of bacteria in water, but they're heaps **more expensive**.
- Scientific advances mean that **non-polluting hydrogen-fuelled cars** can be made. They're better for the environment, but are really expensive. And it'd cost a lot to adapt filling stations to store hydrogen.
- Pharmaceutical drugs are really expensive to develop, and drug companies want to make money. So they put most of their efforts into developing drugs that they can sell for a good price. Society has to consider the **cost** of buying new drugs — the **NHS** can't afford the most expensive drugs without **sacrificing** something else.

So there you have it — how science works...

Hopefully these pages have given you a nice intro to how science works. When you feel like you've got it sussed, it's time to move on to the really good stuff — the chemistry. Bet you can't wait... it's going to be a heck of a ride.

Planning Experiments

Chemistry's not all learning from books and listening to the teacher. No siree. You'll also get to try your hand at some experiments, with titrations being a particular treat to look forward to. Here's how to plan the perfect experiment...

Make Sure You **Plan** Your **Experiment Carefully**

It's really important to plan an experiment well if you want to get accurate and precise results. Here's how to go about it...

1) Work out the **aim** of the experiment — what are you trying to find out?
2) Identify the **independent**, **dependent** and other **variables** (see below).
3) Decide what **data** to collect.
4) Select **appropriate equipment** which will give you accurate results.
5) Make a **risk assessment** and plan any safety precautions.
6) Write out a **detailed method**.
7) Carry out **tests** — to gather **evidence** to address the aim of your experiment.

Have a peek at page 12 to find out more about accurate and precise results.

Make it a **Fair Test** — Control your **Variables**

You probably know this all off by heart but it's easy to get mixed up sometimes. So here's a quick recap:

Variable — A variable is a **quantity** that has the **potential to change**, e.g. mass. There are two types of variable commonly referred to in experiments:

- **Independent variable** — the thing that you **change** in an experiment.
- **Dependent variable** — the thing that you **measure** in an experiment.

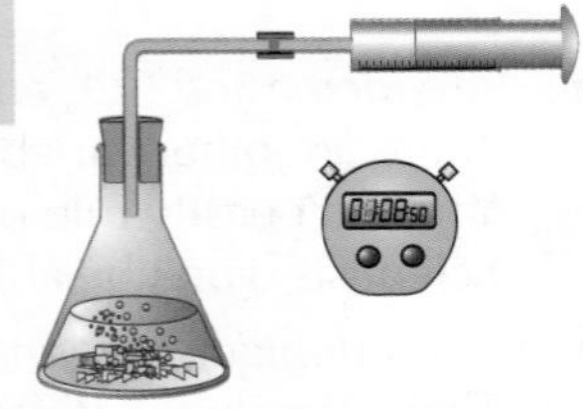

As well as the independent and dependent variables, you need to think of all the other variables in your experiment and plan ways to keep each of those the same.

For example, if you're investigating the effect of **temperature** on rate of reaction using the apparatus on the right, the variables will be:

Independent variable	Temperature
Dependent variable	Volume of gas produced — you can measure this by collecting it in a gas syringe.
Other variables	E.g. concentration and volume of solutions, mass of solids, pressure, the presence of a catalyst and the surface area of any solid reactants.

You MUST control your other variables so they're always the same.

Collect the Appropriate **Data**

Experiments always involve collecting **data** and you need to decide what data to collect.

1) There are different types of data, so it helps to know what they are:

- **Discrete** — you get discrete data by **counting**. E.g. the number of bubbles produced in a reaction.
- **Continuous** — a continuous variable can have **any value** on a scale. For example, the volume of gas produced. You can never measure the exact value of a continuous variable.
- **Categoric** — a categoric variable has values that can be sorted into **categories**. For example, the colours of solutions might be blue, red and green.

2) You need to make sure the data you collect is appropriate for your experiment.

Example: A student suggests measuring the rate of the following reaction by observing how conductivity changes over the course of the reaction:

$NaOH_{(aq)} + CH_3CH_2Br_{(l)} \rightarrow CH_3CH_2OH_{(l)} + NaBr_{(aq)}$

Suggest what is wrong with the student's method, and how it could be improved.

You couldn't collect data about how the **conductivity changes** over the course of the reaction, because there are **salts** in both the reactants and the products.

Instead you could use a **pH meter** to measure how the **pH changes** from basic (due to sodium hydroxide) to neutral.

Planning Experiments

Choose **Appropriate** Equipment — Think about **Size** and **Sensitivity**

Selecting the right apparatus may sound easy but it's something you need to think carefully about.

1) The equipment has to be **appropriate** for the specific experiment.

   For example, if you want to measure the volume of gas produced in a reaction, you need to make sure you use apparatus which will collect the gas, without letting any escape.

2) The equipment needs to be the right **size**.

   For example, if you're using a gas syringe to collect a gas, it needs to be big enough to collect **all** the gas produced during the experiment, or the plunger will just fall out the end. You might need to do some **calculations** to work out what size of syringe to use.

3) The equipment needs to be the right level of **sensitivity**.

   If you want to measure 10 cm^3 of a liquid, it will be more accurate to use a measuring cylinder that is graduated to the nearest 0.5 cm^3 than to the nearest 1 cm^3. A burette would be most accurate though (they can measure to the nearest 0.1 cm^3).

Risk Assessments Help You to Work **Safely**

1) When you're planning an experiment, you need to carry out a **risk assessment**. To do this, you need to identify:
   - All the **dangers** in the experiment, e.g. any hazardous compounds or naked flames.
   - **Who** is at **risk** from these dangers.
   - What can be done to **reduce the risk**, such as wearing goggles or working in a fume cupboard.
2) You need to make sure you're working **ethically** too. This is most important if there are other people or animals involved. You have to put their welfare first.

Methods Must be **Clear** and **Detailed**

When **writing** or **evaluating** a method, you need to think about all of the things on these two pages. The method must be **clear** and **detailed** enough for anyone to follow — it's important that **other people** can recreate your experiment and get the **same** results. Make sure your method includes:

1) All **substances** and **quantities** to be used.
2) How to **control** variables.
3) The exact **apparatus** needed (a diagram is usually helpful to show the set up).
4) Any **safety precautions** that should be taken.
5) What **data** to collect and **how** to collect it.

Practice Questions

Q1 Briefly outline the steps involved in planning an experiment.

Q2 What three things should you consider when choosing the best apparatus for your experiment?

Exam Question

Q1 A student carries out an experiment to investigate how the rate of the following reaction changes with the concentration of hydrochloric acid: $Mg_{(s)} + 2HCl_{(aq)} \rightarrow MgCl_{2\,(aq)} + H_{2\,(g)}$

The student decides to measure how the pH changes over time using litmus paper.
Explain why this method of measuring pH is unsuitable, and suggest an alternative method. [2 marks]

Revision time — independent variable. Exam mark — dependent variable...

I wouldn't advise you to investigate the effect of revision on exam marks. Just trust me — more revision = better marks. But if you were to investigate it, there are all manner of variables that you'd need to control. The amount of sleep you had the night before, how much coffee you drank in the morning, your level of panic on entering the exam hall...

Practical Techniques

The way you carry out your experiment is important, so here's a nice round up of some of the techniques chemists use all the time. You've probably met some of them before, which should hopefully make it all a bit easier. Hopefully... :-)

Results Should be ***Precise***

1) **Precise** results are **repeatable** and **reproducible**. **Repeatable** means that if the **same** person does the experiment again using the same methods and equipment, they'll get the same results. **Reproducible** means that if someone **else** does the experiment, or a different **method** or piece of **equipment** is used, the results will still be the same.
2) To make sure your results are precise, you need to **minimise** any **errors** that might sneak into your data. This includes:
   - using **apparatus** and **techniques** correctly,
   - taking **measurements** correctly,
   - **repeating** your experiments and calculating a **mean**.

Make Sure You ***Measure*** Substances ***Correctly***

The **state** (solid, liquid or gas) that your substance is in will determine **how** you decide to measure it.

1) You weigh **solids** using a **balance**. Here are a couple of things to look out for:
   - Put the container you are weighing your substance into on the balance, and make sure the balance is set to exactly zero before you start weighing out your substance.
   - If you need to **transfer** the solid into another container, make sure that it's **all** transferred. For example, if you're making up a standard solution you could wash any remaining solid into the new container using the solvent. Or, you could **reweigh** the weighing container after you've transferred the solid so you can work out **exactly** how much you added to your experiment.
2) There are a few methods you might use to measure the volume of a liquid. Whichever method you use, always read the volume from the **bottom** of the **meniscus** (the curved upper surface of the liquid) when it's at **eye level**.

Read volume from here — the bottom of the meniscus.

Pipettes are long, narrow tubes that are used to **suck up** an **accurate volume** of liquid and transfer it to another container. They are often **calibrated** to allow for the fact that the last drop of liquid stays in the pipette when the liquid is ejected. This reduces transfer errors.

Burettes measure from **top** to **bottom** (so when they are **full**, the scale reads **zero**). They have a **tap** at the bottom which you can use to release the liquid into another container (you can even release it drop by drop). To use a burette, take an **initial reading**, and once you've released as much liquid as you want, take a **final reading**. The **difference** between the readings tells you how much liquid you used.

Burettes are used a lot for titrations. There's loads more about titrations on pages 40-42.

Volumetric flasks allow you to **accurately** measure a very **specific** volume of liquid. They come in various **sizes** (e.g. 100 cm^3, 250 cm^3) and there's a **line** on the neck that marks the volume that they measure. They're used to make **accurate dilutions** and **standard solutions**. To use them, first measure out and add the liquid or solid that is being diluted or dissolved. Rinse out the measuring vessel into the volumetric flask with a little solvent to make sure everything's been transferred. Then fill the flask with solvent to the **bottom** of the neck. Fill the neck **drop by drop** until the bottom of the meniscus is **level** with the line.

500 cm^3

A standard solution is a solution with a precisely known concentration. You can find out how they're made and used on page 40.

3) Gases can be measured with a **gas syringe**. They should be measured at **room temperature** and **pressure** as the **volume** of a gas **changes** with temperature and pressure. Before you use the syringe, you should make sure it's completely **sealed** and that the **plunger** moves **smoothly**.

Once you've measured a quantity of a substance you need to be careful you don't **lose** any. In particular, think about how to minimise losses as you transfer it from the measuring equipment to the reaction container.

Practical Techniques

Measure **Temperature** Accurately

I'm sure you've heard this before, so I'll be quick... You can use a **thermometer** or a **temperature probe** to measure the temperature of a substance (a temperature probe is like a thermometer but it will always have a **digital display**).

- Make sure the **bulb** of your thermometer or temperature probe is **completely submerged** in any mixture you're measuring.
- Wait for the temperature to **stabilise** before you take an initial reading
- If you're using a thermometer with a scale, read off your measurement at **eye level** to make sure it's accurate.

Qualitative Tests Can be Harder to **Reproduce**

Qualitative tests measure **physical qualities** (e.g. colour) while **quantitative** tests measure numerical data, (e.g. mass).

So if you carried out a reaction and noticed that heat was produced, this would be a **qualitative** observation. If you **measured** the temperature change with a thermometer, this would be **quantitative**.

Qualitative tests can be harder to **reproduce** because they're often **subjective** (based on **opinion**), such as describing the **colour** or **cloudiness** of a solution. There are ways to **reduce** the subjectivity of qualitative results though. For example:

- If you're looking for a **colour change**, put a **white background** behind your reaction container.
- If you're looking for a **precipitate** to form, mark an **X** on a piece of paper and place it under the reaction container. Your solution is 'cloudy' when you can **no longer see** the X.

There are Specific Techniques for Synthesising **Organic Compounds**

Synthesis is used to **make** one **organic compound** from another. There are a number of techniques that chemists use to help them make and purify their products:

These techniques are covered in more detail on pages 154-157.

1) **Reflux** — heating a reaction mixture in a flask fitted with a **condenser** so that any materials that **evaporate**, condense and drip back into the mixture.
2) **Distillation** — gently heating a mixture so that the compounds evaporate off in order of **increasing boiling point** and can be collected separately. This can be done **during** a reaction to collect a product as it forms, or **after** the reaction is **finished** to purify the mixture.
3) **Removing water soluble impurities** — adding **water** to an organic mixture in a separating funnel. Any **water soluble impurities** move out of the organic layer and dissolve in the aqueous layer. The layers have different **densities** so are easy to separate.

Practice Questions

Q1 Give three ways that you could improve the precision of an experiment.

Q2 How would you measure out a desired quantity of a solid? And a gas?

Q3 How could you make the results of an experiment measuring time taken for a precipitate to form less subjective?

Exam Question

Q1 A student dilutes a 1 mol dm^{-3} solution of sodium chloride to 0.1 mol dm^{-3} as follows:

He measures 10 cm^3 of 1 mol dm^{-3} sodium chloride solution in a pipette and puts this into a 100 cm^3 volumetric flask. He then tops up the volumetric flask with distilled water until the top of the meniscus is at 100 cm^3.

A
B
C

a) What has the student done incorrectly? What should he have done instead? [1 mark]

b) Which of the arrows in the diagram on the right indicates the level to which you should fill a volumetric flask? [1 mark]

Reflux, take it easy...

It might seem like there's a lot to do to make sure your results are accurate, but you should get lots of practice in practicals. Before long you'll be measuring temperatures and volumes with your eyes shut (metaphorically speaking).

Presenting Results

Once you've collected the data from your experiment, it's not time to stop, put your feet up and have a cup of tea — you've got some presenting to do. Results tables need converting into graphs and other pretty pictures.

*Organise Your Results in a **Table***

It's a good idea to set up a table to **record** the **results** of your experiment in. When you draw a table, make sure you **include** enough **rows** and **columns** to **record all of the data** you need. You might also need to include a column for **processing** your data (e.g. working out an average).

Make sure each **column** has a **heading** so you know what's going to be recorded where.

The **units** should be in the **column heading**, not the table itself.

Temperature (°C)	Time (s)	Volume of gas evolved (cm^3)			Average volume of gas evolved (cm^3)
		Run 1	Run 2	Run 3	
20	**10**	8.1	7.6	8.5	(8.1 + 7.6 + 8.5) ÷ 3 = 8.1
	20	17.7	19.0	20.1	(17.7 + 19.0 + 20.1) ÷ 3 = 18.9
	30	28.5	29.9	30.0	(28.5 + 29.9 + 30.0) ÷ 3 = 29.5

You'll need to repeat each test **at least three** times to check your results are **precise**.

You can find the **mean result** by **adding up** the data from each repeat and **dividing** by the number of repeats.

*Graphs: **Scatter** or **Bar** — Use the **Best Type***

When drawing graphs, the dependent variable should go on the y-axis, the independent on the x-axis.

You'll often need to make a **graph** of your results.
Graphs make your data **easier to understand** — so long as you choose the right type.

Scatter plots are great for showing how two sets of continuous data are related (or **correlated** — see page 10). Don't try to join all the points on a scatter plot — draw a straight or curved **line of best fit** to show the **trend**.

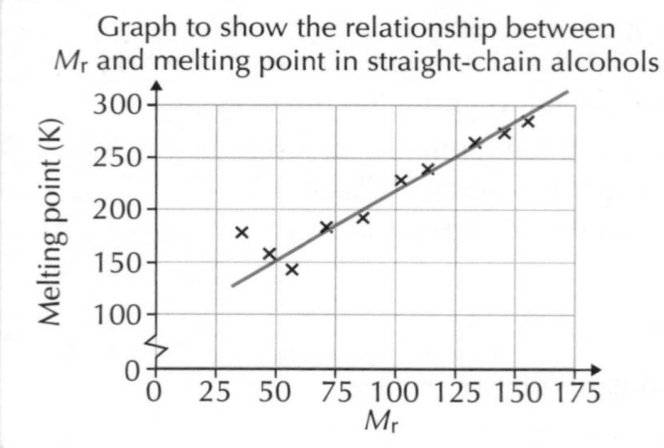

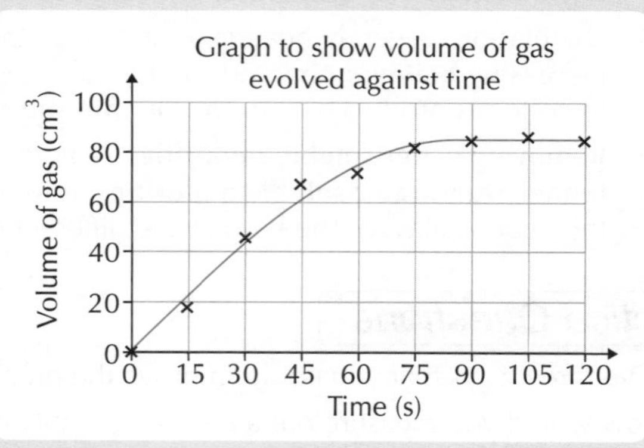

You should use a **bar chart** when one of your data sets is **categoric**. For example:

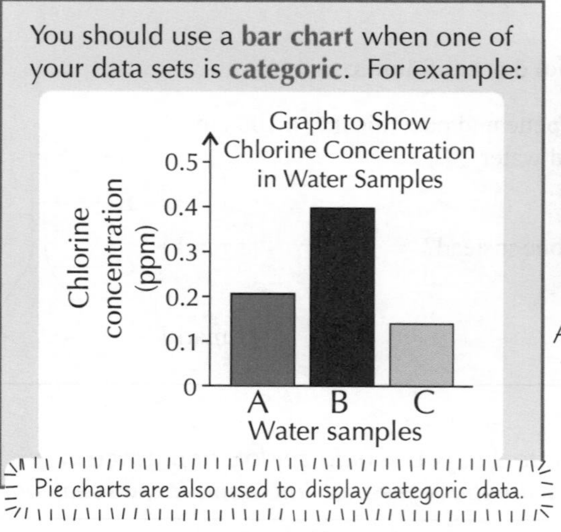

Pie charts are also used to display categoric data.

Apple and blackberry was number one on Jane's pie chart

Whatever type of graph you make, you'll ONLY get full marks if you:

- Choose a sensible **scale** — don't do a tiny graph in the corner of the paper, or massive axes where the data only takes up a tiny part of the graph.
- **Label** both **axes** — including units.
- Plot your points accurately — use a **sharp pencil**.

Sometimes you might need to work out the gradient of a graph, e.g. to work out the rate of a reaction. There are details of how to do this on pages 79-80.

Presenting Results

Don't Forget About **Units**

Units are really important — 10 g is a bit different from 10 kg, so make sure you don't forget to add them to your **tables** and **graphs**. It's often a good idea to write down the units on each line of any **calculations** you do — it makes things less confusing, particularly if you need to convert between two different units.

Here are some useful examples:

Concentration can be measured in **mol dm^{-3}** (M) and **mol cm^{-3}**.

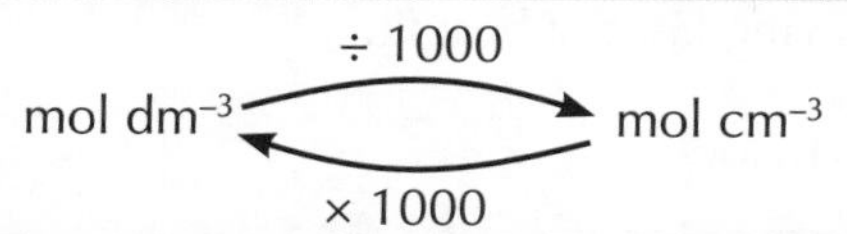

Example: Write 0.2 mol dm^{-3} in mol cm^{-3}.

To convert 0.2 mol dm^{-3} into mol cm^{-3} you divide by 1000.

0.2 mol dm^{-3} ÷ 1000 = **2 × 10^{-4} mol cm^{-3}**

Standard form is useful for writing very big or very small numbers.

Volume can be measured in **m^3**, **dm^3** and **cm^3**.

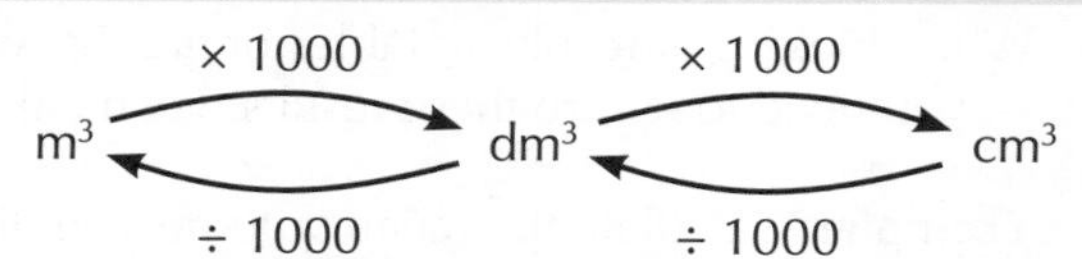

Example: Write 6 dm^3 in m^3 and cm^3.

To convert 6 dm^3 into m^3 you divide by 1000.

6 dm^3 ÷ 1000 = 0.006 m^3 = **6 × 10^{-3} m^3**

To convert 6 dm^3 into cm^3 you multiply by 1000.

6 dm^3 × 1000 = 6000 cm^3 = **6 × 10^3 cm^3**

Round to the **Lowest Number** of **Significant Figures**

You always need to be aware of **significant figures** when working with data.

1) The rule is the same for when doing calculations with the results from your experiment, or when doing calculations in the exam — you have to round your answer to the **lowest number of significant figures** (s.f.) given in the question.
2) It always helps to write down the number of significant figures you've rounded to after your answer — it shows you really know what you're talking about.
3) If you're converting between **standard** and **ordinary form**, you have to keep the **same number** of significant figures. For example, 0.0060 mol dm^{-3} is the same as 6.0 × 10^{-3} mol dm^{-3} — they're both given to 2 s.f..

The first significant figure of a number is the first digit that isn't a zero. The second, third and fourth significant figures follow on immediately after the first (even if they're zeros).

Example: 13.5 cm^3 of a 0.51 mol dm^{-3} solution of sodium hydroxide reacts with 1.5 mol dm^{-3} hydrochloric acid. Calculate the volume of hydrochloric acid required to neutralise the sodium hydroxide

No. of moles of NaOH: (13.5 cm^3 × 0.51 mol dm^{-3}) ÷ 1000 = 6.885 × 10^{-3} mol

Volume of HCl: (6.885 × 10^{-3}) mol × 1000 ÷ 1.5 mol dm^{-3} = 4.59 cm^3 = **4.6 cm^3 (2 s.f.)**

3 s.f. (13.5) — 2 s.f. (0.51)

You don't need to round intermediate answers. Rounding too early will make your final answer less accurate.

Final answer should be rounded to 2 s.f.

Make sure all your units match when you're doing calculations.

Practice Questions

Q1 Why is it always a good idea to repeat your experiments?

Q2 How would you convert an answer from m^3 to dm^3?

Q3 How do you decide how many significant figures you should round your answer to?

Exam Question

Q1 10 cm^3 sodium hydroxide solution is titrated with 0.50 mol dm^{-3} hydrochloric acid to find its concentration. The titration is repeated three times and the volumes of hydrochloric acid used are: 7.30 cm^3, 7.25 cm^3, 7.25 cm^3.

a) What is the mean volume of hydrochloric acid recorded in dm^3? [1 mark]

b) What is the concentration of hydrochloric acid in mol cm^{-3}? [1 mark]

Significant figures — a result of far too many cream cakes...

When you draw graphs, always be careful to get your axes round the right way. The thing you've been changing (the independent variable) goes on the x-axis, and the thing you've been measuring (the dependent variable) is on the y-axis.

Analysing Results

You're not quite finished yet... there's still time to look at your results and try and make sense of them. Graphs can help you to see patterns but don't try and read too much in to them — they won't tell you what grade you're going to get.

Watch Out For **Anomalous** Results

1) Anomalous results are ones that **don't fit** in with the other values and are likely to be wrong.
2) They're often due to **random errors**, e.g. if a drop in a titration is too big and shoots past the end point, or if a syringe plunger gets stuck whilst collecting gas produced in a reaction.
3) When looking at results in tables or graphs, you always need to look to see if there are any anomalies — you need to **ignore** these results when calculating means or drawing lines of best fit.

There's more about random errors on page 13.

Example: Calculate the mean volume from the results in the table below.

Titration Number	1	2	3	4
Titre Volume (cm³)	15.20	15.30	15.25	15.50

Titre 4 isn't **concordant** (doesn't match) the other results so you need to ignore it and just use the other three:
$\frac{15.20 + 15.30 + 15.25}{3}$ = **15.25 cm³**

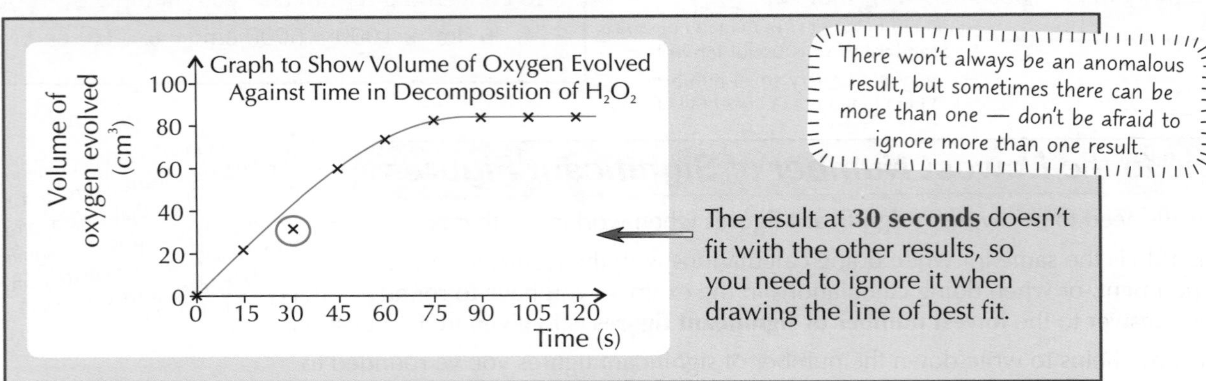
Graph to Show Volume of Oxygen Evolved Against Time in Decomposition of H_2O_2
Volume of oxygen evolved (cm³)
100
80
60
40
20
0
0 15 30 45 60 75 90 105 120
Time (s)
There won't always be an anomalous result, but sometimes there can be more than one — don't be afraid to ignore more than one result.
The result at **30 seconds** doesn't fit with the other results, so you need to ignore it when drawing the line of best fit.

Scatter Graphs Show The **Relationship** Between Variables

Correlation describes the **relationship** between two variables — the independent one and the dependent one. Data can show:

1. **Positive correlation**
As one variable **increases** the other **increases.**

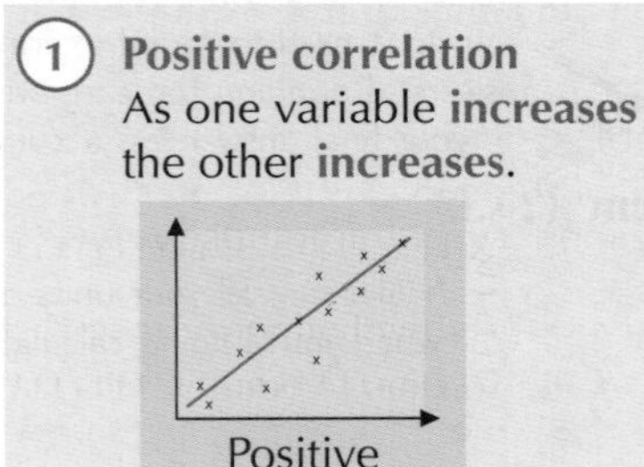
Positive

2. **Negative correlation**
As one variable **increases** the other **decreases.**

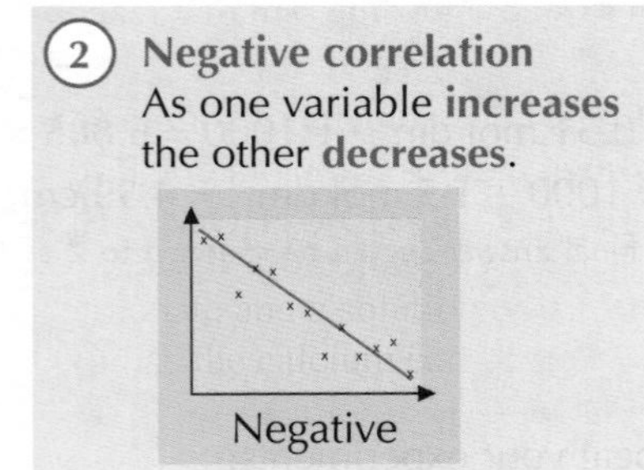
Negative

3. **No correlation**
There is **no relationship** between the two variables.

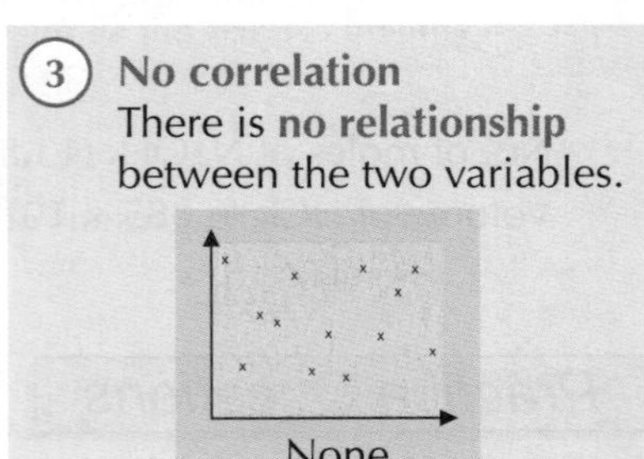
None

Correlation **Doesn't** Mean **Cause** — Don't Jump to Conclusions

1) Ideally, only **two** quantities would **ever** change in any experiment — everything else would remain **constant**.
2) But in experiments or studies outside the lab, you **can't** usually control all the variables. So even if two variables are correlated, the change in one may **not** be causing the change in the other. Both changes might be caused by a **third variable**.

Example:
Some studies have found a correlation between **drinking chlorinated tap water** and the risk of developing certain cancers. So some people argue that water shouldn't have chlorine added.
BUT it's hard to control all the **variables** between people who drink tap water and people who don't.
It could be due to other lifestyle factors.
Or, the cancer risk could be affected by something else in tap water — or by whatever the non-tap water drinkers drink instead...

Analysing Results

Don't Get **Carried Away** When Drawing Conclusions

The **data** should always **support** the conclusion. This may sound obvious but it's easy to **jump** to conclusions. Conclusions have to be **specific** — not make sweeping generalisations.

Example:

1) The rate of an enzyme-controlled reaction was measured at **10 °C, 20 °C, 30 °C, 40 °C, 50 °C** and **60 °C**. All other variables were kept constant, and the results are shown in the graph below.

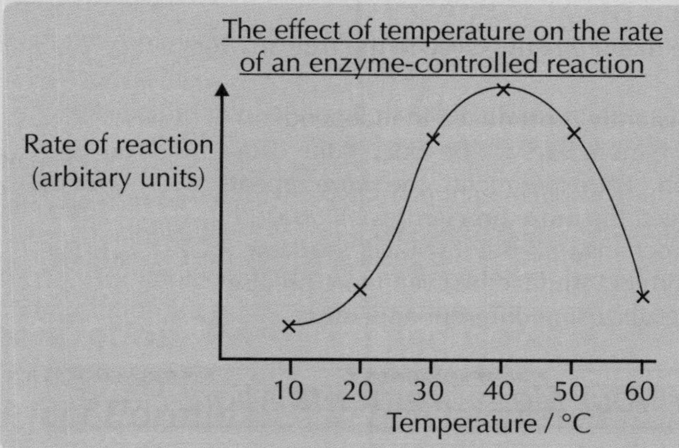

2) A science magazine **concluded** from this data that this enzyme works best at **40 °C**.
3) The data **doesn't** support this. The enzyme **could** work best at 42 °C or 47 °C but you can't tell from the data because **increases** of **10 °C** at a time were used. The rate of reaction at in-between temperatures **wasn't** measured.
4) All you know is that it's faster at **40 °C** than at any of the other temperatures tested.
5) The experiment **ONLY** gives information about this particular enzyme-controlled reaction. You can't conclude that **all** enzyme-controlled reactions happen faster at a particular temperature — only this one. And you can't say for sure that doing the experiment at, say, a different constant pressure, wouldn't give a different optimum temperature.

Practice Questions

Q1 How do you treat anomalous results when calculating averages? And when drawing lines of best fit?

Q2 What is negative correlation?

Exam Question

Q1 A student carried out an investigation to study how the rate of a reaction changed with temperature. He plotted his results on the graph shown on the right.

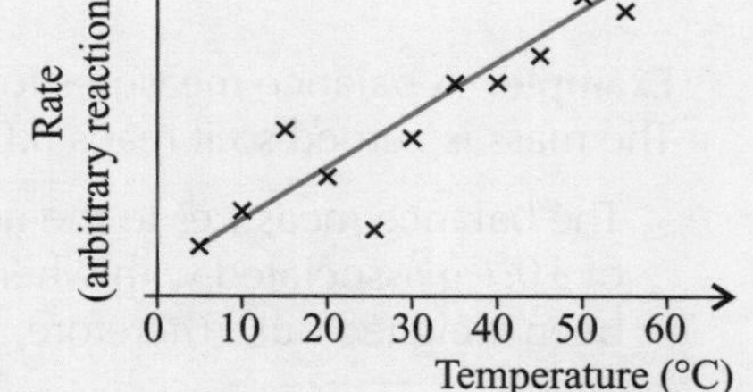

a) Give the temperatures at which any anomalous results occurred. [1 mark]

b) What type of correlation is there between temperature and rate of reaction? [1 mark]

c) Which of the following statements are appropriate conclusions to draw from this experiment?

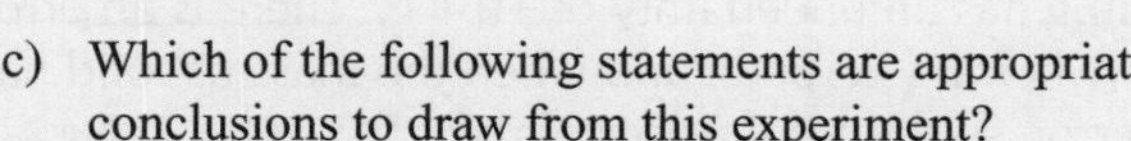

1 The rate of the reaction is highest at 60 °C.
2 Increasing the temperature causes the rate of the reaction to increase.
3 Between 5 °C and 60 °C, the rate of the reaction increased as temperature increased.

A Statements 1, 2 and 3. **B** Statements 2 and 3 only.

C Statement 3 only. **D** Statement 2 only. [1 mark]

Correlation Street — my favourite programme...

Watch out for bias when you're reading about the results of scientific studies. People often tell you what they want you to know. So a bottled water company might say that studies have shown that chlorinated tap water can cause cancer, without mentioning any of the doubts in the results. After all, they want to persuade you to buy their drinks.

Evaluating Experiments

So you've planned an experiment, collected your data (no less than three times, mind you) and put it all onto a lovely graph. Now it's time to sit back, relax and... work out everything you did wrong. That's science, I'm afraid.

You Need to Look **Critically** at Your Experiment

There are a few terms that'll come in handy when you're evaluating how convincing your results are...

1) **Valid results** — Valid results answer the **original question**. For example, if you haven't **controlled all the variables** your results won't be valid, because you won't be testing just the thing you wanted to.

2) **Accurate results** — Accurate results are those that are **really close** to the **true** answer.

3) **Precise results** — **Precise** results can be **consistently reproduced** in independent experiments. If results are reproducible they're more likely to be **true**. If the data isn't precise you **can't draw** a valid **conclusion**. For experiments, the **more repeats** you do, and the closer together the data you get, the **more precise** it is. If you get the **same result** twice, it could be the correct answer. But if you get the same result **20 times**, it's much more likely to be correct. And it'd be even more precise if everyone in the class gets about the same results using **different apparatus**.

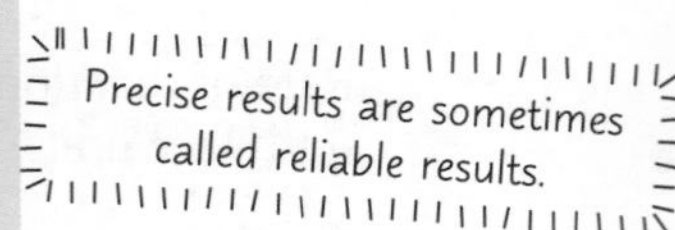
Precise results are sometimes called reliable results.

Uncertainty is the Amount of **Error** Your **Measurements** Might Have

1) Any measurements you make will have **uncertainty** in them due to the limits to the **sensitivity** of the equipment you used.
2) If you use a weighing scale that measures to the nearest 0.1 g, then the **true** weight of any substance you weigh could be up to 0.05 g **more than** or **less than** your reading. Your measurement has an **uncertainty** (or error) of ±0.05 g in either direction.
3) The ± sign tells you the **range** in which the true value could lie. The range can also be called the **margin of error**.
4) For any piece of equipment you use, the uncertainty will be **half** the **smallest increment** the equipment can measure, in either direction.
5) If you're **combining measurements**, you'll need to combine their **uncertainties**. For example, if you're calculating a temperature change by measuring an initial and a final temperature, the **total** uncertainty for the temperature change will be the uncertainties for both measurements added together.

The **Percentage Error** in a Result Should be Calculated

You can calculate the **percentage error** of a measurement using this equation:

$$\text{percentage error} = \frac{\text{uncertainty}}{\text{reading}} \times 100$$

Percentage error is sometimes called percentage uncertainty.

Example: A balance measures to the nearest 0.2 g, and is used to measure the **mass** of a substance. The mass is zeroed so it reads 0.0 g. Then, 18.4 g of a solid are weighed. Calculate the percentage uncertainty.

The balance measures to the nearest 0.2 g, so **each reading** has an uncertainty of ±0.1 g. There is an error of ±0.1 g associated with when the balance reads 0.0 g (when it's zeroed), and when the mass of solid has been weighed out. Therefore, there are two sources of error, so the **total uncertainty** is 0.1 × 2 = 0.2 g.

So for this mass measurement, percentage uncertainty = $\frac{0.2}{18.4} \times 100 = \mathbf{1.1\%}$

You Can **Minimise** the Percentage Error

1) One obvious way to **reduce errors** in your measurements is to use the most **sensitive equipment** available to you.
2) A bit of clever **planning** can also improve your results. If you measure out **5 cm³** of liquid in a measuring cylinder that has increments of 0.1 cm³ then the percentage error is (0.05 ÷ 5) × 100 = **1%**.
   But if you measure **10 cm³** of liquid in the same measuring cylinder the percentage error is (0.05 ÷ 10) × 100 = **0.5%**. Hey presto — you've just halved the percentage error.
   So the percentage error can be reduced by planning an experiment so you use a **larger volume** of liquid.
3) The general principle is that the **smaller** the measurement, the **larger** the percentage error.

Evaluating Experiments

Errors Can Be **Systematic** or **Random**

This should be a photo of a scientist. I don't know what happened — it's a random error...

1) **Systematic errors** are the same every time you repeat the experiment. They may be caused by the **set-up** or **equipment** you used. For example, if the 10.00 cm^3 pipette you used to measure out a sample for titration actually only measured 9.95 cm^3, your sample would have been about 0.05 cm^3 too small **every time** you repeated the experiment.
2) **Random errors** vary — they're what make the results a bit **different** each time you repeat an experiment. The errors when you make a reading from a burette are random. You have to estimate or round the level when it's between two marks — so sometimes your figure will be **above** the real one, and sometimes it will be **below**.
3) **Repeating an experiment** and finding the mean of your results helps to deal with **random errors**. The results that are a bit high will be **cancelled out** by the ones that are a bit low. So your results will be more **precise** (reliable). But repeating your results won't get rid of any **systematic errors**, so your results won't get more **accurate**.

Think About How the Experiment Could Be **Improved**

In your evaluation you need to think about anything that you could have done differently to improve your results. Here are some things to think about...

1) **Whether your method gives you valid results.**
   - Will the data you collected answer the question your experiment aimed to answer?
   - Did you control all your variables?

2) **How you could improve the accuracy of your results.**
   - Was the apparatus you used on an appropriate scale for your measurements?
   - Could you use more sensitive equipment to reduce the random errors and uncertainty of your results?

3) **Whether your results are precise.**
   - Did you repeat the experiment, and were the results you got similar?

Practice Questions

Q1 What's the difference between the accuracy and precision of results?

Q2 What's the uncertainty of a balance that reads to the nearest 0.1 g?

Q3 How do you calculate percentage error?

Q4 Give two ways of reducing percentage error.

Q5 How can you reduce the random errors in your experiments?

Exam Question

Q1 A student carried out an experiment to determine the temperature change in the reaction between citric acid and sodium bicarbonate using the following method:

1. Measure out 25.0 cm^3 of 1.00 mol dm^{-3} citric acid solution in a measuring cylinder and put it in a polystyrene cup.
2. Weigh out 2.10 g sodium bicarbonate and add it to the citric acid solution.
3. Place a thermometer in the solution and measure the temperature change over one minute.

a) The measuring cylinder the student uses measures to the nearest 0.5 cm^3. What is the percentage error of the student's measurement? [1 mark]

b) The student's result is different to the documented value. How could you change the method to give a more accurate measurement for the change in temperature of the complete reaction? [2 marks]

Repeat your results: Your results, your results, your results, your results...

So there you have it, folks. All you need to know about planning, carrying out and analysing experiments. Always look out for where errors could be creeping in to your experimental methods. And make sure you're confident at working out uncertainties and percentage errors. Have another read of that bit if you're feeling a bit... well... uncertain.

The Atom

This stuff about atoms and elements should be ingrained in your brain from GCSE. You do need to know it perfectly though, if you are to negotiate your way through the field of man-eating tigers that is Chemistry.

*Atoms are made up of **Protons, Neutrons** and **Electrons***

Atoms are the stuff **all** elements and compounds are made of.
They're made up of 3 types of **subatomic** particle — **protons**, **neutrons** and **electrons**.

Electrons
1) Electrons have **–1** charge.
2) They whizz around the nucleus in **orbitals**. The orbitals take up most of the **volume** of the atom.

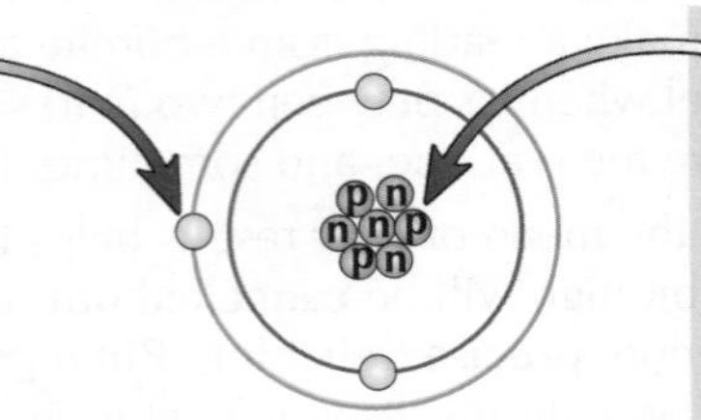

Nucleus
1) Most of the **mass** of the atom is concentrated in the nucleus.
2) The **diameter** of the nucleus is rather titchy compared to the whole atom.
3) The nucleus is where you find the **protons** and **neutrons**.

The mass and charge of these subatomic particles are **tiny**, so **relative mass** and **relative charge** are used instead.

Subatomic particle	Relative mass	Relative charge
Proton	1	+1
Neutron	1	0
Electron, e^-	$\frac{1}{2000}$	–1

The mass of an electron is negligible compared to a proton or a neutron — this means you can usually ignore it.

Nuclear Symbols** Show Numbers of **Subatomic Particles

You can figure out the **number** of protons, neutrons and electrons from the **nuclear symbol**.

$${}^{A}_{Z}\mathrm{X}$$

Mass (nucleon) number
This tells you the **total** number of **protons** and **neutrons** in the nucleus.

Element symbol

Atomic (proton) number
1) This is the number of **protons** in the nucleus — it identifies the element.
2) **All** atoms of the same element have the **same** number of protons.

Sometimes the atomic number is left out of the nuclear symbol, e.g. ^{7}Li. You don't really need it because the element's symbol tells you its value.

1) For **neutral** atoms, which have no overall charge, the number of electrons is **the same as** the number of protons.
2) The number of neutrons is just **mass number minus atomic number**, i.e. 'top minus bottom' in the nuclear symbol.

Nuclear Symbol	Atomic Number	Mass Number	Protons	Electrons	Neutrons
${}^{7}_{3}Li$	3	7	3	3	7 – 3 = 4
${}^{19}_{9}F$	9	19	9	9	19 – 9 = 10
${}^{24}_{12}Mg$	12	24	12	12	24 – 12 = 12

"Hello, I'm Newt Ron..."

*Ions have **Different** Numbers of **Protons** and **Electrons***

Negative ions have **more electrons** than protons...

F^-

The negative charge means that there's 1 more electron than there are protons. F has 9 protons (see table above), so F^- must have 10 electrons. The overall charge = +9 – 10 = –1.

...and **positive** ions have **fewer electrons** than protons.

Mg^{2+}

The 2+ charge means that there are 2 fewer electrons than there are protons. Mg has 12 protons (see table above), so Mg^{2+} must have 10 electrons. The overall charge = +12 – 10 = +2.

The Atom

Isotopes are Atoms of the Same Element with Different Numbers of Neutrons

Make sure you **learn** this definition and totally **understand** what it means —

Isotopes of an element are atoms with the same number of protons but different numbers of neutrons.

35 – 17 = 18 neutrons ← **Different** mass numbers mean different masses and different numbers of neutrons. → **37 – 17 = 20 neutrons**

$^{35}_{17}Cl$ The **atomic numbers** are the same. **Both** isotopes have 17 protons and 17 electrons. $^{37}_{17}Cl$

Chlorine-35 and chlorine-37 are examples of isotopes.

1) It's the **number** and **arrangement** of electrons that decides the **chemical properties** of an element. Isotopes have the **same configuration of electrons**, so they've got the **same** chemical properties.
2) Isotopes of an element do have slightly different **physical properties** though, such as different densities, rates of diffusion, etc. This is because **physical properties** tend to depend more on the **mass** of the atom.
3) Here's another example — naturally occurring **magnesium** consists of 3 isotopes.

^{24}Mg (79%)	^{25}Mg (10%)	^{26}Mg (11%)
12 protons	12 protons	12 protons
<u>12</u> neutrons	**<u>13</u>** neutrons	**<u>14</u>** neutrons
12 electrons	12 electrons	12 electrons

The periodic table gives the atomic number for each element. The other number isn't the mass number — it's the relative atomic mass (see page 21). They're a bit different, but you can often assume they're equal — it doesn't matter unless you're doing really accurate work.

Practice Questions

Q1 Draw a diagram showing the structure of an atom, labelling each part.

Q2 Where is the mass concentrated in an atom, and what makes up most of the volume of an atom?

Q3 Draw a table showing the relative charge and relative mass of the three subatomic particles found in atoms.

Q4 Using an example, explain the terms 'atomic number' and 'mass number'.

Q5 Define the term 'isotopes' and give examples.

Exam Questions

Q1 Hydrogen, deuterium and tritium are all isotopes of each other.

a) Identify one similarity and one difference between these isotopes. [2 marks]

b) Deuterium can be written as $^{2}_{1}H$. Determine the number of protons, neutrons and electrons in a deuterium atom. [1 mark]

c) Write the nuclear symbol for tritium, given that it has 2 neutrons. [1 mark]

Q2 This question relates to the atoms or ions A to D: **A** $^{32}_{16}S^{2-}$ **B** $^{40}_{18}Ar$ **C** $^{30}_{16}S$ **D** $^{42}_{20}Ca$

a) Identify the similarity for each of the following pairs, justifying your answer in each case.

i) A and B. [1 mark]

ii) A and C. [1 mark]

iii) B and D. [1 mark]

b) Which two of the atoms or ions are isotopes of each other? Explain your reasoning. [2 marks]

Got it learned yet? — Isotope so...

This is a nice page to ease you into things. Remember that positive ions have fewer electrons than protons, and negative ions have more electrons than protons. Get that straight in your mind or you'll end up in a right mess. There's nowt too hard about isotopes neither. They're just the same element with different numbers of neutrons.

Atomic Models

Things ain't how they used to be, you know. Take atomic structure, for starters.

The **Accepted Model** of the **Atom** Has **Changed** Throughout History

The model of the atom on page 14 is one of the currently **accepted** ones.
In the past, completely different models were accepted, because they fitted the evidence available at the time.

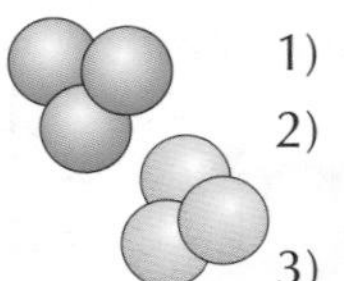

1) Some **ancient Greeks** thought that all matter was made from **indivisible particles.**
2) At the start of the 19th century John Dalton described atoms as **solid spheres**, and said that different spheres made up the different elements.
3) But as scientists did more experiments, our currently accepted models began to emerge, with modifications or refinements being made to take account of new evidence.

The Greek word atomos means 'uncuttable'.

Experimental Evidence Showed that Atoms **Weren't Solid Spheres**

In 1897 J J Thomson did a whole series of experiments and concluded that atoms **weren't** solid and indivisible.

1) His measurements of **charge** and **mass** showed that an atom must contain even smaller, negatively charged particles. He called these particles 'corpuscles' — we call them **electrons.**
2) The 'solid sphere' idea of atomic structure had to be changed. The new model was known as the '**plum pudding model**' — a positively charged sphere with negative electrons embedded in it.

positively charged 'pudding'
delicious pudding

Rutherford Showed that the **Plum Pudding** Model Was **Wrong**

1) In 1909 Ernest Rutherford and his students Hans Geiger and Ernest Marsden conducted the famous **Geiger-Marsden experiment**. They fired **alpha particles** (which are positively charged) at an extremely thin sheet of gold.
2) From the plum pudding model, they were expecting **most** of the alpha particles to be deflected **very slightly** by the positive 'pudding' that made up most of an atom.
3) In fact, most of the alpha particles passed **straight through** the gold atoms, and a very small number were deflected **backwards** (through more than 90°). This showed that the plum pudding model **couldn't be right**.
4) So Rutherford came up with a model that **could** explain this new evidence — the **nuclear model** of the atom:

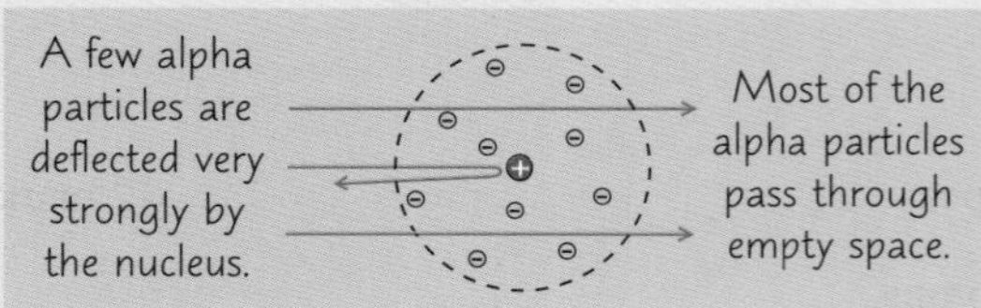
A few alpha particles are deflected very strongly by the nucleus.
Most of the alpha particles pass through empty space.

1) There is a **tiny, positively charged nucleus** at the centre of the atom, where most of the atom's mass is concentrated.
2) The nucleus is surrounded by a **'cloud'** of freely orbiting **negative electrons.**
3) Most of the atom is **empty space.**

Rutherford's **Nuclear Model** Was **Modified** Several Times

Rutherford's model seemed pretty convincing, but (there's always a but)... the scientists of the day didn't just say, "Well done Ernest old chap, you've got it", then all move to Patagonia to farm goats. No, they stuck at their experiments, wanting to be sure of the truth. (And it's just conceivable they wanted some fame and fortune too.)

1) Henry Moseley discovered that the charge of the nucleus **increased** from one element to another in units of one.
2) This led Rutherford to investigate the nucleus further. He finally discovered that it contained **positively charged** particles that he called **protons**. The charges of the nuclei of different atoms could then be explained — the atoms of **different elements** have a **different number of protons** in their nucleus.
3) There was still one problem with the model — the nuclei of atoms were **heavier** than they would be if they just contained protons. Rutherford predicted that there were other particles in the nucleus, that had **mass but no charge** — and the **neutron** was eventually discovered by James Chadwick.

This is nearly always the way scientific knowledge develops — **new evidence** prompts people to come up with **new, improved ideas.** Then other people go through each new, improved idea with a fine-tooth comb as well — modern '**peer review**' (see page 2) is part of this process.

Atomic Models

The **Bohr Model** Was a Further Improvement

1) Scientists realised that electrons in a '**cloud**' around the nucleus of an atom would **spiral down** into the nucleus, causing the atom to **collapse**. Niels Bohr proposed a new model of the atom with four basic principles:

- Electrons can only exist in **fixed orbits**, or **shells**, and not anywhere in between.
- Each shell has a **fixed energy**.
- When an electron moves between shells **electromagnetic radiation** is **emitted** or **absorbed**.
- Because the energy of shells is fixed, the radiation will have a **fixed frequency**.

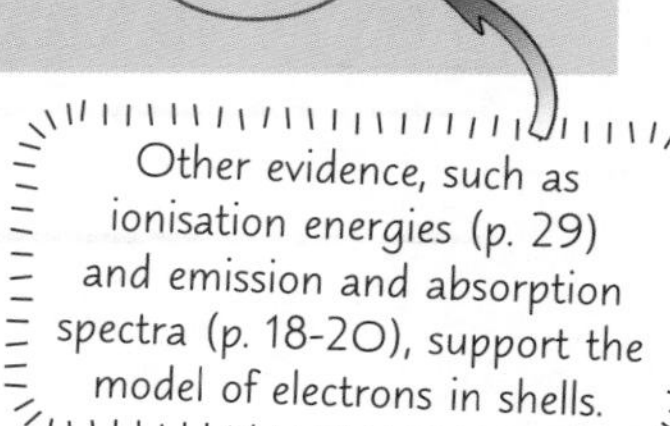

2) The frequencies of radiation emitted and absorbed by atoms were already known from experiments. The Bohr model fitted these observations — it looked good.
3) The Bohr model also explained why some elements (the noble gases) are **inert**. It said that the shells of an atom can only hold **fixed numbers of electrons**, and that an element's reactivity is due to its electrons. When an atom has **full shells** of electrons it is **stable** and does not react.

Other evidence, such as ionisation energies (p. 29) and emission and absorption spectra (p. 18-20), support the model of electrons in shells.

There's **More Than One** Model of Atomic Structure in Use Today

1) We now know that the Bohr model is **not perfect** — but it's still widely used to describe atoms because it's simple and explains many **observations** from experiments, like bonding and ionisation energy trends.
2) The most accurate model we have today involves complicated quantum mechanics. Basically, you can never **know** where an electron is or which direction it's going in at any moment, but you can say **how likely** it is to be at any particular point in the atom.
3) This model might be **more accurate**, but it's a lot harder to get your head round and visualise. It **does** explain some observations that can't be accounted for by the Bohr model though. So scientists use whichever model is most relevant to whatever they're investigating.

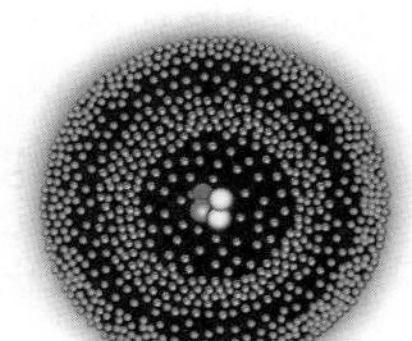

This picture shows the quantum model of an atom with two shells of electrons. The denser the dots, the more likely an electron is to be there.

Practice Questions

Q1 What particle did J J Thomson discover?

Q2 Describe the model of the atom that was adopted because of Thomson's work.

Q3 Who developed the 'nuclear' model of the atom? What evidence did they have for it?

Exam Question

Q1 Scientists theories are constantly being revised in the light of new evidence. New theories are accepted because they have been successfully tested by experiments or because they help to explain certain observations.

a) Niels Bohr thought that the model of the atom proposed by Ernest Rutherford did not describe the electrons in an atom correctly. Why did he think this and how was his model of the atom different from Rutherford's? [2 marks]

b) According to the Bohr model of the atom, what happens when electrons in an atom move from one shell to another? [1 mark]

c) How did the Bohr model explain the lack of reactivity of the noble gases? [2 marks]

These models are tiny — even smaller than size zero, I reckon...

The process of developing a model to fit the evidence available, looking for more evidence to show if it's correct or not, then revising the model if necessary is really important. It happens with all new scientific ideas. Remember, scientific 'facts' are only accepted as true because no one's proved yet that they aren't. It might all be bunkum.

Atomic Spectra and Nuclear Radiation

So, on to the patterns electrons make when they absorb and emit energy. Yep, they don't sit still these electrons...

Electromagnetic Spectrum — the range of Electromagnetic Radiation

1) Electromagnetic radiation is **energy** that's transmitted as waves, with a **spectrum** of different frequencies.
2) Along the electromagnetic spectrum, the radiation increases in **frequency** and decreases in **wavelength**.
3) This is the electromagnetic spectrum:

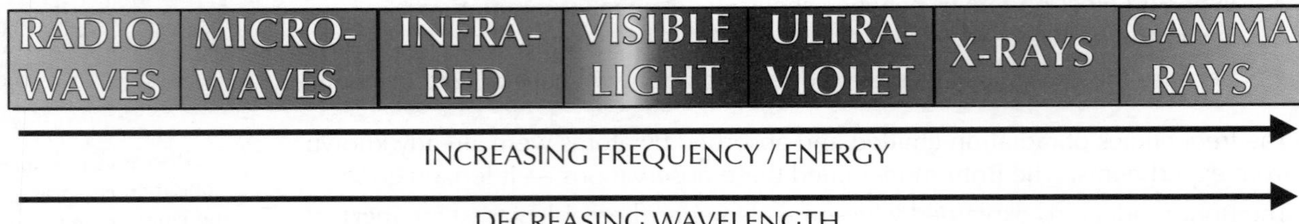

Electrons Absorb or Release Energy in Fixed Amounts

1) Electron shells are sometimes called **energy levels** (see page 26).
2) Atoms in their **ground state** have all their electrons at their **lowest** possible energy levels.
3) If an atom's electrons **take in energy** from their surroundings they can move to **higher energy levels**, further from the nucleus. At higher energy levels, electrons are said to be **excited**. (More excited than you right now, I'll bet.)
4) Electrons can also **release energy** by dropping from a higher energy level down to a **lower energy level**.
5) The energy levels all have **certain fixed values** — they're **discrete**. Electrons can jump from one energy level to another by **absorbing or releasing** a fixed amount of energy.

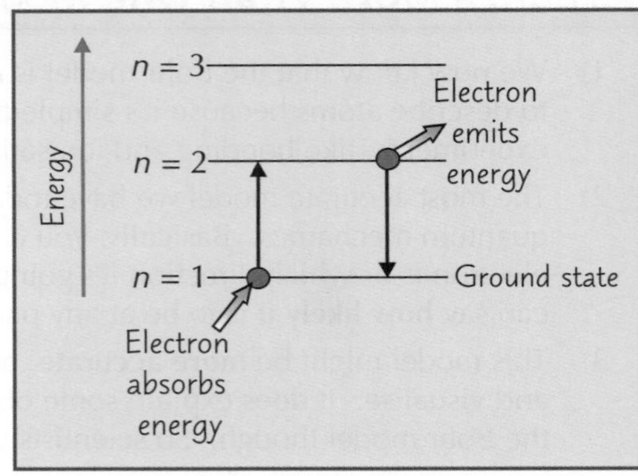

Transition Between Energy Levels Produces Line Spectra

When electrons move between energy levels, they can produce two types of line spectra — **absorption spectra** and **emission spectra**.

Absorption Spectra — Made Up of Dark Lines

1) Energy is related to **frequency** (see next page). So when **electromagnetic radiation** is passed through a gaseous element, the electrons only absorb **certain frequencies**, corresponding to **differences between the energy levels**.
2) That means the radiation passing through has certain frequencies missing. These frequencies correspond to the differences between the energy levels. A spectrum of this radiation is called an **atomic absorption spectrum**.
3) The missing frequencies show up as **dark lines** on a coloured background.

Absorption Spectrum

Emission Spectra — Made Up of Bright Lines

1) When electrons **drop** to lower energy levels, they **give out** certain amounts of energy. This produces lines in the spectrum too — but this time it's called an **emission spectrum**. For any particular element, the frequencies in an emission spectrum are the **same** as those missing in the absorption spectrum (the patterns are just opposites of each other).
2) Each element has a **different** electron arrangement, so the frequencies of radiation absorbed and emitted are different. This means the **spectrum** for each element is unique.

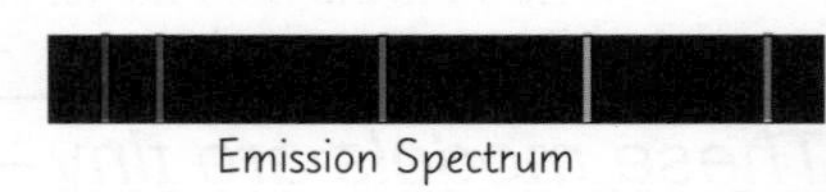
Emission Spectrum

Atomic Spectra and Nuclear Radiation

Both Types of Spectra are Made Up of Sets of Lines

1) Absorption and emission spectra are both **line spectra** with lines in the **same position** for a given element.
2) You get lots of **sets of lines** in these spectra — each set represents electrons moving to or from **a different energy level**. So, in an emission spectrum, you get one **set of lines** produced when electrons fall to the ***n* = 1** level, and another set produced when they fall to the ***n* = 2** level, and so on.
3) The lines on both absorption and emission spectra get **closer together** as the frequency **increases**.
4) Spectra often seem to make as much sense as bar codes. But the emission spectrum of **hydrogen** is fairly simple because hydrogen only has **one** electron that can move. It has **three important sets of lines**:

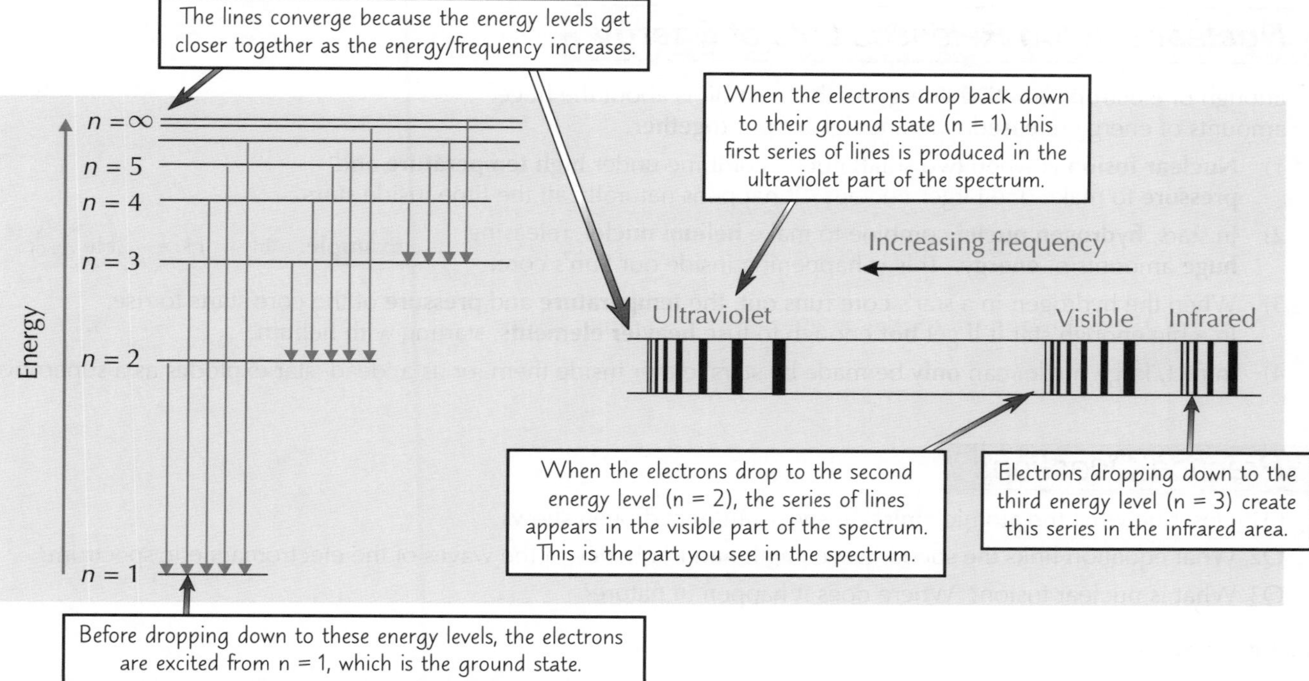

The lines converge because the energy levels get closer together as the energy/frequency increases.
When the electrons drop back down to their ground state (n = 1), this first series of lines is produced in the ultraviolet part of the spectrum.
n = ∞
n = 5
n = 4
n = 3
n = 2
n = 1
Energy
Increasing frequency
Ultraviolet
Visible
Infrared
When the electrons drop to the second energy level (n = 2), the series of lines appears in the visible part of the spectrum. This is the part you see in the spectrum.
Electrons dropping down to the third energy level (n = 3) create this series in the infrared area.
Before dropping down to these energy levels, the electrons are excited from n = 1, which is the ground state.

Energy is Related to Frequency

When an electron moves to a higher or lower shell it **absorbs** or **emits** electromagnetic radiation with a certain frequency. The **amount of energy** absorbed or emitted is related to the **frequency** of the radiation by this equation:

$$\Delta E = h\nu$$

The difference in energy between two shells. The units are joules (J).

The Greek letter 'nu', the symbol for frequency. The units are hertz (Hz or s^{-1}).

Just a number — Planck's constant. The units are joule per hertz ($J\,Hz^{-1}$).

You can use this equation to calculate the difference in energy between energy levels in an atom.

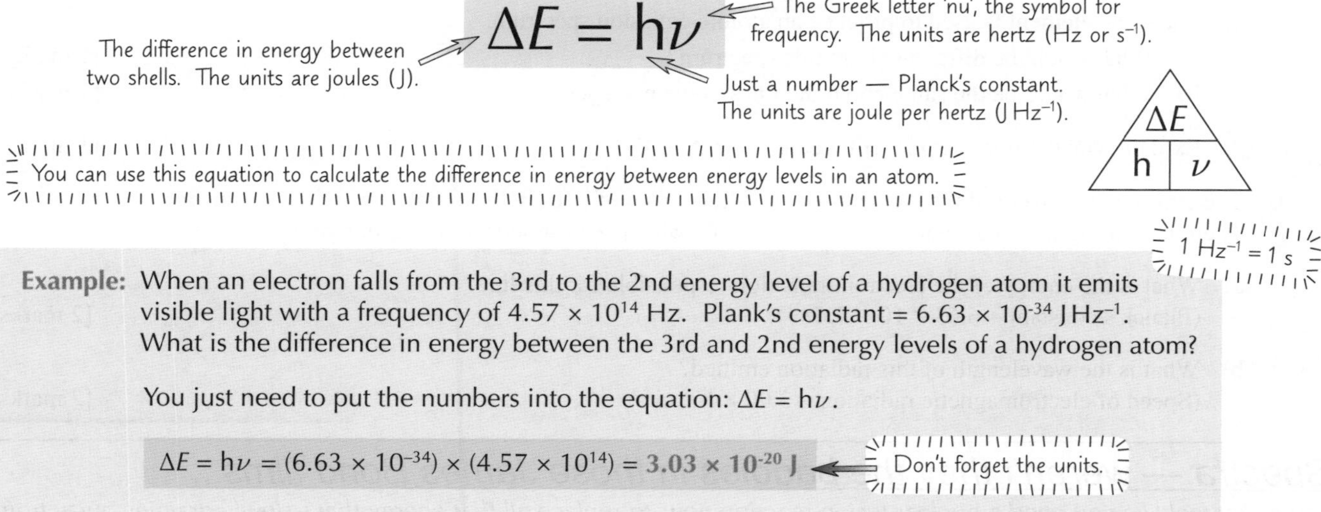

$1\ Hz^{-1} = 1\ s$

Example: When an electron falls from the 3rd to the 2nd energy level of a hydrogen atom it emits visible light with a frequency of 4.57×10^{14} Hz. Plank's constant = $6.63 \times 10^{-34}\ J\,Hz^{-1}$. What is the difference in energy between the 3rd and 2nd energy levels of a hydrogen atom?

You just need to put the numbers into the equation: $\Delta E = h\nu$.

$\Delta E = h\nu = (6.63 \times 10^{-34}) \times (4.57 \times 10^{14}) = \mathbf{3.03 \times 10^{-20}\ J}$

Don't forget the units.

Atomic Spectra and Nuclear Radiation

Speed and Frequency are Related to Wavelength

The frequency of radiation is also connected to the **wavelength** and **speed of electromagnetic radiation** in this equation:

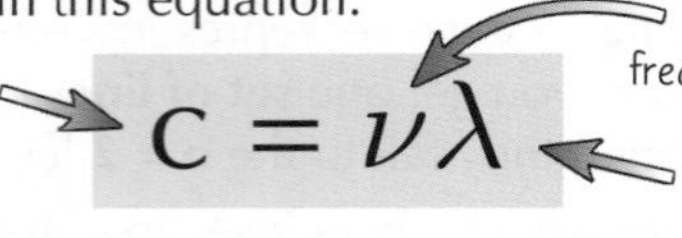
The speed of electromagnetic radiation (the same as the speed of light). The units are metres per second (m/s).
$c = \nu\lambda$
The Greek letter 'nu', the symbol for frequency. The units are hertz (Hz or s^{-1}).
The Greek letter 'lambda', the symbol for wavelength. The units are metres (m).

You can rearrange this equation to work out the **wavelength** from a given frequency and vice versa.

Nuclear Fusion Releases Lots of Energy

Enough of electrons emitting energy — this next bit is about the huge amounts of energy released when nuclei are put **together**.

1) **Nuclear fusion** is when two small nuclei combine under **high temperature** and **pressure** to make one larger nucleus. It happens naturally all the time inside **stars**.
2) In stars, **hydrogen nuclei** combine to make **helium nuclei**, releasing **huge** amounts of **energy**. This is happening inside our Sun's core.

Example: ${}^{2}_{1}H + {}^{3}_{1}H \rightarrow {}^{4}_{2}He + {}^{1}_{0}n$

3) When the hydrogen in a star's core runs out, the **temperature** and **pressure** of the core starts to rise. In a big enough star it'll get **hot** enough to fuse **heavier elements**, starting with helium.
4) In fact, large nuclei can **only** be made by stars (either inside them, or as a 'dead' star explodes as a supernova).

Practice Questions

Q1 Describe what the atomic emission spectrum of hydrogen shows.

Q2 What equation links the speed, wavelength and frequency of the waves of the electromagnetic spectrum?

Q3 What is nuclear fusion? Where does it happen in nature?

Exam Questions

Q1 The diagram below shows part of an atomic absorption spectrum of a single element. The dark lines in the spectrum are labelled A to E.

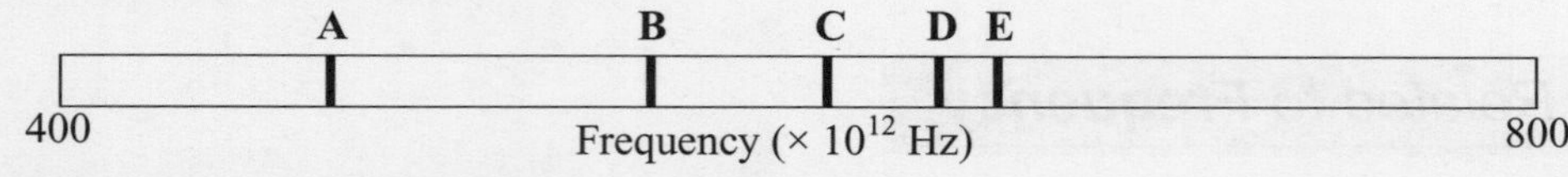
A
B
C
D
E
400
Frequency ($\times 10^{12}$ Hz)
800

a) What happens in the atom when radiation is absorbed? [2 marks]

b) Which line in the spectrum represents the largest absorption of energy? [1 mark]

c) The same element is used to produce an atomic emission spectrum.

i) What would be different about this spectrum? [1 mark]

ii) What would be the same about the lines in the two spectra? [1 mark]

d) Explain why the lines get closer together from A to E. [1 mark]

Q2 The emission spectrum of the element sodium shows a set of lines in the visible part of the spectrum. There is a strong line at a frequency 5.10×10^{14} Hz, which corresponds to the colour yellow.

a) What is the energy of the electron transition responsible for this line?
(Planck's constant = 6.63×10^{-34} J Hz^{-1}) [2 marks]

b) What is the wavelength of this radiation emitted?
(Speed of electromagnetic radiation = 3.00×10^{8} m/s) [2 marks]

Spectra — weren't they the baddies in those James Bond films...

You might feel like you need a nuclear fusion reaction now, to replace all that energy that's slowly draining away from you. A biscuit might be a safer bet though. Whatever you do, prepare yourself for some maths and some spectra.

Relative Mass and the Mass Spectrometer

Relative mass...What? Eh?...Read on...

Relative Masses are Masses of Atoms Compared to **Carbon-12**

The actual mass of an atom is **very, very tiny**. Don't worry about exactly how tiny for now, but it's far **too small** to weigh. So, the mass of one atom is compared to the mass of a different atom. This is its **relative mass**. Here are some definitions:

Relative atomic mass is an average, so it's not usually a whole number. Relative isotopic mass is usually a whole number. E.g. a natural sample of chlorine contains a mixture of ^{35}Cl (75%) and ^{37}Cl (25%), so the relative isotopic masses are 35 and 37. But its relative atomic mass is 35.5.

The **relative atomic mass**, A_r, is the **average mass** of an atom of an element on a scale where an atom of **carbon-12** is 12.

Relative isotopic mass is the mass of an atom of an **isotope** of an element on a scale where an atom of **carbon-12** is 12.

The **relative molecular mass**, M_r, is the average mass of a **molecule** on a scale where an atom of **carbon-12** is 12.

To find the relative molecular mass, just add up the relative atomic mass values of all the atoms in the molecule, e.g. $M_r(C_2H_6O) = (2 \times 12.0) + (6 \times 1.0) + 16.0 = 46.0$

Relative formula mass is used instead for compounds that are ionic (or giant covalent). To find the relative formula mass, just add up the relative atomic masses (A_r) of all the atoms in the formula unit. E.g. $M_r(CaF_2) = 40.1 + (2 \times 19.0) = 78.1$

"All those pies have made me relatively massive."

Relative Masses can be Measured Using a **Mass Spectrometer**

You can use a **mass spectrometer** to find out loads of stuff. It can tell you the **relative atomic mass**, **relative molecular mass**, **relative isotopic abundance** and your **horoscope** for the next fortnight.

There are **4** things that happen when a sample is squirted into a **time of flight (TOF) mass spectrometer**.

① **Vaporisation and Ionisation** — the sample is dissolved and pushed through a small nozzle at high pressure. A high voltage is applied to it, causing the particles to lose an electron and turning the sample into a **gas** made up of **positive ions**. This is called **electrospray ionisation**.

② **Acceleration** — the positive ions are accelerated by an **electric field**. (The particles need to be **positively charged** to be accelerated by the field.) Ions with a lower mass/charge ratio experience a greater acceleration.

③ **Ion Drift** — when the ions leave the electric field they have a **constant speed** and **kinetic energy**. They enter a region with no electric field and so they **drift**. Ions with lower mass/charge ratios drift at higher speeds.

④ **Detection** — because ions that have a **lower mass/charge ratio** travel at **higher speeds** in the drift region, they reach the detector in **less time** than ions with a higher mass/charge ratio. The detector detects **charged** particles and a **mass spectrum** (see next page) is produced.

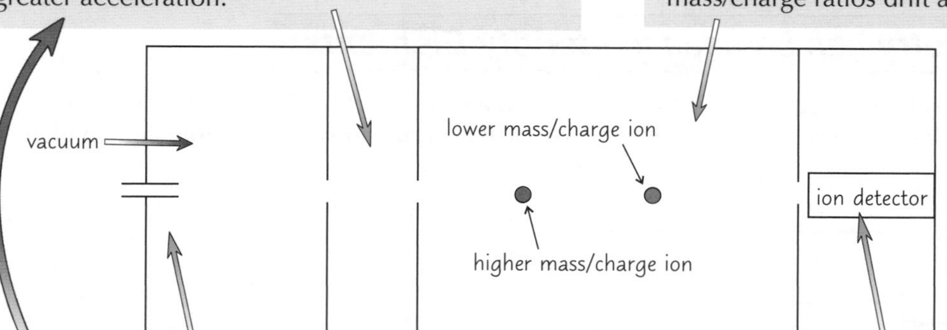

The detectors used in mass spectrometers detect charged particles. An electrical current is produced in the detector when a charged particle hits it.

Relative Mass and the Mass Spectrometer

A Mass Spectrum is Mass/Charge plotted against Abundance

The *y*-axis gives the **abundance of ions**, often as a percentage. For an element, the **height** of each peak gives the **relative isotopic abundance**, e.g. 75.5% of this sample is made up of the ^{35}Cl isotope.

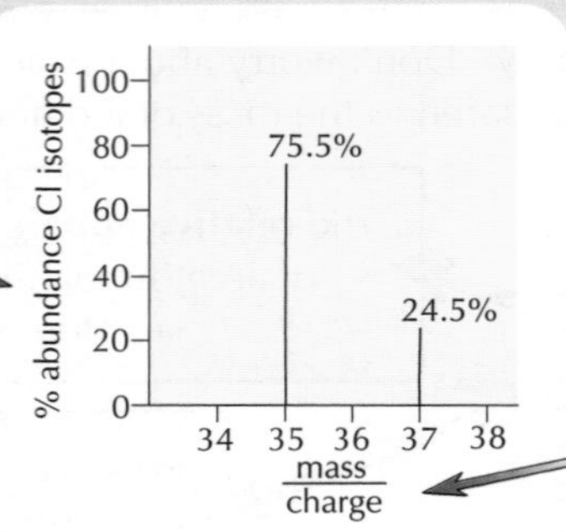

If the sample is an **element**, each line will represent a **different isotope** of the element.

The ***x*-axis** units are given as a **'mass/charge'** ratio. Since the charge on the ions is mostly **+1**, you can usually assume the *x*-axis is simply the **relative isotopic mass**.

You Can Work Out Relative Atomic Mass from a Mass Spectrum

You can calculate the **relative atomic mass** (A_r) of an element from the **mass spectrum**.
Here's how to calculate A_r for magnesium, using the mass spectrum below:

1: For each peak, read the **% relative isotopic abundance** from the y-axis and the **relative isotopic mass** from the x-axis. **Multiply** them together to get the total mass for each isotope: 79 × 24 = 1896; 10 × 25 = 250; 11 × 26 = 286

2: **Add** up these totals. 1896 + 250 + 286 = 2432

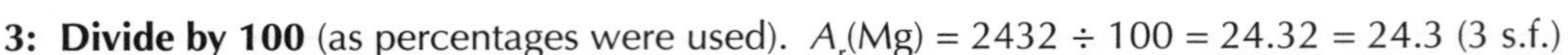
3: **Divide by 100** (as percentages were used). $A_r(Mg) = 2432 \div 100 = 24.32 = 24.3$ (3 s.f.)

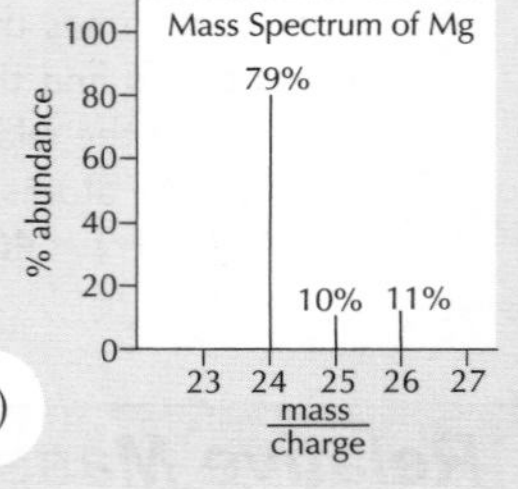

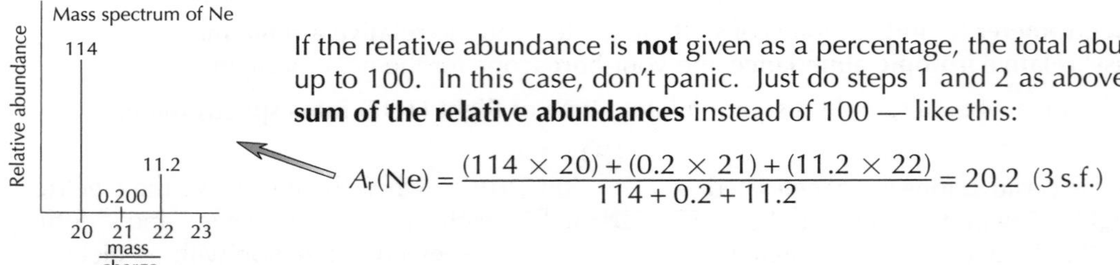

If the relative abundance is **not** given as a percentage, the total abundance may not add up to 100. In this case, don't panic. Just do steps 1 and 2 as above, but then divide by the **sum of the relative abundances** instead of 100 — like this:

$$A_r(\text{Ne}) = \frac{(114 \times 20) + (0.2 \times 21) + (11.2 \times 22)}{114 + 0.2 + 11.2} = 20.2 \text{ (3 s.f.)}$$

Mass Spectrometry can be used to Identify Elements

Elements with different **isotopes** produce more than one line in a mass spectrum because the isotopes have **different masses**. This produces characteristic patterns which can be used as **'fingerprints'** to **identify** certain **elements**.

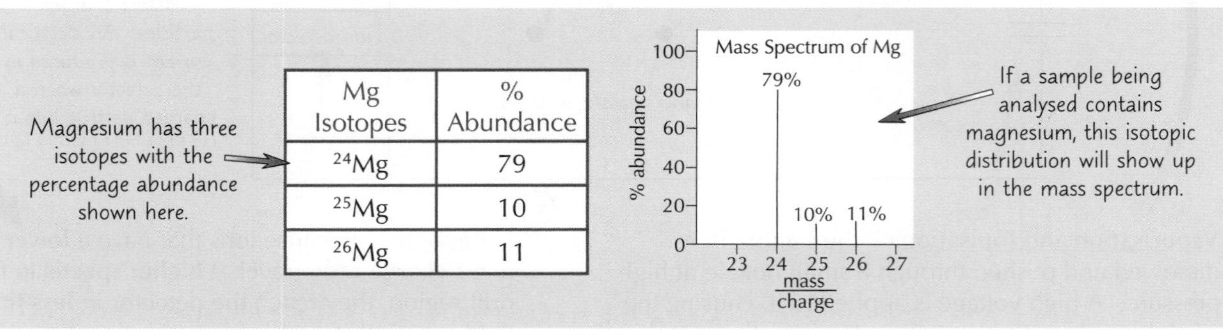

Magnesium has three isotopes with the percentage abundance shown here.

Mg Isotopes	% Abundance
^{24}Mg	79
^{25}Mg	10
^{26}Mg	11

If a sample being analysed contains magnesium, this isotopic distribution will show up in the mass spectrum.

Many elements only have one stable isotope. They can still be identified in a mass spectrum by looking for a line at their **relative atomic mass**.

Relative Mass and the Mass Spectrometer

Mass Spectrometry can be used to **Identify Molecules**

You can also get a mass spectrum for a **molecular sample**.

1) A **molecular ion**, M^+, is formed in the mass spectrometer when one electron is removed from the molecule.
2) This gives a peak in the spectrum with a mass/charge ratio equal to the **relative molecular mass** of the molecule.
3) This can be used to help **identify** an unknown compound.
There's more about using mass spectrometry to identify compounds on page 25.

Example: A sample of a straight-chain alcohol is analysed in a mass spectrometer. The mass/charge ratio of its molecular ion is 46.0. Identify the alcohol.

The table on the right shows the M_r of the first three straight-chain alcohols. The mass/charge ratio of the molecular ion must **equal** the M_r of the alcohol in the sample. So the alcohol must be **ethanol, C_2H_5OH.**

Alcohol	M_r
methanol CH_3OH	32.0
ethanol C_2H_5OH	46.0
propanol C_3H_7OH	60.0

If you have a mixture of compounds with different M_r values, you'll get a peak for the molecular ion of each one.

Practice Questions

Q1 Explain what relative atomic mass (A_r) and relative isotopic mass mean.

Q2 Explain the difference between relative molecular mass and relative formula mass.

Q3 Describe how electrospray ionisation works.

Q4 Explain how a mass spectrum can be used to determine relative molecular mass.

Exam Questions

Q1 Copper, Cu, exists in two main isotopic forms, ^{63}Cu and ^{65}Cu.

a) Calculate the relative atomic mass of Cu using the information from the mass spectrum on the right. [2 marks]

b) Explain why the relative atomic mass of copper is not a whole number. [2 marks]

Mass Spectrum of Cu
Relative abundance
120.8
54.0
61 63 65 67
mass / charge

Q2 The percentage make-up of naturally occurring potassium is 93.11% ^{39}K, 0.12% ^{40}K and 6.77% ^{41}K.

a) What method is used to determine the mass and abundance of each isotope? [1 mark]

b) Use the information to determine the relative atomic mass of potassium. [2 marks]

Q3 A mixture containing chlorine (Cl), gallium (Ga), bromine (Br) and rubidium (Rb), was analysed in a time of flight mass spectrometer.

a) Why do samples need to be positively charged in time of flight mass spectrometry? [2 marks]

b) Explain how time of flight mass spectrometry distinguishes between ions with different masses. [4 marks]

c) The abundance of the isotopes of the elements in the mixture are shown below. Which element is responsible for the part of the spectrum on the right?

% abundance
0 20 40 60 80 100
mass / charge

A Chlorine: 75.8% ^{35}Cl, 24.2% ^{37}Cl **B** Gallium: 60.1% ^{69}Ga, 39.9% ^{71}Ga

C Bromine: 50.7% ^{79}Br, 49.3% ^{81}Br **D** Rubidium: 72.2% ^{85}Rb, 27.8% ^{87}Rb [1 mark]

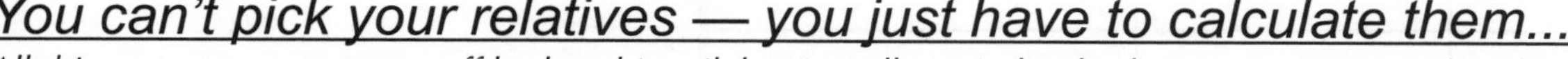

You can't pick your relatives — you just have to calculate them...

All this mass spectrometry stuff looks a bit evil, but it really isn't that bad once you get your head round it. Make sure you've done the practice and exam questions. They'll make sure you've really learnt all the stuff covered on these pages. Then you can go and do something much more fun, like cutting the lawn with nail scissors...

More on Relative Mass

"More relative mass?! How much more could there possibly be?" I hear you cry. Well, as you're about to see, there's plenty more. This is all dead useful to scientists and (more importantly) to you in your exams.

You Can Calculate **Isotopic Masses** from **Relative Atomic Mass**

If you know the **relative atomic mass** of an **element**, and you know all but one of the **abundances** and relative isotopic masses of its **isotopes**, you can work out the abundance and isotopic mass of the final isotope. Neat huh?

Example: Silicon can exist in three isotopes. 92.23% of silicon is ^{28}Si and 4.67% of silicon is ^{29}Si. Given that the A_r of silicon is 28.1, calculate the abundance and isotopic mass of the third isotope.

Step 1: First, find the **abundance** of the third isotope.
You're dealing with percentage abundances, so you know they need to total 100%.
So, the abundance of the final isotope will be 100% – 92.23% – 4.67% = **3.10%**

Step 2: You know that the **relative atomic mass** (A_r) of silicon is 28.1, and you know two of the three **isotopic masses**. So, you can put all of that into the equation you use to work out the relative atomic mass from relative abundances and isotopic masses (see page 22), which you can then rearrange to work out the **final isotopic mass**, *X*.

$28.1 = ((28 \times 92.23) + (29 \times 4.67) + (X \times 3.10)) \div 100$
$28.1 = (2717.87 + (X \times 3.10)) \div 100$
$2810 - 2717.87 = X \times 3.10$
$29.719 = X$ So the isotopic mass of the third isotope is **30** — ^{30}**Si**.

Remember — isotopic masses are usually whole numbers, so you should round your answer to the nearest whole number.

You Can **Predict** the Mass Spectra for **Diatomic Molecules**

Now, this is where it gets even more mathsy and interesting (seriously — I love it). You can use your knowledge to **predict** what the **mass spectra** of diatomic molecules (i.e. molecules containing two atoms) look like.

Example: Chlorine has two isotopes. ^{35}Cl has an abundance of 75% and ^{37}Cl has an abundance of 25%. Predict the mass spectrum of Cl_2.

To convert a percentage to a decimal, just divide by 100.

1) First, express each of the percentages as a decimal — 75% = 0.75 and 25% = 0.25.

2) Make a **table** showing all the different Cl_2 molecules. For each molecule, **multiply** the abundances (as decimals) of the isotopes to get the relative abundance of each one.

	^{35}Cl	^{37}Cl
^{35}Cl	$^{35}Cl-^{35}Cl$: 0.75 × 0.75 = 0.5625	$^{35}Cl-^{37}Cl$: 0.25 × 0.75 = 0.1875
^{37}Cl	$^{37}Cl-^{35}Cl$: 0.25 × 0.75 = 0.1875	$^{37}Cl-^{37}Cl$: 0.25 × 0.25 = 0.0625

3) Look for any molecules in the table that are the **same** and **add up** their abundances.
In this case, $^{37}Cl-^{35}Cl$ and $^{35}Cl-^{37}Cl$ are the same, so the actual abundance for this molecule is:
0.1875 + 0.1875 = **0.375**.

4) **Divide** all the relative abundances by the smallest relative abundance to get the **smallest whole number ratio**. And by working out the relative molecular mass, you can **predict** the **mass spectrum** for Cl_2:

Molecule	Relative Molecular Mass	Relative abundance
$^{35}Cl-^{35}Cl$	35 + 35 = 70	0.5625 ÷ 0.0625 = 9
$^{35}Cl-^{37}Cl$	35 + 37 = 72	0.375 ÷ 0.0625 = 6
$^{37}Cl-^{37}Cl$	37 + 37 = 74	0.0625 ÷ 0.0625 = 1

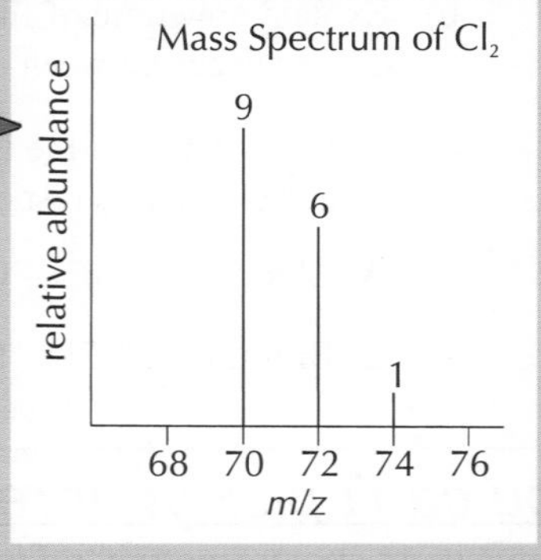

More on Relative Mass

Mass Spectrometry Can Also Help to Identify Compounds

1) You've seen how you can use a mass spectrum showing the relative isotopic abundances of an element to work out its relative atomic mass. You can also get mass spectra for **molecules** made up from more than one element.
2) The molecules in the sample are bombarded with electrons, which remove an electron from the molecule to form a **molecular ion**, $\mathbf{M^{+}_{(g)}}$.
3) To find the relative molecular mass of a compound you look at the **molecular ion peak** (the **M peak**). The mass/charge value of the molecular ion peak is the **molecular mass**.

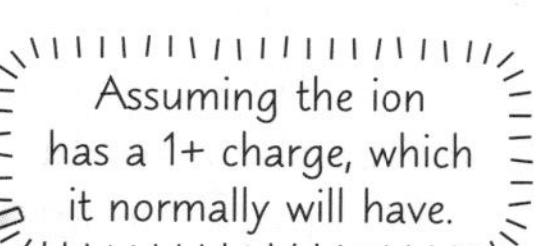

Assuming the ion has a 1+ charge, which it normally will have.

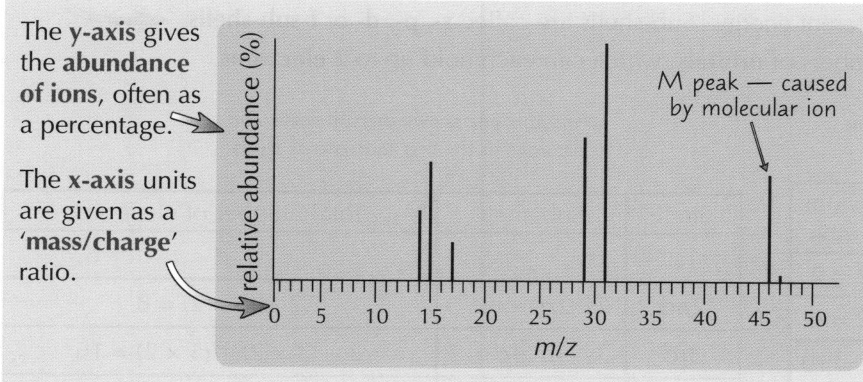

This is the mass spectrum of an unknown alcohol.

1) The m/z value of the molecular ion peak is 46, so the M_r of the compound must be **46**.
2) If you calculate the molecular masses of the first few alcohols, you'll find that the one with a molecular mass of 46 is ethanol (C_2H_5OH).
   M_r of ethanol = (2 × 12.0) + (5 × 1.0) + 16.0 + 1.0 = **46.0**
3) So the compound must be **ethanol**.

There's loads more on mass spectrometry on pages 150-151.

Practice Questions

Q1 Explain why diatomic molecules can have different relative molecular masses.

Q2 What is the significance of the molecular ion peak on a mass spectrum?

Exam Questions

Q1 The table below shows the percentage abundances of isotopes of oxygen found in a sample of O_2.

Isotopes	% Abundance
^{16}O	98
^{18}O	2

a) Calculate the relative abundances of all the possible molecules of O_2. [3 marks]

b) Sketch a mass spectrum of O_2. [4 marks]

Q2 Potassium (A_r = 39.1) can exist in one of three isotopes. 94.20% exists as ^{39}K and 0.012% exists as ^{40}K.

a) Calculate the abundance of the third isotope of potassium. [1 mark]

b) Calculate the isotopic mass of the third isotope of potassium. [2 marks]

Q3 A sample of an unknown straight-chain alkane is analysed using mass spectrometry. The molecular ion peak is seen at a m/z value of 58.

The structures of alkanes are covered on page 116.

a) What is the M_r of this compound? [1 mark]

b) Using your answer to part a), suggest a structure for this compound. [1 mark]

How do you make a colourful early noughties girl group? Diatomic Kitten...

Dye Atomic Kitten... Geddit...? Only one topic into this revision guide and we already have a strong contender for world's worst joke. But don't be too dismayed, there are plenty more terrible puns on their way, I assure you. Before you go looking for them, make sure you know how to do all these relative mass calculations — they're pretty important.

Electronic Structure

Those little electrons prancing about like mini bunnies decide what'll react with what — it's what chemistry's all about.

Electron Shells are Made Up of Sub-Shells and Orbitals

1) In the currently accepted model of the atom, electrons have fixed energies.
2) They move around the nucleus in **shells** (sometimes called **energy levels**). These shells are all given numbers known as **principal quantum numbers**.
3) Shells **further** from the nucleus have a higher **energy** (and a larger principal quantum number) than shells closer to the nucleus.
4) Shells are divided up into **sub-shells**. Different electron shells have different numbers of sub-shells, each of which has a different energy. Sub-shells are called **s-**, **p-**, **d-** or **f-sub-shells**.
5) These sub-shells have different numbers of **orbitals**, which can each hold up to **2 electrons**.

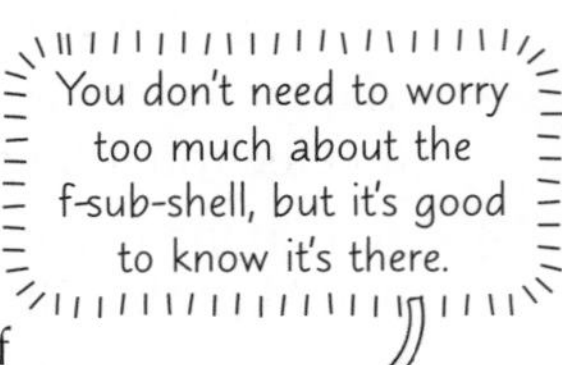

You don't need to worry too much about the f-sub-shell, but it's good to know it's there.

This table shows the number of electrons that fit in each type of sub-shell.

Sub-shell	Number of orbitals	Maximum electrons
s	1	$1 \times 2 = 2$
p	3	$3 \times 2 = 6$
d	5	$5 \times 2 = 10$
f	7	$7 \times 2 = 14$

And this one shows the sub-shells and electrons in the first four energy levels.

Shell	Sub-shell	Total number of electrons
1st	1*s*	2
2nd	2*s* 2*p*	$2 + (3 \times 2) = 8$
3rd	3*s* 3*p* 3*d*	$2 + (3 \times 2) + (5 \times 2) = 16$
4th	4*s* 4*p* 4*d* 4*f*	$2 + (3 \times 2) + (5 \times 2) + (7 \times 2) = 32$

Orbitals Have Characteristic Shapes

"So what are these orbitals like?" I hear you ask. Well, here goes...

1) An orbital is the **bit of space** that an electron moves in. Orbitals within the same sub-shell have the **same energy**.
2) If there are two electrons in an orbital, they have to 'spin' in **opposite** directions — this is called **spin-pairing**.
3) s orbitals are **spherical** — p orbitals have **dumbbell shapes**. There are three p orbitals and they're at right angles to one another.

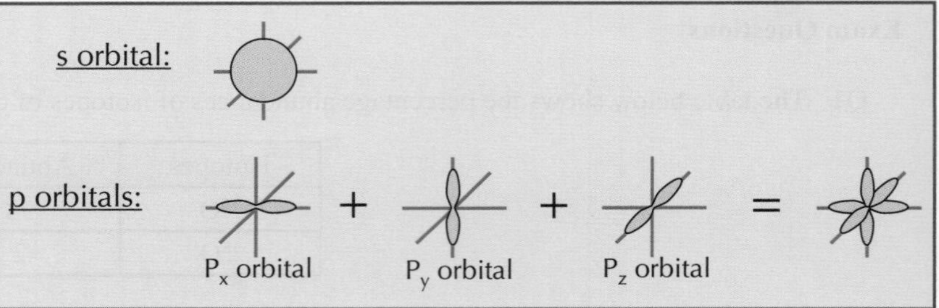

You Can Show Electron Configuration in Different Ways

The **number** of electrons that an atom or ion has, and how they are **arranged**, is called its **electron configuration**. Electron configurations can be shown in different ways. E.g. an atom of neon has 10 electrons — two in the 1s sub-shell, two in the 2s sub-shell and six in the 2p sub-shell. You can show this using...

Sub-shell notation:

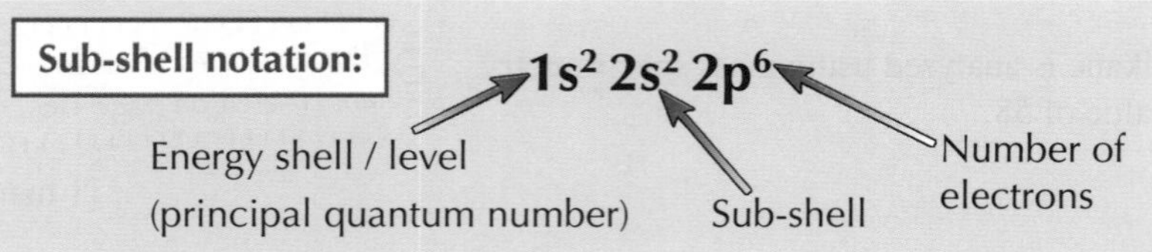

You might see electron configuration called electronic configuration. Don't worry, they mean the same thing.

Electrons in boxes:

1) Each **box** represents one **orbital** and each **arrow** represents one **electron**.
2) The up and down arrows represent electrons **spinning** in opposite directions. Two electrons can only occupy the same orbital if they have **opposite** spin.

1s [↑↓] 2s [↑↓] 2p [↑↓|↑↓|↑↓]

Electronic Structure

Work Out **Electron Configurations** by Filling the **Lowest** Energy Levels First

You can figure out most electron configurations pretty easily, so long as you know a few simple rules —

1) Electrons fill up the **lowest** energy sub-shells first.

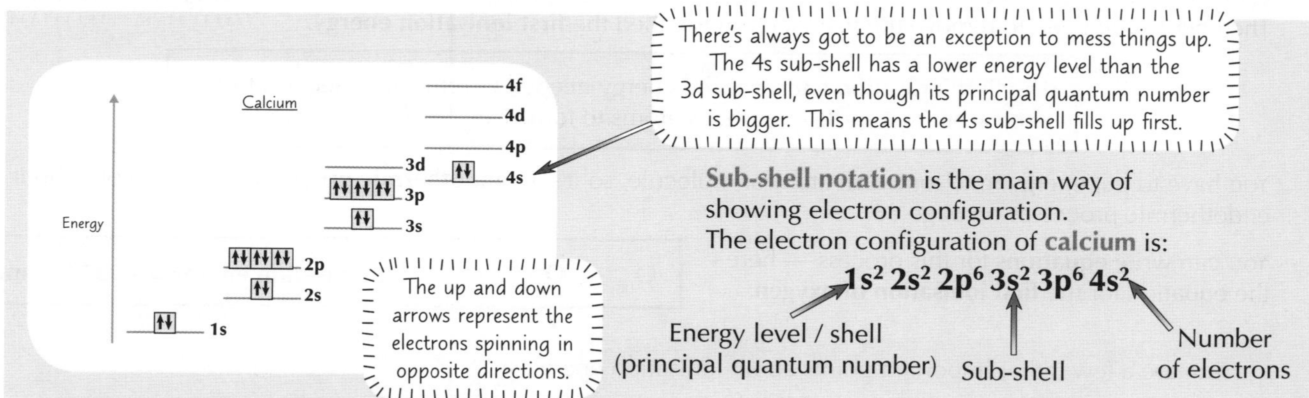

Calcium
Energy
4f
4d
4p
3d
4s
3p
3s
2p
2s
1s
There's always got to be an exception to mess things up. The 4s sub-shell has a lower energy level than the 3d sub-shell, even though its principal quantum number is bigger. This means the 4s sub-shell fills up first.
The up and down arrows represent the electrons spinning in opposite directions.
Energy level / shell (principal quantum number)
Sub-shell
Number of electrons

Sub-shell notation is the main way of showing electron configuration. The electron configuration of **calcium** is:

$$1s^2\ 2s^2\ 2p^6\ 3s^2\ 3p^6\ 4s^2$$

2) Electrons fill orbitals with the same energy **singly** before they start sharing.

Nitrogen: 1s ↑↓ 2s ↑↓ 2p ↑ ↑ ↑ Oxygen: 1s ↑↓ 2s ↑↓ 2p ↑↓ ↑ ↑

3) For the configuration of **ions** from the **s** and **p** blocks of the periodic table, just **remove or add** the electrons to or from the highest-energy occupied sub-shell. E.g. $Mg^{2+} = 1s^2\ 2s^2\ 2p^6$, $Cl^- = 1s^2\ 2s^2\ 2p^6\ 3s^2\ 3p^6$.

Watch out — **noble gas symbols**, like that of argon (Ar), are sometimes used in electron configurations. For example, calcium ($1s^2\ 2s^2\ 2p^6\ 3s^2\ 3p^6\ 4s^2$) can be written as [Ar]$4s^2$, where [Ar] = $1s^2\ 2s^2\ 2p^6\ 3s^2\ 3p^6$.

Practice Questions

Q1 How many electrons do full s, p and d sub-shells contain?

Q2 What is an atomic orbital?

Q3 Draw diagrams to show the shapes of an s and a p orbital.

Q4 Write down the sub-shells in order of increasing energy up to 4p.

Exam Questions

Q1 Potassium reacts with oxygen to form potassium oxide, K_2O.

a) Give the electron configurations of the K atom and K^+ ion using sub-shell notation. [2 marks]

b) Give the electron configuration of the oxide ion using 'electrons in boxes' notation. [1 mark]

Q2 This question concerns electron configurations in atoms and ions.

a) Identify the element with the 4th shell configuration of $4s^2\ 4p^2$. [1 mark]

b) Suggest the identity of an atom, a positive ion and a negative ion with the configuration $1s^2\ 2s^2\ 2p^6\ 3s^2\ 3p^6$. [3 marks]

c) Give the electron configuration of the Al^{3+} ion using sub-shell notation. [1 mark]

Q3 a) Write the electron configuration of a silicon atom using sub-shell notation. [1 mark]

b) How many orbitals contain an unpaired electron in a silicon atom? [1 mark]

She shells sub-sells on the shesore...

Electrons fill up the orbitals kind of like how strangers fill up seats on a bus. Everyone tends to sit in their own seat till they're forced to share. Except for the huge, scary man who comes and sits next to you. Make sure you learn the order that the sub-shells are filled up, so you can write electron configurations for any atom or ion they throw at you.

Ionisation Energy

This page gets a trifle brain-boggling, so I hope you've got a few aspirin handy...

Ionisation is the *Removal* of One or More *Electrons*

You might see 'ionisation energy' referred to as 'ionisation enthalpy' instead.

When electrons have been removed from an atom or molecule, it's been **ionised**. The energy you need to remove the first electron is called the **first ionisation energy**.

The **first ionisation energy** is the energy needed to remove 1 electron from **each atom** in **1 mole** of **gaseous** atoms to form 1 mole of gaseous 1+ ions.

You have to put energy in to ionise an atom or molecule, so it's an **endothermic process** — there's more about endothermic processes on page 66.

You can write **equations** for this process — here's the equation for the **first ionisation of oxygen**:

$O_{(g)} \rightarrow O^{+}_{(g)} + e^{-}$ **1st ionisation energy = +1314 kJ mol⁻¹**

Here are a few rather important points about ionisation energies:

1) You **must** use the gas state symbol, (g), because ionisation energies are measured for gaseous atoms.
2) Always refer to **1 mole** of atoms, as stated in the definition, rather than to a single atom.
3) The **lower** the ionisation energy, the **easier** it is to form an ion.

The *Factors* Affecting Ionisation Energy are...

Ways in which bears are like electrons #14 — the more warm apple pies there are cooling on a window sill, the tastier the window sill smells and the stronger the attraction for the bears.

Nuclear Charge — The **more protons** there are in the nucleus, the more positively charged the nucleus is and the **stronger the attraction** for the electrons.

Distance from Nucleus — Attraction falls off very **rapidly with distance**. An electron **close** to the nucleus will be **much more** strongly attracted than one further away.

Shielding — As the number of electrons **between** the outer electrons and the nucleus **increases**, the outer electrons feel less attraction towards the nuclear charge. This lessening of the pull of the nucleus by inner shells of electrons is called **shielding (or screening)**.

A **high ionisation energy** means there's a **high attraction** between the **electron** and the **nucleus** and so **more energy** is needed to remove the electron.

Successive Ionisation Energies Involve Removing *Additional* Electrons

1) You can remove **all** the electrons from an atom, leaving only the nucleus. Each time you remove an electron, there's a **successive ionisation energy**.
2) The definition for the **second ionisation energy is** —

The **second ionisation energy** is the energy needed to remove 1 electron from **each ion** in **1 mole** of **gaseous** 1+ ions to form 1 mole of gaseous 2+ ions.

And here's the equation for the **second ionisation of oxygen**:

$O^{+}_{(g)} \rightarrow O^{2+}_{(g)} + e^{-}$ **2nd ionisation energy = +3388 kJ mol⁻¹**

3) You need to be able to write equations for **any** successive ionisation energy. The equation for the ***nth* ionisation energy** is....

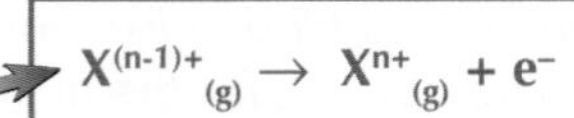

$X^{(n-1)+}_{(g)} \rightarrow X^{n+}_{(g)} + e^{-}$

Ionisation Energy

Successive Ionisation Energies Show **Shell Structure**

A **graph** of successive ionisation energies (like this one for sodium) provides evidence for the **shell structure** of atoms.

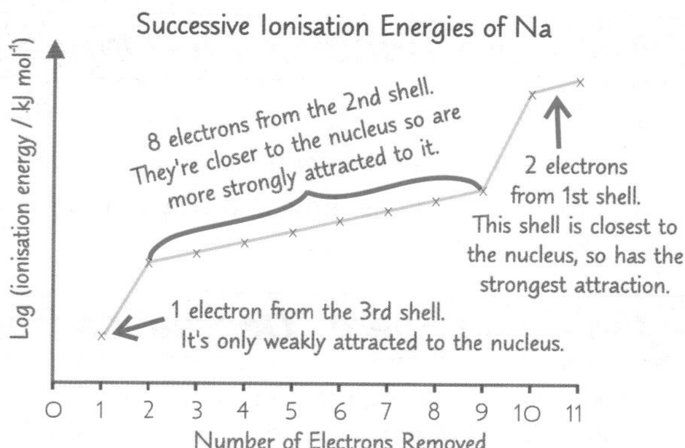

1) **Within each shell**, successive ionisation energies **increase**. This is because electrons are being removed from an **increasingly positive ion** — there's **less repulsion** amongst the remaining electrons, so they're **held more strongly** by the nucleus.
2) The **big jumps** in ionisation energy happen when a new shell is broken into — an electron is being removed from a shell **closer** to the nucleus.

1) Graphs like this can tell you which **group** of the periodic table an element belongs to. Just count **how many electrons are removed** before the first big jump to find the group number.

   E.g. In the graph for sodium, **one electron** is removed before the first big jump — sodium is in **group 1**.

2) These graphs can be used to predict the **electronic structure** of elements. Working from **right to left**, count how many points there are before each big jump to find how many electrons are in each shell, starting with the first.

   E.g. The graph for sodium has **2 points** on the right-hand side, then a jump, then **8 points**, a jump, and **1 final point**. Sodium has **2 electrons** in the first shell, **8** in the second and **1** in the third.

Practice Questions

Q1 Define first ionisation energy and give an equation as an example.

Q2 Describe the three main factors that affect ionisation energies.

Q3 How is ionisation energy related to the force of attraction between an electron and the nucleus of an atom?

Exam Questions

Q1 This table shows the nuclear charge and first ionisation energy for four elements.

Element	B	C	N	0
Charge of Nucleus	+5	+6	+7	+8
1st Ionisation Energy (kJ mol^{-1})	801	1087	1402	1314

a) Write an equation, including state symbols, to represent the first ionisation energy of carbon (C). [2 marks]

b) In these four elements, what is the relationship between nuclear charge and first ionisation energy? [1 mark]

c) Explain why nuclear charge has this effect on first ionisation energy. [2 marks]

Q2 This graph shows the successive ionisation energies of a certain element.

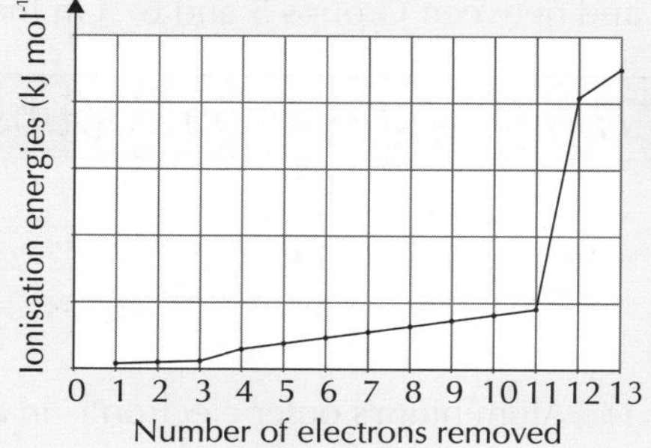

a) To which group of the periodic table does this element belong? [1 mark]

b) Why does it takes more energy to remove each successive electron? [2 marks]

c) What causes the sudden increases in ionisation energy? [1 mark]

d) What is the total number of electron shells in this element? [1 mark]

Shirt crumpled — ionise it...

When you're talking about ionisation energies in exams, always use the three main factors — shielding, nuclear charge and distance from nucleus. Recite the definition of the first ionisation energies to yourself until you can't take any more.

Trends in First Ionisation Energy

Let joy be unconfined — it's another two pages about ionisation energy. This time though it's all about trends in first ionisation energies and what they can tell you about the structure of atoms.

*There are **Trends** in **First Ionisation Energies***

1) The first ionisation energies of elements **down a group** of the periodic table **decrease**.
2) The first ionisation energies of elements **across a period generally increase**.
3) You need to know **how** and **why** ionisation energy **changes** as you go down **Group 2** and across **Period 3**. Read on to discover all...

*Ionisation Energy **Decreases** Down Group 2*

This graph shows the first ionisation energies of the elements in **Group 2**. It provides **evidence** that electron shells **REALLY DO EXIST** and that successive elements down the group have **extra**, **bigger**, **shells**...

1) If each element down Group 2 has an **extra electron shell** compared to the one above, the extra inner shells will **shield** the outer electrons from the attraction of the nucleus.
2) Also, the extra shell means that the outer electrons are **further away** from the nucleus, so the nucleus's attraction will be greatly reduced.

It makes sense that both of these factors will make it **easier** to remove outer electrons, resulting in a **lower ionisation energy**.

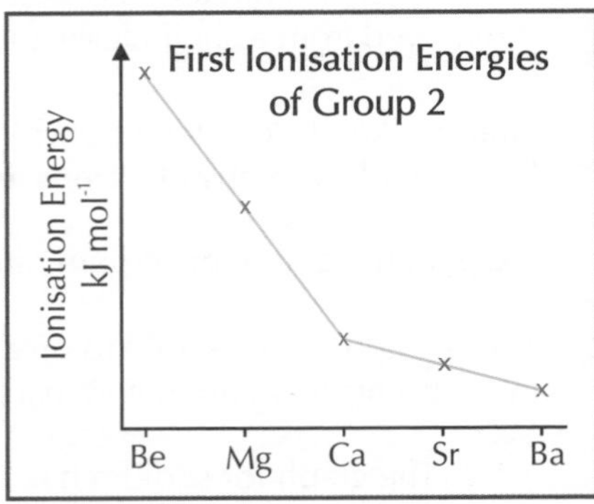

*Ionisation Energy **Increases** Across a Period*

The graph below shows the first ionisation energies of the elements in **Periods 2** and **3**.

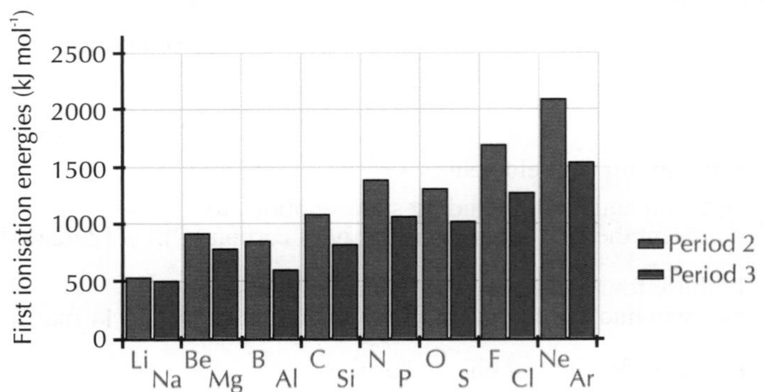

1) As you **move across** a period, the **general trend** is for the ionisation energies to **increase** — i.e. it gets harder to remove the outer electrons.
2) This is because the number of protons is increasing. As the **positive charge** of the nucleus increases, the electrons are **pulled closer** to the nucleus, making the atomic radius smaller.
3) The extra electrons that the elements gain across a period are added to the **outer energy level** so they don't really provide any extra shielding effect (shielding works with inner shells mainly).

There are **two exceptions** to the trend — the first ionisation energy **decreases** between Groups 2 and 3, and between Groups 5 and 6. On the graph, you can see this as **small drops** between those groups.

*The Drop between Groups 2 and 3 Shows **Sub-Shell Structure***

Example

Mg $1s^2 2s^2 2p^6 3s^2$ — 1st ionisation energy = 738 kJ mol^{-1}
Al $1s^2 2s^2 2p^6 3s^2 3p^1$ — 1st ionisation energy = 578 kJ mol^{-1}

1) Aluminium's outer electron is in a **3p orbital** rather than a 3s. The 3p orbital has a **slightly higher** energy than the 3s orbital, so the electron is, on average, to be found **further** from the nucleus.
2) The 3p orbital has additional shielding provided by the **$3s^2$ electrons**.
3) Both these factors together are strong enough to **override** the effect of the increased nuclear charge, resulting in the ionisation energy **dropping** slightly.
4) This pattern in ionisation energies provides **evidence** for the theory of electron sub-shells.

Trends in First Ionisation Energy

The Drop between Groups 5 and 6 is due to **Electron Repulsion**

P	$1s^2 2s^2 2p^6 3s^2 3p^3$	1st ionisation energy = 1012 kJ mol^{-1}
S	$1s^2 2s^2 2p^6 3s^2 3p^4$	1st ionisation energy = 1000 kJ mol^{-1}

1) The **shielding is identical** in the phosphorus and sulfur atoms, and the electron is being removed from an identical orbital.
2) In phosphorus's case, the electron is being removed from a **singly-occupied** orbital. But in sulfur, the **electron** is being **removed** from an orbital containing two electrons.

   Phosphorus: [Ne] 3s ↑↓ 3p ↑ ↑ ↑ Sulfur: [Ne] 3s ↑↓ 3p ↑↓ ↑ ↑

   The **repulsion** between two electrons in an orbital means that electrons are **easier to remove** from shared orbitals.
3) Yup, yet more **evidence** for the electronic structure model.

Ways in which bears are like electrons #23 — the repulsion between two bears in a river means that bears are easier to remove from shared rivers.

Practice Questions

Q1 Describe the trend in ionisation energy as you go down Group 2.

Q2 Why do ionisation energies change down a group?

Q3 Which electron is easier to remove, a lone electron in an orbital or one in a pair?

Exam Questions

Q1 The first ionisation energies of the elements lithium to neon are given below in kJ mol^{-1}:

Li	Be	B	C	N	O	F	Ne
519	900	799	1090	1400	1310	1680	2080

a) Explain why the ionisation energies show an overall tendency to increase across the period. [3 marks]

b) Explain the irregularities in this trend for:

i) boron [2 marks]

ii) oxygen [2 marks]

Q2 First ionisation energy decreases down Group 2.

Explain how this trend provides evidence for the arrangement of electrons in levels. [3 marks]

Q3 a) Which of these elements has the highest first ionisation energy?

A Krypton **B** Lithium **C** Potassium **D** Neon [1 mark]

b) Explain your reasoning for the answer given in part a). [2 marks]

Q4 a) Which of these elements has the largest jump between its first and second ionisation energies?

A Sodium **B** Magnesium **C** Argon **D** Chlorine [1 mark]

b) Explain your reasoning for the answer given in part a). [3 marks]

First ionisation energies are so popular, they're trending...

If all these trends across and up and down the periodic table get confusing, just think back to basics — it's all about how strongly the outer electron is attracted to the nucleus. THAT depends on shielding, nuclear charge and distance from the nucleus and THEY depend on which shell, sub-shell and orbital the electron is in.

The Mole and Equations

It'd be handy to be able to count out atoms — but they're way too tiny. You can't even see them, never mind get hold of them with tweezers. But not to worry — using the idea of relative mass, you can figure out how many atoms you've got.

A **Mole** is Just a (Very Large) **Number of Particles**

Chemists often talk about 'amount of substance'. Basically, all they mean is 'number of particles'.

1) Amount of substance is measured using a unit called the **mole** (or **mol**). The number of moles is given the symbol **n**.
2) The number of **particles** in one mole is **6.02×10^{23}**. This number is **the Avogadro constant, N_A**.
3) It **doesn't matter** what the particles are. They can be atoms, molecules, penguins — **anything**.
4) Here's a nice simple formula for finding the number of moles from the number of atoms or molecules:

$$\text{Number of moles} = \frac{\text{Number of particles you have}}{\text{Number of particles in a mole}}$$

Example: I have 1.50×10^{24} carbon atoms. How many moles of carbon is this?

$$\text{Number of moles} = \frac{1.50 \times 10^{24}}{6.02 \times 10^{23}} \approx \textbf{2.49 moles}$$

The Amount of a Substance in **Moles** can be Calculated from **Mass** and **M_r**

1) **1 mole** of any substance has a **mass** that's the same as its **relative molecular mass** (M_r) in **grams**. For example, the M_r of water (H_2O) is $(1 \times 2) + 16 = 18$, so 1 mole of water has a mass of 18 g.
2) This means that you can work out how many **moles** of a substance you have from the **mass** of the substance and its **relative molecular mass** (M_r). Here's the formula you need:

$$\text{Number of moles} = \frac{\text{mass of substance}}{M_r}$$

If you need to find M_r or mass instead, you can re-arrange the formula using this formula triangle: mass / moles × M_r

Example: How many moles of aluminium oxide are present in 5.10 g of Al_2O_3?

M_r of $Al_2O_3 = (2 \times 27.0) + (3 \times 16.0) = 102.0$

Number of moles of $Al_2O_3 = \frac{5.10}{102.0} =$ **0.0500 moles**

Molar Mass is the Mass of **One Mole**

Molar mass, **M**, is the mass of **one mole** of something. Just remember:

Molar mass is just the same as the relative molecular mass, M_r.

That's why the mole is such a ridiculous number of particles (6.02×10^{23}) — it's the number of particles for which the weight in g is the same as the relative molecular mass.

The only difference is it has units of 'grams per mole', so you stick a 'g mol^{-1}' on the end...

Example: Find the molar mass of $CaCO_3$.

Relative formula mass, M_r, of $CaCO_3 = 40.1 + 12.0 + (3 \times 16.0) = 100.1$

So the molar mass, M, is **100.1 g mol^{-1}**. — i.e. 1 mole of $CaCO_3$ weighs 100.1 g.

This means you can use a very similar formula to the one above to find the number of moles of a substance:

$$\text{Number of moles} = \frac{\text{mass of substance}}{\text{molar mass}}$$

You can re-arrange this equation using this formula triangle: mass / moles | molar mass

Example: How many moles of methane are present in 6.70 g of CH_4?

Molar mass, M, of $CH_4 = (1 \times 12.0) + (4 \times 1.0) = 16.0$ g mol^{-1}

Number of moles of $CH_4 = \frac{6.70}{16.0} =$ **0.419 moles**

The Mole and Equations

The **Concentration** of a Solution is Measured in **mol dm^{-3}**

1) The **concentration** of a solution is how many **moles** are dissolved per **1 dm^3** (that's 1 litre) of solution. The units are **mol dm^{-3}**.
2) Here's the formula to find the **number of moles**:

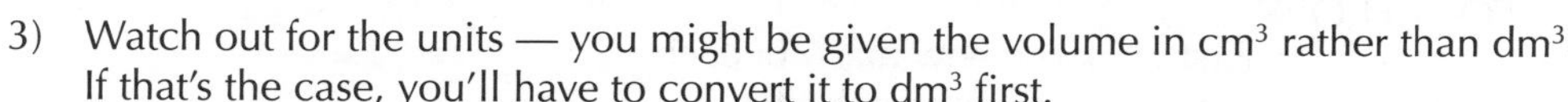

Number of moles = Concentration (mol dm^{-3}) × Volume (dm^3)

3) Watch out for the units — you might be given the volume in cm^3 rather than dm^3. If that's the case, you'll have to convert it to dm^3 first.

This one can go in a handy formula triangle too:

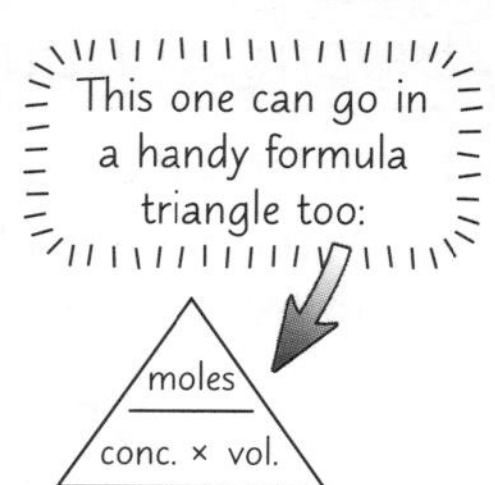

Example: What mass of sodium hydroxide (NaOH) needs to be dissolved in water to give 50.0 cm^3 of a solution with a concentration of 2.00 mol dm^{-3}?

Volume of solution in dm^3 = 50 ÷ 1000 = 0.05 dm^3
Number of moles NaOH = 2.00 mol dm^{-3} × 0.0500 dm^3 = 0.100
M_r of NaOH = 23.0 + 16.0 + 1.0 = 40.0
Mass = number of moles × M_r = 0.100 × 40.0 = **4.00 g**

1 dm^3 = 1000 cm^3
So to convert from cm^3 to dm^3 you need to divide by 1000.

All Gases Take Up the **Same Volume** under the Same Conditions

The space that one mole of a gas occupies at a certain temperature and pressure is known as the **molar gas volume**. It has units of **dm^3 mol^{-1}**.
If temperature and pressure stay the same, **one mole** of **any** gas always has the **same volume**.
At **room temperature and pressure** (r.t.p.), this happens to be **24 dm^3 mol^{-1}** (r.t.p is 298 K (25 °C) and 101.3 kPa).
Here's the formula for working out the number of moles in a volume of gas.

$$\textbf{Number of moles} = \frac{\textbf{Volume in dm}^3}{\textbf{Molar gas volume}}$$

At r.t.p, just substitute 24 dm^3 mol^{-1} into this equation as the molar gas volume.

Example: How many moles are there in 6.0 dm^3 of oxygen gas at r.t.p.?

Number of moles = $\frac{6.0}{24}$ = **0.25 moles of oxygen molecules**

This is oxygen molecules, not atoms, as gaseous oxygen exists as O_2, not lone O atoms.

Ideal Gas equation — $pV = nRT$

In the real world, it's not always room temperature and pressure.
The **ideal gas equation** lets you find the **number of moles** in a certain volume at **any temperature and pressure**.

$pV = nRT$ Where: p = pressure (Pa)
V = volume (m^3)
n = number of moles
R = 8.314 J K^{-1} mol^{-1}
T = temperature (K)

1 cm^3 = 1 × 10^{-6} m^3
1 dm^3 = 1 × 10^{-3} m^3

R is the gas constant. It's sometimes only written to 3 s.f. (8.31 J K^{-1} mol^{-1}), so make sure you use the value that you're given in the exams.

K = °C + 273

Example: At a temperature of 60.0 °C and a pressure of 250 kPa, a gas occupied a volume of 1100 cm^3 and had a mass of 1.60 g. Find its relative molecular mass.

1 kPa = 1000 Pa

1100 cm^3 = 1.1 × 10^{-3} m^3

$$n = \frac{pV}{RT} = \frac{(250 \times 10^3) \times (1.1 \times 10^{-3})}{8.314 \times 333} = 0.0993 \text{ moles}$$

If 0.0993 moles is 1.60 g, then 1 mole = $\frac{1.60}{0.0993}$ = 16.1 g. So the relative molecular mass (M_r) is **16.1**.

The Mole and Equations

Balanced Equations have **Equal Numbers** of each Atom on **Both Sides**

1) Balanced equations have the **same number** of each atom on **both** sides. They're... well... you know... balanced.
2) You can only add more atoms by adding **whole reactants** or **products**. You do this by putting a number **in front** of a substance that's already there (or adding a new substance). You **can't** mess with formulas — ever.

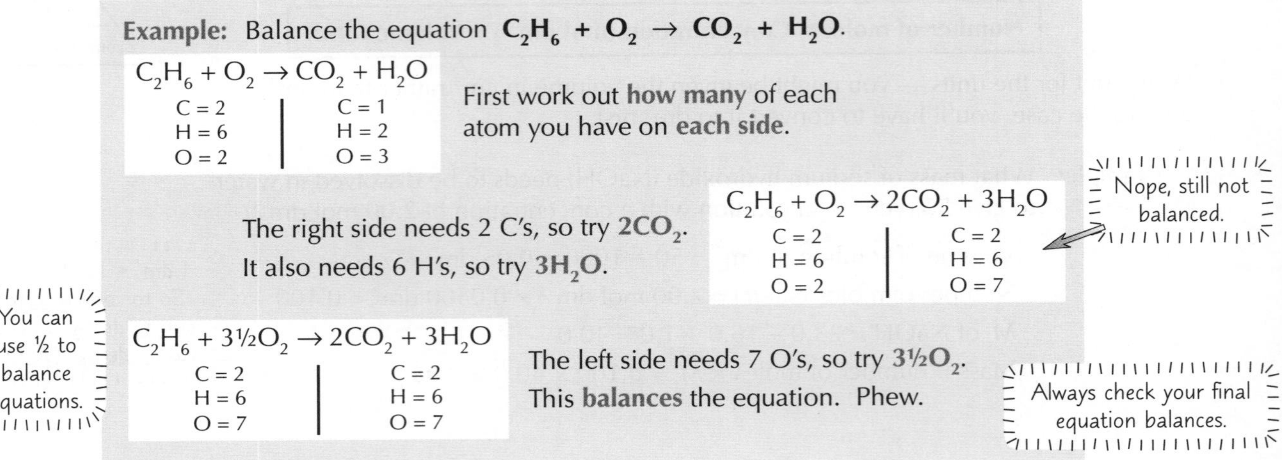

Example: Balance the equation $\mathbf{C_2H_6 + O_2 \rightarrow CO_2 + H_2O}$.

$C_2H_6 + O_2 \rightarrow CO_2 + H_2O$

Left	Right
C = 2	C = 1
H = 6	H = 2
O = 2	O = 3

First work out **how many** of each atom you have on **each side**.

The right side needs 2 C's, so try $\mathbf{2CO_2}$.
It also needs 6 H's, so try $\mathbf{3H_2O}$.

$C_2H_6 + O_2 \rightarrow 2CO_2 + 3H_2O$

Left	Right
C = 2	C = 2
H = 6	H = 6
O = 2	O = 7

Nope, still not balanced.

You can use ½ to balance equations.

$C_2H_6 + 3\frac{1}{2}O_2 \rightarrow 2CO_2 + 3H_2O$

Left	Right
C = 2	C = 2
H = 6	H = 6
O = 7	O = 7

The left side needs 7 O's, so try $\mathbf{3\frac{1}{2}O_2}$.
This **balances** the equation. Phew.

Always check your final equation balances.

Ionic Equations Only Show the Reacting Particles

1) You can also write an **ionic equation** for any reaction involving **ions** that happens **in solution**.
2) In an ionic equation, only the **reacting particles** (and the **products** they form) are included.

Example: Here is the **full balanced equation** for the reaction of **nitric acid** with **sodium hydroxide**:

$$HNO_3 + NaOH \rightarrow NaNO_3 + H_2O$$

The **ionic** substances in this equation will **dissolve**, breaking up into ions in solution. You can rewrite the equation to show all the **ions** that are in the reaction mixture:

$$H^+ + NO_3^- + Na^+ + OH^- \rightarrow Na^+ + NO_3^- + H_2O$$

Leave anything that isn't an ion in solution (like the H_2O) as it is.

To get from this to the ionic equation, just cross out any ions that appear on **both sides** of the equation — in this case, that's the sodium ions (Na^+) and the nitrate ions (NO_3^-).

An ion that's present in the reaction mixture, but doesn't get involved in the reaction is called a spectator ion.

So the **ionic equation** for this reaction is:

$$\mathbf{H^+ + OH^- \rightarrow H_2O}$$

3) When you've written an ionic equation, check that the **charges** are **balanced**, as well as the atoms — if the charges don't balance, the equation isn't right.

In the example above, the **net charge** on the left hand side is +1 + –1 = **0** and the net charge on the right hand side is **0** — so the charges balance.

State Symbols Give a bit More Information about the Substances

State symbols are put after each reactant or product in an equation. They tell you what **state of matter** things are in.

s = solid
l = liquid
g = gas
aq = aqueous (solution in water)

To show you what I mean, here's an example —

$$\mathbf{CaCO_{3\,(s)} + 2HCl_{(aq)} \rightarrow CaCl_{2\,(aq)} + H_2O_{(l)} + CO_{2\,(g)}}$$

$CaCO_{3\,(s)}$	$2HCl_{(aq)}$	$CaCl_{2\,(aq)}$	$H_2O_{(l)}$	$CO_{2\,(g)}$
solid	**aqueous**	**aqueous**	**liquid**	**gas**

The Mole and Equations

Balanced Equations can be used to Work out Masses

This is handy for working out how much **reactant** you need to make a certain **mass of product** (or **vice versa**).

Example: Calculate the mass of iron oxide produced if 27.9 g of iron is burnt in air.

$$4Fe + 3O_2 \rightarrow 2Fe_2O_3$$

M_r of Fe = 55.8, so the number of moles in 27.9 g of Fe = $\frac{\text{mass}}{M_r} = \frac{27.9}{55.8}$ = 0.500 moles

From the equation: 4 moles of Fe gives 2 moles of Fe_2O_3, so 0.500 moles of Fe would give 0.250 moles of Fe_2O_3.

M_r of Fe_2O_3 = (2 × 55.8) + (3 × 16.0) = 159.6

Mass of Fe_2O_3 produced = moles × M_r = 0.250 × 159.6 = **39.9 g**.

Once you know the number of moles and the M_r of Fe_2O_3, it's easy to work out the mass.

That's not all... Balanced Equations can be used to Work Out Gas Volumes

It's pretty handy to be able to use the ideal gas equation to work out **how much gas** a reaction will produce, so that you can use **large enough apparatus**. Or else there might be a rather large bang.

Example: What volume of gas, in dm^3, is produced when 15.0 g of sodium reacts with excess water at a temperature of 25.0 °C and a pressure of 100 kPa? The gas constant is 8.31 J K^{-1} mol^{-1}.

$$2Na_{(s)} + 2H_2O_{(l)} \rightarrow 2NaOH_{(aq)} + H_{2\,(g)}$$

'Excess water' just means that you know all of the sodium will react.

M_r of Na = 23.0, so number of moles in 15.0 g of Na = $\frac{15.0}{23.0}$ = 0.652 moles

From the equation, 2 moles of Na produces 1 mole of H_2,
so 0.652 moles of Na must produce $\frac{0.652}{2}$ = 0.326 moles of H_2.

Volume of $H_2 = \frac{nRT}{p} = \frac{0.326 \times 8.31 \times 298}{100 \times 10^3}$ = 0.00807 m^3 = **8.07 dm^3** (3 s.f.)

Practice Questions

Q1 Give an equation you could use to work out the number of moles of something from a given mass?

Q2 What volume does 1 mole of gas occupy at r.t.p.?

Q3 What is the difference between a full equation and an ionic equation?

Q4 What is the state symbol for a solution of sodium chloride dissolved in water?

Exam Questions

Q1 Calculate the mass of 0.360 moles of ethanoic acid, CH_3COOH. [2 marks]

Q2 What mass of H_2SO_4 is needed to produce 60.0 cm^3 of 0.250 mol dm^{-3} solution? [2 marks]

Q3 Calculate the mass of ethene, C_2H_4, required to produce 258 g of chloroethane, C_2H_5Cl.

$$C_2H_4 + HCl \rightarrow C_2H_5Cl$$

[3 marks]

Q4 15.0 g of calcium carbonate is heated strongly so that it fully decomposes. $CaCO_{3\,(s)} \rightarrow CaO_{(s)} + CO_{2\,(g)}$

a) Calculate the mass of calcium oxide produced. [3 marks]

b) Calculate the volume of gas produced in m^3 at 25.0 °C and 100 kPa.
The gas constant is 8.31 J K^{-1} mol^{-1}. [3 marks]

Q5 Balance this equation: $KI + Pb(NO_3)_2 \rightarrow PbI_2 + KNO_3$ [1 mark]

Don't get in a state about equations...

Balancing equations is a really, really important skill in Chemistry, so make sure you can do it. You will ONLY be able to calculate reacting masses and gas volumes if you've got a balanced equation to work from. You've been warned...

Formulas of Ionic Compounds

Ahh — ions. My favourite topic. In fact, the only things better than ions are probably ionic compounds, and here's a page all about them. It's like Christmas has come early...

Ions are made when *Electrons* are *Transferred*

1) Ions are formed when electrons are **transferred** from one atom to another.
2) The simplest ions are single atoms which have either lost or gained electrons so as to have a **full outer shell**.

A sodium atom (Na) **loses** 1 electron to form a sodium ion (Na^+)	$Na \rightarrow Na^+ + e^-$
A magnesium atom (Mg) **loses** 2 electrons to form a magnesium ion (Mg^{2+})	$Mg \rightarrow Mg^{2+} + 2e^-$
A chlorine atom (Cl) **gains** 1 electron to form a chloride ion (Cl^-)	$Cl + e^- \rightarrow Cl^-$
An oxygen atom (O) **gains** 2 electrons to form an oxide ion (O^{2-})	$O + 2e^- \rightarrow O^{2-}$

3) You **don't** have to remember what ion **each element** forms — nope, you just look at the Periodic Table.
4) Elements in the same **group** all have the same number of **outer electrons**. So they have to **lose or gain** the same number to get the full outer shell that they're aiming for. And this means that they form ions with the **same charges**.

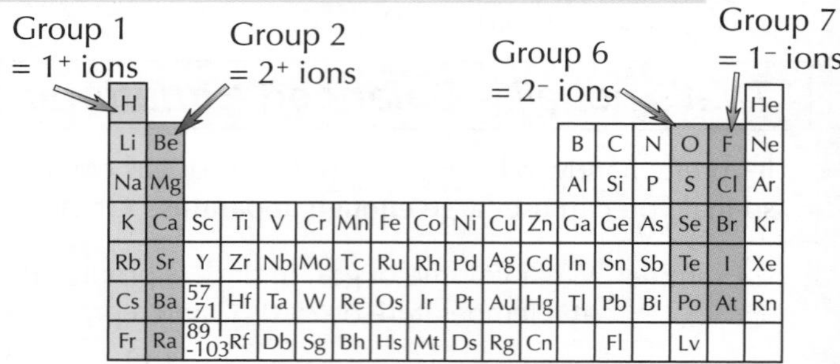

Not all *Ions* are Made from *Single Atoms*

There are lots of ions that are made up of a group of atoms with an overall charge.
These are called **molecular ions**. Here are the names and formulas of some common ones:

Name	Nitrate	Carbonate	Sulfate	Hydroxide	Ammonium	Hydrogencarbonate
Formula	NO_3^-	CO_3^{2-}	SO_4^{2-}	OH^-	NH_4^+	HCO_3^-

Don't forget to learn the charge on each ion too.

Here are the names and formulas of some common monoatomic ions:

Name	Zinc ion	Silver ion	Copper(II) ion	Iron(II) ion	Iron(III) ion	Lead(II) ion
Formula	Zn^{2+}	Ag^+	Cu^{2+}	Fe^{2+}	Fe^{3+}	Pb^{2+}

Charges in *Ionic Compounds* Always *Balance*

1) **Ionic compounds** are made when positive and negative ions **bond** together. They do this through **ionic bonding**, but that's another story (see pages 46-49).
2) The charges on an **ionic compound** must always balance out to zero. For example...
   - In **NaCl**, the +1 charge on the Na^+ ion balances the –1 charge on the Cl^- ion.
   - In **$MgCl_2$**, the +2 charge on the Mg^{2+} ion balances the two –1 charges on the two Cl^- ions.

Example: What is the formula of potassium sulfate?

Potassium is in Group 1 of the periodic table, so will therefore form ions with a +1 charge: **K^+**.
The formula for the sulfate ion is **SO_4^{2-}**.
For every **one** sulfate ion, you will need **two** potassium ions to balance the charge: $(+1 \times 2) + (-2) = 0$.
So the formula is **K_2SO_4**.

Formulas of Ionic Compounds

Salts are Ionic Compounds

1) When **acids** and **bases** react, they form **water** and a **salt** (p. 38).
2) **Salts** are **ionic compounds**. All solid salts consist of a **lattice** of positive and negative ions. In some salts, **water molecules** are incorporated in the lattice too.
3) The water in a lattice is called **water of crystallisation**. A solid salt containing water of crystallisation is **hydrated**. A salt is **anhydrous** if it doesn't contain water of crystallisation.
4) **One mole** of a particular hydrated salt always has the **same number of moles** of water of crystallisation — its **formula** shows **how many** (it's always a whole number).
5) For example, **hydrated copper sulfate** has **five** moles of water for every mole of the salt. So its formula is $\mathbf{CuSO_4.5H_2O}$. ← Notice that there's a dot between $CuSO_4$ and $5H_2O$.
6) Many hydrated salts **lose** their water of crystallisation **when heated**, to become **anhydrous**. If you know the mass of the salt when hydrated and anhydrous, you can work its formula out like this:

Here's a tiny part of the lattice in a hydrated salt.

Water molecules are **polar** (see p. 56). They're held in place in the lattice because they're attracted to the ions.

Example: Heating 3.210 g of hydrated magnesium sulfate, $MgSO_4.\mathbf{X}H_2O$, forms 1.567 g of anhydrous magnesium sulfate. Find the value of **X** and write the formula of the hydrated salt.

First you find the number of moles of water lost.

Mass of water lost:	3.210 – 1.567 = 1.643 g
Number of moles of water lost:	mass ÷ molar mass = 1.643 g ÷ 18 g mol^{-1} = **0.09127 moles**

Then you find the number of moles of anhydrous salt.

Molar mass of $MgSO_4$:	24.3 + 32.1 + (4 × 16.0) = 120.4 g mol^{-1}
Number of moles (in 1.567 g):	mass ÷ molar mass = 1.567 g ÷ 120.4 g mol^{-1} = **0.01301 moles**

Now you work out the ratio of moles of anhydrous salt to moles of water in the form 1:n.

From the experiment, **0.01301 moles of salt : 0.09127 moles of water,**

So, $$\mathbf{1\ mole\ of\ salt:}\ \frac{\mathbf{0.09127}}{\mathbf{0.01301}} = \mathbf{7.015\ moles\ of\ water.}$$

You might be given the percentage of the mass that is water — use the method on page 43.

X must be a whole number, and some errors are to be expected in any experiment, so you can safely round off your result — so the formula of the hydrated salt is $\mathbf{MgSO_4.7H_2O}$.

Practice Questions

Q1 What charge do the ions formed by Group 7 elements have?

Q2 What is the formula for the hydroxide ion?

Q3 Why can water molecules become fixed in an ionic lattice?

Exam Questions

Q1 What is the formula of scandium sulfate, given that the scandium ion has a charge of +3? [1 mark]

Q2 Use the periodic table to work out the formula of sodium oxide. [1 mark]

Q3 A sample of hydrated calcium sulfate, $CaSO_4.XH_2O$, was prepared by reacting calcium hydroxide with sulfuric acid. 1.883 g of hydrated salt was produced. This was then heated until all the water of crystallisation was driven off and the product was then reweighed. Its mass was 1.133 g.

a) How many moles of anhydrous calcium sulfate were produced? [2 marks]

b) Calculate the value of X in the formula $CaSO_4.XH_2O$. (X is a whole number.) [3 marks]

Ioning — every scientist's favourite household chore...

I prefer dusting personally. But even if you're a fan of vacuuming or sweeping, make sure you take the time to learn the rules for working out the charges on different ions. The periodic table is great for working out the charges of the ions of elements in groups 1, 2, 6 and 7, but the best way to remember the charges on molecular ions is to just learn them.

Acids and Bases

Acid's a word that's thrown around willy-nilly — but now for the truth...

Acids are all about Hydrated Protons

1) Acids are **proton donors**. When mixed with **water**, all acids **release hydrogen ions** — H^+ (these are just **protons**, but you never get them by themselves in water — they're always combined with H_2O to form hydroxonium ions, H_3O^+).
2) **Bases** do the opposite — they're proton acceptors and want to **grab H^+ ions**.
3) Bases that are soluble in water are known as **alkalis**. They release **OH^-** ions in solution.

Acids produce $H^+_{(aq)}$ ions in an aqueous solution.
Alkalis produce $OH^-_{(aq)}$ ions in an aqueous solution.

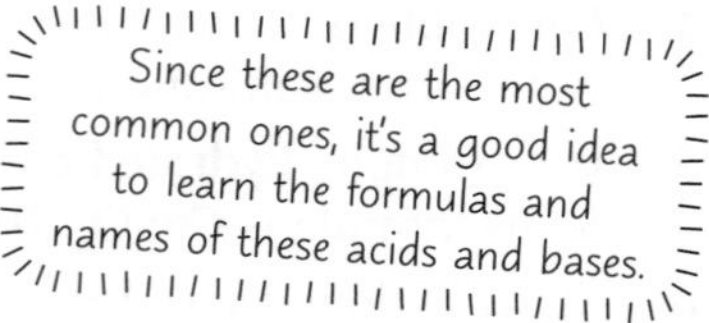

Since these are the most common ones, it's a good idea to learn the formulas and names of these acids and bases.

4) Some common acids are: **HCl** (hydrochloric acid), **H_2SO_4** (sulfuric acid), **HNO_3** (nitric acid) and **CH_3COOH** (ethanoic acid).
5) And some common bases are: **NaOH** (sodium hydroxide), **KOH** (potassium hydroxide) and **NH_3** (ammonia).

Acids and Bases Can Be Strong or Weak

1) The reaction between acids and water, and bases and water is **reversible**, so at any one point in time, both the forwards and backwards reactions will be happening.

Acids: $HA + H_2O \rightleftharpoons H_3O^+ + A^-$

Bases: $B + H_2O \rightleftharpoons BH^+ + OH^-$

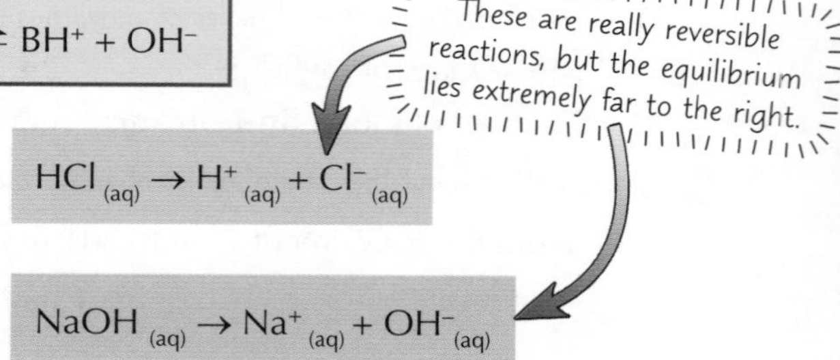

These are really reversible reactions, but the equilibrium lies extremely far to the right.

2) For **strong acids**, e.g. HCl, very little of the reverse reaction happens, so nearly all the acid will dissociate (or ionise) in water, and **nearly all** the H^+ ions are released.

$$HCl_{(aq)} \rightarrow H^+_{(aq)} + Cl^-_{(aq)}$$

3) The same thing applies with **strong bases**, e.g. NaOH. Again, the forwards reaction is favoured, so nearly all the base dissociates in water and **lots** of OH^- ions are released.

$$NaOH_{(aq)} \rightarrow Na^+_{(aq)} + OH^-_{(aq)}$$

4) For **weak acids**, e.g. CH_3COOH, the backwards reaction is favoured, so only a small amount of the acid will dissociate in water and **only a few** H^+ ions are released.

$$CH_3COOH_{(aq)} \rightleftharpoons CH_3COO^-_{(aq)} + H^+_{(aq)}$$

5) Again, **weak bases**, such as NH_3, ionise only slightly in water. The backwards reaction is favoured so only a small amount of the base dissociates and **only a few** OH^- ions are released.

$$NH_{3(aq)} + H_2O_{(l)} \rightleftharpoons NH_4^+{}_{(aq)} + OH^-_{(aq)}$$

Acids React to Form Neutral Salts

Acids and **bases neutralise** each other. In the **neutralisation** reaction between acids and alkalis, a **salt** and **water** are produced.

1) It's the hydrogen ions released by the acid and the hydroxide ions released by the alkali that combine to form water.

$$H^+_{(aq)} + OH^-_{(aq)} \rightleftharpoons H_2O_{(l)}$$

2) You get a **salt** when the hydrogen ions in the acid are replaced by **metal ions** or **ammonium (NH_4^+) ions** from the alkali.

E.g. $HCl_{(aq)} + KOH_{(aq)} \rightarrow KCl_{(aq)} + H_2O_{(l)}$

3) Different acids produce **different salts** — sulfuric acid (H_2SO_4) produces salts called **sulfates**, hydrochloric acid (HCl) produces **chlorides**, and nitric acid (HNO_3) produces **nitrates**.

Ammonia is a bit of an exception as it doesn't directly produce hydroxide ions, but **aqueous ammonia** is still an **alkali**. This is because the reaction between ammonia and water produces hydroxide ions. Ammonia accepts a hydrogen ion from water molecules, forming an ammonium ion and a hydroxide ion. In this way, ammonia can **neutralise acids**.

$$NH_{3(aq)} + H_2O_{(l)} \rightleftharpoons NH_4^+{}_{(aq)} + OH^-_{(aq)}$$

Acids and Bases

Acids React with **Metals** and **Metal Compounds**

1) As you've seen, when **acids** react with **bases**, they **neutralise** each other and produce a **salt**.
2) **Metal oxides**, **metal hydroxides** and **metal carbonates** are all common bases that'll react with acids. **Metals** will also react with acids.

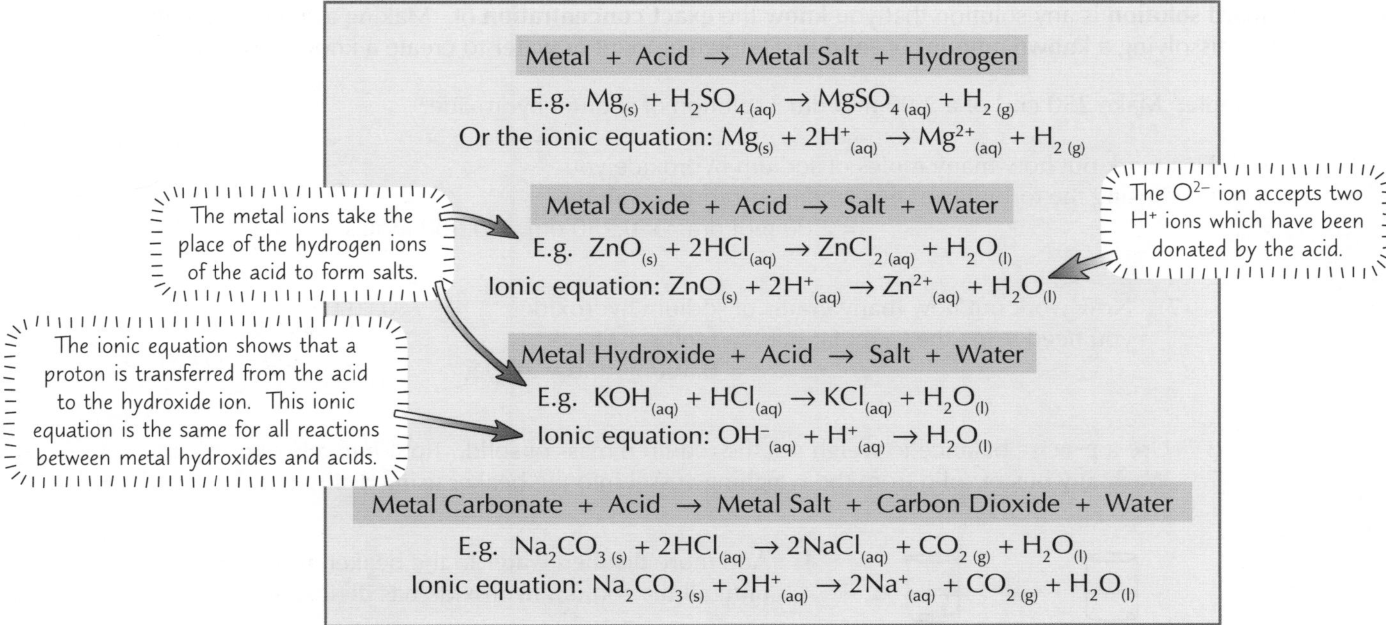

Metal + Acid → Metal Salt + Hydrogen
E.g. $Mg_{(s)} + H_2SO_{4\,(aq)} \rightarrow MgSO_{4\,(aq)} + H_{2\,(g)}$
Or the ionic equation: $Mg_{(s)} + 2H^+_{(aq)} \rightarrow Mg^{2+}_{(aq)} + H_{2\,(g)}$
The metal ions take the place of the hydrogen ions of the acid to form salts.
Metal Oxide + Acid → Salt + Water
E.g. $ZnO_{(s)} + 2HCl_{(aq)} \rightarrow ZnCl_{2\,(aq)} + H_2O_{(l)}$
Ionic equation: $ZnO_{(s)} + 2H^+_{(aq)} \rightarrow Zn^{2+}_{(aq)} + H_2O_{(l)}$
The O^{2-} ion accepts two H^+ ions which have been donated by the acid.
The ionic equation shows that a proton is transferred from the acid to the hydroxide ion. This ionic equation is the same for all reactions between metal hydroxides and acids.
Metal Hydroxide + Acid → Salt + Water
E.g. $KOH_{(aq)} + HCl_{(aq)} \rightarrow KCl_{(aq)} + H_2O_{(l)}$
Ionic equation: $OH^-_{(aq)} + H^+_{(aq)} \rightarrow H_2O_{(l)}$
Metal Carbonate + Acid → Metal Salt + Carbon Dioxide + Water
E.g. $Na_2CO_{3\,(s)} + 2HCl_{(aq)} \rightarrow 2NaCl_{(aq)} + CO_{2\,(g)} + H_2O_{(l)}$
Ionic equation: $Na_2CO_{3\,(s)} + 2H^+_{(aq)} \rightarrow 2Na^+_{(aq)} + CO_{2\,(g)} + H_2O_{(l)}$

Ammonia reacts with **Acids** to make **Ammonia Salts**

The reaction of ammonia with nitric acid produces ammonium nitrate. Ammonium sulfate is made if ammonia reacts with sulfuric acid.

Ammonia + Acid → Ammonium salt

E.g. $NH_{3\,(aq)} + HNO_{3\,(aq)} \rightarrow NH_4NO_{3\,(aq)}$

Ionic equation: $NH_{3\,(aq)} + H^+_{(aq)} \rightarrow NH_4^+{}_{(aq)}$

This reaction is actually: $NH_4^+ + OH^- + HNO_3 \rightarrow NH_4NO_3 + H_2O$ as the reactant is aqueous ammonia.

Practice Questions

Q1 Define an acid, a base and an alkali.

Q2 Name three common acids.

Q3 What products are formed when an acid and an alkali react?

Exam Questions

Q1 A solution of magnesium chloride can be made in the laboratory using dilute hydrochloric acid.

a) Name a compound that could be used, with hydrochloric acid, to make magnesium chloride. [1 mark]

b) Write a balanced equation for this reaction. [1 mark]

Q2 Sodium hydroxide reacts with nitric acid at room temperature to produce water and a soluble salt.

a) Write a balanced equation, including state symbols for this reaction. [1 mark]

b) What is the name given to this type of reaction? [1 mark]

It's a stick-up — your protons or your life...

All acids have protons to give away and bases just love to take them. It's what makes them acids and bases. It's like how bus drivers drive buses... it's what makes them bus drivers. Learn the formulas for the common acids — hydrochloric, sulfuric, nitric and ethanoic, and the common alkalis — sodium hydroxide, potassium hydroxide and aqueous ammonia.

Titrations

Titrations are used to find out the concentration of acid or alkali solutions. You'll probably get to do a titration or two (lucky you), but there's more to titrations than glassware. You'll need to do calculations with your results. Read on...

A **Standard Solution** Has a **Known** Concentration

Standard solutions can also be called volumetric solutions.

Before you do a titration, you might have to make up a **standard solution** to use.
A **standard solution** is any solution that you **know** the **exact concentration** of. Making a standard solution involves dissolving a **known amount** of **solid** in a known amount of **water** to create a known concentration.

Example: Make 250 cm^3 of a 2.00 mol dm^{-3} solution of sodium hydroxide.

1) First work out how many **moles** of sodium hydroxide you need using the formula: **moles = concentration × volume**
= 2.00 mol dm^{-3} × 0.250 dm^3 = 0.500 moles

Remember, the volume needs to be in dm^3 for this bit.

2) Now work out how many **grams** of sodium hydroxide you need using the formula: **mass = moles ×** M_r
= 0.500 × 40.0 = 20.0 g

M_r of NaOH: 23.0 + 16.0 + 1.0 = 40.0

3) Use a **precise** balance to weigh out the required mass of solid. Tip it into a beaker. **Wash** any bits of solid from the weighing vessel into the beaker using **distilled water**.

4) Add more **distilled water** to the beaker and **stir** until all the sodium hydroxide has **dissolved**.

5) Tip the solution into a **volumetric flask** — make sure it's the right size for the volume that you're making (250 cm^3 in this case). Use a **funnel** to make sure it all goes in.

6) **Rinse** the beaker and stirring rod with distilled water and add that to the **flask** too. This makes sure there's no solute clinging to the beaker or rod.

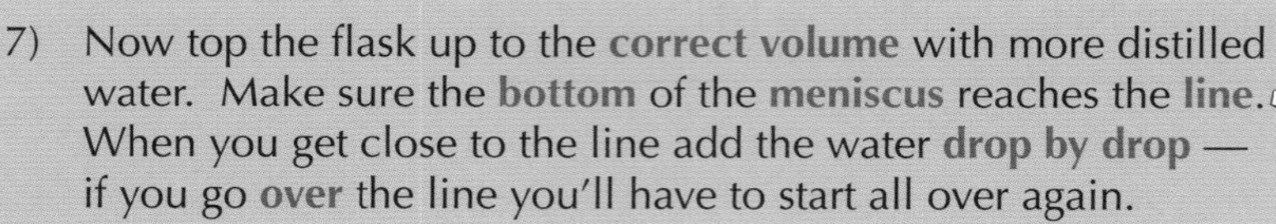

7) Now top the flask up to the **correct volume** with more distilled water. Make sure the **bottom** of the **meniscus** reaches the **line**. When you get close to the line add the water **drop by drop** — if you go **over** the line you'll have to start all over again.

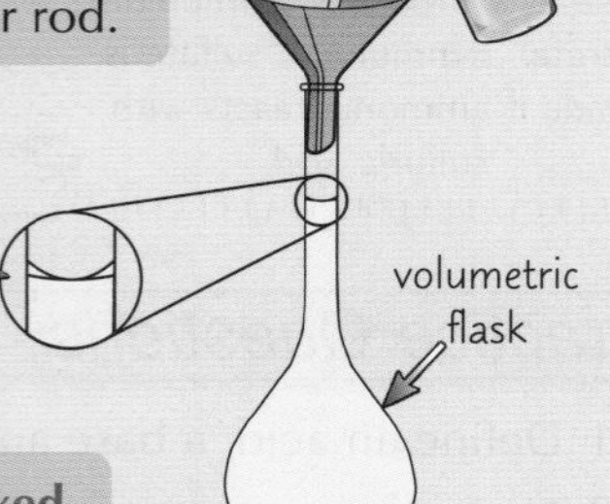

8) **Stopper** the flask and turn it upside down a few times to make sure it's **mixed**.

Titrations let you work out the **Concentration** of an **Acid** or **Alkali**

1) A **titration** allows you to find out **exactly** how much acid is needed to **neutralise** a measured quantity of alkali (or the other way round).
2) You can use this data to work out the **concentration** of the alkali.
3) Start off by using a **pipette** to measure out a set volume of the solution that you want to know the concentration of. Put it in a flask.
4) Add a few drops of an appropriate **indicator** (see next page) to the flask.
5) Then fill a **burette** (see next page) with a **standard solution** of the acid — remember, that means you know its exact concentration.
6) Use a **funnel** to carefully pour the acid into the burette. Always do this **below eye level** to avoid any acid splashing on to your face or eyes. (You should wear **safety glasses** too.)
7) Now you're ready to **titrate**...

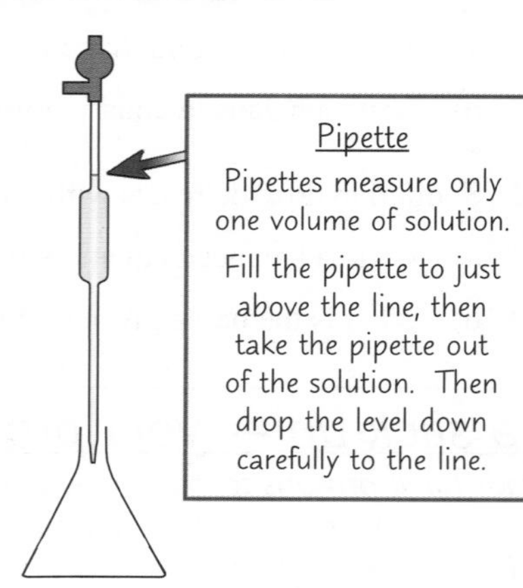

Pipette
Pipettes measure only one volume of solution.
Fill the pipette to just above the line, then take the pipette out of the solution. Then drop the level down carefully to the line.

Titrations

Titrations need to be done Really Accurately

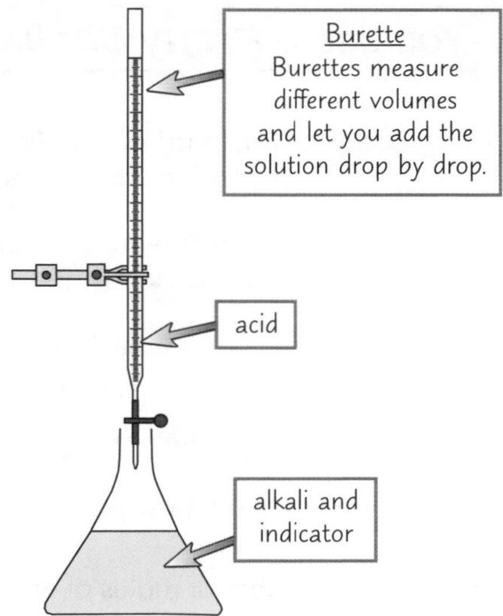

Burette
Burettes measure different volumes and let you add the solution drop by drop.
acid
alkali and indicator

1) First do a **rough titration** to get an idea where the **end point** (the exact point where the alkali is **neutralised** and the indicator changes colour) is. Add the **acid** to the alkali using a **burette**, giving the flask a regular **swirl**.
2) Now do an **accurate** titration. Take an initial reading to see exactly how much acid is in the burette. Then run the acid in to within 2 cm^3 of the end point. When you get to this stage, add it **dropwise** — if you don't notice exactly when the colour changes you'll **overshoot** and your result won't be accurate.
3) Work out the **amount** of acid used to **neutralise** the alkali. This is just the final reading minus the initial reading. This volume is known as the **titre**.
4) **Repeat** the titration a few times, until you have at least three results that are **concordant** (very similar).
5) Use the results from each repeat to calculate the **mean** volume of acid used. Remember to leave out any **anomalous results** when calculating your mean — they can distort your answer.

There's more stuff about how to record and handle the data you get from experiments like this in the Practical Skills section. Have a look if you want to know more about means, anomalous results, precision and experimental error.

Choppy seas made it difficult for Captain Cod to read the burette accurately.

Indicators Show you when the Reaction's Just Finished

In titrations, indicators that change colour quickly over a **very small pH range** are used so you know **exactly** when the reaction has ended.

The main two indicators for **acid/alkali reactions** are:

1) **methyl orange** — this is yellow in acid and red in alkali.
2) **phenolphthalein** — this is **pink** in alkali and **colourless** in acid.

Universal indicator is no good here — its colour change is too gradual.

It's a good idea to stand your flask on a white tile — it'll make it easier to see exactly when the end point is.

You can Calculate Concentrations from Titrations

The next step is to use the **mean volume** from your titrations to find the **concentration** of the solution in the flask.

Example: In a titration experiment, 25.0 cm^3 of 0.500 mol dm^{-3} HCl neutralised 35.0 cm^3 of NaOH solution. Calculate the concentration of the sodium hydroxide solution in mol dm^{-3}.

First write a **balanced equation** and decide **what you know** and what you **need to know**:

HCl +	NaOH → NaCl + H_2O
25.0 cm^3	**35.0 cm^3**
0.500 mol dm^{-3}	**?**

Now work out how many **moles of HCl** you have:

Number of moles HCl = concentration × volume (dm^3) = $0.500 \times \frac{25.0}{1000}$ = 0.0125 moles

This is the formula from page 33.

From the equation, you know 1 mole of HCl neutralises 1 mole of NaOH.
So 0.0125 moles of HCl must neutralise **0.0125** moles of NaOH.

Now it's a doddle to work out the **concentration of NaOH**:

Concentration of NaOH = moles ÷ volume (dm^3) = $0.0125 \div \frac{35.0}{1000}$ = **0.357 mol dm^{-3}**

Titrations

You use a **Pretty Similar Method** to Calculate **Volumes** for Reactions

Example: 20.4 cm^3 of a 0.500 mol dm^{-3} solution of sodium carbonate reacts with 1.50 mol dm^{-3} nitric acid.
Calculate the volume of nitric acid required to neutralise the sodium carbonate.

Like before, first write a **balanced equation** for the reaction and decide **what you know** and what you **want to know**:

Na_2CO_3	$+ 2HNO_3$	$\rightarrow 2NaNO_3 + H_2O + CO_2$
20.4 cm^3	**?**	
0.500 mol dm^{-3}	**1.50 mol dm^{-3}**	

Now work out how many **moles** of Na_2CO_3 you've got:

Number of moles of Na_2CO_3 = concentration × volume (dm^3) = $0.500 \times \frac{20.4}{1000} = 0.0102$ moles.

1 mole of Na_2CO_3 neutralises 2 moles of HNO_3,
so 0.0102 moles of Na_2CO_3 neutralises **0.0204 moles of HNO_3**.

Now you know the number of moles of HNO_3 and the concentration, you can work out the **volume**:

Volume of HNO_3 = $\frac{\text{number of moles}}{\text{concentration}} = \frac{0.0204}{1.50}$ = **0.0136 dm^3**

That's 0.0136 × 1000 = 13.6 cm^3.

Practice Questions

Q1 What is a standard solution? Describe how to make one.

Q2 When you're doing a titration, why do you add the acid dropwise when you're getting near the end point?

Q3 Write down the formula for calculating number of moles from the concentration and volume of a solution. Rearrange it so that you could use it to calculate concentration. Then do the same for volume.

Exam Questions

Q1 Calculate the concentration in mol dm^{-3} of a solution of ethanoic acid (CH_3COOH) if 25.4 cm^3 of it is neutralised by 14.6 cm^3 of 0.500 mol dm^{-3} sodium hydroxide solution.
The equation for this reaction is: $CH_3COOH + NaOH \rightarrow CH_3COONa + H_2O$. [3 marks]

Q2 You are supplied with 0.750 g of calcium carbonate and a solution of 0.250 mol dm^{-3} sulfuric acid.
What volume of acid will be needed to neutralise the calcium carbonate?
The equation for this reaction is: $CaCO_3 + H_2SO_4 \rightarrow CaSO_4 + H_2O + CO_2$. [4 marks]

Q3 50.0 cm^3 of nitric acid was titrated with 0.400 mol dm^{-3} sodium hydroxide solution.
The equation for this reaction is: $HNO_3 + NaOH \rightarrow NaNO_3 + H_2O$.
The results of the titration are shown in the table on the right.

a) Identify any anomalous results, explaining your reasoning. [1 mark]

b) Calculate the mean titre, ignoring anomalous results. [1 mark]

c) Calculate the concentration of the nitric acid. [3 marks]

Titration	Volume NaOH (cm^3)
1	45.00
2	45.10
3	42.90
4	44.90

Burettes and pipettes — big glass things, just waiting to be dropped...

Titrations are fiddly. But you do get to use big, impressive-looking equipment and feel like you're doing something important. Then there are the results to do calculations with. The best way to start is always to write out the balanced equation and put what you know about each substance underneath it. Then think about what you're trying to find out.

Formulas, Yield and Atom Economy

Here's another load of pages that are piled high with numbers — it's all just glorified maths really.

Empirical and **Molecular** Formulas are **Ratios**

Time to learn what's what with empirical and molecular formulas, so here goes...

1) The **empirical formula** gives just the simplest whole number ratio of atoms of each element in a compound.
2) The **molecular formula** gives the **actual** numbers of atoms of each element in a compound.
3) The **molecular formula** is made up of a whole **number** of empirical units.

Example: A molecule with $M_r = 166.0$ has the empirical formula $C_4H_3O_2$. Find its molecular formula.

First find the **empirical mass** (that's just the total mass of all the atoms in the empirical formula):

$$(4 \times 12.0) + (3 \times 1.0) + (2 \times 16.0) = 48.0 + 3.0 + 32.0 = 83.0$$

Now compare the empirical mass with the **molecular mass**: $M_r = 166$,

so there are $\frac{166.0}{83.0} = 2$ empirical units in the molecule.

The molecular formula must be the **empirical formula × 2**, so the molecular formula is $\mathbf{C_8H_6O_4}$.

Empirical Formulas can be Calculated from **Percentage Composition**

You can work out the empirical formula of a compound from the **percentages** of the different elements it contains.

Example: A compound is found to have percentage composition 56.5% potassium, 8.70% carbon and 34.8% oxygen by mass. Find its empirical formula.

Use $n = \frac{\text{mass}}{M_r}$

In **100 g** of the compound there would be:

$\frac{56.5}{39.1} = 1.445$ moles of K $\quad \frac{8.70}{12.0} = 0.725$ moles of C $\quad \frac{34.8}{16.0} = 2.175$ moles of O

Divide each number of moles by the **smallest** of these **numbers** — in this case it's 0.725.

K: $\frac{1.445}{0.725} = 2.00$ $\quad$ C: $\frac{0.725}{0.725} = 1.00$ $\quad$ O: $\frac{2.175}{0.725} = 3.01$

The ratio of K : C : O is 2 : 1 : 3. So the empirical formula's got to be $\mathbf{K_2CO_3}$.

Empirical Formulas can be Calculated from **Experiments**

You can work out empirical formulas using **masses** from **experimental results** too.

Example: When a hydrocarbon is burnt in excess oxygen, 4.40 g of carbon dioxide and 1.80 g of water are made. What is the empirical formula of the hydrocarbon?

First work out how many moles of the products you have.

No. of moles of $CO_2 = \frac{\text{mass}}{M_r} = \frac{4.40}{12.0 + (16.0 \times 2)} = \frac{4.40}{44.0} = 0.100$ moles

1 mole of CO_2 contains 1 mole of carbon atoms, so the original hydrocarbon must have contained **0.100 moles** of **carbon atoms.**

No. of moles of $H_2O = \frac{\text{mass}}{M_r} = \frac{1.80}{(2 \times 1.0) + 16.0} = \frac{1.80}{18.0} = 0.100$ moles

1 mole of H_2O contains 2 moles of hydrogen atoms, so the original hydrocarbon must have contained **0.200 moles** of **hydrogen atoms.**

This works because the only place the carbon in the carbon dioxide and the hydrogen in the water could have come from is the hydrocarbon.

Ratio C : H = 0.100 : 0.200. Now divide both numbers by the smallest — here it's 0.100.

Ratio **C : H = 1 : 2**. So the empirical formula must be $\mathbf{CH_2}$.

Formulas, Yield and Atom Economy

Percentage Yield Is Never 100%

1) The **theoretical yield** is the **mass of product** that **should** be formed in a chemical reaction. It assumes **no** chemicals are '**lost**' in the process. You can use the **masses of reactants** and a **balanced equation** to calculate the theoretical yield for a reaction.

Example: 1.40 g of iron filings reacts with ammonia and sulfuric acid to make hydrated ammonium iron(II) sulfate.

$$Fe_{(s)} + 2NH_{3\,(aq)} + 2H_2SO_{4\,(aq)} + 6H_2O_{(l)} \rightarrow (NH_4)_2Fe(SO_4)_2.6H_2O_{(s)} + H_{2\,(g)}$$

Calculate the theoretical yield of the reaction.

You started with 1.40 g of iron filings and iron has a relative atomic mass of 55.8, so:

Number of moles of iron (A_r = 55.8) reacted = $\frac{\text{mass}}{M_r} = \frac{1.40}{55.8} = 0.0251$

From the equation, **moles of iron : moles of hydrated ammonium iron(II) sulfate** is **1 : 1**, so 0.0251 moles of hydrated ammonium iron(II) sulfate should form.

M_r of $(NH_4)_2Fe(SO_4)_2.6H_2O_{(s)}$ = 392.0
Theoretical yield = moles × M_r = 0.0251 × 392.0 = **9.84 g**

2) For any reaction, the **actual** mass of product (the **actual yield**) will always be **less** than the theoretical yield. There are many reasons for this. For example, sometimes not all the 'starting' chemicals react fully. And some chemicals are always 'lost', e.g. some solution gets left on filter paper, or is lost during transfers between containers.

3) Once you know the **theoretical yield** and the **actual yield**, you can use them to work out the **percentage yield**.

$$\text{Percentage Yield} = \frac{\text{Actual Yield}}{\text{Theoretical Yield}} \times 100$$

4) So, in the ammonium iron(II) sulfate example above, the theoretical yield was 9.84 g. Say you weighed the hydrated ammonium iron(II) sulfate crystals that you had produced and found the actual yield was **5.22 g**. Now you can just pop these numbers into the formula to find the percentage yield:

Percentage yield = (5.22 ÷ 9.84) × 100 = **53.0%**

Here's another example of calculating the percentage yield:

Example: 0.475 g of CH_3Br reacts with excess NaOH in the following reaction:

$$CH_3Br + NaOH \rightarrow CH_3OH + NaBr$$

0.153 g of CH_3OH is produced. What is the percentage yield?

Find the number of moles of **CH_3Br** that you started off with:

Number of moles of CH_3Br = $\frac{\text{mass}}{M_r} = \frac{0.475}{(12.0 + (3 \times 1.0) + 79.9)} = \frac{0.475}{94.9} = 0.00501$ mol

From the equation, **moles of CH_3Br : CH_3OH** is **1 : 1**, so 0.00501 moles of CH_3OH should form.

M_r of CH_3OH = 32.0
Theoretical yield = 0.00501 × 32.0 = **0.160 g.**

Now put these numbers into the percentage yield formula:

Percentage yield = $\frac{\text{Actual Yield}}{\text{Theoretical Yield}} \times 100 = \frac{0.153\text{ g}}{0.160\text{ g}} \times 100 =$ **95.6%**

Formulas, Yield and Atom Economy

Atom Economy is a Measure of the Efficiency of a Reaction

1) **Percentage yield** tells you how wasteful a **process** is — it's based on how much of the product is **lost** during the process (see previous page).
2) But percentage yield doesn't measure how wasteful the **reaction** itself is. A reaction with a 100% yield could still be wasteful if a lot of the atoms from the **reactants** wind up in **by-products** rather than the **desired product**.
3) **Atom economy** is a measure of the proportion of reactant **atoms** that become part of the desired product (rather than by-products) in the **balanced** chemical equation. It's calculated using this formula:

$$\%\text{ atom economy} = \frac{\text{molecular mass of desired product}}{\text{sum of molecular masses of all reactants}} \times 100$$

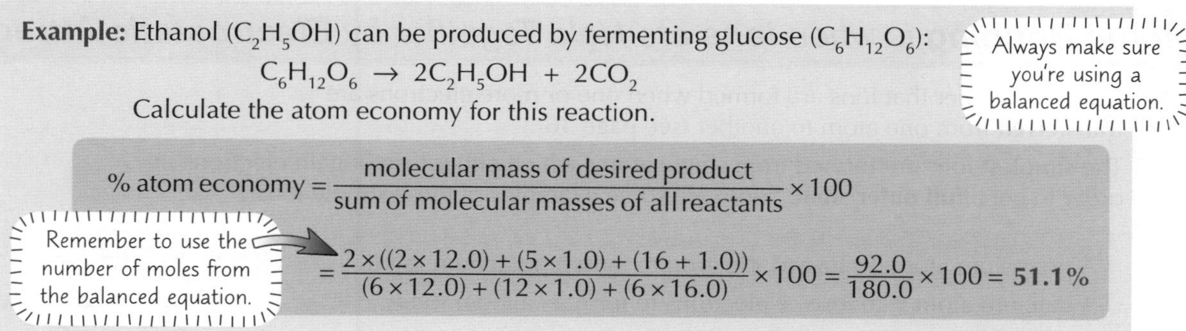

Example: Ethanol (C_2H_5OH) can be produced by fermenting glucose ($C_6H_{12}O_6$):

$$C_6H_{12}O_6 \rightarrow 2C_2H_5OH + 2CO_2$$

Calculate the atom economy for this reaction.

$$\%\text{ atom economy} = \frac{\text{molecular mass of desired product}}{\text{sum of molecular masses of all reactants}} \times 100$$

$$= \frac{2 \times ((2 \times 12.0) + (5 \times 1.0) + (16 + 1.0))}{(6 \times 12.0) + (12 \times 1.0) + (6 \times 16.0)} \times 100 = \frac{92.0}{180.0} \times 100 = \mathbf{51.1\%}$$

Always make sure you're using a balanced equation.
Remember to use the number of moles from the balanced equation.

4) Wherever possible, companies in the chemical industry try to use processes with **high atom economies**.
5) Processes with high atom economies are better for the **environment** because they produce less **waste**. Any waste that's made needs to be **disposed of safely** so the less that's made, the better.
6) They make more efficient use of **raw materials**, so they're more **sustainable** (they use up natural resources more slowly).
7) They're also **less expensive**. A company using a process with a high atom economy will spend less on separating the desired product from the waste products and also less on treating waste.

Practice Questions

Q1 Define 'empirical formula'.

Q2 What is the difference between a molecular formula and an empirical formula?

Q3 Write down the formula for calculating percentage yield.

Q4 Write down the formula for calculating atom economy.

Q5 Explain why it is important for chemical companies to develop processes that have high atom economies.

Exam Questions

Q1 Hydrocarbon X has a relative molecular mass of 78.0. It is found to have 92.3% carbon and 7.70% hydrogen by mass. Find the empirical and molecular formulas of X. [4 marks]

Q2 Phosphorus trichloride (PCl_3) can react with chlorine to give phosphorus pentachloride (PCl_5). This is the equation for this reaction: $PCl_3 + Cl_2 \rightarrow PCl_5$

a) If 0.275 g of PCl_3 (M_r = 137.5) reacts with chlorine, what is the theoretical yield of PCl_5? [3 marks]

b) When this reaction is performed 0.198 g of PCl_5 is collected. Calculate the percentage yield. [1 mark]

c) State the atom economy of this reaction. Explain your answer. [2 marks]

The Empirical Strikes Back...

This is the kind of stuff where it isn't enough to just learn the facts — you have to know how to do the calculations too. That takes practice — so make sure you understand all the examples on these pages, then test yourself on the questions.

Ionic Bonding

Every atom's aim in life is to have a full outer shell of electrons. Once they've managed this, they're happy.

Compounds are Atoms of Different Elements Bonded Together

1) When different elements join or bond together, you get a **compound**.
2) The main types of bonding found in compounds are **ionic**, **covalent** and **metallic** bonds. The type of bonding in a compound can affect its properties.

E.g. when the elements hydrogen and oxygen combine, the compound water (H_2O) is formed.

Ionic Bonding is when Ions are Held Together by Electrostatic Attraction

1) You'll remember that ions are formed when one or more electrons are **transferred** from one atom to another (see page 36).
2) The simplest ions are formed from single atoms which either lose or gain electrons in order to get a **full outer shell**. Here are some examples of these simple ions:

A potassium atom (K) **loses** 1 electron to form a potassium ion (K^+)	$K \rightarrow K^+ + e^-$
A calcium atom (Ca) **loses** 2 electrons to form a calcium ion (Ca^{2+})	$Ca \rightarrow Ca^{2+} + 2e^-$
A fluorine atom (F) **gains** 1 electron to form a fluoride ion (F^-)	$F + e^- \rightarrow F^-$
A sulfur atom (S) **gains** 2 electrons to form a sulfide ion (S^{2-})	$S + 2e^- \rightarrow S^{2-}$

3) Remember that to work out what ion **each element** forms you can often just look at the Periodic Table.
4) Elements in the same **group** all have the same number of **outer electrons** so they'll form ions with the **same charges**.

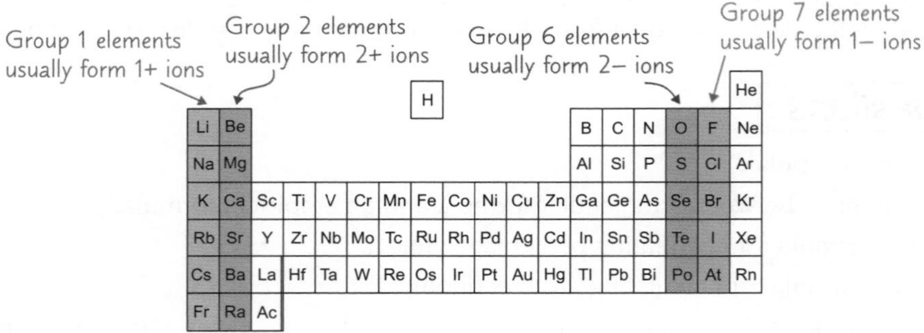

4) Positively charged ions are called **cations** and negatively charged ions are called **anions**.
5) **Electrostatic attraction** holds positive and negative ions together — it's **very** strong. When atoms are held together like this, it's called **ionic bonding**.

Not all ions are made from single atoms. You learnt about molecular ions on page 36.

An **ionic bond** is an **electrostatic attraction** between two **oppositely charged** ions.

6) The overall charge of any compound is **zero**. So all the negative charges in the compound must **balance** all the positive charges.
7) You can use the charges on the individual ions present to work out the **formula** of an ionic compound:

Sodium nitrate contains **Na^+ (1+)** and **NO_3^- (1–)** ions. The charges are balanced with one of each ion, so the formula of sodium nitrate is **$NaNO_3$**.

Ionic Bonding

Sodium Chloride has a **Giant Ionic Lattice** Structure

1) Ionic crystals are giant lattices of ions. A **lattice** is just a **regular structure**.
2) The structure's called '**giant**' because it's made up of the same basic unit repeated over and over again.
3) In **sodium chloride**, the Na^+ and Cl^- ions are packed together. The sodium chloride lattice is **cube** shaped — different ionic compounds have different shaped structures, but they're all still giant lattices.

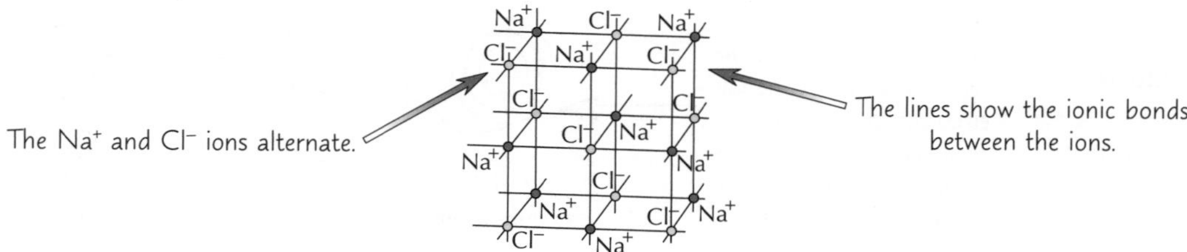
The Na^+ and Cl^- ions alternate.
The lines show the ionic bonds between the ions.
Na^+
Cl^-

The structure of ionic compounds determines their **physical properties**...

Ionic Structure Explains the **Behaviour** of Ionic Compounds

1) **Ionic compounds conduct electricity when they're molten or dissolved — but not when they're solid.** The ions in a liquid are free to move (and they carry a charge). In a solid the ions are fixed in position by strong ionic bonds.
2) **Ionic compounds have high melting and boiling points.** The giant ionic lattices are held together by strong electrostatic forces. It takes loads of energy to overcome these forces, so their melting and boiling points are very high.
3) **Ionic compounds tend to dissolve in water.** Water molecules are polar — part of the molecule has a small negative charge and other bits have small positive charges (see page 56). These charged parts pull ions away from the lattice, causing it to dissolve.

Practice Questions

Q1 What's a compound?

Q2 Oxygen is in group 6 of the periodic table. What will the charge on an oxide ion be?

Q3 What type of force holds ionic substances together?

Exam Questions

Q1 a) Draw a labelled diagram to show the structure of sodium chloride. Your diagram should show at least eight ions. [3 marks]

b) What is the name of this type of structure? [1 mark]

c) Would you expect sodium chloride to have a high or a low melting point? Explain your answer. [3 marks]

d) Would you expect sodium chloride to dissolve in water? Explain your answer. [2 marks]

Q2 Solid lead(II) bromide does not conduct electricity, but molten lead(II) bromide does. Explain this with reference to ionic bonding. [3 marks]

Atom 1 says, "I think I lost an electron." Atom 2 replies, "are you positive?"...

Make sure that you can explain why ionic compounds do what they do. Their properties are down to the fact that ionic crystals are made up of oppositely charged ions attracted to each other. The bonding in ionic compounds isn't the only thing that determines their properties, however. The ions in the compound matter as well. Keep reading...

More on Ionic Bonding

Time to find out how the ions in an ionic compound affect the strength of the ionic bonding. First though — a bit of drawing to show how ionic compounds form. I hope they don't make you go dotty (or make you cross for that matter).

Dot-and-Cross Diagrams Show Where the Electrons in a Bond Come From

Dot-and-cross diagrams show the **arrangement** of electrons in an atom or ion. Each electron is represented by a dot or a cross. They can also show which **atom** the electrons in a **bond** originally came from.

1) For example, **sodium chloride** (NaCl) is an ionic compound:

Here, the dots represent the Na electrons and the crosses represent the Cl electrons (all electrons are really identical, but this is a good way of following their movement).

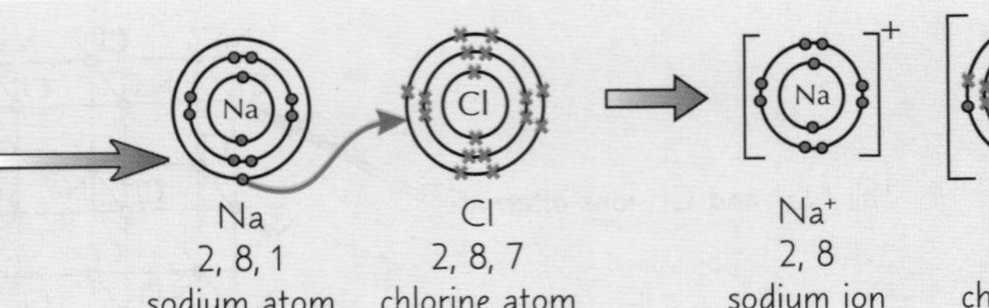

2) **Magnesium oxide**, MgO, is another good example:

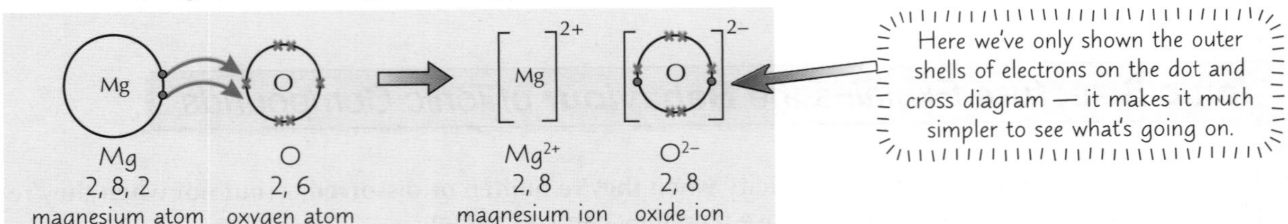

3) When there's a 1:2 ratio of ions, such as in **magnesium chloride**, $MgCl_2$, you draw dot-and-cross diagrams like this:

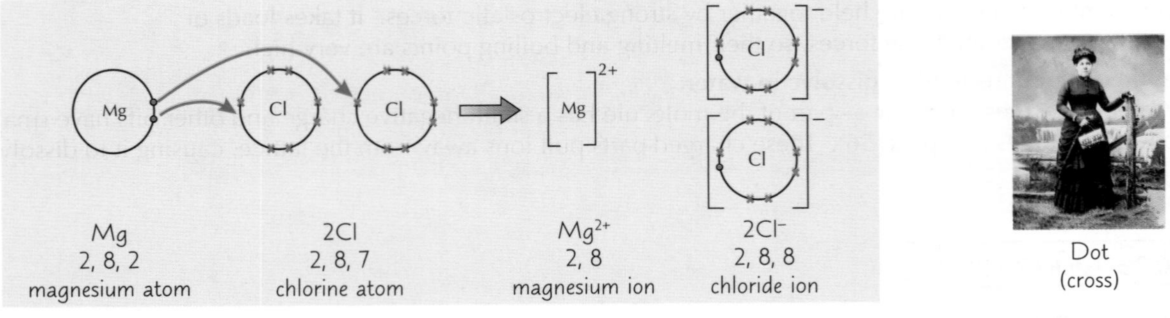

Dot
(cross)

The Size of an Ion Depends on its Electron Shells and Atomic Number

There are a couple of factors that can affect the size of an ion...

1) The **ionic radius increases** as you go **down a group**.

Ion	Li^+	Na^+	K^+	Rb^+
Ionic radius (nm)	0.060	0.095	0.133	0.148

All these **Group 1** ions have the **same charge**.

As you go down the group the **ionic radius increases** as the **atomic number increases**.

This is because **extra electron shells** are added.

2) **Isoelectronic ions** are ions of different atoms with the **same number of electrons**. The **ionic radius** of a set of **isoelectronic ions decreases** as the **atomic number increases**.

See page 14 for how to work out the subatomic particles in an ion.

Ion	N^{3-}	O^{2-}	F^-	Na^+	Mg^{2+}	Al^{3+}
No. of electrons	10	10	10	10	10	10
No. of protons	7	8	9	11	12	13
Ionic radius (nm)	0.171	0.140	0.136	0.095	0.065	0.050

As you go through this series of ions the number of **electrons stays the same**, but the number of **protons increases**.

This means that the electrons are **attracted** to the **nucleus** more strongly, pulling them in a little, so the **ionic radius decreases**.

More on Ionic Bonding

Ionic Charges and Ionic Radii Affect Ionic Bonding

Ionic bonds are all to do with the **attraction** between **oppositely charged ions**. So, the stronger the **electrostatic attraction**, the stronger the ionic bond. There are **two** things that affect the strength of an ionic bond:

IONIC CHARGES

In general, the **greater** the **charge** on an ion, the **stronger** the **ionic bond** and therefore the higher the melting/boiling point.

E.g. the melting point of **NaF** (which is made up of **singly charged** Na^+ and F^- ions) is **993 °C**, while **CaO** (which is made up of Ca^{2+} and O^{2-} ions) has a much higher melting point of **2572 °C**.

IONIC RADII

Smaller ions can **pack closer** together than larger ions. Electrostatic attraction gets weaker with distance, so **small, closely packed ions** have **stronger** ionic bonding than larger ions, which sit further apart. Therefore, small, closely packed ionic compounds have higher melting and boiling points.

E.g. the **ionic radius** of Cs^+ is **greater** than that of Na^+. NaF has a melting point of **992 °C**, whereas CsF has a melting point of **683 °C** since the Na^+ and F^- ions can pack closer together in NaF than the Cs^+ and F^- ions in CsF.

Generally, small, highly charged ions will form the strongest ionic bonds, while large, low-charged ions will form the weakest bonds.

Practice Questions

Q1 Draw a dot-and-cross diagram showing the bonding between magnesium and oxygen.

Q2 Explain the trend in ionic radius as you go down a group in the periodic table.

Q3 Why does sodium fluoride (NaF) have a lower melting point than calcium oxide (CaO)?

Q4 How does the radius of an ion affect the strength of the ionic bonds that it makes?

Exam Questions

Q1 In terms of electron transfer, what happens when sodium reacts with fluorine to form sodium fluoride? [3 marks]

Q2 Which of the following sets of atoms and ions are isoelectronic?

A Ca^{2+}, K^+, Cl **B** Mg^+, Ne, Na^+ **C** Ar, S^{2-}, Sc^{3+} **D** Ti^{4+}, Cl^-, S [1 mark]

Q3 Put the following sets of ions in order of increasing ionic radius. Explain your answers.

a) Br^-, Cl^-, F^-, I^- [3 marks]

b) Cl^-, Rb^+, S^{2-}, Sr^{2+} [3 marks]

Q4 Calcium oxide is an ionic compound with ionic formula CaO.

a) Draw a dot-and-cross diagram to show the formation of a bond and the subsequent bonding in calcium oxide. Show the outer electrons only. [2 marks]

b) How would you expect the melting point of calcium sulfide (CaS) to compare with calcium oxide? Explain your answer. [3 marks]

The name's Bond... Ionic Bond... Electrons taken, not shared...

Dot-and-cross diagrams can be easy marks in the exams, so practise drawing them so that you know exactly what you're doing. Make sure you've got your head around why ionic charges and ionic radii affect ionic bonding, too. It's no good just being able to state which ionic compound will have stronger bonds if you can't explain it.

Covalent Bonding

And now for covalent bonding — this is when atoms share electrons with one another so they've all got full outer shells.

Molecules are Groups of Atoms Bonded Together

1) Molecules form when **two or more** atoms bond together — it doesn't matter if the atoms are the **same** or **different**. Chlorine gas (Cl_2), carbon monoxide (CO), water (H_2O) and ethanol (C_2H_5OH) are all molecules.

Molecules are held together by **covalent bonds**. In covalent bonding, two atoms **share** electrons, so they've **both** got full outer shells of electrons.

E.g. two hydrogen atoms bond covalently to form a molecule of hydrogen.

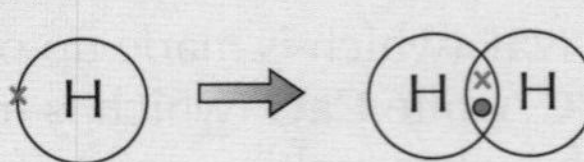

Covalent bonding happens between nonmetals. Ionic bonding is between a metal and a nonmetal.

2) Here's a useful definition:

A **covalent bond** is the strong **electrostatic attraction** between a **shared pair of electrons** and the **nuclei** of the bonded atoms.

3) Here are a few more examples:

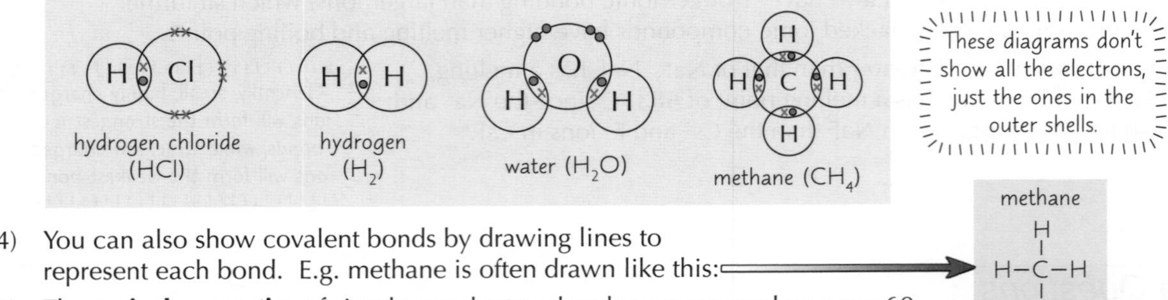

These diagrams don't show all the electrons, just the ones in the outer shells.

4) You can also show covalent bonds by drawing lines to represent each bond. E.g. methane is often drawn like this:

methane

```
   H
   |
H—C—H
   |
   H
```

5) The **typical properties** of simple covalent molecules are covered on page 60.

Some Molecules have Double or Triple Bonds

1) Atoms don't just form single bonds — **double** or even **triple covalent bonds** can be formed between atoms too.
2) These multiple bonds contain **multiple shared pairs** of electrons.

Multiple covalent bonds can be shown using multiple lines, e.g. you can draw N_2 like this: N≡N.

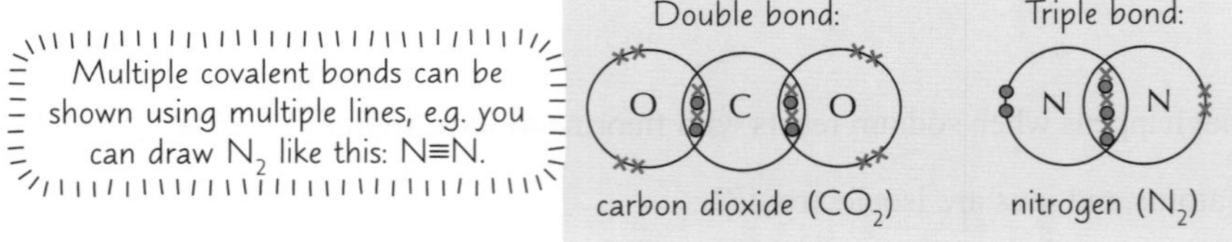

Bond Enthalpy is Related to the Length of a Bond

1) In covalent molecules, the **positive nuclei** are attracted to the area of electron density between the two nuclei (where the shared electrons are). But there's also a repulsion. The two **positively charged nuclei repel** each other, as do the **electrons**. To maintain the covalent bond there has to be a **balance** between these forces.
2) The distance between the **two nuclei** is the distance where the **attractive** and **repulsive** forces balance each other. This distance is the **bond length**.
3) The **higher the electron density** between the nuclei (i.e. the more electrons in the bond), the **stronger** the attraction between the atoms, the higher the **bond enthalpy** and the **shorter** the bond length. It makes sense really. If there's more attraction, the nuclei are pulled **closer** together.

A C=C bond has a **greater bond enthalpy** and is **shorter** than a C–C bond. Four electrons are shared in C=C and only two in C–C, so the **electron density** between the two carbon atoms is greater and the **bond** is **shorter**.

C≡C has an even **higher** bond enthalpy and is **shorter** than C=C — six electrons are shared here.

Bond	C–C	C=C	C≡C
Average Bond Enthalpy (kJ mol^{-1})	+347	+612	+838
Bond length (nm)	0.154	0.134	0.120

Covalent Bonding

Dative Covalent Bonding is Where Both Electrons Come From One Atom

1) In the molecules on the last page, the atoms are acting in a bit of an "I'll lend you mine if you lend me yours" way — each atom puts an electron into the bond and, in return, they get use of the electron put in by the other atom.
2) But there's another kind of covalent bond as well — a **dative covalent** (or **coordinate**) bond. This is where one atom donates **both electrons** to a bond.
3) The **ammonium ion** (NH_4^+) is formed by dative covalent (or coordinate) bonding. It forms when the nitrogen atom in an ammonia molecule **donates a pair of electrons** to a proton (H^+).

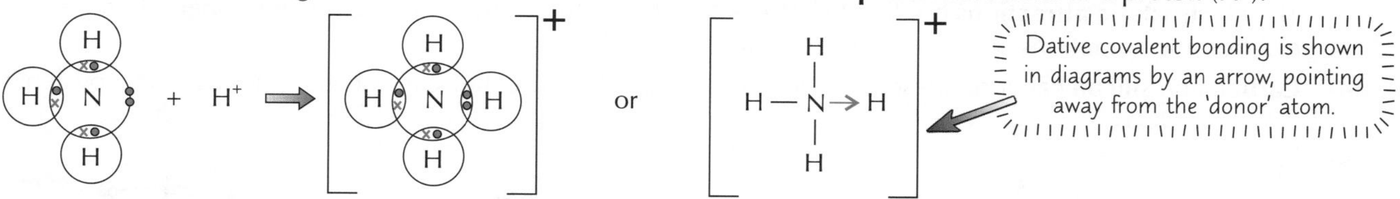

4) The ammonium ion can go on to form ionic bonds with other ions (see page 46).

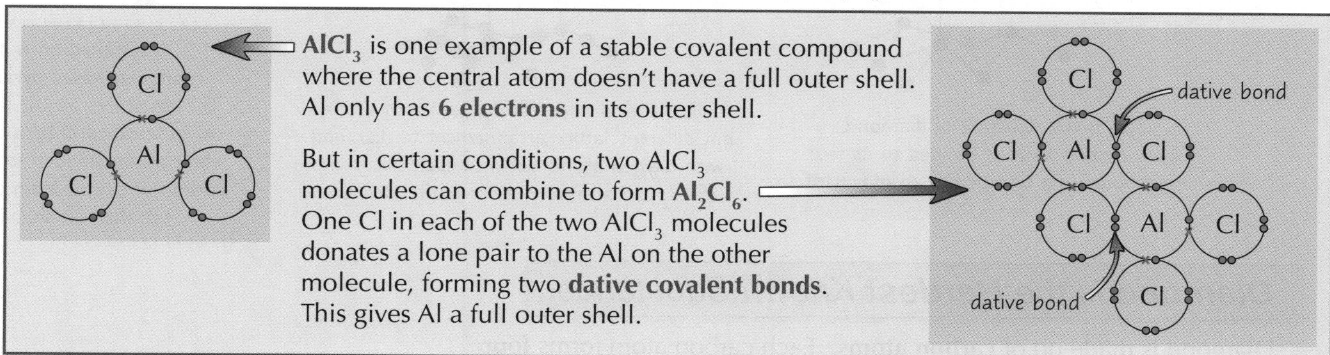

$AlCl_3$ is one example of a stable covalent compound where the central atom doesn't have a full outer shell. Al only has **6 electrons** in its outer shell.

But in certain conditions, two $AlCl_3$ molecules can combine to form Al_2Cl_6. One Cl in each of the two $AlCl_3$ molecules donates a lone pair to the Al on the other molecule, forming two **dative covalent bonds**. This gives Al a full outer shell.

Practice Questions

Q1 Describe how atoms are held together in covalent molecules.

Q2 Put the following three bonds in order from shortest to longest: C–C, C=C, C≡C.

Q3 What is a dative covalent bond?

Exam Questions

Q1 Ethene, C_2H_4, is a covalently bonded organic compound.
It contains four carbon-hydrogen single bonds and one carbon-carbon double bond.

a) What is a covalent bond? [1 mark]

b) Explain how a single covalent bond differs from a double covalent bond. [1 mark]

Q2 a) Draw a dot-and-cross diagram of the ammonia molecule (NH_3) showing the outer shell electrons only. [1 mark]

b) Draw a dot-and-cross diagram of the hydrogen chloride molecule (HCl) showing the outer shell electrons only. [1 mark]

c) Ammonia reacts with hydrogen chloride to form ammonium chloride.
Draw a dot-and-cross diagram to show the bonding in ammonium chloride. [2 marks]

Q3 a) Would you expect an N–N single bond to be shorter or longer than an N=N bond? Explain your answer. [3 marks]

b) Draw a dot-and-cross diagram to show the bonding in a molecule of nitrogen gas (N_2). [1 mark]

c) How would you expect the bond enthalpy of the bond(s) in a molecule of N_2 to compare to N–N and N=N bonds? Explain your answer. [3 marks]

Dative covalent bonds — an act of charity on an atomic scale...

More pretty diagrams here. Drawing dot-and-cross diagrams isn't too hard. It's just a bit of trial and error really. Just sort the outer electrons until every atom has a full outer shell (that's 8 electrons for most atoms, except hydrogen which only has 2 in its outer shell). Watch out for double, triple and dative covalent bonds too...

Giant Covalent Structures

Not all covalent structures are tiny molecules... some form vast structures (well... vast compared to simple molecules).

Some **Covalently Bonded** Substances Have **Giant Structures**

1) **Covalent bonds** form when atoms **share** electrons with other atoms. Very often, this leads to the formation of small **molecules**, including CO_2, N_2 and the others on page 50.
2) But they can also lead to huge great **lattices** too — containing billions and billions of atoms.
3) These **giant** structures have a huge network of **covalently** bonded atoms. The **electrostatic attractions** holding the atoms together in these structures are much **stronger** than the electrostatic attractions between simple covalent molecules.
4) **Carbon** and **silicon** can form these giant networks. This is because they can each form four strong, covalent bonds.

Silicon can also form networks in this kind of pattern.

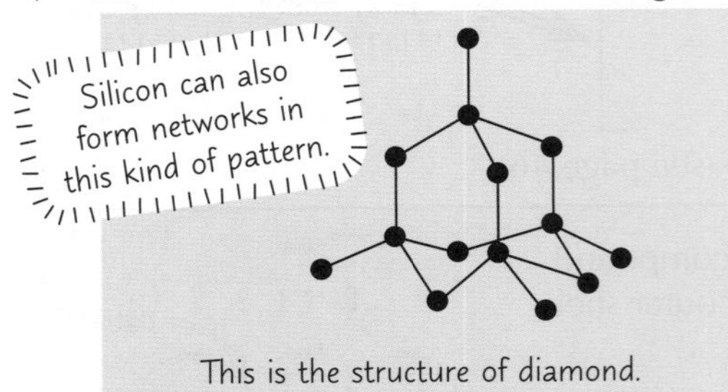

This is the structure of diamond. Each carbon atom is bonded to its four neighbours in a tetrahedral arrangement.

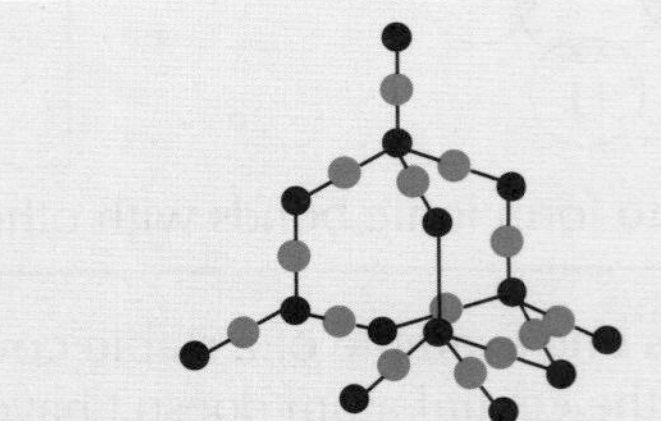

Silicon(IV) dioxide (SiO_2) can form a 'similar but different' lattice arrangement to diamond — with oxygen atoms between each silicon atom. (SiO_2 can also form other lattice structures.)

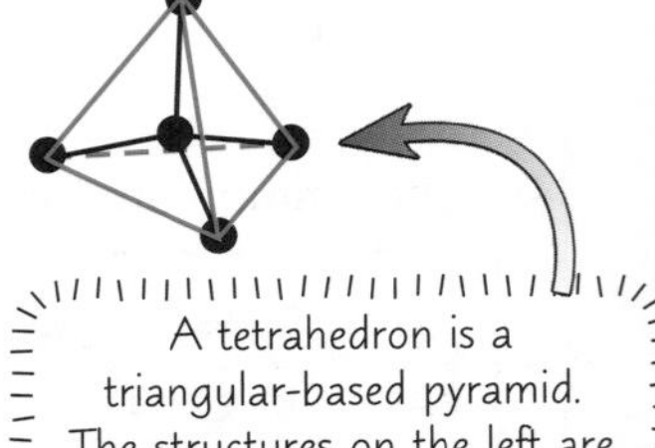

A tetrahedron is a triangular-based pyramid. The structures on the left are called tetrahedral because the four atoms bonded to each carbon or silicon atom form a tetrahedron shape.

Diamond is the **Hardest** Known Substance

Diamond is made up of **carbon atoms**. Each carbon atom forms **four** strong covalent bonds to neighbouring carbon atoms.

'Sublime' means to change straight from a solid to a gas

Because of its **strong covalent** bonds:

1) Diamond has a **very high melting point** as the strong covalent bonds are very hard to break (it sublimes at over 3900 K).
2) Diamond is extremely **hard** — it's used in diamond-tipped drills and saws.
3) **Vibrations** travel easily through the stiff lattice, so it's a **good thermal conductor**.
4) It **can't conduct** electricity — all the outer electrons are held in localised bonds.
5) Diamond is **insoluble** in any solvent. The covalent bonds are **too strong** to break.
6) You can 'cut' diamond to form **gemstones**. Its structure makes it **refract light** a lot, which is why it sparkles.

Graphite — Sheets of Hexagons with **Delocalised Electrons**

Graphite is also made up of **carbon atoms**. Each carbon atom forms **three** strong covalent bonds to neighbouring carbon atoms and has one **delocalised** electron.

The carbon atoms are arranged in sheets of flat hexagons covalently bonded with three bonds each. The fourth outer electron of each carbon atom is delocalised.

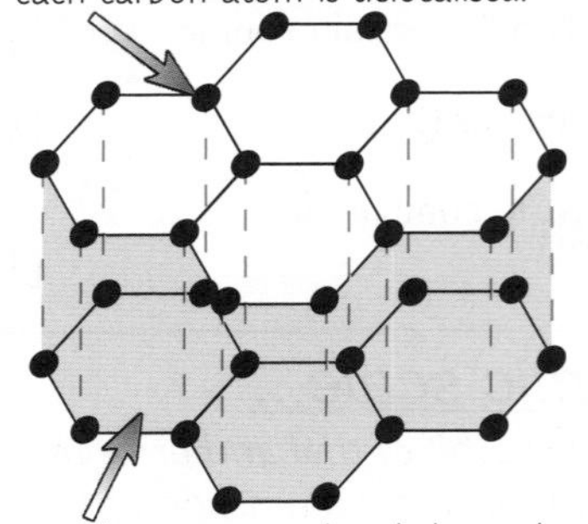

The sheets of hexagons are bonded together by weak induced dipole-dipole forces (see p. 57).

The **structure** of graphite explains its **properties**:

1) The weak bonds **between** the layers in graphite are easily broken, so the sheets can slide over each other — graphite feels **slippery** and is used as a **dry lubricant** and in **pencils**.
2) The '**delocalised**' electrons in graphite aren't attached to any particular carbon atoms and are **free to move** along the sheets carrying a **charge**. So graphite is an **electrical conductor**.
3) The layers are quite **far apart** compared to the length of the covalent bonds, so graphite has a **low density** and is used to make **strong, lightweight** sports equipment.
4) Because of the **strong covalent bonds** in the hexagon sheets, graphite has a **very high melting point** (it also sublimes at over 3900 K).
5) Like diamond, graphite won't **dissolve** in any solvent.

Giant Covalent Structures

Graphene is One Layer of Graphite

Graphene is a **sheet** of carbon atoms joined together in **hexagons**.
The sheet is just **one atom** thick, making it a **two-dimensional** compound.

Each carbon atom has three covalent bonds (and one delocalised electron).

Graphene's **structure** gives it some pretty **useful properties**.

1) Like in graphite, the **delocalised electrons** in graphene are **free to move** along the sheet. Without layers, they can move **quickly** above and below the sheet, making graphene the **best known** electrical conductor.
2) The **delocalised electrons** also strengthen the covalent bonds between the carbon atoms. This makes graphene extremely **strong**.
3) A single layer of graphene is **transparent** and incredibly **light**.

Like diamond and graphite, graphene has high melting and boiling points and it's insoluble due to its strong covalent bonds.

Due to its high strength, low mass, and good electrical conductivity, graphene has potential applications in **high-speed electronics** and **aircraft technology**. Its flexibility and transparency also make it a potentially useful material for **touchscreens** on smartphones and other electronic devices.

Practice Questions

Q1 In diamond, how many other carbons is each carbon atom bonded to?

Q2 Explain why diamond has a very high melting point.

Q3 Draw the structure of graphene.

Q4 Which properties of graphene make it a potentially useful material in aircraft technology?

Exam Questions

Q1 Carbon can be found as diamond and as graphite.

a) What type of structure do diamond and graphite display? [1 mark]

b) Draw diagrams to illustrate the structures of diamond and graphite. [2 marks]

c) Compare and explain the electrical conductivities of diamond and graphite in terms of their structure and bonding. [4 marks]

Q2 A student wrote the following statement about graphene:

'Graphene is a one-dimensional compound made up of one sheet of carbon atoms bonded together to form hexagons. Each carbon atom forms three covalent bonds and has one delocalised electron. The delocalised electrons are free to move along the sheet, making graphene a very good electrical conductor. However, they weaken the covalent bonds meaning graphene isn't very strong.'

Identify and correct two mistakes in this statement. [2 marks]

Q3 Graphite is a giant covalent structure. It is often used as a dry lubricant in machinery. Explain why the structure of graphite makes it suitable for use as a lubricant. [2 marks]

Carbon is a girl's best friend...

It's important to understand why the differences in the structures of graphite, diamond and graphene give them such different properties. Pretty amazing isn't it — they're all just carbon, but one's crumbly and grey, one's hard and shiny, and the other is stronger, lighter and more conductive than anything that's come before. Talk about showing off...

Shapes of Molecules

Chemistry would be heaps more simple if all molecules were flat. But they're not.

Molecular Shape depends on Electron Pairs around the Central Atom

Molecules and ions come in loads of **different shapes**.
Their shape depends on the **number of pairs** of electrons in the outer shell of the central atom.

For example, in **ammonia** the outermost shell of the **nitrogen atom** contains **four** pairs of electrons.

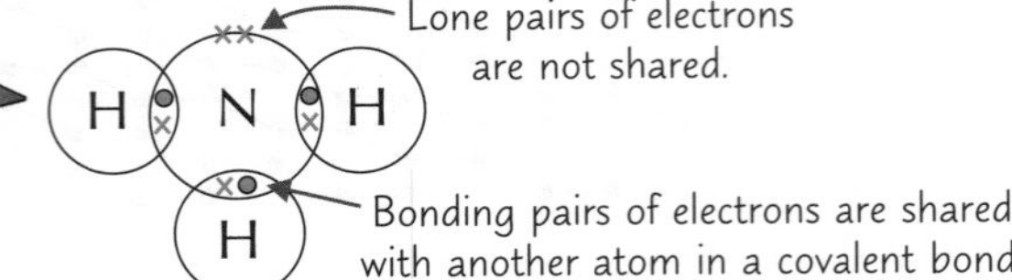

H
N
H
H
Lone pairs of electrons are not shared.
Bonding pairs of electrons are shared with another atom in a covalent bond.

A lone pear

Electron Pairs exist as Charge Clouds

Bonding pairs and lone pairs of electrons exist as **charge clouds**.
A charge cloud is an area where you have a really **big chance** of finding an electron pair. The electrons don't stay still — they **whizz around** inside the charge cloud.

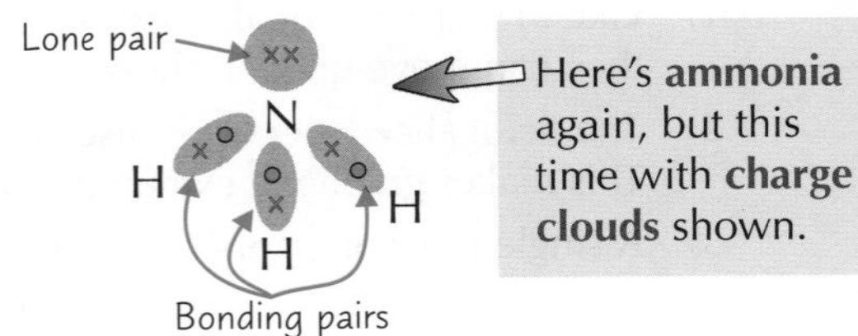

Here's **ammonia** again, but this time with **charge clouds** shown.

Electron Charge Clouds Repel Each Other

1) Electrons are all **negatively charged**, so the charge clouds will **repel** each other as much as they can. So the **pairs of electrons** in the outer shell of an atom will sit as **far apart** from each other as they possibly can.
2) This sounds straightforward, but the **shape** of the charge cloud affects **how much** it repels other charge clouds. Lone-pair charge clouds repel **more** than bonding-pair charge clouds.
3) So, the **greatest** angles are between **lone pairs** of electrons, and bond angles between bonding pairs are often **reduced** because they are pushed together by lone-pair repulsion.

Lone-pair/lone-pair angles are the biggest.	**Lone-pair/bonding-pair angles are the second biggest.**	**Bonding-pair/bonding-pair angles are the smallest.**

The central atoms in these molecules all have **four pairs** of electrons in their outer shells, but they're all **different shapes**:

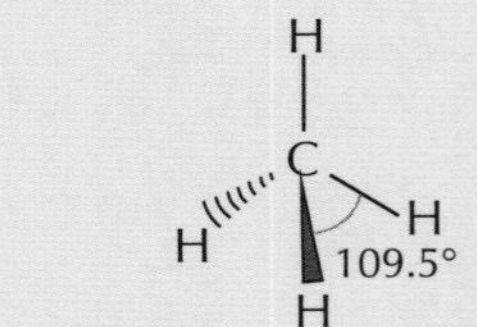

Methane — no lone pairs

The lone pair repels the bonding pairs

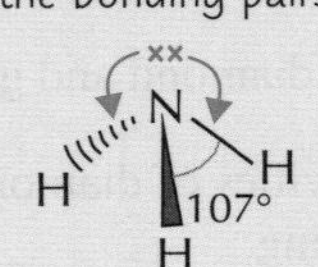

Ammonia — 1 lone pair

2 lone pairs reduce the bond angle even more

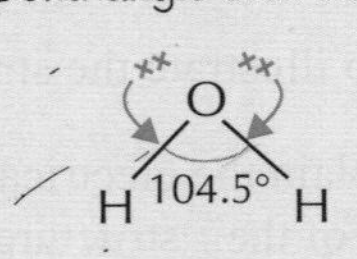

Water — 2 lone pairs

Wedges (◀) show bonds that are sticking out of the page towards you. Broken lines (((((·) show bonds that go into the page.

4) This is sometimes known by the long-winded name '**Valence-Shell Electron-Pair Repulsion Theory**'.

Use the Number of Electron Pairs to Predict the Shape of a Molecule

To predict the shape of a molecule, you'll need to know how many **bonding** and **lone electron pairs** there are on the central atom of the molecule. Here's how:

1) First work out which one is the **central atom** (that's the one all the other atoms are bonded to).
2) Use the periodic table to work out the **number of electrons** in the **outer shell** of the central atom.
3) **Add one** to this number for every atom that the central atom is **bonded** to.
4) **Divide by 2** to find the number of electron pairs on the central atom.
5) **Compare** the number of **electron pairs** to the number of **bonds** to find the number of lone pairs and the number of bonding pairs on the cental atom.

Now you can use this information to work out the shape of the molecule...

If you're dealing with an ion, you need to take its charge into account too. After step 3, add 1 for each negative charge on the ion (or subtract 1 for each positive charge).

Shapes of Molecules

Molecules With Different Numbers of **Electron Pairs Have Different Shapes**

Here are the **shapes** that molecules with different numbers of electron pairs will take (and some handy examples):

2 ELECTRON PAIRS

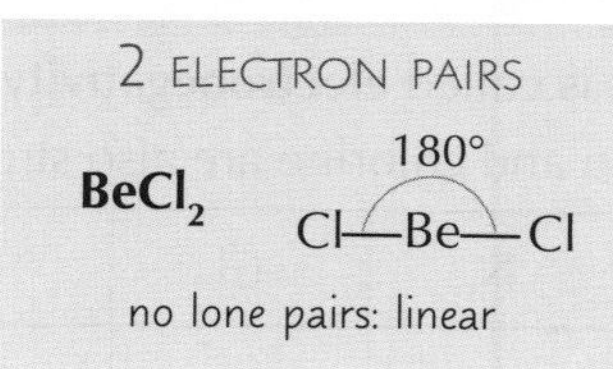

no lone pairs: linear

3 ELECTRON PAIRS

BF_3 120°

no lone pairs: trigonal planar

4 ELECTRON PAIRS

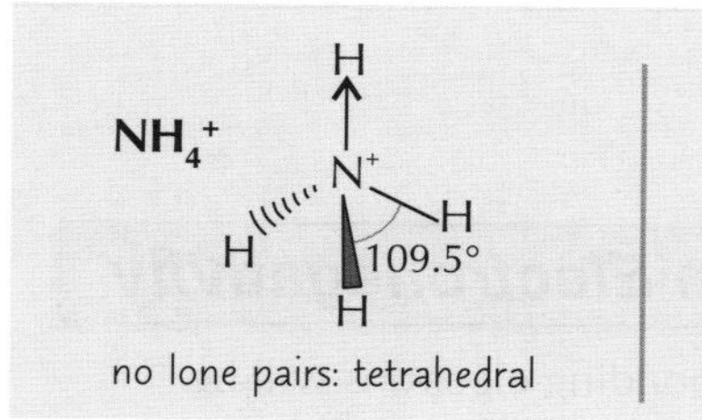

no lone pairs: tetrahedral

PF_3 107°

1 lone pair: trigonal pyramidal

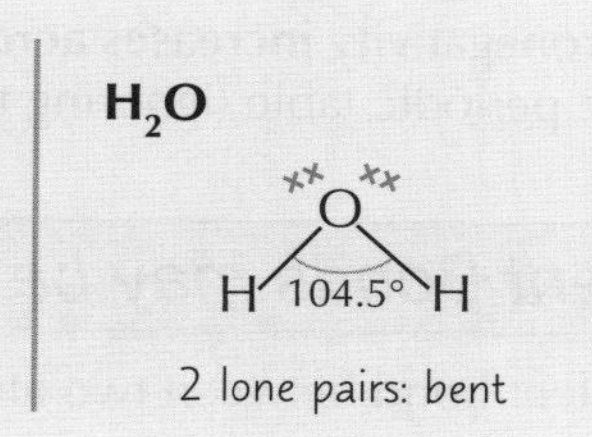

2 lone pairs: bent

5 ELECTRON PAIRS

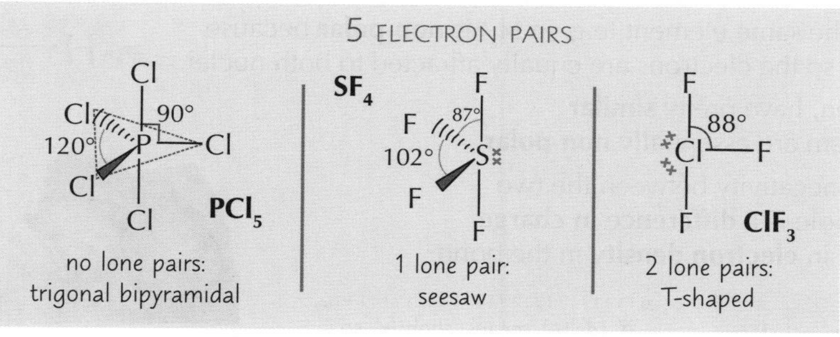

no lone pairs: trigonal bipyramidal | 1 lone pair: seesaw | 2 lone pairs: T-shaped

6 ELECTRON PAIRS

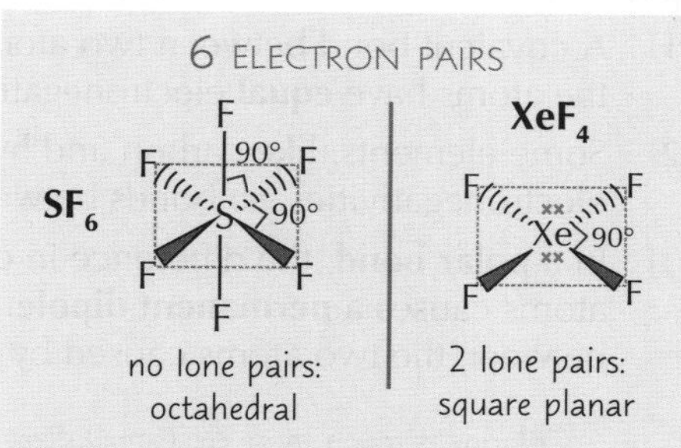

no lone pairs: octahedral | 2 lone pairs: square planar

Molecules with 5 electron pairs and 1 lone pair are pretty rare — they have a shape like SF_6, but with the bottom F replaced by the lone pair.

Example: Predicting the Shape of the Molecule H_2S

1) The central atom is **sulfur**.
2) Sulfur is in Group 6, so it has **6 electrons** in its outer shell to start with.
3) The sulfur atom is bonded to 2 hydrogen atoms, so it has (6 + 2) = **8 electrons** in its outer shell in H_2S.
4) The number of electron pairs on the central sulfur atom is 8 ÷ 2 = **4 pairs**.
5) The sulfur atom has **4 electron pairs** and has made **2 bonds** — so it has **2 bonding pairs** and **2 lone pairs**.

This means that H_2S will have a **bent** shape (like water).

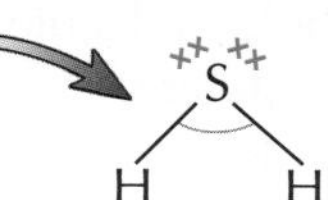

Practice Questions

Q1 What is a lone pair of electrons?

Q2 Write down the order of the strength of repulsion between different kinds of electron pair.

Q3 Draw an example of a tetrahedral molecule.

Exam Question

Q1 Nitrogen and boron can form the chlorides NCl_3 and BCl_3.

a) Draw the shape of NCl_3. Show the approximate value of the bond angles and name the shape. [3 marks]

b) Draw the shape of BCl_3. Show the approximate value of the bond angles and name the shape. [3 marks]

c) Explain why the shapes of NCl_3 and BCl_3 are different. [3 marks]

These molecules ain't square...

Don't panic if you get asked to predict the shape of a molecule that you don't know — it'll be just like one you do know (e.g. PH_3 is like NH_3). So learn the shapes on this page — and make sure you remember the bond angles too.

Polarisation and Intermolecular Forces

Intermolecular forces hold molecules together. They're pretty important, cos we'd all be gassy clouds without them. Some of these intermolecular forces are down to polarisation. So you best make sure you know about that first...

Some Atoms **Attract** Bonding Electrons More than Other Atoms

1) An atom's ability to attract the electron pair in a covalent bond is called **electronegativity**.
2) **Fluorine** is the most electronegative element. Oxygen, nitrogen and chlorine are also strongly electronegative.

Element	H	C	N	Cl	O	F
Electronegativity (Pauling Scale)	2.1	2.5	3.0	3.0	3.5	4.0

3) Electronegativity **increases across periods** and **decreases down groups** in the periodic table (ignoring the noble gases).

Covalent Bonds may be **Polarised** by **Differences** in **Electronegativity**

In a covalent bond between two atoms of **different** electronegativities, the bonding electrons will be **pulled towards** the more electronegative atom. This makes the bond **polar**.

1) A covalent bond between two atoms of the same element (e.g. in H_2) is **non-polar** because the atoms have **equal** electronegativities, so the electrons are equally attracted to both nuclei.

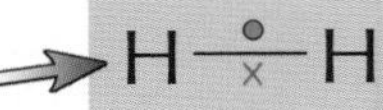

2) Some elements, like carbon and hydrogen, have pretty **similar** electronegativities, so bonds between them are essentially **non-polar**.
3) In a **polar bond**, the difference in electronegativity between the two atoms causes a **permanent dipole**. A dipole is a **difference in charge** between the two atoms caused by a shift in **electron density** in the bond.

Chlorine is much more electronegative than hydrogen, so hydrogen chloride has a permanent dipole.

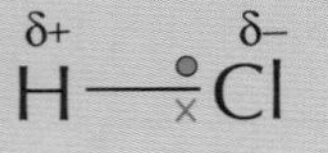

'δ' (delta) means 'slightly', so 'δ+' means 'slightly positive'.

Permanent polar bonding

4) The greater the **difference** in electronegativity between the atoms, the **more polar** the bond.

Whole Molecules can be **Polar** Too

1) If you have a molecule that contains polar bonds, you can end up with an uneven distribution of charge across the whole molecule. When this happens, the molecule is **polar**.
2) Not all molecules that contain polar bonds are polar though. If the polar bonds are arranged **symmetrically** in the molecule, then the charges **cancel out** and there is no permanent dipole

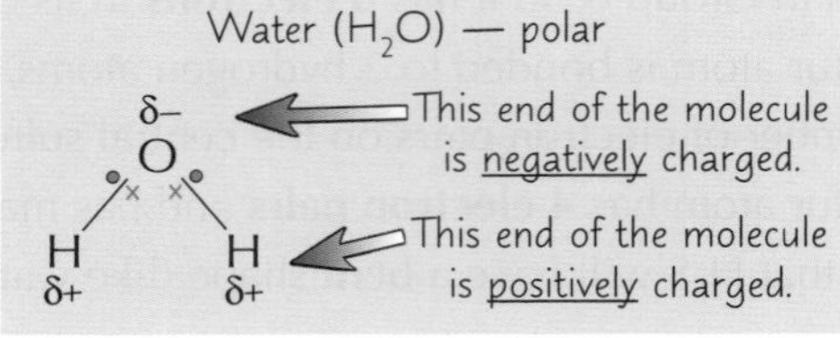

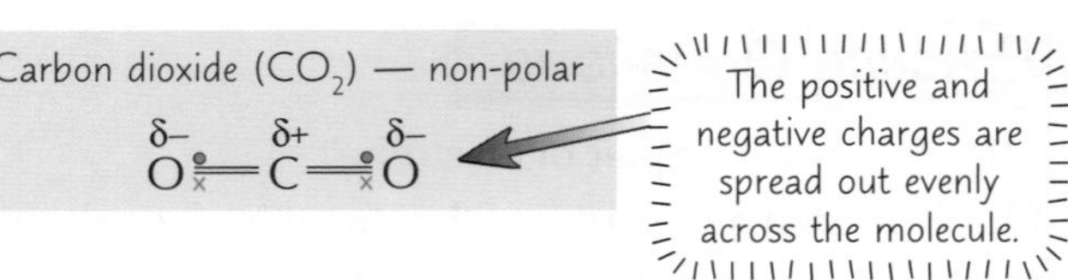

The positive and negative charges are spread out evenly across the molecule.

Polar Molecules have **Permanent Dipole-Dipole** Forces

In a substance made up of molecules that have **permanent dipoles**, there will be **weak electrostatic forces** of attraction **between** the δ+ and δ– charges on neighbouring molecules.

E.g. hydrogen chloride gas has polar molecules:

δ+ δ– δ+ δ– δ+ δ–
H—Cl······H—Cl······H—Cl

The δ– chlorine is attracted to the δ+ hydrogen on the next molecule.

If you put a **charged rod** next to a jet of a polar liquid, like water, the liquid will **move** towards the rod. It's because **polar liquids** contain molecules with **permanent dipoles**. It doesn't matter if the rod is **positively** or **negatively** charged. The polar molecules in the liquid can **turn around** so the oppositely charged end is attracted towards the rod.

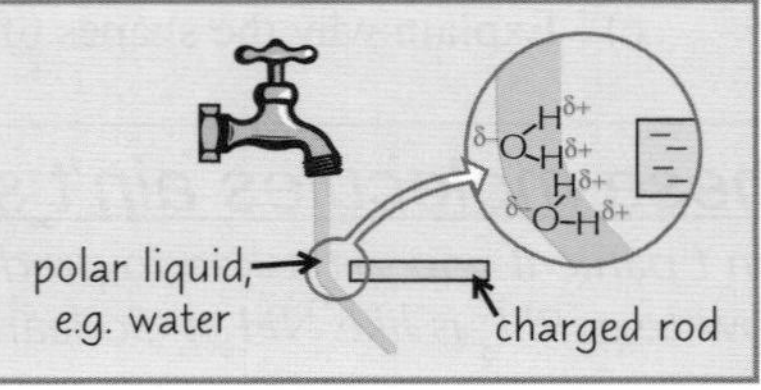

Polarisation and Intermolecular Forces

Intermolecular Forces are *Very Weak*

Intermolecular forces are forces **between** molecules. They're much **weaker** than covalent, ionic or metallic bonds. There are three types you need to know about:

1) **Induced dipole-dipole** forces.
2) **Permanent dipole-dipole forces** (these are the ones caused by polar molecules — see previous page).
3) **Hydrogen bonding.**

Intermolecular forces are important because they affect the **physical properties** of a compound.

Induced Dipole-Dipole Forces are Found Between *All* Atoms and Molecules

Induced dipole-dipole forces cause **all** atoms and molecules to be **attracted** to each other.

1) **Electrons** in charge clouds are always **moving** really quickly. At any moment, the electrons in an atom are likely to be more to one side than the other. At this moment, the atom would have a **temporary dipole**.
2) This dipole can cause **another** temporary dipole in the opposite direction on a neighbouring atom. The two dipoles are then **attracted** to each other.

3) The second dipole can cause yet another dipole in a **third atom**. It's kind of like a domino effect.
4) Because the electrons are constantly moving, the dipoles are being **created** and **destroyed** all the time. Even though the dipoles keep changing, the **overall effect** is for the atoms to be **attracted** to each another.

Induced Dipole-Dipole Forces Can Hold Molecules in a *Lattice*

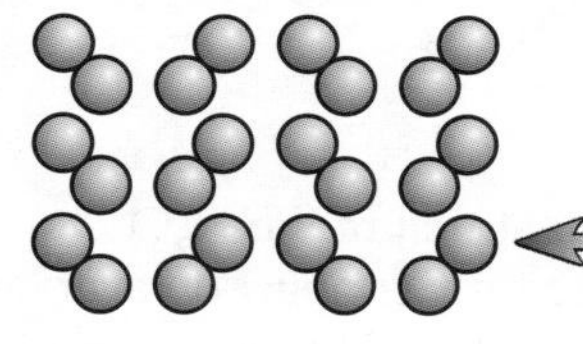

Iodine ($\mathbf{I_2}$) is a **solid** at room temperature. It's the **induced dipole-dipole forces** between the iodine molecules that are responsible for holding them together in a **lattice**:

1) Iodine atoms are held together in pairs by **strong** covalent bonds to form I_2 molecules.
2) But the molecules are then held together in a **molecular lattice** arrangement by **weak** induced dipole-dipole forces.

Stronger *Induced Dipole-Dipole Forces* mean *Higher Boiling Points*

1) Not all induced dipole-dipole forces are the same strength — larger molecules have **larger electron clouds**, meaning **stronger** induced dipole-dipole forces.
2) The **shape** of molecules also affects the strength of induced dipole-dipole forces. Long, straight molecules can lie closer together than branched ones — the **closer** together two molecules get, the **stronger** the forces between them are.
3) When you **boil** a liquid, you need to **overcome** the intermolecular forces, so that the particles can **escape** from the liquid surface. It stands to reason that you need **more energy** to overcome **stronger** intermolecular forces, so liquids with stronger induced dipole-dipole forces will have **higher boiling points**.

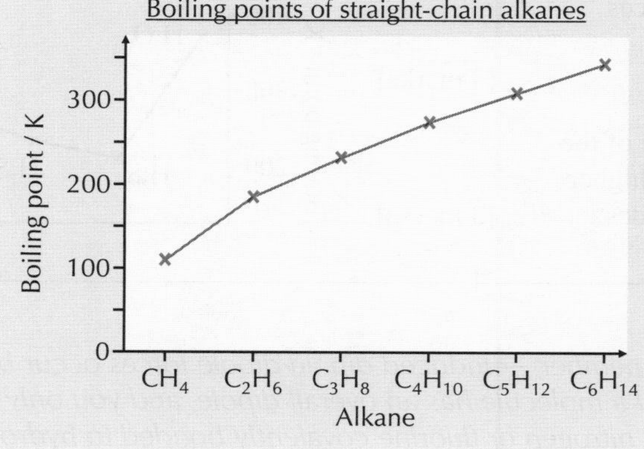

As the alkane chains get **longer**, the **number of electrons** in the molecules increases. This means the induced dipole-dipole forces are **stronger**, and so the boiling points **increase**.

Induced dipole-dipole forces affect other physical properties too, such as melting point and viscosity.

Polarisation and Intermolecular Forces

Hydrogen Bonding is the Strongest Intermolecular Force

1) Hydrogen bonding **only** happens when **hydrogen** is covalently bonded to **fluorine, nitrogen** or **oxygen**.
2) Fluorine, nitrogen and oxygen are very **electronegative**, so they draw bonding electrons away from the hydrogen atom. The bond is so **polarised**, and hydrogen has such a **high charge density** (because it's so small), that the hydrogen atoms form weak bonds with **lone pairs of electrons** on the fluorine, nitrogen or oxygen atoms of **other molecules.**
3) Molecules which have hydrogen bonding usually contain **-OH** or **-NH** groups. **Water** and **ammonia** both have hydrogen bonding.

Water:

A lone pair of electrons on the oxygen is attracted to the hydrogen.

Ammonia:

A lone pair of electrons on the nitrogen is attracted to the hydrogen.

4) Hydrogen bonding has a **huge effect** on the properties of substances:

Substances with hydrogen bonds have **higher boiling** and **melting points** than other similar molecules because of the **extra energy** needed to break the hydrogen bonds.
This is the case with **water** and also **hydrogen fluoride**, which has a **much higher boiling point** than other hydrogen halides:

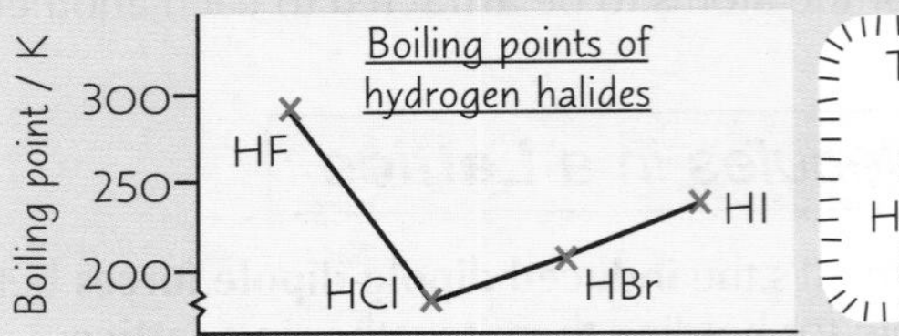

The trend is similar for the Group 5 and Group 6 hydrides, where NH_3 and H_2O have unexpectedly high boiling points respectively.

As liquid water cools to form **ice**, the molecules make **more hydrogen bonds** and arrange themselves into a regular **lattice** structure:

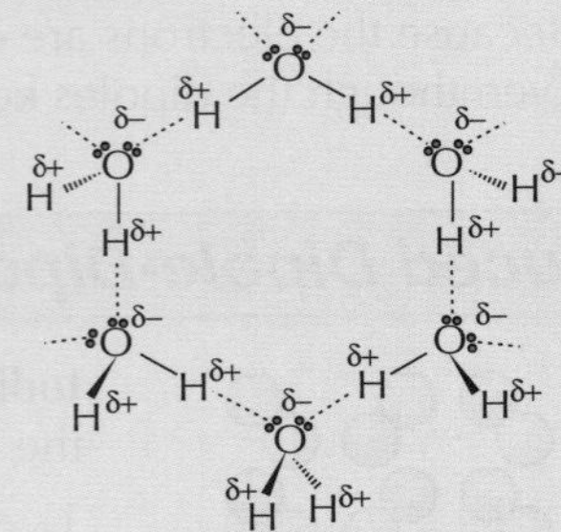

In this regular structure the H_2O molecules are **further apart** on average than the molecules in liquid water — so ice is **less dense** than liquid water.

Practice Questions

Q1 Define the term electronegativity.

Q2 What is a dipole?

Q3 Write down the three types of intermolecular force.

Exam Questions

Q1 Predict whether octene (C_8H_{16}) or decene ($C_{10}H_{20}$) will have a higher boiling point. Explain your answer. [3 marks]

Q2 a) State whether the C–Cl covalent bond is polar. Explain your answer. [1 mark]

b) The molecule CCl_4 has a tetrahedral shape. Will CCl_4 be polar? Explain your answer. [2 marks]

Q3 a) Draw a labelled diagram to show the intermolecular forces that exist between two molecules of water. Include all lone pairs and partial charges in your diagram. [3 marks]

b) The graph on the right shows the boiling points of some of the group 6 hydrides. Explain why water's boiling point is higher than expected in comparison to the other Group 6 hydrides. [3 marks]

Boiling point / K: 400, 300, 200; H_2O, H_2S, H_2Se, H_2Te

May the force be with you...

Intermolecular forces are a bit weak, but they're important. Remember — induced dipole-dipole forces occur between all molecules. Permanent dipole-dipole interactions only form if a molecule has an overall dipole, and you only need to think about hydrogen bonding if the molecule contains oxygen, nitrogen or fluorine covalently bonded to hydrogen.

Metallic Bonding and Properties of Materials

A bit of a mish-mash of a topic now to round up different types of bonding — starting with a bit about bonding in metals.

Metals have Giant Structures

Metal elements exist as **giant metallic lattice structures**.

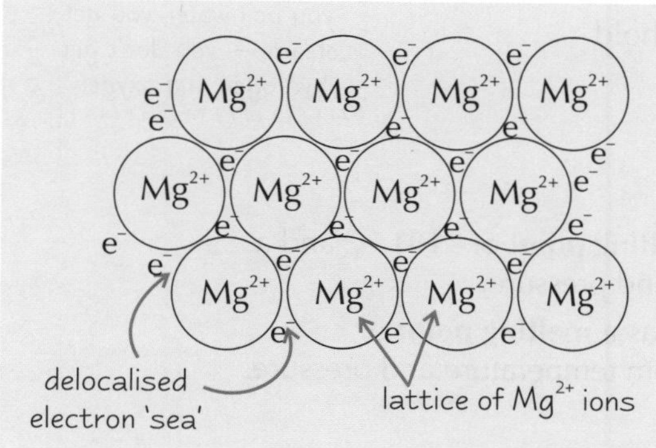

1) The outermost shell of electrons of a metal atom is **delocalised** — the electrons are free to move about the metal. This leaves a **positive metal ion**, e.g. Na^+, Mg^{2+}, Al^{3+}.
2) The positive metal ions are **attracted** to the delocalised negative electrons. They form a lattice of closely packed positive ions in a **sea** of delocalised electrons — this is **metallic bonding**.

Metallic Bonding Explains the Properties of Metals

1) Metals have **high melting points** because of the strong **electrostatic attraction** between the positive metal ions and the delocalised sea of electrons.
2) The **number of delocalised electrons per atom** affects the melting point. The **more** there are, the **stronger** the bonding will be and the **higher** the melting point. For example, Mg^{2+} has **two** delocalised electrons per atom, so it's got a **higher melting point** than Na^+, which only has **one**.
3) The delocalised electrons can pass **kinetic energy** to each other, making metals **good thermal conductors**.
4) Metals are **good electrical conductors** because the **delocalised electrons** can move and carry a **current**.
5) Metals are **insoluble** (except in **liquid metals**), because of the **strength** of the metallic bonds.

Right, well that's all you need to know about metals. So, a change of topic now — it's the properties of materials...

The Physical Properties of Solids, Liquids and Gases Depend on Particles

1) A typical **solid** has its particles very **close** together. This gives it a high density and makes it **incompressible**. The particles **vibrate** about a **fixed point** and can't move about freely.
2) A typical **liquid** has a similar density to a solid and is virtually **incompressible**. The particles move about **freely** and **randomly** within the liquid, allowing it to flow.
3) In **gases**, the particles have **loads more** energy and are much **further apart**. So the density is generally pretty low and it's **very compressible**. The particles move about **freely**, with not a lot of attraction between them, so they'll quickly **diffuse** to fill a container.
4) In order to **change** from a solid to a liquid or a liquid to a gas, you need to **break** the forces that are holding the particles together. To do this you need to give the particles more **energy**, e.g. by **heating** them.

Taylor's demonstration of how the particles in a liquid behave had got a bit out of hand.

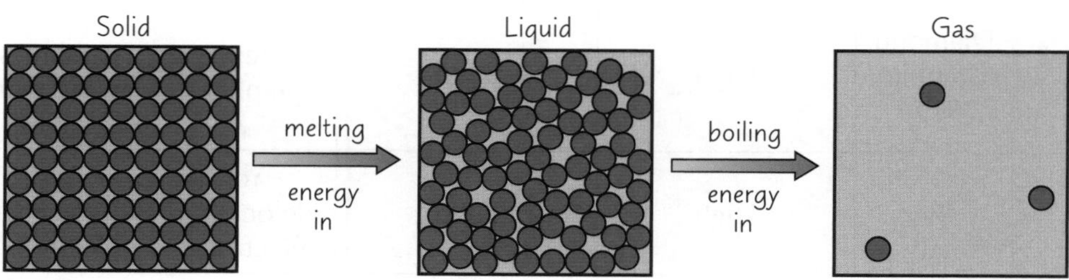

Metallic Bonding and Properties of Materials

Covalent Bonds Don't Break during Melting and Boiling*

*Except for giant covalent substances, like diamond.

This is something that confuses loads of people — prepare to be enlightened...

1) To **melt** or **boil** a simple covalent compound you only have to overcome the **intermolecular forces** that hold the molecules together.
2) You **don't** need to break the much stronger covalent bonds that hold the atoms together in the molecules.
3) That's why simple covalent compounds have relatively **low melting** and **boiling points**. For example:

It might help to remember that when you boil water, you get steam — you don't get hydrogen and oxygen.

- **Chlorine**, Cl_2, is a **simple covalent** substance. It has a **melting point** of **–101 °C** and a **boiling point** of **–34 °C** — it's a **gas** at room temperature and pressure.
- **Pentane**, C_5H_{12}, is also a **simple covalent** compound. It has a **melting point** of **–130 °C** and a **boiling point** of **36 °C** — it's a **liquid** at room temperature and pressure.

- By contrast, **diamond**, is a **giant covalent** substance, so you **do** have to break the covalent bonds between atoms to turn it into a liquid or a gas. It never really melts, but **sublimes** at over **3600 °C**.

The Physical Properties of a Solid Depend on the Nature of its Particles

Here are a just a few examples of the ways in which the particles that make up a substance affect it properties:

1) The **melting** and **boiling points** of a substance are determined by the strength of the **attraction** between its particles.
2) A substance will only **conduct electricity** if it contains **charged particles** that are **free to move**.
3) How **soluble** a substance is in **water** depends on the **type** of particles that it contains. Water is a **polar solvent**, so substances that are **polar** or **charged** will dissolve in it well, whereas **non-polar** or **uncharged** substances won't.

Each of the Main Substance Types Have Certain Properties

Here's a round up of all the properties of the different types of substances:

Bonding	Examples	Melting and boiling points	Typical state at room temperature and pressure	Does solid conduct electricity?	Does liquid conduct electricity?	Is it soluble in water?
Ionic	NaCl $MgCl_2$	High	Solid	No (ions are held in place)	Yes (ions are free to move)	Yes
Simple covalent (molecular)	CO_2 I_2 H_2O	Low (involves breaking intermolecular forces but <u>not</u> covalent bonds)	May be solid (like I_2) but usually liquid or gas.	No	No	Depends on how polarised the molecule is
Giant covalent (macromolecular)	Diamond Graphite SiO_2	High	Solid	No (except graphite)	— (sublimes rather than melting)	No
Metallic	Fe Mg Al	High	Solid	Yes (delocalised electrons)	Yes (delocalised electrons)	No

Metallic Bonding and Properties of Materials

You Can Use the **Properties** of a Material to **Predict its Structure**

You can predict the type of structure from a list of its properties.
Here's a quick example.

Example: Substance X has a melting point of 1045 K. When solid, it is an insulator, but once melted it conducts electricity. Identify the type of structure present in substance X.

1) Substance X **doesn't** conduct electricity when it's **solid**, but **does** conduct electricity once **melted**. So it looks like it's **ionic** — that would fit with the fact that it has a **high melting point** too.
2) You can also tell that it definitely **isn't simple covalent** because it has a **high melting point**, it definitely **isn't metallic** because it **doesn't** conduct electricity when it's **solid**, and it definitely **isn't giant covalent** because it **does** conduct electricity when **melted**.

So substance X must be **ionic**.

Practice Questions

Q1 Describe the structure of a giant metallic lattice.

Q2 Explain why metals have high melting points.

Q3 Describe how the particles are arranged in a typical solid, a typical liquid and a typical gas.

Q4 In which state will the particles of a substance have the least energy — solid, liquid or gas?

Q5 If a substance has a low melting point, what type of structure is it most likely to have?

Q6 Out of the four main types of structure (ionic, simple covalent, giant covalent and metallic), which will conduct electricity when they are liquids?

Exam Questions

Q1 a) Illustrate the structure of magnesium metal using a labelled diagram. [2 marks]

b) Explain why metals are good conductors of electricity. [1 mark]

Q2 The table below describes the properties of four compounds, A, B, C and D.

Substance	Melting point	Electrical conductivity of solid	Electrical conductivity of liquid	Solubility in water
A	high	poor	good	soluble
B	low	poor	poor	insoluble
C	high	good	good	insoluble
D	very high	poor	— (compound sublimes rather than melting)	insoluble

Identify the type of structure present in each substance. [4 marks]

Q3 Explain why iodine, I_2, has a much lower boiling point than graphite. [4 marks]

I never used to like Chemistry, but after this I feel we've truly bonded...

It's useful to know how the structure of a compound relates to its properties, so have another look at the table on page 60. Remember — materials only conduct electricity if they have charged particles that can move around, they need to have polar particles to dissolve in water and the stronger the bonds, the higher their melting and boiling points.

Solubility

Ever wondered why that teaspoon of sugar dissolves in your afternoon cuppa'? Or why all the salt doesn't just fall out of the sea onto the seabed? Well my friend, you're about to find out. It's all to do with solubility...

Solubility *is Affected by* ***Bonding***

1) For one substance to **dissolve** in another, all these things have to happen:

- bonds in the **substance** have to **break**,
- bonds in the **solvent** have to **break**, and
- **new bonds** have to form **between** the **substance** and the **solvent**.

2) Usually a substance will only dissolve if the strength of the new bonds **formed** is about **the same as**, or **greater than**, the strength of the bonds that are **broken**.

There Are ***Polar*** *and* ***Non-Polar Solvents***

You may see water referred to as an aqueous solvent. Any solvent that isn't water is known as a non-aqueous solvent.

There are two main **types of solvent**:

1) **Polar solvents** are made of polar molecules, such as water. Water molecules bond to each other with **hydrogen bonds**. But not all polar solvents can form hydrogen bonds. For example, **propanone** (often called acetone) is a polar solvent but only forms **induced dipole-dipole forces** and **permanent dipole-permanent dipole forces**.
2) **Non-polar solvents** such as hexane. Hexane molecules bond to each other by **induced dipole-dipole forces**.

Look back at pages 56-58 for more on polarity and intermolecular forces.

Many substances are soluble in one type of solvent but not the other — and it's all down to intermolecular forces.

Ionic Substances *Dissolve in* ***Polar Solvents*** *such as Water*

1) Water is a **polar solvent** — water molecules have a slightly positively-charged end (the δ+ hydrogens) and a slightly negatively-charged end (the δ– oxygen).
2) When an ionic substance is mixed with water, the ions in the ionic substance are attracted to the **oppositely charged ends** of the water molecules.
3) The ions are pulled away from the ionic lattice by the water molecules, which surround the ions. This process is called **hydration**.

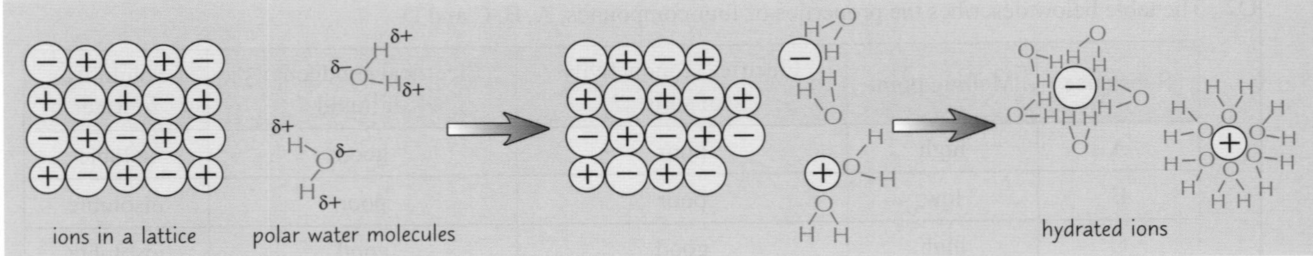

4) Some ionic substances **don't dissolve** because the bonding between their ions is **too strong**. For example, aluminium oxide (Al_2O_3) is insoluble in water because the bonds between the ions are stronger than the bonds they'd form with the water molecules. (Al^{3+} has a high charge density, so it's highly polarising — see page 49.)

Alcohols *also Dissolve in* ***Polar Solvents*** *such as Water*

1) Alcohols are **covalent** but they dissolve in water...
2) ... because the polar O-H bond in an alcohol is attracted to the polar O-H bonds in water. **Hydrogen bonds** form between the lone pairs on the δ– oxygen atoms and the δ+ hydrogen atoms.
3) The **carbon chain** part of the alcohol isn't attracted to water, so the more carbon atoms there are, the **less soluble** the alcohol will be.

Solubility

Not All Molecules with Polar Bonds Dissolve in Water

1) **Halogenoalkanes** (see page 125) contain **polar bonds** but their dipoles aren't strong enough to form **hydrogen bonds** with water.
2) The hydrogen bonding **between** water molecules is **stronger** than the bonds that would be formed with halogenoalkanes, so halogenoalkanes don't dissolve.

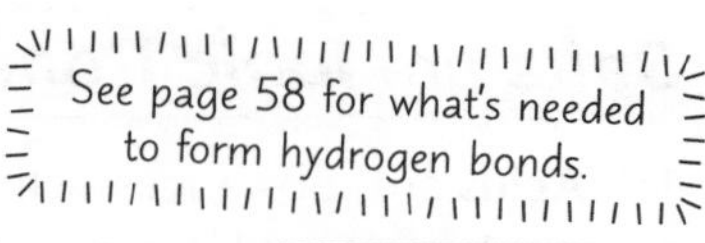

See page 58 for what's needed to form hydrogen bonds.

Henry couldn't understand why the champagne wouldn't dissolve.

Example:
When the halogenoalkane chlorobutane is added to water, they don't mix, but separate into two layers.

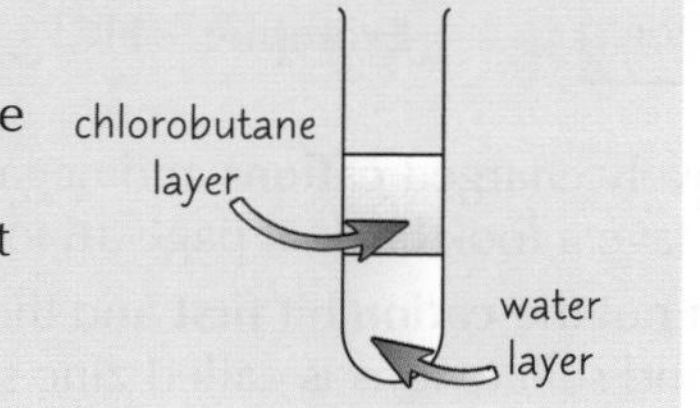

3) But, halogenoalkanes can form **permanent dipole-dipole forces**. They happily dissolve in polar solvents that also form **permanent dipole-dipole forces** (not hydrogen bonds).

Non-Polar Substances Dissolve Best in Non-Polar Solvents

1) Non-polar substances such as **ethene** have **induced dipole-dipole forces** between their molecules. They form **similar bonds** with **non-polar solvents** such as hexane — so they tend to dissolve in them.
2) Water molecules are attracted to **each other** more strongly than they are to **non-polar molecules** such as iodine — so non-polar substances don't tend to dissolve easily in water.

Like dissolves like (usually) — substances usually dissolve best in solvents with similar **intermolecular forces**.

Practice Questions

Q1 Which type of solvent, polar or a non-polar, would you choose to dissolve: i) sodium chloride? ii) ethane?

Q2 Why do most ionic substances dissolve in water?

Q3 What is meant by 'hydration'?

Q4 Some ionic substances don't dissolve in water. Why not?

Q5 What type of bonding occurs between an alcohol and water?

Q6 Why are most non-polar substances insoluble in water?

Exam Questions

Q1 Hydrogen bonds are present between molecules of water.

a) i) Explain why alcohols often dissolve in water while halogenoalkanes do not. [4 marks]

ii) Draw a labelled diagram to show the bonds that form when propan-1-ol ($CH_3CH_2CH_2OH$) dissolves in water. [2 marks]

b) Explain the process by which potassium iodide dissolves in water to form hydrated ions. Include a diagram of the hydrated ions. [5 marks]

Q2 a) An unknown substance, X, is suspected to be a non-polar simple covalent molecule. Describe how you could confirm this by testing with two different solvents. Name the solvents chosen and give the expected results. [3 marks]

b) Explain these results in terms of the intermolecular bonding within X and the solvents. [4 marks]

When the ice-caps melt, where will all the polar solvents live?

I reckon it's logical enough, this business of what dissolves what. Remember, water is a polar molecule — so other polar molecules, as well as ions, are attracted to its δ+ and δ– ends. If that attraction's stronger than the existing bonds (which have to break), the substance will dissolve. It's worth remembering that rule of thumb about 'like dissolves like'.

Making Salts

Making salts isn't tricky, as long as you know what you're doing. And after these pages you should know exactly what you're doing. Fingers crossed. I recommend reading this page with a bowl of chips and some malt vinegar. That'll help.

Salts** are **Ionic Compounds

1) **Acids** are substances with a pH of **less than 7**. **Bases** are substances that have a pH of **more than 7**.
2) Acids react with bases in **neutralisation reactions** to form a salt and water.

acid + base → salt + water

Example: $HCl_{(aq)} + NaOH_{(aq)} \rightarrow NaCl_{(aq)} + H_2O_{(l)}$

3) Salts are formed from positively charged **cations** and negatively charged **anions**, so the product is **neutral**. Have a look back at page 36 to see some common ions and their charges.
4) When naming salts you just put the **cation** bit **first** and then the anion. For example, a salt formed between zinc ions and sulfate ions is called zinc sulfate. Easy.
5) Working out the formula is a bit harder as it involves **balancing charges** (see page 36).

***Salts** can be **Soluble** or **Insoluble** in Water*

If you're making a salt it's important to know if it's soluble or not, so you know how to make it.

- Lithium, sodium, potassium and ammonium salts are **soluble**.
- Nitrates are **soluble**.
- Most chlorides, bromides and iodides are **soluble** — except for silver halides (see page 101), copper iodide (which forms as a white precipitate), lead chloride and lead bromide (both white precipitates) and lead iodide (which is a yellow precipitate).
- Most sulfates are **soluble** — except barium sulfate, calcium sulfate and lead sulfate, which form white precipitates.
- Most hydroxides are **insoluble** — except lithium, sodium, potassium, strontium, calcium, barium and ammonium hydroxides.

Most carbonates are **insoluble** — except lithium, sodium, potassium and ammonium carbonates. Some insoluble carbonates form **coloured** precipitates:

- Copper carbonate is **blue-green**.
- Silver carbonate is **yellow**.
- Most other carbonate precipitates are **white**, e.g. barium, calcium, lead(II), iron(II) (off-white) and zinc carbonates.

*Making **Insoluble Salts** — **Precipitation** Reactions*

Salts can be made in other ways too, not just reactions between acids and bases.

1) If the salt you want to make is **insoluble**, you can use a **precipitation reaction**.
2) Precipitation reactions occur in aqueous solutions, when **cations** and **anions** combine to form an **insoluble ionic salt**. This insoluble salt is called a **precipitate**.
3) You just need to pick **two solutions** that contain the **ions** you need. E.g. to make **lead chloride** you need a solution which contains **lead ions** and one which contains **chloride ions**. So you can mix **lead nitrate solution** (nitrates are soluble) with **sodium chloride solution** (most chlorides are soluble).

Example: $Pb(NO_3)_{2\,(aq)} + 2NaCl_{(aq)} \rightarrow PbCl_{2\,(s)} + 2NaNO_{3\,(aq)}$

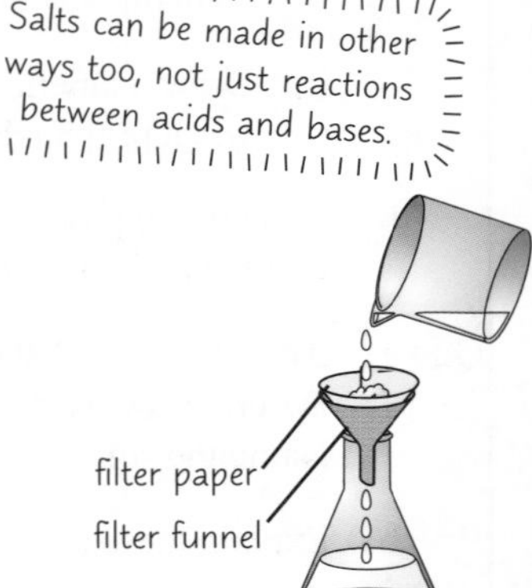

4) Once the salt has precipitated out (and is lying at the bottom of your flask), all you have to do is **filter** it from the solution, **wash** it and then **dry** it on filter paper.

Making Salts

Making **Soluble Salts** Using a **Metal** or an **Insoluble Base**

Soluble salts are a little bit trickier to make.

1) You need to pick the right **acid**, plus a suitable **metal** or an **insoluble base** (a **metal oxide** or **metal hydroxide**). E.g. if you want to make **copper chloride**, mix **hydrochloric acid** and **copper oxide**.

   Example: $CuO_{(s)} + 2HCl_{(aq)} \rightarrow CuCl_{2\,(aq)} + H_2O_{(l)}$

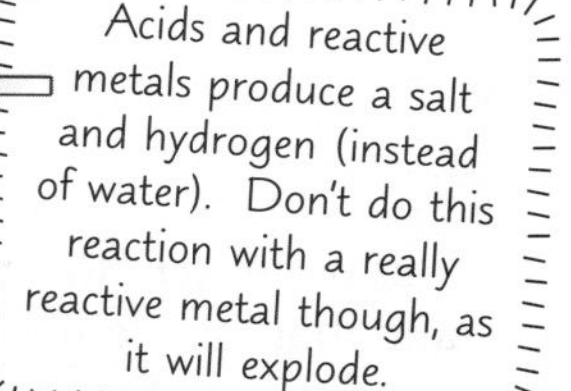

Acids and reactive metals produce a salt and hydrogen (instead of water). Don't do this reaction with a really reactive metal though, as it will explode.

2) Picking the right acid is easy — to make **chlorides** use **hydrochloric acid** (HCl), to make **sulfates** use **sulfuric acid** (H_2SO_4) and to make **nitrates** use **nitric acid** (HNO_3).
3) Add the solid **metal**, **metal oxide** or **hydroxide** to the **acid** — it will **dissolve** in the acid as it reacts. You will know when all the acid has been neutralised because no more solid will dissolve, so it will just **sink** to the bottom of the flask.
4) Then **filter** out the **excess** metal, metal oxide or metal hydroxide to get the salt solution.
5) To get **pure**, **solid** crystals of the **salt**, evaporate some of the water (to make the solution more concentrated) and then leave the rest to evaporate very **slowly**. This is called **crystallisation**.

Making **Soluble Salts** Using an **Alkali**

1) You can't use the method above with **alkalis** (soluble bases) like **sodium**, **potassium** or **ammonium hydroxides**, because you can't tell whether the reaction has **finished** — you can't just add an **excess** to the acid and filter out what's left.
2) You have to add **exactly** the right amount of alkali to just **neutralise** the acid — the most accurate way to do this is with a **titration** (see pages 41-42). This method involves using an **indicator** (which is a substance that changes colour at a particular pH) to show you exactly how much alkali neutralises a known volume of acid.
3) Once you've found out how much alkali you need to neutralise the acid, **repeat** the titration by combining these volumes again — just don't add the indicator this time, otherwise it will contaminate the salt.
4) Then just **evaporate** off the water to **crystallise** the salt as normal.

Mildred loves sharing a good bit o' salt with the gals.

Practice Questions

Q1 What is the name of the salt formed from ammonium and sulfate ions?

Q2 Name one soluble salt and one insoluble salt.

Q3 What is a precipitation reaction and how is it important in making insoluble salts?

Q4 Which acid would you use to make silver chloride?

Q5 What can you use to show when a neutralisation reaction is complete, if both the base and the salt are soluble in water?

Exam Questions

Q1 What is the formula of the soluble salt produced in the reaction between nitric acid and copper(II) hydroxide?

A NO_3Cu_2 B $CuOH_2$ C H_2NO_3 D $Cu(NO_3)_2$ [1 mark]

Q2 Which of the following compounds would react with iron(III) chloride to produce an insoluble salt?

A sodium chloride B silver nitrate C copper(II) sulfate D calcium sulfate [1 mark]

Q3 Potassium sulfate can be made by mixing potassium hydroxide with sulfuric acid.
Describe the method you would use to produce pure, solid potassium sulfate in the lab. [3 marks]

I'm all about that base, 'bout that base, and acid...

If you want to prepare a certain soluble or insoluble salt, you need to think carefully about what chemicals you'd need in order to get the salt you want — and what method you'd use. And to do that you've got to know whether things are soluble or insoluble. Now get yourself a cup of tea — all that talk of salts is bound to make you thirsty.

Enthalpy Changes

A whole new section to enjoy — but don't forget, Big Brother is watching...

Chemical Reactions Often Have Enthalpy Changes

When chemical reactions happen, some bonds are **broken** and some bonds are **made**. More often than not, this'll cause a **change in energy**. The souped-up chemistry term for this is **enthalpy change**.

> **Enthalpy change**, ΔH (delta H), is the heat energy change in a reaction at **constant pressure**. The units of ΔH are **kJ mol^{-1}**.

The Smiths were enjoying the standard conditions in British summertime.

You write $\Delta H^{\ominus}$ to show that the measurements were made under **standard conditions** and that the elements were in their **standard states** (their physical states under standard conditions). Standard conditions are **100 kPa** (about 1 atm) **pressure** and a specified temperature (which is normally **298 K**). The next page explains why this is necessary.

Reactions can be Either Exothermic or Endothermic

1) **Exothermic** reactions **give out** heat energy. ΔH is **negative**. In exothermic reactions, the temperature often goes **up**.

The **combustion** of a fuel like methane is **exothermic**:

$CH_{4(g)} + 2O_{2(g)} \rightarrow CO_{2(g)} + 2H_2O_{(l)}$ $\quad \Delta_c H^{\ominus} = -890$ kJ mol^{-1}

2) **Endothermic** reactions **absorb** heat energy. ΔH is **positive**. In endothermic reactions, the temperature often **falls**.

The **thermal decomposition** of calcium carbonate is **endothermic**:

$CaCO_{3(s)} \rightarrow CaO_{(s)} + CO_{2(g)}$ $\quad \Delta_r H^{\ominus} = +178$ kJ mol^{-1}

The symbols $\Delta_c H^{\ominus}$ and $\Delta_r H^{\ominus}$ are explained on the next page.

Enthalpy Level Diagrams Show the Overall Change of a Reaction

1) Enthalpy level diagrams show the **relative** energies of the reactants and products in a reaction. The **difference** in the enthalpies is the **enthalpy change** of the reaction.
2) The **less enthalpy** a substance has, the **more stable** it is.

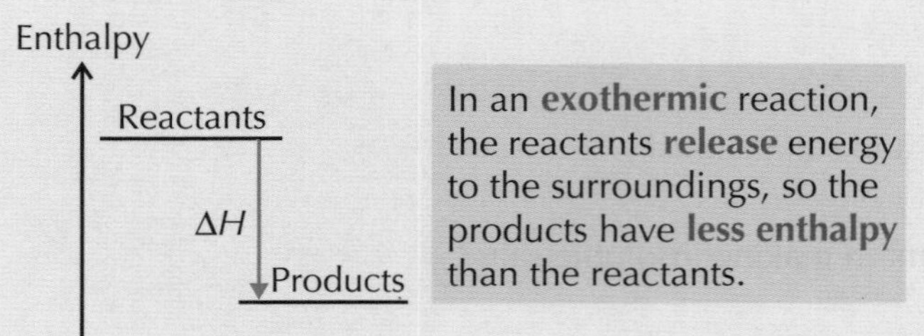

Enthalpy
Reactants
ΔH
Products
In an exothermic reaction, the reactants release energy to the surroundings, so the products have less enthalpy than the reactants.

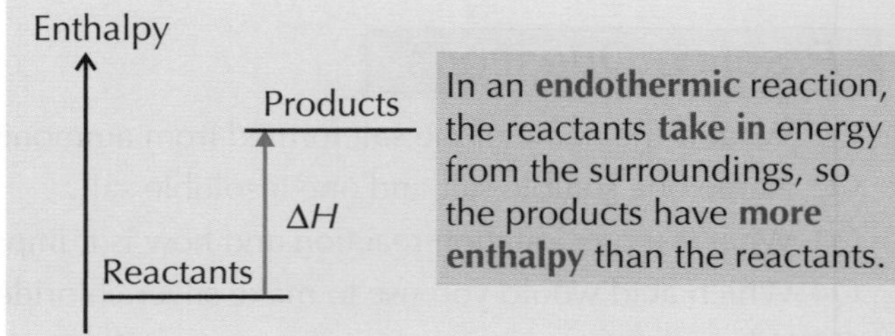

Enthalpy
Products
ΔH
Reactants
In an endothermic reaction, the reactants take in energy from the surroundings, so the products have more enthalpy than the reactants.

Reaction Profile Diagrams Show Enthalpy Changes During a Reaction

1) **Reaction profile diagrams** show you how the **enthalpy changes** during reactions.
2) The **activation energy**, E_a, is the minimum amount of energy needed to begin breaking reactant bonds and start a chemical reaction. (For more on activation energy, see p. 74.)

Reaction profile diagrams are also called enthalpy profile diagrams.

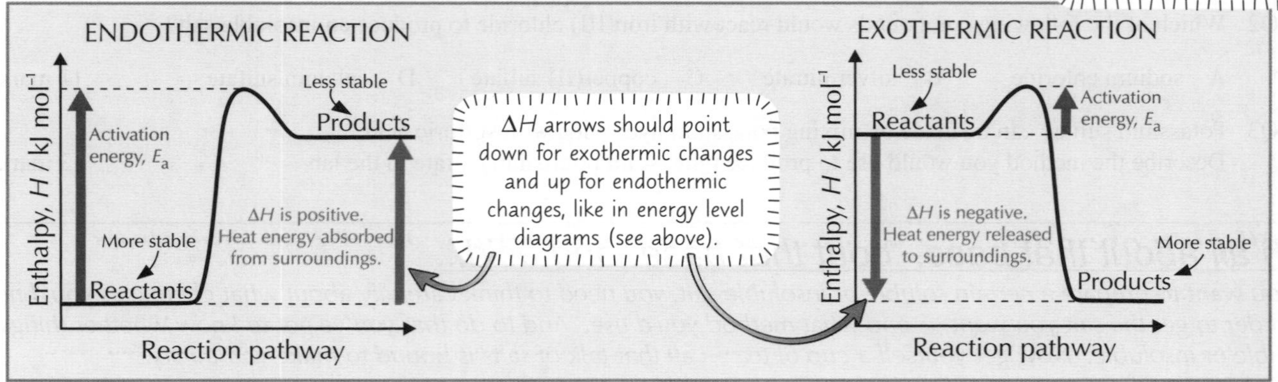

Enthalpy Changes

You Need to Specify the Conditions for Enthalpy Changes

1) You can't directly measure the **actual** enthalpy of a system. In practice, that doesn't matter, because it's only ever **enthalpy change** that matters. You can find enthalpy changes either by **experiment** or in **data books**.
2) Enthalpy changes you find in data books are usually **standard** enthalpy changes — enthalpy changes under **standard conditions** (**298 K** and **100 kPa**).
3) This is important because changes in enthalpy are affected by **temperature** and **pressure** — using standard conditions means that everyone can know **exactly** what the enthalpy change is describing.

There are Different Types of ΔH Depending On the Reaction

1) **Standard enthalpy change of reaction**, $\Delta_r H^{\ominus}$, is the enthalpy change when the reaction occurs in the **molar quantities** shown in the **chemical equation**, under standard conditions.
2) **Standard enthalpy change of formation**, $\Delta_f H^{\ominus}$, is the enthalpy change when **1 mole** of a **compound** is formed from its **elements** in their standard states, under standard conditions, e.g. $2C_{(s)} + 3H_{2(g)} + \frac{1}{2}O_{2(g)} \rightarrow C_2H_5OH_{(l)}$.
3) **Standard enthalpy change of combustion**, $\Delta_c H^{\ominus}$, is the enthalpy change when **1 mole** of a substance is completely **burned in oxygen**, under standard conditions.
4) **Standard enthalpy change of neutralisation**, $\Delta_{neut} H^{\ominus}$, is the enthalpy change when an **acid** and an **alkali** react together, under standard conditions, to form **1 mole of water**.

Practice Questions

Q1 Explain the terms exothermic and endothermic, giving an example reaction in each case.

Q2 Draw and label reaction profile diagrams for an exothermic and an endothermic reaction.

Q3 Define standard enthalpy of formation and standard enthalpy of combustion.

Exam Questions

Q1 Hydrogen peroxide, H_2O_2, can decompose into water and oxygen.

$$2H_2O_{2(l)} \rightarrow 2H_2O_{(l)} + O_{2(g)} \qquad \Delta H^{\ominus} = -98 \text{ kJ mol}^{-1}$$

Draw a reaction profile diagram for this reaction. Mark on the activation energy, E_a, and ΔH. [3 marks]

Q2 Methanol, $CH_3OH_{(l)}$, when blended with petrol, can be used as a fuel. $\Delta_c H^{\ominus}[CH_3OH] = -726 \text{ kJ mol}^{-1}$

a) Write an equation, including state symbols, for the standard enthalpy change of combustion of methanol. [1 mark]

b) Write an equation, including state symbols, for the standard enthalpy change of formation of methanol. [1 mark]

c) Petroleum gas is a fuel that contains propane, C_3H_8. Why does the following equation not represent a standard enthalpy change of combustion? [1 mark]

$$2C_3H_{8(g)} + 10O_{2(g)} \rightarrow 6CO_{2(g)} + 8H_2O_{(g)} \qquad \Delta_r H^{\ominus} = -4113 \text{ kJ mol}^{-1}$$

Q3 Coal is mainly carbon. It is burned as a fuel. $\Delta_c H^{\ominus} = -393.5 \text{ kJ mol}^{-1}$

a) Write an equation, including state symbols, for the standard enthalpy change of combustion of carbon. [1 mark]

b) Explain why the standard enthalpy change of formation of carbon dioxide will also be $-393.5 \text{ kJ mol}^{-1}$. [1 mark]

c) How much energy would be released when 1 tonne of carbon is burned? (1 tonne = 1000 kg) [2 marks]

Enthalpy changes — ethylpan, thenalpy, panthely, lanthepy, nyapleth...

Quite a few definitions here, full of pernickety details, but those details are important. Knowing the difference between different types of enthalpy changes probably seems about as useful as a dead fly in your custard right now, but all will be revealed over the next few pages (how mysterious...). Get to know them, so you've got a bit of a head start.

More on Enthalpy Changes

I bonded with my friend straight away. Now we're on the waiting list to be surgically separated.

Reactions are all about **Breaking** and **Making** Bonds

When reactions happen, **reactant bonds** are **broken** and **product bonds** are **formed**.

1) You **need** energy to break bonds, so bond breaking is **endothermic** (ΔH is **positive**).
2) Energy is **released** when bonds are formed, so this is **exothermic** (ΔH is **negative**).
3) The **enthalpy change** for a reaction is the **overall effect** of these two changes. If you need **more** energy to **break** bonds than is released when bonds are made, ΔH is **positive**. If you need **less**, ΔH is **negative**.

You need **Energy** to **Break** the **Attraction** between **Atoms** and **Ions**

1) In ionic bonding, **positive** and **negative ions** are attracted to each other. In covalent molecules, the **positive nuclei** are attracted to the **negative** charge of the shared electrons in a covalent bond.
2) You need energy to **break** this attraction — **stronger** bonds take more energy to break. The **amount of energy** you need per mole is called the **bond dissociation enthalpy**. (Of course it's got a fancy name — this is chemistry.)
3) Bond dissociation enthalpies always involve bond breaking in **gaseous compounds**. This makes comparisons fair.

Average Bond Enthalpies are **not Exact**

1) Water (H_2O) has **two O–H bonds**. You'd think it'd take the same amount of energy to break them both... but it **doesn't**.
2) The **data book** says the bond enthalpy for O–H is +463 kJ mol^{-1}. It's a bit different because it's the average for a **much bigger range** of molecules, not just water. For example, it includes the O–H bonds in alcohols and carboxylic acids too.

> The **first** bond, $H\text{–}OH_{(g)}$: $E(H\text{–}OH) = +492$ kJ mol^{-1}
> The **second** bond, $H\text{–}O_{(g)}$: $E(H\text{–}O) = +428$ kJ mol^{-1}
> (OH^- is a bit easier to break apart because of the extra electron repulsion.)
> The **average** bond enthalpy is $(492 + 428) \div 2 =$ **+460 kJ mol^{-1}**.

3) So when you look up an **average bond enthalpy**, what you get is:

> The energy needed to break **one mole** of bonds in the **gas phase**, averaged over **many different** compounds.

You can find out **Enthalpy Changes** in the Lab

1) To measure the **enthalpy change** for a reaction you need to know the **number of moles** of the stuff that's reacting, and the change in **temperature**.
2) How you go about doing the experiment depends on what type of reaction it is.
   - To find the enthalpy of **combustion** of a **flammable liquid**, you burn it — using apparatus like this...

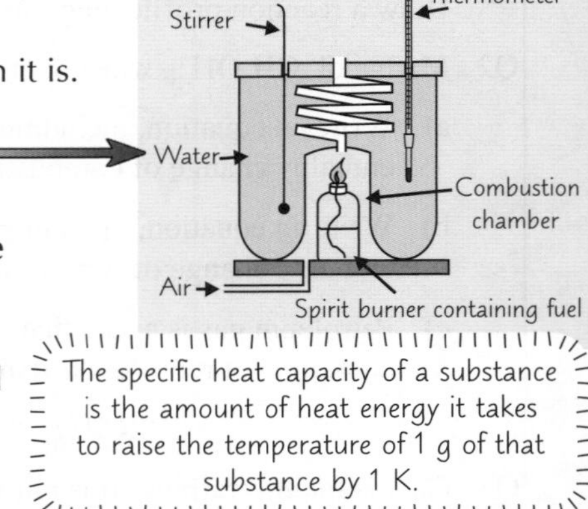

   - As the fuel burns, it heats the water. You can work out the **heat absorbed** by the water if you know the **mass of water**, the **temperature change of the water** (ΔT), and the **specific heat capacity of water** (= 4.18 J g^{-1} K^{-1}). See the next page for all the details.
   - Ideally **all** the heat given out by the fuel as it burns would be **absorbed** by the water — allowing you to work out the enthalpy change of combustion (see the next page). In practice though, you **always** lose some heat (as you heat the apparatus and the surroundings).

> The specific heat capacity of a substance is the amount of heat energy it takes to raise the temperature of 1 g of that substance by 1 K.

3) You can also calculate an enthalpy change for a reaction that happens **in solution**, such as **neutralisation** or **displacement**. For a neutralisation reaction, monitor the temperature of a known quantity of acid (or alkali) **before**, **during** and **after** combining it with a known quantity of alkali (or acid) in an **insulated container**. Draw a **graph** to show the temperature change against time, and **extrapolate** the line from the point where the temperature begins to return to its original value back to the time when the reaction **started** to find the temperature change accounting for any heat lost or gained from the surroundings. The **heat given out** can be calculated using the formula on the next page.

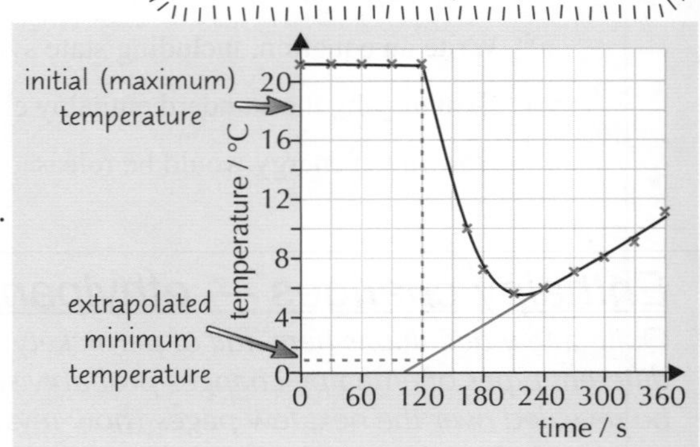

More on Enthalpy Changes

Calculate **Enthalpy Changes** Using the **Equation q = mcΔT**

It seems there's a snazzy equation for everything these days, and enthalpy change is no exception:

$q = mc\Delta T$ where, q = heat lost or gained (in joules). This is the same as the enthalpy change if the pressure is constant.
m = mass of water in the calorimeter, or solution in the insulated container (in grams).
c = specific heat capacity of water (4.18 J g^{-1} K^{-1}).
ΔT = the change in temperature of the water or solution (in K).

This is the same as the change in °C.

Example: In a laboratory experiment, 1.16 g of an organic liquid fuel was completely burned in oxygen. The heat formed during this combustion raised the temperature of 100 g of water from 295.3 K to 357.8 K. Calculate the standard enthalpy of combustion, $\Delta_c H^{\ominus}$, of the fuel. Its M_r is 58.0.

Remember — m is the mass of water, NOT the mass of fuel.

1. First off, you need to calculate the **amount of heat** given out by the fuel using $q = mc\Delta T$.

   $q = mc\Delta T$

   $q = 100 \times 4.18 \times (357.8 - 295.3) = 26\,125$ J

   $26\,125 \div 1000 = 26.125$ kJ

   If you're asked to calculate an enthalpy change, the answer should always be in kJ mol^{-1}. So change the amount of heat from J to kJ by dividing by 1000.

2. The standard enthalpy of combustion involves 1 mole of fuel. So next you need to find out **how many moles** of fuel produced this heat. It's back to the old n = **mass** ÷ M_r equation.

   n = 1.16 ÷ 58.0 = 0.0200 mole of fuels

3. So the heat produced by 1 mole of fuel = −26.125 ÷ 0.0200

   ≈ **−1310 kJ mol^{-1}** (3 s.f.).

   This is the standard enthalpy change of combustion.

   It's negative because combustion is an exothermic reaction.

The actual $\Delta_c H^{\ominus}$ of this compound is −1615 kJ mol^{-1} — lots of heat has been **lost** and not measured. For example, it's likely a bit would have escaped through the **calorimeter**, the fuel might not have **combusted completely**, or the conditions might not have been **standard**.

Practice Questions

Q1 Briefly describe an experiment that could be carried out to find the enthalpy change of a reaction.

Q2 Why is the enthalpy change determined in a laboratory likely to be lower than the value shown in a data book?

Q3 What equation is used to calculate the heat change in a chemical reaction?

Exam Questions

Q1 A 50.0 cm^3 sample of 0.200 mol dm^{-3} copper(II) sulfate solution placed in a polystyrene beaker gave a temperature increase of 2.60 K when excess zinc powder was added and stirred. Calculate the enthalpy change when 1 mole of zinc reacts. Assume that the specific heat capacity for the solution is 4.18 J g^{-1} K^{-1}. Ignore the increase in volume due to the zinc.
The equation for the reaction is: $Zn_{(s)} + CuSO_{4(aq)} \rightarrow Cu_{(s)} + ZnSO_{4(aq)}$ [4 marks]

Q2 a) Explain why bond enthalpies determine whether a reaction is exothermic or endothermic. [2 marks]

b) Calculate the temperature change that should be produced when 1.000 kg of water is heated by burning 6.000 g of coal. Assume the coal is pure carbon.
[The specific heat capacity of water is 4.18 J g^{-1} K^{-1}. For carbon, $\Delta_c H^{\ominus} = -393.5$ kJ mol^{-1}] [3 marks]

If you can't stand the heat, get out of the calorimeter...

Reactions are like pulling a model spaceship apart and building something new. Sometimes the bits get stuck together and you need to use loads of energy to pull 'em apart. Okay, so energy's not really released when you stick them together, but you can't have everything — and it wasn't that bad an analogy up till now.

Enthalpy Calculations

You can't always work out an enthalpy change by measuring a single temperature change. But there are other ways...

Hess's Law — the Total Enthalpy Change is **Independent** of the Route Taken

Hess's Law says that: The **total enthalpy change** of a reaction is always **the same**, no matter **which route** is taken.

This law is handy for working out enthalpy changes that you **can't find directly** by doing an experiment.

Here's an example:
The **total enthalpy change** for route 1 is the **same as for route 2**.

So, $\Delta_r H^\circ$ = +114.4 + (–180.8) = **–66.4 kJ mol⁻¹**.

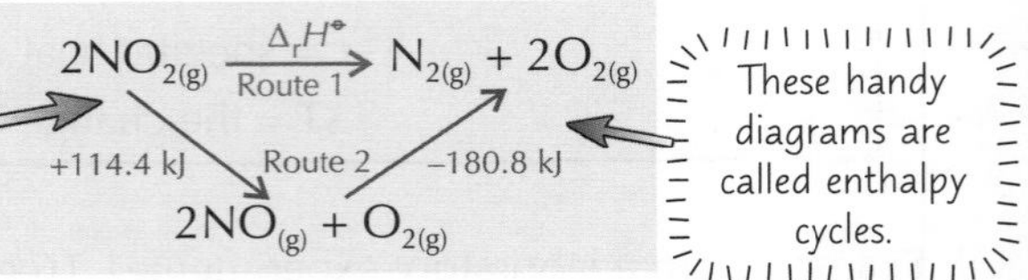

Enthalpy Changes Can be Worked Out From **Enthalpies of Formation**

Enthalpy changes of formation are useful for calculating enthalpy changes you can't find directly.
You need to know $\Delta_f H^\circ$ for **all** the reactants and products that are **compounds** — $\Delta_f H^\circ$ for elements is **zero**.

Example: Use the enthalpy cycle on the right to calculate $\Delta_r H^\circ$ for the reaction: $SO_{2(g)} + 2H_2S_{(g)} \rightarrow 3S_{(s)} + 2H_2O_{(l)}$

REACTANTS $SO_{2(g)} + 2H_2S_{(g)}$ —$\Delta_r H^\circ$→ PRODUCTS $3S_{(s)} + 2H_2O_{(l)}$
Route 1
Route 2
$\Delta_f H^\circ_{(reactants)}$
$\Delta_f H^\circ_{(products)}$
$3S_{(s)} + 2H_{2(g)} + O_{2(g)}$
ELEMENTS

$\Delta_f H^\circ[SO_{2(g)}]$ = –297 kJ mol⁻¹
$\Delta_f H^\circ[H_2S_{(g)}]$ = –20.2 kJ mol⁻¹
$\Delta_f H^\circ[H_2O_{(l)}]$ = –286 kJ mol⁻¹

Using **Hess's Law**: Route 1 = Route 2

$\Delta_r H^\circ$ + the sum of $\Delta_f H^\circ$(reactants) = the sum of $\Delta_f H^\circ$(products)

So, $\Delta_r H^\circ$ = the sum of $\Delta_f H^\circ$(products) – the sum of $\Delta_f H^\circ$(reactants)

Just plug the numbers given on the right into the equation above:

$\Delta_r H^\circ$ = [0 + (2 × –286)] – [–297 + (2 × –20.2)] = **–235 kJ mol⁻¹**

$\Delta_f H^\circ$ of sulfur is zero — it's an element.

There are 2 moles of H_2O and 2 moles of H_2S.

It **always** works, no matter how complicated the reaction...

Example: Use the enthalpy cycle on the right to calculate $\Delta_r H^\circ$ for the reaction:
$2NH_4NO_{3(s)} + C_{(s)} \rightarrow 2N_{2(g)} + CO_{2(g)} + 4H_2O_{(l)}$

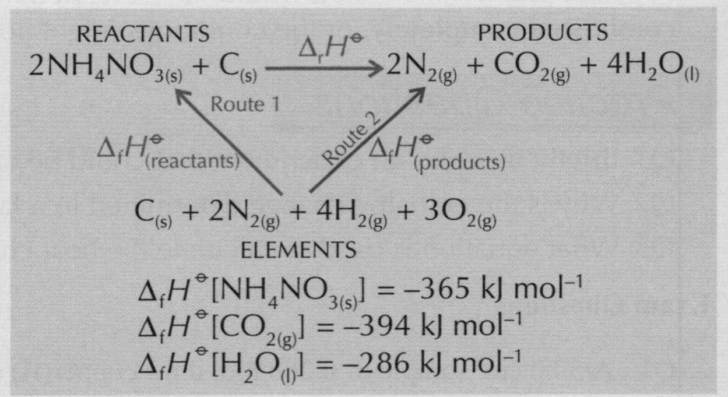

Using Hess's Law: Route 1 = Route 2

$\Delta_f H^\circ$(reactants) + $\Delta_r H^\circ$ = $\Delta_f H^\circ$(products)

(2 × –365) + 0 + $\Delta_r H^\circ$ = 0 + –394 + (4 × –286)

$\Delta_r H^\circ$ = –394 + (–1144) – (–730)

= **–808 kJ mol⁻¹**

Enthalpy Changes Can be Worked Out From **Enthalpies of Combustion**

You can use a similar method to find an enthalpy change from **enthalpy changes of combustion**.

Example: Use the enthalpy cycle on the right to calculate $\Delta_f H^\circ$ for C_2H_5OH.

You need to add enough oxygen to balance the equations.

REACTANTS $2C_{(s)} + 3H_{2(g)} + ½O_{2(g)}$ —$\Delta_f H^\circ$→ PRODUCTS $C_2H_5OH_{(l)}$
Route 1
Route 2
$3O_{2(g)}$
$3O_{2(g)}$
$2CO_{2(g)} + 3H_2O_{(l)}$
COMBUSTION PRODUCTS

$\Delta_c H^\circ[C_{(s)}]$ = –394 kJ mol⁻¹
$\Delta_c H^\circ[H_{2(g)}]$ = –286 kJ mol⁻¹
$\Delta_c H^\circ[C_2H_5OH_{(l)}]$ = –1367 kJ mol⁻¹

Using Hess's Law: Route 1 = Route 2

$\Delta_f H^\circ[C_2H_5OH] + \Delta_c H^\circ[C_2H_5OH] = 2\Delta_c H^\circ[C] + 3\Delta_c H^\circ[H_2]$

$\Delta_f H^\circ[C_2H_5OH]$ + (–1367) = (2 × –394) + (3 × –286)

$\Delta_f H^\circ[C_2H_5OH]$ = –788 + –858 – (–1367) = **–279 kJ mol⁻¹**

Enthalpy Calculations

Enthalpy Changes Can Be Calculated using Average Bond Enthalpies

In any chemical reaction, energy is **absorbed** to **break bonds** and **given out** during **bond formation**. The difference between the energy absorbed and released is the overall **enthalpy change of reaction**:

Enthalpy Change of Reaction = Sum of bond enthalpies of reactants − Sum of bond enthalpies of products

This is the total energy absorbed to break bonds. (→ Sum of bond enthalpies of reactants)

This is the total energy released in making bonds (→ Sum of bond enthalpies of products)

Example: Calculate the overall enthalpy change for this reaction: $N_{2(g)} + 3H_{2(g)} \rightarrow 2NH_{3(g)}$
Use the average bond enthalpy values in the table.

Bonds broken: 1 N≡N bond broken = 1 × 945 = 945 kJ mol^{-1}
3 H–H bonds broken = 3 × 436 = 1308 kJ mol^{-1}

Total Energy Absorbed = 945 + 1308 = **2253 kJ mol^{-1}**

Bonds formed: 6 N–H bonds formed = 6 × 391 = 2346 kJ mol^{-1}

Total Energy Released = **2346 kJ mol^{-1}**

Now you just subtract 'total energy released' from 'total energy absorbed':

Enthalpy Change of Reaction = 2253 − 2346 = **−93 kJ mol^{-1}**

Bond	Average Bond Enthalpy
N≡N	945 kJ mol^{-1}
H–H	436 kJ mol^{-1}
N–H	391 kJ mol^{-1}

Practice Questions

Q1 What is Hess's Law?

Q2 What is the standard enthalpy change of formation of any element?

Q3 Describe how you can make an enthalpy cycle to find the standard enthalpy change of a reaction using standard enthalpy changes of formation.

Exam Questions

Q1 Using the facts that the standard enthalpy change of formation of $Al_2O_{3(s)}$ is −1676 kJ mol^{-1} and the standard enthalpy change of formation of $MgO_{(s)}$ is −602 kJ mol^{-1}, calculate the enthalpy change of the following reaction.

$$Al_2O_{3(s)} + 3Mg_{(s)} \rightarrow 2Al_{(s)} + 3MgO_{(s)}$$

[2 marks]

Q2 Calculate the enthalpy change for the reaction below (the fermentation of glucose).

$$C_6H_{12}O_{6(s)} \rightarrow 2C_2H_5OH_{(l)} + 2CO_{2(g)}$$

Use the following standard enthalpies of combustion in your calculations:

$\Delta_c H^{\circ}$(glucose) = −2820 kJ mol^{-1} $\quad$ $\Delta_c H^{\circ}$(ethanol) = −1367 kJ mol^{-1} [2 marks]

Q3 Calculate the standard enthalpy of formation of propane from carbon and hydrogen. $3C_{(s)} + 4H_{2(g)} \rightarrow C_3H_{8(g)}$

Use the following data:

$\Delta_c H^{\circ}$(propane) = −2220 kJ mol^{-1}, $\Delta_c H^{\circ}$(carbon) = −394 kJ mol^{-1}, $\Delta_c H^{\circ}$(hydrogen) = −286 kJ mol^{-1} [2 marks]

Q4 The table on the right shows some average bond enthalpy values.

Bond	C–H	C=O	O=O	O–H
Average Bond Enthalpy (kJ mol^{-1})	435	805	498	464

The complete combustion of methane can be represented by the following equation:

$$CH_{4(g)} + 2O_{2(g)} \rightarrow CO_{2(g)} + 2H_2O_{(l)}$$

Use the table of bond enthalpies above to calculate the enthalpy change for the reaction. [2 marks]

Meet Hessie. She's the Lawch Hess Monster...

To get your head around those enthalpy cycles, you're going to have to do more than skim them. It'll also help if you know the definitions for those standard enthalpy thingumabobs. I'd read those enthalpy cycle examples again and make sure you understand how the elements/compounds at each corner were chosen to be there.

The Atmosphere

The bonds in some molecules can absorb certain frequencies of light, which have a fixed energy. This is important in the atmosphere as it's what stops too much harmful ultraviolet radiation reaching the Earth's surface. Without it, we'd fry.

Gases Can be Measured by Their Percentage Concentration

1) The composition of the atmosphere is sometimes broken down by its **percentage concentration** by **volume** of dry air (air with no **water vapour** in it).
2) For example, in air, **nitrogen** has a percentage concentration of **78%**. This means that for every **100 particles** in the atmosphere, 78 of them will be N_2. The percentage concentration of **oxygen** in air is about 21%.

Parts Per Million is used for Really Small Quantities

1) The **major gases** in the atmosphere are normally given as **percentages** of the **total volume**. But some gases are present in such **tiny amounts** that it's **not very convenient** to write their quantities like this. For instance, **xenon** makes up only **0.000 009%** of the atmosphere. Numbers this small are a pain to work with.
2) So to get round this problem, another type of measurement is used. It is called **parts per million** or **ppm**.
3) It's easy to switch between **percentage concentration** and **parts per million**:

Instead of dividing the percentage by 100 and multiplying by 1 000 000, you can just multiply it by 10 000 instead.

Example: The percentage concentration of xenon in the atmosphere is 0.000 009%. What is its concentration in parts per million?

0.000 009% means there are 0.000 009 parts of xenon per 100 parts of air.
So in one part of air there will be 0.000 009 ÷ 100 = 0.000 000 09 parts of air
And in a million parts of air there are 0.000 000 09 × 1 000 000 = 0.09 parts of air.
So xenon has a concentration of **0.09 ppm**

4) The atmosphere also contains **0.1 ppm** carbon monoxide and **0.3 ppm** nitrous oxide.

The Earth's Atmosphere Absorbs Radiation

1) The Sun gives out **electromagnetic radiation** because of the nuclear processes going on in its core. Electromagnetic radiation is energy that's transmitted as waves, with a **spectrum** of different frequencies.
2) The Sun mainly gives out **visible** radiation (light) and **infrared** radiation (heat), along with a smaller amount of **ultraviolet** radiation.

The Sun's main radiations

RADIO WAVES	MICRO-WAVES	INFRA-RED	VISIBLE LIGHT	ULTRA-VIOLET	X-RAYS	GAMMA RAYS

Increasing frequency and energy

3) The **Earth's atmosphere** absorbs some of the Sun's infrared radiation and most of the ultraviolet radiation.
4) The **Earth's surface** also absorbs radiation from the Sun and is warmed. It then re-emits **radiation**, mostly as **infrared**. The Earth emits much **lower frequency** radiation than the Sun (because it's much cooler).

UV and Visible Light Radiation Give Electrons More Energy

1) The **electrons** in molecules have **fixed energy levels** that they can **jump between**. These are called **quantised** energy levels.
2) When **ultraviolet radiation** or **visible light** hit a molecule of **gas** the **electrons** can **absorb** the energy and **jump up** to their **next energy level**. Because the energy needed for these changes is **quantised** too, **only specific frequencies** are absorbed.
3) If enough energy is absorbed bonds **break**, forming **free radicals**.

There's more about free radicals on page 118.

If O_2 molecules absorb the right amount of UV energy they split into oxygen atoms or free radicals — this is the first step in the formation of ozone, O_3 (see page 128).

The Atmosphere

The Energy from Radiation can be Calculated

The **energy** of light depends on its **frequency**. I reckon we're about due for an **equation**:

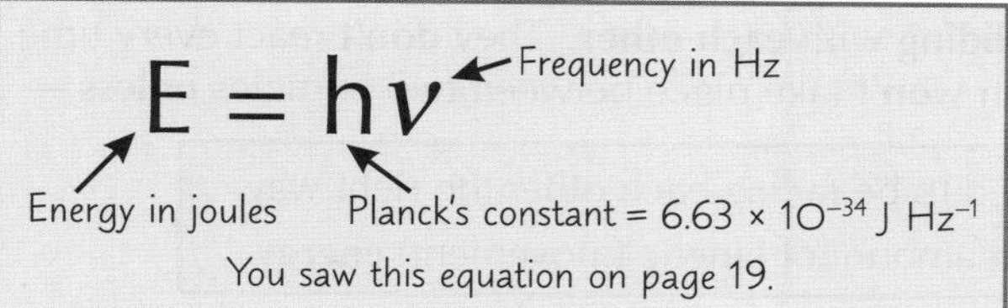

E = hν
Frequency in Hz
Energy in joules
Planck's constant = 6.63 × 10⁻³⁴ J Hz⁻¹

You saw this equation on page 19.

Example: What is the energy supplied to a molecule by ultraviolet radiation of frequency 1.2×10^{15} Hz?

$E = h\nu = (6.63 \times 10^{-34}) \times (1.2 \times 10^{15})$
$= \mathbf{7.96 \times 10^{-19}}$ **J**

So, if you know **Planck's constant** and the **frequency**, you can calculate **how much energy** the molecule absorbed.

Sometimes it's easier to measure **wavelength** than **frequency**. Fortunately, there's an equation to switch between the two:

$$\nu = \frac{c}{\lambda}$$

c — speed of light in m s^{-1} = 3.00×10^8 m s^{-1}; ν — Frequency in Hz; λ — wavelength in m

This is the equation you saw on page 20, just rearranged to find frequency rather than wavelength.

You can **combine** these two equations to make a new equation for energy:

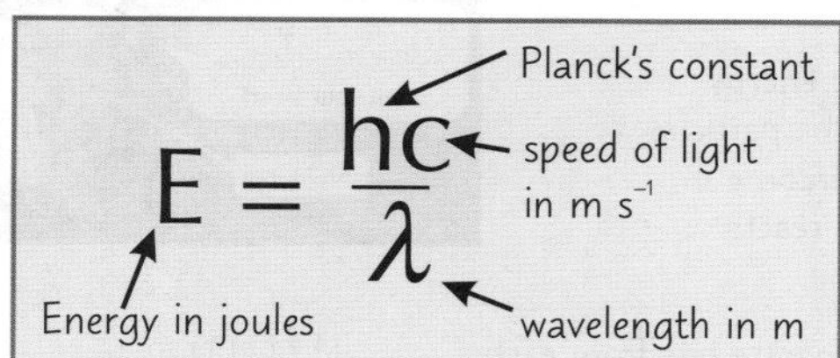

Example: What is the energy supplied to a molecule by ultraviolet radiation with wavelength 1.95×10^{-7}m?

$$E = \frac{hc}{\lambda} = \frac{(6.63 \times 10^{-34}) \times (3.00 \times 10^8)}{1.95 \times 10^{-7}} = \mathbf{1.02 \times 10^{-18}\ J}$$

Wavelengths are often given in nm. 1 nm = 1×10^{-9} m.

Example: When irradiated with UV light of wavelength 242 nm, oxygen gas decomposes. Calculate the enthalpy of the O=O bonds broken at this wavelength.

First work out the energy of light at this wavelength. Remember to convert the wavelength from nm to m:

$$E = \frac{hc}{\lambda} = \frac{6.63 \times 10^{-34} \times 3.00 \times 10^8}{2.42 \times 10^{-7}} = 8.219 \times 10^{-19}\ J$$

This is the energy needed to break **one O=O bond**, but the definition of bond enthalpy is the energy needed to break **one mole of bonds**. So multiply by **Avogadro's number** to find the energy needed to break **one mole** of O=O bonds:

$(8.219 \times 10^{-19}) \times (6.02 \times 10^{23}) = 494\ 783.8$ J mol^{-1} = **495 kJ mol^{-1}** (3 s.f.)

Practice Questions

Q1 What is the difference between 'percent' and 'parts per million'?

Q2 What types of electromagnetic radiation does the Sun emit?

Q3 What is the equation that relates frequency to wavelength?

Exam Questions

Q1 Ozone is a molecule that absorbs ultraviolet light with a wavelength of 255 nm.

a) i) What frequency of ultraviolet radiation does ozone absorb? [1 mark]

ii) What is the energy of the ultraviolet light that ozone absorbs? [1 mark]

b) What is the concentration of ozone in ppm if its percentage concentration by volume is 0.000 021%? [1 mark]

Q2 Calculate the energy absorbed when one molecule of H_2O changes from its ground electronic level to the next level, given that the frequency of radiation absorbed is 1.80×10^{15} Hz. [1 mark]

You're one in a million (that's 1.0 ppm or 0.000 1%)...

If there were no atmospheric gases to absorb the Sun's radiation, sunburn would be the least of our worries. There wouldn't be any oxygen, so we wouldn't be able to breathe. But at least you wouldn't have any exams...

Reaction Rates

The rate of a reaction is just how quickly it happens. Lots of things can make it go faster or slower.

Particles **Must** Collide to **React**

1) Particles in liquids and gases are **always moving** and **colliding** with **each other**. They **don't** react every time though — only when the **conditions** are right. A reaction **won't** take place between two particles **unless** —

- They collide in the **right direction**. They need to be **facing** each other the right way.
- They collide with at least a certain **minimum** amount of kinetic (movement) **energy**.

This stuff's called **Collision Theory**.

2) The **minimum amount of kinetic energy** particles need to react is called the **activation energy**. The particles need this much energy to **break the bonds** to start the reaction.
3) Reactions with **low activation energies** often happen **pretty easily**. But reactions with **high activation energies** don't. You need to give the particles extra energy by **heating** them.

To make this a bit clearer, here's a **reaction profile diagram**.

Can I talk to you about collision theory dear?
If you do, my croquet mallet might collide with your head.
Ah ha ha!

Reaction Profile Diagram
If the particles have enough energy, the bonds will break.
Here, the bonds within each particle are being stretched.
This is the energy barrier that the particles have to overcome in order to react.
The separate bits from each particle can't exist by themselves — so they form new bonds and release energy.
Enthalpy
Reactants
Activation energy
Products
Progress of Reaction

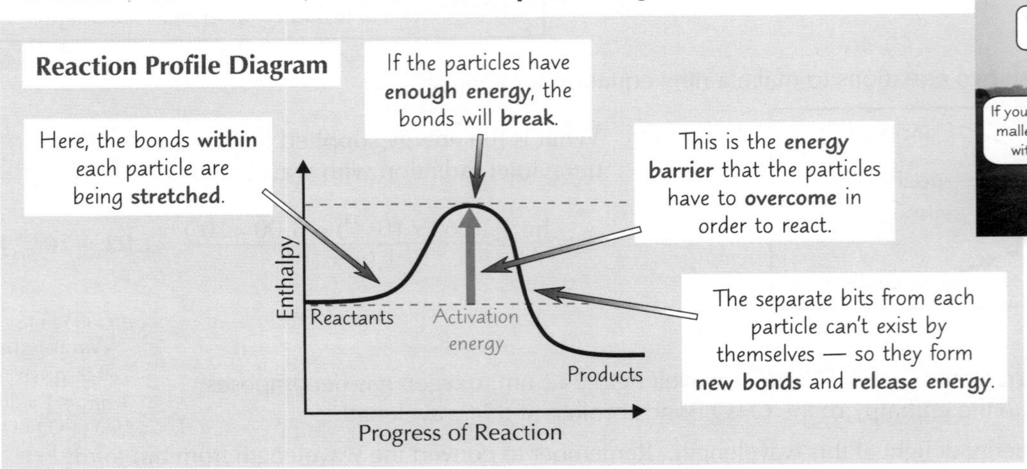

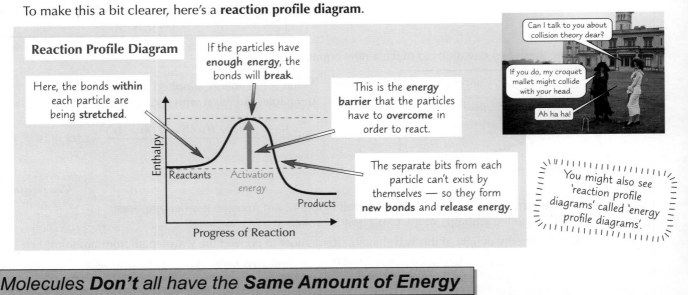

You might also see 'reaction profile diagrams' called 'energy profile diagrams'.

Molecules **Don't** all have the **Same Amount of Energy**

Imagine looking down on Oxford Street when it's teeming with people. You'll see some people ambling along **slowly**, some hurrying **quickly**, but most of them will be walking with a **moderate speed**. It's the same with the **molecules** in a liquid or gas. Some **don't have much kinetic energy** and move **slowly**. Others have **loads** of **kinetic energy** and **whizz** along. But most molecules are somewhere **in between**.

If you plot a **graph** of the **numbers of molecules** in a substance with different **kinetic energies** you get a **Boltzmann distribution**. It looks like this —

Boltzmann distributions are sometimes called Maxwell-Boltzmann distributions.

A Boltzmann Distribution
Most molecules are moving at a moderate speed so their energies are in this range.
Some molecules have more than the activation energy. These are the only ones that can react.
The curve starts at (0, 0) because no molecules have zero energy.
Number of Molecules
Kinetic Energy
Activation energy
A few molecules are moving slowly.

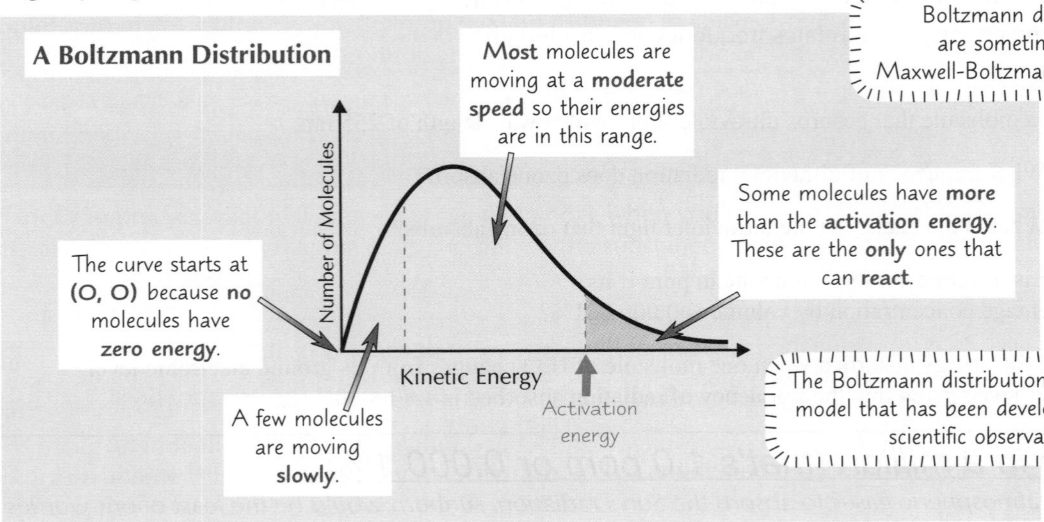

The Boltzmann distribution is a theoretical model that has been developed to explain scientific observations.

Reaction Rates

Increasing the Temperature makes Reactions Faster

1) If you increase the **temperature**, the particles will, on average, have more **kinetic energy** and will move **faster**.
2) So, a **greater proportion** of molecules will have at least the **activation energy** and be able to **react**. This changes the **shape** of the **Boltzmann distribution curve** — it pushes it over to the **right**.

The total number of molecules is still the same, which means the area under each curve must be the same.

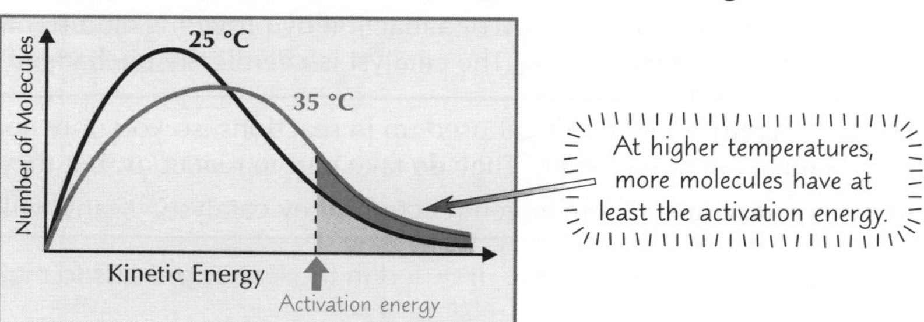

At higher temperatures, more molecules have at least the activation energy.

3) Because the molecules are flying about **faster**, they'll **collide more often**. This is **another reason** why increasing the temperature makes a reaction faster.

Concentration, Pressure and Catalysts also Affect the Reaction Rate

Increasing Concentration Speeds Up Reactions

If you increase the **concentration** of reactants in a **solution**, the particles will be **closer together**, on average. If they're closer, they'll **collide more frequently**. If there are **more collisions**, they'll have **more chances** to react.

Increasing Pressure Speeds Up Reactions

If any of your reactants are **gases**, increasing the **pressure** will increase the rate of reaction. It's pretty much the same as increasing the **concentration** of a solution — at higher pressures, the particles will be **closer together**, increasing the chance of **successful collisions**.

If one of the reactants is a solid, increasing its surface area makes the reaction faster too.

Catalysts Can Speed Up Reactions

Catalysts are really useful. They **lower the activation energy** by providing a **different way** for the bonds to be broken and remade. If the activation energy's **lower**, more particles will have **enough energy** to react. There's heaps of information about catalysts on the next two pages.

Practice Questions

Q1 Explain the term 'activation energy'.

Q2 Name four factors that affect the rate of a reaction.

Exam Questions

Q1 Nitrogen oxide (NO) and ozone (O_3) sometimes react to produce nitrogen dioxide (NO_2) and oxygen (O_2). How would increasing the pressure affect the rate of this reaction? Explain your answer. [2 marks]

Q2 On the right is a Boltzmann distribution curve for a sample of a gas at 25 °C.

a) Which of the curves, X or Y, shows the Boltzmann distribution curve for the same sample at 15 °C ? [1 mark]

b) Explain how this curve shows that the reaction rate will be lower at 15 °C than at 25 °C. [1 mark]

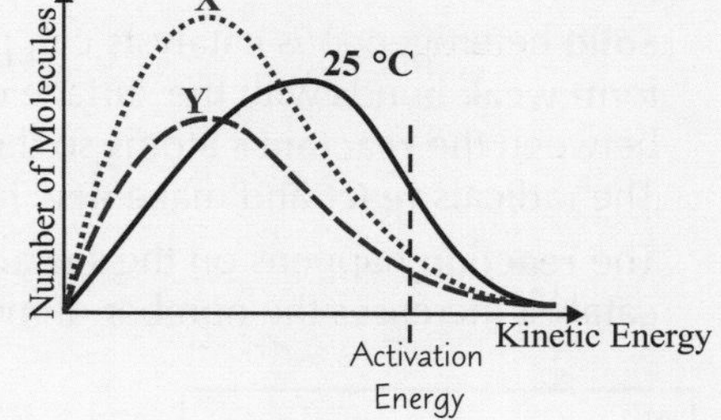

What do you call a sprinter's mother? Bolt's mum...

This page isn't too hard to learn — no equations, no formulas... What more could you ask for. The only tricky thing might be the Boltzmann thingymajiggle. Remember, increasing concentration and pressure do exactly the same thing. The only difference is, you increase the concentration of a solution and the pressure of a gas.

Catalysts

Catalysts were tantalisingly mentioned on the last page — here's the full story...

Catalysts Increase the Rate of Reactions

1) You can use **catalysts** to make chemical reactions happen **faster**. Here's a useful definition:

> A **catalyst** increases the **rate** of a reaction by providing an **alternative reaction pathway** with a **lower activation energy**. The catalyst is **chemically unchanged** at the end of the reaction.

2) Catalysts are **great**. They **don't** get used up in reactions, so you only need a **tiny bit** of catalyst to catalyse a **huge** amount of stuff. They **do** take part in reactions, but they're **remade** at the end.
3) Catalysts are **very fussy** about which reactions they catalyse. Many will **only** work on a single reaction.

> An example of a catalyst is **iron**. It's used in the **Haber process** to make ammonia.
>
> $$N_{2(g)} + 3H_{2(g)} \underset{}{\overset{Fe_{(s)}}{\rightleftharpoons}} 2NH_{3(g)}$$

'Catalysis' means speeding up a chemical reaction using a catalyst.

Reaction Profiles and Boltzmann Distributions Show Why Catalysts Work

If you look at a **reaction profile** together with a **Boltzmann distribution**, you can see **why** catalysts work.

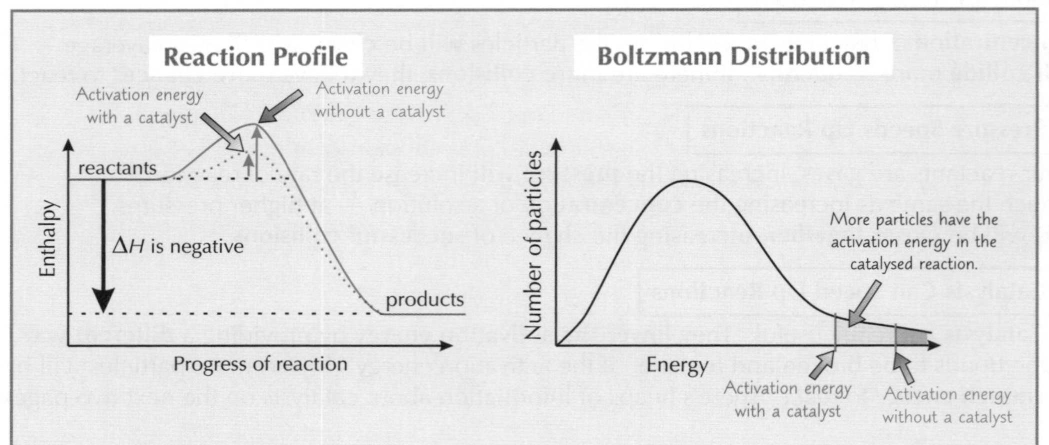

The 1985 Nobel Prize in Chemistry was awarded to Mr Tiddles for discovering catalysis.

The catalyst **lowers the activation energy**, meaning there are **more particles** with **enough energy** to react when they collide. So, in a certain amount of time, **more particles react**.

Catalysts can be Homogeneous or Heterogenous

Heterogeneous Catalysts

A heterogeneous catalyst is one that is in a **different phase** from the reactants — i.e. in a different **physical state**. For example, in the Haber Process (see above), **gases** are passed over a **solid iron catalyst**.

Solid heterogeneous catalysts can provide a **surface** for a reaction to take place on. First, the reactant molecules form **weak bonds** with the surface of the catalyst in a process called **adsorption**. This weakens the bonds between the **reactant's** atoms so they **break up** to form **radicals** — atoms or molecules with **unpaired** electrons. The radicals **react** and make **new molecules** which detach from the catalyst in a process called **desorption**.

The **reaction** happens on the **surface** of the **heterogeneous catalyst**. So, **increasing** the **surface area** of the catalyst increases the number of molecules that can **react** at the same time, **increasing the rate** of the reaction.

Homogeneous Catalysts

Homogeneous catalysts are in the **same physical state** as the reactants.
Usually a **homogeneous** catalyst is an **aqueous catalyst** for a reaction between two **aqueous solutions**.

A homogeneous catalyst works by forming an **intermediate species**. The **reactants** combine with the **catalyst** to make an **intermediate species**, which then reacts to form the **products** and **reform the catalyst**.

Catalysts

Catalysts — Good for Industries...

Loads of industries rely on **catalysts**. They can dramatically lower production costs, give you more product in a shorter time and help make better products. Here are a few examples —

Iron is used as a catalyst in **ammonia** production. If it wasn't for the catalyst, the **temperature** would have to be raised loads to make the reaction happen **quick enough**. Not only would this be bad for the fuel bills, it'd **reduce the amount of ammonia** produced.

Using a catalyst can change the properties of a product to make it more useful, e.g. **poly(ethene)**.

	Made without a catalyst	Made with a catalyst (a Ziegler-Natta catalyst, to be precise)
Properties of poly(ethene)	less dense, less rigid	more dense, more rigid, higher melting point

...and for Environmental Sustainability

1) Using catalysts means that lower temperatures and pressures can be used. So energy is saved, meaning **less CO_2** is released, and fossil fuel reserves are preserved. Catalysts can also **reduce waste** by allowing a different reaction to be used with a better **atom economy**. (See page 45 for more on atom economy.)

   For example, making the painkiller ibuprofen by the traditional method involves 6 steps and has an atom economy of 32%. Using catalysts, it can be made in **3 steps** with an **atom economy of 77%**.

2) **Catalytic converters** on cars are made from **alloys of platinum, palladium and rhodium**. They reduce the pollution released into the atmosphere by speeding up the reaction, $2CO + 2NO \rightarrow 2CO_2 + N_2$.

Practice Questions

Q1 Explain what a catalyst is.

Q2 Explain what the difference between a heterogeneous and a homogeneous catalyst is.

Q3 Describe three reasons why catalysts are useful for industry.

Exam Question

Q1 Sulfuric acid is manufactured by the contact process. In one of the stages, sulfur dioxide gas is mixed with oxygen gas and converted into sulfur trioxide gas. A solid vanadium(V) oxide (V_2O_5) catalyst is used. The enthalpy change for the uncatalysed reaction is –197 kJ mol^{-1}.

a) Which of the following reaction profile diagrams is correct for the catalysed reaction? [1 mark]

A

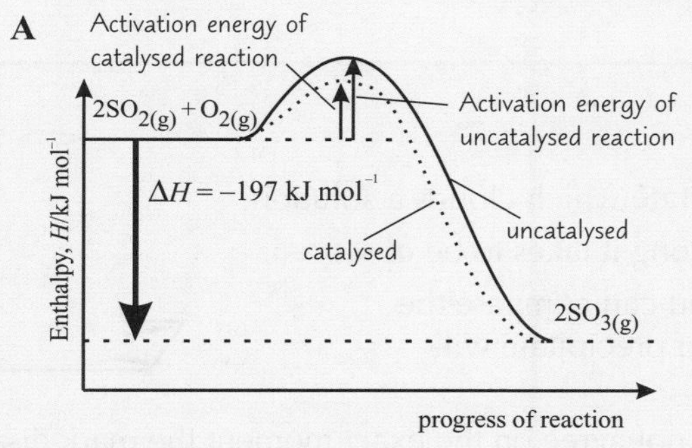

B

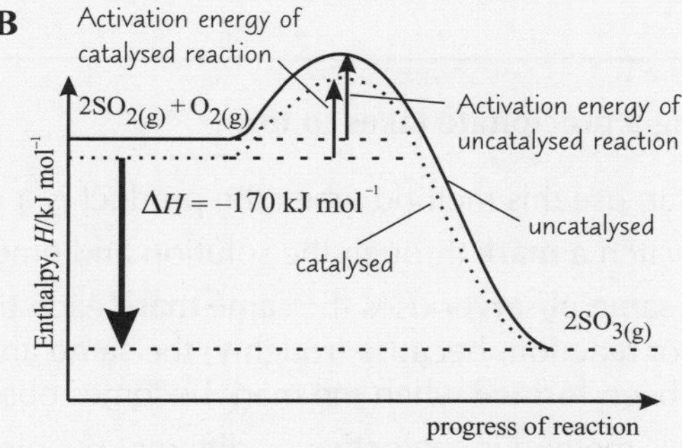

b) Is the vanadium(V) oxide catalyst heterogeneous or homogeneous? Explain your answer. [1 mark]

Catalysts and walking past bad buskers — increased speed but no change...

Whatever you do, don't confuse the Boltzmann diagram for catalysts with the one for a temperature change. Catalysts lower the activation energy without changing the shape of the curve. BUT, the shape of the curve does change with temperature. Get these mixed up and you'll be the laughing stock of the annual catalyst-lovers conference.

Calculating Reaction Rates

Stopwatches at the ready. It's time to see how you can measure the rate of a reaction using experiments.

Reaction Rate is the Amount of Stuff Reacting Divided by Time

The **reaction rate** is the **rate** at which a **product is formed** or a **reactant is used up**.
A simple equation for the rate of a chemical reaction is...

$$\text{rate of reaction} = \frac{\text{amount of reactant used or product formed}}{\text{time}}$$

There are Different ways to Investigate Reaction Rates

You can either measure how quickly the **reactants are used up** or how quickly the **products are formed** — it's usually **easier** to measure products forming. Here are a couple of ways to measure how quickly a product forms...

Change in mass

1) When the product is a **gas**, its formation can be measured using a **mass balance**.
2) The amount of product formed is the mass **disappearing** from the container.
3) When the reaction starts, you should start a **stop clock** or timer. Then take **mass measurements** at **regular time intervals**.
4) Make a **table** with a column for '**time**' and a column for '**mass**' and fill it in as the reaction goes on.
5) You'll know the reaction is **finished** when the reading on the mass balance **stops decreasing**.
6) This method is **very accurate** and easy to use but does **release gas** into the room, which could be **dangerous** if the gas is toxic or flammable.

Volume of gas given off

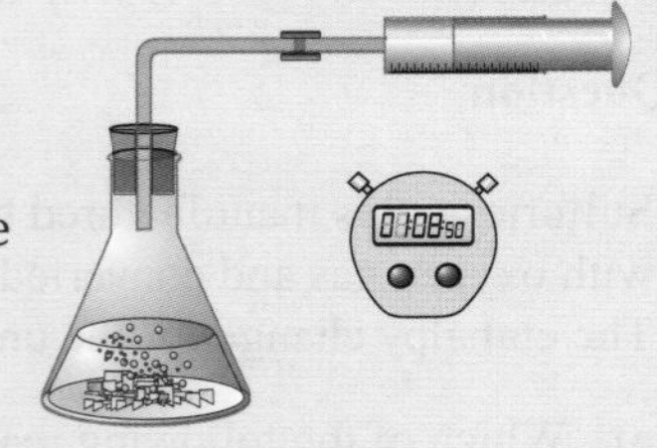

1) You can use a **gas syringe** to measure the **volume** of product formed.
2) The experiment is carried out the same way as above but you measure the **volume** of gas in the syringe rather than the mass from the balance.
3) This method is **accurate** but vigorous reactions can **blow the plunger** out of the syringe.

How long a precipitate takes to form

1) You can use this method when the product is a **precipitate** which clouds a solution.
2) You watch a **mark** through the solution and time how long it takes to be **obscured**.
3) If the **same observer** uses the **same mark** each time, you can compare the rates of reaction, because (roughly) the same amount of precipitate will have been **formed** when the mark becomes obscured.
4) But this method is **subjective** — different people might not agree on the exact moment the mark disappears.

There are a few other ways to measure the amount of reactant used or product formed. For example, you can monitor **changes in pressure** (for gases), **changes in colour** (for solutions) or **changes in conductivity**.
The best method **depends** on the **reaction** you're looking at.

Calculating Reaction Rates

Example: The Reaction Between **Sodium Thiosulfate** and **Hydrochloric Acid**

Sodium thiosulfate and hydrochloric acid are both **clear**, **colourless solutions**.
They react together to form a **yellow precipitate** of **sulfur**.

You can use the amount of **time** that it takes for the precipitate to form as a measure of the **rate** of this reaction. This experiment is often used to demonstrate the effect of **increasing temperature** on reaction rate:

1) Measure out fixed volumes of **sodium thiosulfate** and **hydrochloric acid**, using a measuring cylinder.
2) Use a **water bath** to **gently heat** both solutions to the desired temperature before you mix them.
3) Mix the solutions in a conical flask. Place the flask over a black cross which can be seen through the solution. Watch the black cross **disappear** through the **cloudy sulfur** and **time** how long it takes to go.

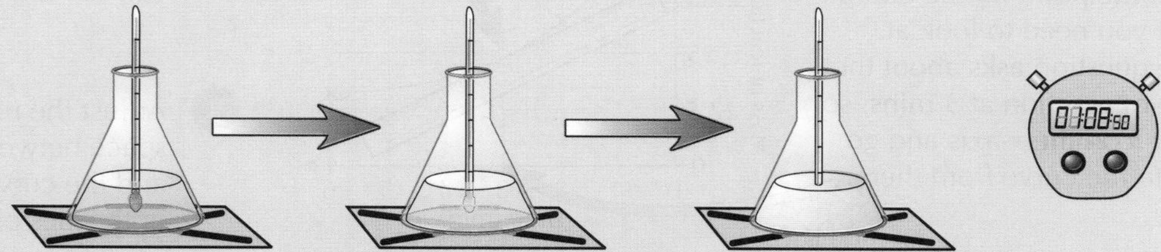

4) The reaction can be repeated for solutions at **different temperatures**. The **depth** of liquid must be kept the same each time. The **concentrations** of the solutions must also be kept the same.
5) The results should show that the **higher** the temperature, the **faster** the reaction rate and therefore the **less time** it takes for the mark to **disappear**.

You can Work out **Reaction Rate** from the **Gradient of a Graph**

If you have a graph where the **x-axis** is **time** and the **y-axis** is a measure of either the **amount of reactant** or **product**, then the reaction rate is just the **gradient** of the graph. You can work out the gradient using the equation...

gradient = change in y ÷ change in x

Example: The data on the graph below came from measuring the volume of gas given off over the course of a chemical reaction. Calculate the rate of the reaction.

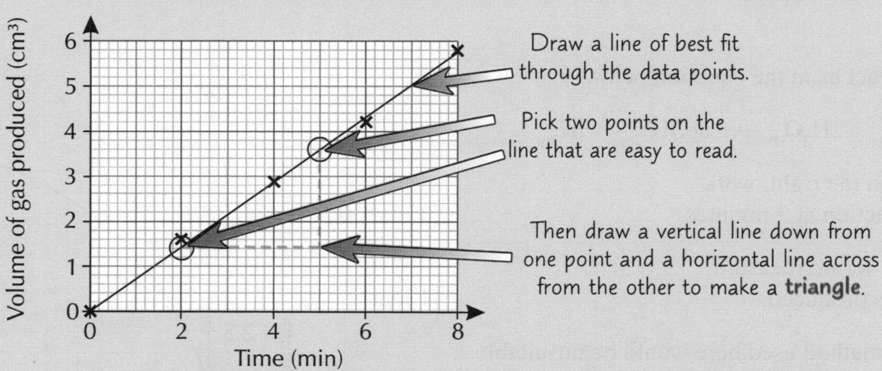
Volume of gas produced (cm³)
Time (min)
0
2
4
6
8
1
3
5
Draw a line of best fit through the data points.
Pick two points on the line that are easy to read.
Then draw a vertical line down from one point and a horizontal line across from the other to make a **triangle**.

change in y = 3.6 – 1.4 = 2.2 cm^3
change in x = 5.0 – 2.0 = 3.0 minutes
gradient = 2.2 ÷ 3.0 = 0.73 cm^3 min^{-1}

So the rate of reaction = **0.73 cm^3 min^{-1}**

The units of rate are the units of the y-axis (here it's cm^3) divided by the units of the x-axis (here it's minutes, making the units of rate cm^3 min^{-1}).

The gradient of the flume meant that Shona and Kim had a very fast rate of descent.

Calculating Reaction Rates

You may need to Work out the Gradient from a Curved Graph

When the points on a graph lie in a **curve**, you can't draw a straight line of best fit through them. But you can still work out the gradient, and so the rate, at a **particular point** in the reaction by working out the **gradient of a tangent**.

Example: The graph below shows the mass of a reaction vessel measured at regular intervals during a chemical reaction. What is the rate of reaction at 3 mins?

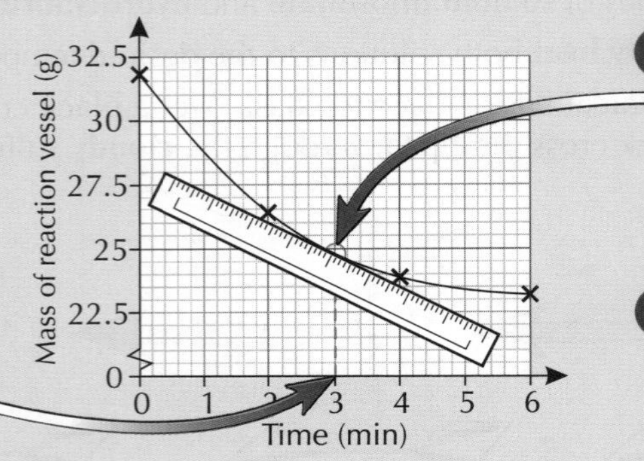

1. Find the point on the curve that you need to look at. The question asks about the rate of reaction at 3 mins, so find 3 on the x-axis and go up to the curve from there.

2. Place a ruler at that point so that it's just touching the curve. Position the ruler so that you can see the whole curve.

3. Adjust the ruler until the space between the ruler and the curve is equal on both sides of the point.

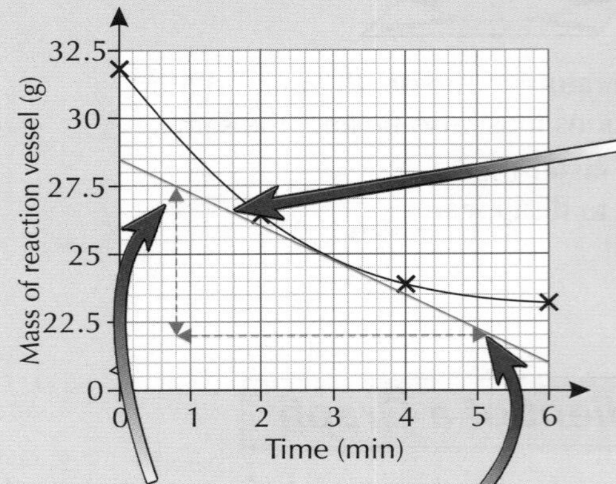

Pick two points on the line that are easy to read.

4. Draw a line along the ruler to make the tangent. Extend the line right across the graph — it'll help to make your gradient calculation easier as you'll have more points to choose from.

5. Calculate the gradient of the tangent to find the rate:

gradient = change in y ÷ change in x
= (27.50 – 22.00) ÷ (5.20 – 0.80)
= 5.50 g ÷ 4.40 mins = 1.25 g min^{-1}

So, the rate of reaction at 3 mins was **1.25 g min^{-1}**.

Don't forget the units — you've divided g by mins, so it's g min^{-1}.

Practice Questions

Q1 Write the equation for reaction rate.

Q2 Describe how measuring a change in mass can help to work out the rate of a reaction.

Exam Question

Q1 Calcium and water react as in the equation below.

$$Ca_{(s)} + 2H_2O_{(l)} \rightarrow Ca(OH)_{2(aq)} + H_{2(g)}$$

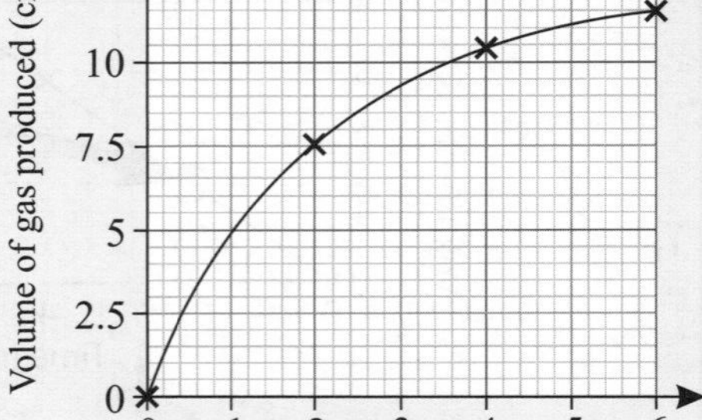

a) From the graph on the right, work out the rate of reaction at 3 minutes. [3 marks]

b) Suggest how you would measure the volume of gas produced. [1 mark]

c) Explain why the method used here would be unsuitable for working out the rate of the reaction below.

$$6CO_{2(g)} + 6H_2O_{(l)} \rightarrow C_6H_{12}O_{6(aq)} + 6O_{2(g)}$$ [1 mark]

Calculate your reaction to this page. Boredom? How dare you...

Really, this stuff isn't too bad. Make sure you can write out the reaction rate equation in your sleep and that you understand what it means. It'll make handling the rest of the stuff on these pages easier. It might take a bit of practice to get the hang of these graphs but, as I'm sure you're tired of hearing, practice makes perfect. So get practising.

Reversible Reactions

There's a lot of to-ing and fro-ing on these pages. Mind your head doesn't start spinning.

Reversible *Reactions Can Reach* ***Dynamic Equilibrium***

1) Lots of chemical reactions are **reversible** — they go **both ways**.
2) To show a reaction's reversible, you stick in a $\rightleftharpoons$. Here's an example:

$$H_{2(g)} + I_{2(g)} \rightleftharpoons 2HI_{(g)}$$

This reaction can go in **either direction**:

forwards $H_{2(g)} + I_{2(g)} \rightleftharpoons 2HI_{(g)}$

...or **backwards** $2HI_{(g)} \rightleftharpoons H_{2(g)} + I_{2(g)}$

3) As the **reactants** get used up, the **forward** reaction **slows down** — and as more **product** is formed, the **reverse** reaction **speeds up**.
4) After a while, the forward reaction will be going at exactly the **same rate** as the backward reaction so the amounts of reactants and products **won't be changing** any more — it'll seem like **nothing's happening**.

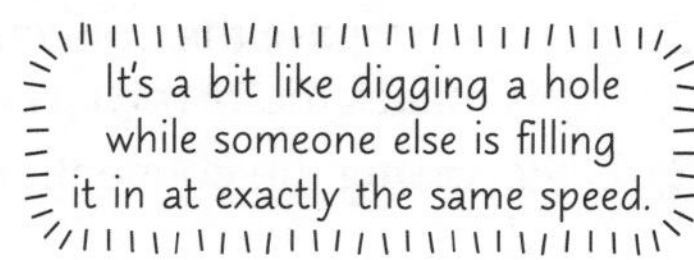

It's a bit like digging a hole
while someone else is filling
it in at exactly the same speed.

5) This is called **dynamic equilibrium**. At equilibrium, the **concentrations** of **reactants** and **products** stay **constant**.
6) A **dynamic equilibrium** can only happen in a **closed system**. This just means nothing can get in or out.

Le Chatelier's Principle *Predicts what will Happen if* ***Conditions are Changed***

If you **change** the **concentration**, **pressure** or **temperature** of a reversible reaction, you're going to **alter** the **position of equilibrium**. This just means you'll end up with **different amounts** of reactants and products at equilibrium.

If the position of equilibrium moves to the **left**, you'll get more **reactants**.

$$H_{2(g)} + I_{2(g)} \rightleftharpoons 2HI_{(g)}$$

lots of H_2 and I_2 — not much HI

If the position of equilibrium moves to the **right**, you'll get more **products**.

$$H_{2(g)} + I_{2(g)} \rightleftharpoons 2HI_{(g)}$$

not much H_2 and I_2 — lots of HI

Mr and Mrs Le Chatelier celebrate another successful year in the principle business.

Le Chatelier's principle tells you how the **position of equilibrium** will change if a **condition changes**:

> If a reaction at **equilibrium** is subjected to a change in **concentration**, **pressure** or **temperature**, the position of equilibrium will move to **counteract** the change.

So, basically, if you **raise the temperature**, the position of equilibrium will shift to try to **cool things down**. And, if you **raise the pressure or concentration**, the position of equilibrium will shift to try to **reduce it again**.

Reversible Reactions

Here's Some **Handy Rules** for Using **Le Chatelier's Principle**

1) You can use Le Chatelier's principle to work out what effect changing the **concentration**, **pressure** or **temperature** will have on the **position of equilibrium**.
2) This only applies to **homogeneous equilibria** — that means reactions where every species is in the **same physical state** (e.g. all liquid or all gaseous).

CONCENTRATION

1) If you **increase** the **concentration** of a **reactant**, the equilibrium tries to **get rid** of the extra reactant. It does this by making **more product**. So the equilibrium shifts to the **right**.

$2SO_{2(g)} + O_{2(g)} \rightleftharpoons 2SO_{3(g)}$ — If you increase the concentration of SO_2 or O_2, the speed of the forward reaction will increase (to use up the extra reactant), moving the equilibrium to the right.

2) If you **increase** the **concentration** of the **product** (SO_3), the equilibrium tries to remove the extra product. This makes the **reverse reaction** go faster. So the equilibrium shifts to the **left**.
3) **Decreasing** the concentrations has the **opposite effect**.

PRESSURE (Changing this only affects **equilibria involving gases.**)

1) **Increasing** the pressure shifts the equilibrium to the side with **fewer** gas molecules. This **reduces** the pressure.

$2SO_{2(g)} + O_{2(g)} \rightleftharpoons 2SO_{3(g)}$ — There are 3 moles of gas on the left, but only 2 on the right. So, an increase in pressure shifts the equilibrium to the right.

2) **Decreasing** the pressure shifts the equilibrium to the side with **more** gas molecules. This **raises** the pressure again.

TEMPERATURE

1) **Increasing** the temperature means **adding heat**. The equilibrium shifts in the **endothermic** (**positive** ΔH) **direction** to absorb this heat.

$2SO_{2(g)} + O_{2(g)} \rightleftharpoons 2SO_{3(g)} \quad \Delta H = -197 \text{ kJ mol}^{-1}$ — This reaction's exothermic in the forward direction. If you increase the temperature, the equilibrium shifts to the left to absorb the extra heat.

2) **Decreasing** the temperature means **removing heat**. The equilibrium shifts in the **exothermic** (**negative** ΔH) **direction** to produce more heat, in order to counteract the drop in temperature.
3) If the forward reaction's **endothermic**, the reverse reaction will be **exothermic**, and vice versa.

Catalysts **Don't Affect** The Position of Equilibrium

Catalysts have **NO EFFECT** on the **position of equilibrium**.
They **can't** increase **yield** — but they **do** mean equilibrium is reached **faster**.

Reversible Reactions

In Industry the **Reaction Conditions** Chosen are a **Compromise**

Companies have to think about how much it **costs** to run a reaction and how much money they can make from it. This means they have a few factors to think about when they're choosing the best conditions for a reaction.

For example, **ethanol** can be produced via a reversible exothermic reaction between **ethene and steam:**

$$C_2H_{4(g)} + H_2O_{(g)} \rightleftharpoons C_2H_5OH_{(g)} \qquad \Delta H = -46 \text{ kJ mol}^{-1}$$

In industry, this reaction is carried out at pressures of **60-70 atmospheres** and a temperature of **300 °C**, with a catalyst of **phosphoric acid**.

1) Because this is an **exothermic reaction, lower** temperatures favour the forward reaction. This means that at lower temperatures **more** ethene and steam is converted to ethanol — you get a better **yield**.
2) But **lower temperatures** mean a **slower rate of reaction**. There's **no point** getting a **very high yield** of ethanol if it takes you 10 years. So 300 °C is a **compromise** between a **reasonable yield** and a **faster reaction**.
3) **High pressure** shifts the equilibrium to the side with **fewer molecules**, which favours the **forward reaction** here. **High pressure** increases the **rate** of this reaction too. So a pressure of **60-70 atmospheres** is used.
4) Cranking up the pressure even higher than that might sound like a great idea. But **very high pressures** are **really expensive** to produce. You need really strong **pipes** and **containers** to withstand high pressures.
5) So the **60-70 atmospheres** is a **compromise** — it gives a **reasonable yield** for the lowest possible **cost**.

Practice Questions

Q1 Explain what the terms 'reversible reaction' and 'dynamic equilibrium' mean.

Q2 If an equilibrium moves to the right, do you get more products or reactants?

Q3 A reaction at equilibrium is exothermic in the forward direction.
What happens to the position of equilibrium as the temperature is increased?

Q4 What effect do catalysts have on equilibrium position?

Exam Questions

Q1 Nitrogen and oxygen gases were reacted together in a closed flask and allowed to reach equilibrium, with the gas nitrogen monoxide formed: $N_{2(g)} + O_{2(g)} \rightleftharpoons 2NO_{(g)} \quad \Delta H = +181 \text{ kJ mol}^{-1}$

a) State Le Chatelier's principle. [1 mark]

b) Explain how the following changes would affect the position of equilibrium of the above reaction:

i) Pressure is increased. [1 mark]

ii) Temperature is reduced. [1 mark]

iii) The concentration of nitrogen monoxide is reduced. [1 mark]

c) State the effect that a catalyst would have on the composition of the equilibrium mixture. [1 mark]

Q2 Ammonia can be manufactured from nitrogen and hydrogen: $N_{2(g)} + 3H_{2(g)} \rightleftharpoons 2NH_{3(g)} \quad \Delta H = -92.4 \text{ kJ mol}^{-1}$
Typical conditions are 450 °C, 200 atmospheres and an iron catalyst.

a) Explain why, for this reaction, decreasing the temperature would increase the yield of ammonia. [2 marks]

b) i) What effect would increasing pressure have on the yield of ammonia? [2 marks]

ii) Suggest why a pressure higher than the one quoted is not often used. [1 mark]

Reverse psychology — don't bother learning this rubbish...

Make sure that you know what happens to a reaction at equilibrium if you change the conditions. A quick reminder about pressure, since I'm nice. If there are the same number of molecules of gas on each side of the equation, then you can raise the pressure as high as you like and it won't make a blind bit of difference to the position of equilibrium.

The Equilibrium Constant

It's not enough to just know what dynamic equilibrium means. It's nice to be able to describe what's going on but you know scientists — they do insist on using mathsy stuff. Here come the numbers...

K_c is the Equilibrium Constant

[X] = the concentration of species X in mol dm^{-3}.

If you know the **molar concentration** of each substance at equilibrium, you can work out the **equilibrium constant, K_c**.
The equilibrium constant can be written as an expression, like this:

$$aA + bB \rightleftharpoons dD + eE, \quad K_c = \frac{[D]^d[E]^e}{[A]^a[B]^b}$$

You can just bung the **equilibrium concentrations** into your expression to work out the **value** for K_c.
The **units** are a bit trickier though — they **vary**, so you have to work them out after each calculation.

Example: Hydrogen gas and iodine gas are mixed in a closed flask. Hydrogen iodide is formed.

$$H_{2(g)} + I_{2(g)} \rightleftharpoons 2HI_{(g)}$$

Calculate the equilibrium constant for the reaction at 640 K. The equilibrium concentrations are:
[HI] = 0.80 mol dm^{-3}, [H_2] = 0.10 mol dm^{-3}, and [I_2] = 0.10 mol dm^{-3}.

Just stick the concentrations into the **expression** for K_c: $K_c = \frac{[HI]^2}{[H_2][I_2]} = \frac{0.80^2}{0.10 \times 0.10} = 64$

To work out the **units** of K_c put the units in the expression instead of the numbers:

Units of $K_c = \frac{\cancel{(mol\,dm^{-3})^2}}{\cancel{(mol\,dm^{-3})}\cancel{(mol\,dm^{-3})}}$ — the concentration units cancel, so there are **no units** for K_c.

So K_c is just **64**.

You can **estimate** the **position of equilibrium** using the value of K_c:

- The **greater** the value of K_c, the **more products** than reactants there are at equilibrium, so the equilibrium lies further to the **right**.
- The **smaller** the value of K_c, the **more reactants** than products there are at equilibrium, so the equilibrium lies further to the **left**.

You Might Need to Work Out the Equilibrium Concentrations

You might have to figure out some of the **equilibrium concentrations** before you can find K_c:

Example: 0.20 moles of phosphorus(V) chloride decomposes at 600 K in a vessel of 5.00 dm^3.
The equation for this reaction is: $PCl_{5(g)} \rightleftharpoons PCl_{3(g)} + Cl_{2(g)}$
The equilibrium mixture is found to contain 0.080 moles of chlorine.
Write the expression for K_c and calculate its value, including units.

First find out how many moles of PCl_5 and PCl_3 there are at equilibrium:

The **equation** tells you that when **1 mole of PCl_5** decomposes, **1 mole of PCl_3** and **1 mole of Cl_2** are formed.
So if 0.080 moles of chlorine are produced at equilibrium, then there will be **0.080 moles** of PCl_3 as well.
0.080 moles of PCl_5 must have decomposed, so there will be **0.12 moles** left (0.20 – 0.080).

Divide each number of moles by the volume of the flask to give the molar concentrations:

[PCl_3] = [Cl_2] = 0.080 ÷ 5.00 = **0.016 mol dm^{-3}**   [PCl_5] = 0.12 ÷ 5.00 = **0.024 mol dm^{-3}**

Put the concentrations in the expression for K_c and calculate it: $K_c = \frac{[PCl_3][Cl_2]}{[PCl_5]} = \frac{0.016 \times 0.016}{0.024} = \mathbf{0.011}$

Now find the units of K_c: Units of $K_c = \frac{\cancel{(mol\,dm^{-3})}(mol\,dm^{-3})}{\cancel{(mol\,dm^{-3})}}$ = **mol dm^{-3}**   So K_c = **0.011 mol dm^{-3}**

The Equilibrium Constant

K_c can be used to Find **Concentrations** in an **Equilibrium Mixture**

Example: When ethanoic acid was allowed to reach equilibrium with ethanol at 25 °C, it was found that the equilibrium mixture contained 2.0 mol dm^{-3} ethanoic acid and 3.5 mol dm^{-3} ethanol. The K_c of the equilibrium is 4.0 at 25 °C. What are the concentrations of the other components?

$$CH_3COOH_{(l)} + C_2H_5OH_{(l)} \rightleftharpoons CH_3COOC_2H_{5(l)} + H_2O_{(l)}$$

Put all the values you know in the K_c expression: $K_c = \frac{[CH_3COOC_2H_5][H_2O]}{[CH_3COOH][C_2H_5OH]} \Rightarrow 4.0 = \frac{[CH_3COOC_2H_5][H_2O]}{2.0 \times 3.5}$

Rearranging this gives: $[CH_3COOC_2H_5][H_2O] = 4.0 \times 2.0 \times 3.5 = 28$

From the equation you know that $[CH_3COOC_2H_5] = [H_2O]$, so: $[CH_3COOC_2H_5] = [H_2O] = \sqrt{28} = 5.3$ mol dm^{-3}

The concentration of $CH_3COOC_2H_5$ and H_2O is **5.3 mol dm^{-3}**

Temperature Changes Alter K_c

1) The value of $\mathbf{K_c}$ is only **valid** for one particular **temperature**.
2) If you change the temperature of the system, you will also change the **equilibrium concentrations** of the products and reactants, so $\mathbf{K_c}$ **will change**.
3) If the temperature change means there's **more product** at equilibrium, $\mathbf{K_c}$ **will rise**. If it means there's **less product** at equilibrium, $\mathbf{K_c}$ **will decrease**. For example:

Remember: if the temperature rises, the equilibrium shifts in the endothermic (+ve ΔH) direction to absorb the heat. If the temperature falls, the equilibrium shifts in the exothermic (–ve ΔH) direction to replace the heat.

The reaction on the right is exothermic in the forward direction. If you **increase** the temperature, you favour the **endothermic** reaction. This means that **less product** is formed.

Exothermic ⟶

$$N_{2(g)} + 3H_{2(g)} \rightleftharpoons 2NH_{3(g)} \quad \Delta H = -46.2 \text{ kJ mol}^{-1}$$

⟵ Endothermic

$$K_c = \frac{[NH_3]^2}{[N_2][H_2]^3}$$

$[NH_3]^2$ ⟵ The concentration of NH_3 will be reduced.

$[N_2][H_2]^3$ ⟵ The concentrations of N_2 and H_2 will increase.

As the temperature **increases**, $[NH_3]$ will **decrease** and $[N_2]$ and $[H_2]$ will **increase**, so K_c will **decrease**.

4) Changing the **concentration** of a reactant or product, will **not affect** the value of K_c .
5) **Catalysts** don't affect K_c either — they'll speed up the reaction in both directions by the same amount, so they just help the system to reach equilibrium **faster**.

Practice Question

Q1 If a reversible reaction has an exothermic forward reaction, how will increasing the temperature affect K_c?

Exam Questions

Q1 A sample of pure hydrogen iodide is placed in a sealed flask, and heated to 443 °C. The following equilibrium is established: $2HI_{(g)} \rightleftharpoons H_{2(g)} + I_{2(g)}$ ($K_c = 0.0200$) At equilibrium, $[I_2] = 0.770$ mol dm^{-3}. Find the equilibrium concentration of HI. [4 marks]

Q2 Nitrogen dioxide dissociates according to the equation $2NO_{2(g)} \rightleftharpoons 2NO_{(g)} + O_{2(g)}$.

When 34.5 g of nitrogen dioxide were heated in a vessel of volume 9.80 dm^3 at 500 °C, 7.04 g of oxygen were found in the equilibrium mixture.

a) Calculate: i) the number of moles of nitrogen dioxide originally. [1 mark]

ii) the number of moles of each gas in the equilibrium mixture. [3 marks]

b) Find the value of K_c at this temperature, and give its units. [4 marks]

I still don't like equilibrium positions — so nothing's changed there...

Working out K_c is easy as pie once you've got all the concentrations figured out. Make sure you practise writing down expressions for the equilibrium constant and doing all those mathsy bits — the questions here should help you with that.

Oxidation Numbers

This double page has more occurrences of "oxidation" than the Beatles' "All You Need is Love" features the word "love".

Oxidation Numbers Tell you how Many Electrons Atoms have

When atoms **react** or **bond** to other atoms, they can **lose** or **gain** electrons. The **oxidation number** tells you how many electrons an atom has donated or accepted to form an **ion**, or to form part of a **compound**.
There are certain rules that help you assign oxidation numbers. Here they are...

1) All uncombined elements have an oxidation number of **0**. This means they haven't accepted or donated any electrons. Elements that are bonded to identical atoms will also have an oxidation number of **0**.

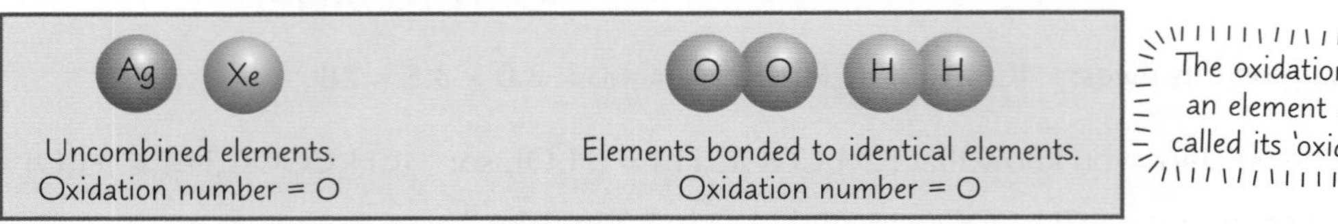

The oxidation number of an element can also be called its 'oxidation state'.

2) The oxidation number of a simple, monatomic ion (that's an ion consisting of just one atom) is the same as its **charge**.

3) For **molecular ions** (see page 36), the sum of the oxidation numbers is the same as the overall charge of the ion. Each of the constituent atoms will have an oxidation number of its own, and the **sum** of their oxidation numbers equals the **overall charge**.

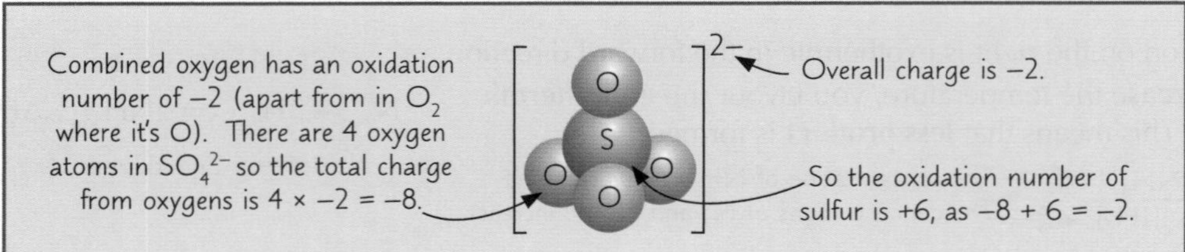

Combined oxygen has an oxidation number of −2 (apart from in O_2 where it's 0). There are 4 oxygen atoms in SO_4^{2-} so the total charge from oxygens is 4 × −2 = −8.
Overall charge is −2.
So the oxidation number of sulfur is +6, as −8 + 6 = −2.

4) For a neutral compound, the overall charge is **0**. If the compound is made up of more than one element, each element will have its own oxidation number.

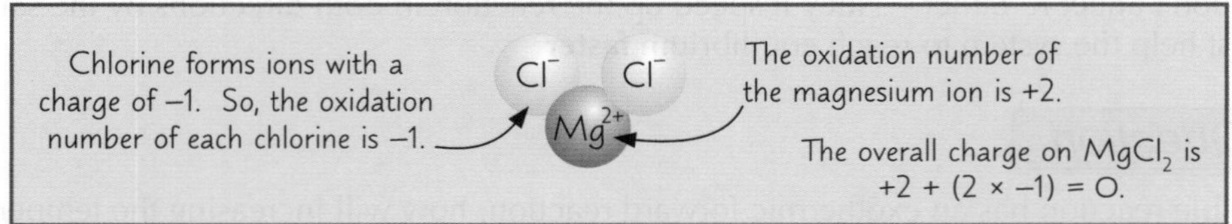

Chlorine forms ions with a charge of −1. So, the oxidation number of each chlorine is −1.
The oxidation number of the magnesium ion is +2.
The overall charge on $MgCl_2$ is +2 + (2 × −1) = 0.

5) **Oxygen** and **hydrogen** have different oxidation numbers depending on what **type** of compound they're in.

- **Oxygen** nearly always has an oxidation number of **−2**, except in **peroxides** (O_2^{2-}) where it's **−1**, and **molecular oxygen** (O_2) where it's **0**.
- **Hydrogen** always has an oxidation number of **+1**, except in **metal hydrides** (MH_x, where M = metal) where it's **−1** and in **molecular hydrogen** (H_2) where it's **0**.

Roman Numerals tell you the Oxidation Number

If an element can have **multiple** oxidation numbers, or **isn't** in its 'normal' oxidation state, its oxidation number can be shown by using **Roman numerals**, e.g. (I) = +1, (II) = +2, (III) = +3 and so on. The Roman numerals are written after the name of the element they correspond to.

Hands up if you like Roman numerals...

E.g. In iron(II) sulfate, iron has an oxidation number of +2. Formula = $FeSO_4$
In iron(III) sulfate, iron has an oxidation number of +3. Formula = $Fe_2(SO_4)_3$

Oxidation Numbers

-ate Compounds Contain Oxygen and Another Element

1) Ions with names ending in -ate (e.g. sulfate, nitrate, chlorate, carbonate) contain **oxygen** and another element. For example, sulfates contain sulfur and oxygen, nitrates contain nitrogen and oxygen... and so on.
2) Sometimes the 'other' element in the ion can exist with different oxidation numbers, and so form different '-ate ions'. In these cases, the oxidation number is attached as a Roman numeral **after** the name of the -ate compound.
   The roman numerals correspond to the **non-oxygen** element in the -ate compound.
   E.g. In sulfate(VI) ions, the **sulfur** has oxidation number **+6** — this is the SO_4^{2-} ion.
   In sulfate(IV) ions, the **sulfur** has oxidation number **+4** — this is the SO_3^{2-} ion.
   In nitrate(III), **nitrogen** has an oxidation number of **+3** — this is the NO_2^- ion.

If there are no oxidation numbers shown, assume nitrate = NO_3^- and sulfate = SO_4^{2-}.

You Can Work Out Oxidation Numbers from Formulas or Systematic Names

You can **work out** the oxidation numbers of different elements in a compound from its **formula** or **systematic name**. You can also work out the formulas of compounds from their systematic names and vice versa.

Example: What is the formula of iron(III) sulfate?

From the systematic name, you can tell iron has an **oxidation number** of **+3**.
The formula of the sulfate ion is SO_4^{2-} and it has an **overall charge** of **–2**.
The overall charge of the compound is 0, so you need to find a ratio of $Fe^{3+}:SO_4^{2-}$ that will make the overall charge 0.

$(+3 \times 2) + (-2 \times 3) = 6 + -6 = 0$ The ratio of $Fe:SO_4$ is **2:3**.

So the formula is $\mathbf{Fe_2(SO_4)_3}$.

Example: What is the systematic name for ClO_2^-?

This formula contains **chlorine** and **oxygen**, so it's a **chlorate**.
Oxygen usually exists with an oxidation number of **–2**.
There are 2 oxygens, so this will make the total charge from oxygens $-2 \times 2 = -4$.
The overall charge on the molecule is –1, so chlorine must have an oxidation number of **+3**, since $-4 + 3 = -1$. So, the systematic name is **chlorate(III)**.

Practice Questions

Q1 What is the oxidation number of H in H_2?

Q2 What is the usual oxidation number for oxygen when it's combined with another element?

Q3 What is the oxidation number of sulfur in a sulfate(IV) ion?

Exam Questions

Q1 What is the systematic name of $Cr_2(SO_4)_3$? [1 mark]

Q2 What is the formula of iron(II) nitrate? [1 mark]

Q3 Lead sulfate can be formed by reacting lead oxide (PbO) with warm sulfuric acid in a ratio of 1:1.

a) What is the formula of lead sulfate? [1 mark]

b) Calculate the oxidation number of lead in:

i) lead oxide ii) lead sulfate [2 marks]

Sockidation number — a measure of how many odd socks are in my drawers...

There isn't any tricky maths involved with oxidation numbers, just a bit of adding, some subtracting... Maybe a bit of multiplying if you're unlucky. The real trick is to learn the rules about predicting oxidation numbers for those elements and molecular ions that come up all the time, especially the ones for those pesky metal hydrides and peroxides.

Redox Reactions

Redox reactions can be tricky to get your head around at first. It will help you loads if you're confident about all the oxidation number stuff on the last two pages before you start tackling this.

If Electrons are Transferred, it's a Redox Reaction

1) A **loss** of electrons is called **oxidation**. A **gain** in electrons is called **reduction**.
2) Reduction and oxidation happen **simultaneously** — hence the term "**redox**" reaction.
3) An **oxidising agent accepts** electrons and gets reduced.
4) A **reducing agent donates** electrons and gets oxidised.

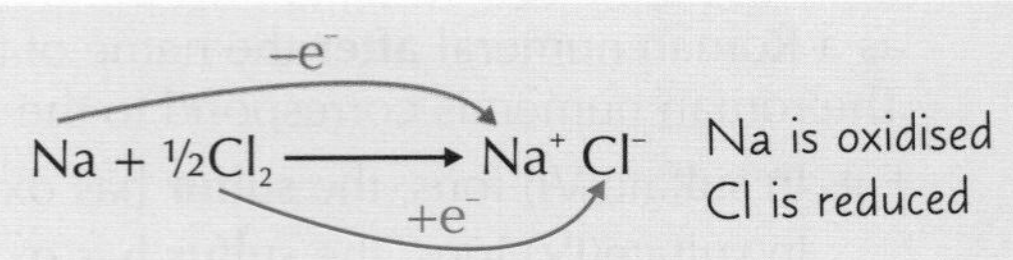

Oxidation Numbers go Up or Down as Electrons are Lost or Gained

1) The oxidation number for an atom will **increase by 1** for each **electron lost**.
2) The oxidation number will **decrease by 1** for each **electron gained**.
3) To work out whether something has been **oxidised** or **reduced**, you need to assign each element an oxidation number **before** the reaction, and **after** the reaction.
4) If the oxidation number has increased, then the element has **lost** electrons and been **oxidised**.
5) If the oxidation number has decreased, then the element has **gained** electrons and been **reduced**.

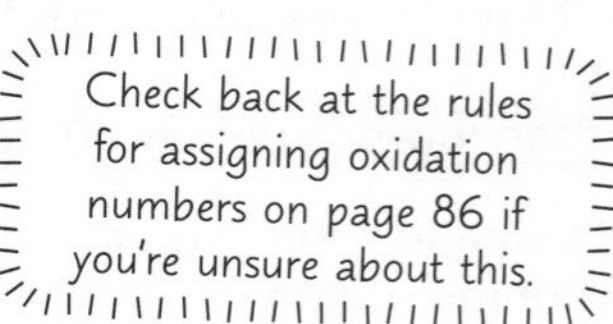

Check back at the rules for assigning oxidation numbers on page 86 if you're unsure about this.

PC Honey was a reducing agent where crime was concerned.

Example: Identify the oxidising and reducing agents in this reaction: $4Fe + 3O_2 \rightarrow 2Fe_2O_3$

Iron has gone from having an oxidation number of 0, to an oxidation number of +3.
It's **lost electrons** and has been **oxidised**. This makes it the **reducing agent** in this reaction.

Oxygen has gone from having an oxidation number of 0, to an oxidation number of –2.
It's **gained electrons** and has been **reduced**. This means it's the **oxidising agent** in this reaction.

6) When **metals** form compounds, they generally **donate** electrons (they lose electrons and are **oxidised**) to form **positive ions** — meaning they usually have **positive oxidation numbers**.
7) When **non-metals** form compounds, they generally **gain** electrons — meaning they usually have **negative oxidation numbers**.
8) To make remembering these oxidation and reduction rules a little bit easier, just remember **OIL RIG**.

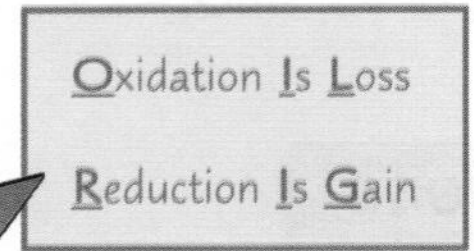

Oxidation Is Loss
Reduction Is Gain

Metals are Oxidised when they react with Acids

1) On page 39, you saw how metals react with acids to produce a salt and hydrogen gas. This is a redox reaction:
   - The metal atoms are **oxidised**, losing electrons to form **positive metal ions** (in **salts**).
   - The hydrogen ions in solution are **reduced**, gaining electrons and forming hydrogen molecules.
2) For example, magnesium reacts with dilute hydrochloric acid like this:

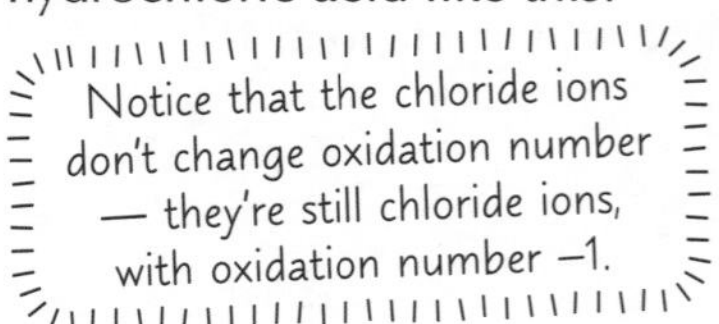

Notice that the chloride ions don't change oxidation number — they're still chloride ions, with oxidation number –1.

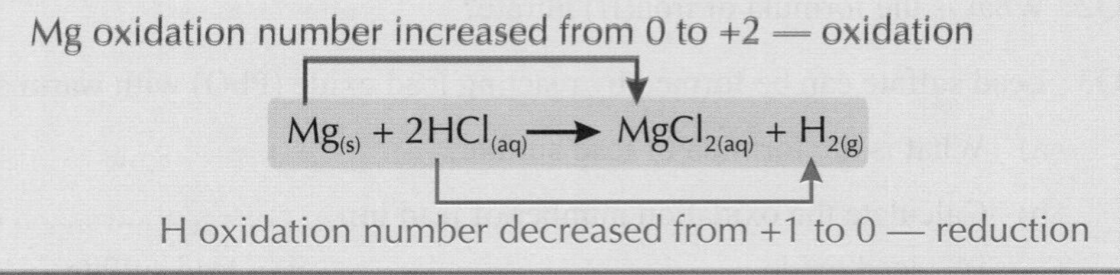

3) If you use **sulfuric acid** instead of hydrochloric acid, exactly the same processes of **oxidation** and **reduction** take place. For example, potassium is oxidised to K^+ ions:

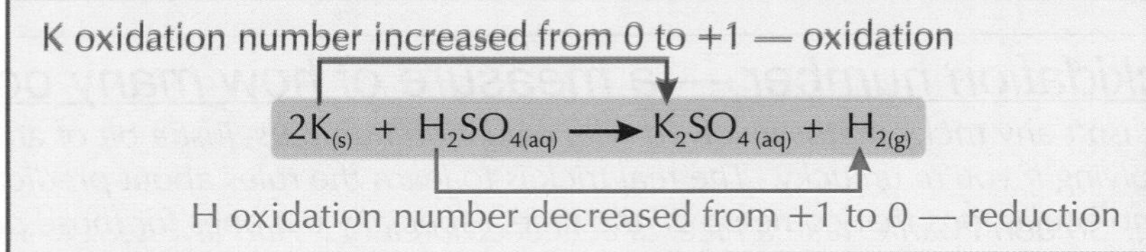

Redox Reactions

You can Write **Half-Equations** and Combine them into **Redox Equations**

1) **Ionic half-equations** show oxidation or reduction.
2) You show the **electrons** that are being lost or gained in a half-equation. For example, this is the half-equation for the **oxidation of sodium**: $Na \rightarrow Na^+ + e^-$

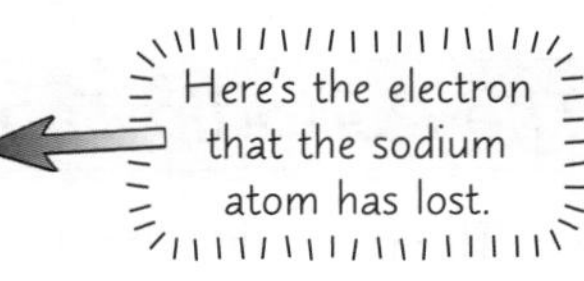

Here's the electron
that the sodium
atom has lost.

3) You can **combine** half-equations for different oxidising or reducing agents together to make **full equations** for redox reactions.

Magnesium burns in **oxygen** to form **magnesium oxide**.
Oxygen is reduced to O^{2-}:

$$O_2 + 4e^- \rightarrow 2O^{2-}$$

Magnesium is oxidised to Mg^{2+}:

$$Mg \rightarrow Mg^{2+} + 2e^-$$

Make sure the atoms and charges balance.

You need both equations to contain the same number of electrons. So double everything in the second equation.

$$2Mg \rightarrow 2Mg^{2+} + 4e^-$$

Combining the half-equations makes:

$$2Mg + O_2 \rightarrow 2MgO$$

The electrons aren't included in the full equation. You end up with four on each side — so they cancel.
$2Mg + O_2 + 4e^- \rightarrow 2MgO + 4e^-$

Aluminium reacts with **chlorine** to form **aluminium chloride**.
Aluminium is oxidised to Al^{3+}:

$$Al \rightarrow Al^{3+} + 3e^-$$

Chlorine is reduced to Cl^-:

$$Cl_2 + 2e^- \rightarrow 2Cl^-$$

Make sure the atoms and charges balance.

Now make sure the equations each contain the same number of electrons.

$$Al \rightarrow Al^{3+} + 3e^- \xrightarrow{\times 2} 2Al \rightarrow 2Al^{3+} + 6e^-$$

$$Cl_2 + 2e^- \rightarrow 2Cl^- \xrightarrow{\times 3} 3Cl_2 + 6e^- \rightarrow 6Cl^-$$

Combining the half-equations makes:

$$2Al + 3Cl_2 \rightarrow 2AlCl_3$$

Practice Questions

Q1 Is an oxidising agent reduced or oxidised in a redox reaction?

Q2 Would the oxidation number of an element that is reduced get bigger, smaller, or stay the same?

Q3 What generally happens to the number of electrons a metal has when it forms a compound?

Q4 Describe what happens, in terms of oxidation and reduction, when metals react with acids.

Exam Questions

Q1 Which of these equations shows a redox reaction?

A $HCl + NaOH \rightarrow NaCl + H_2O$ **B** $NaCl + AgNO_3 \rightarrow AgCl + NaNO_3$

C $BaBr_2 + H_2S \rightarrow BaS + 2HBr$ **D** $N_2 + O_2 \rightarrow 2NO$ [1 mark]

Q2 Concentrated sulfuric acid reacts with iron to produce iron(II) sulfate and one other product.

a) Write a balanced chemical equation for this reaction. [1 mark]

b) Use your answer to part a) to identify the oxidising agent and the reducing agent. [1 mark]

Q3 This equation shows the reaction of aluminium and iodine: $2Al_{(s)} + 3I_{2\,(g)} \rightarrow 2AlI_{3\,(s)}$

Use oxidation numbers to show that aluminium has been oxidised. [1 mark]

Q4 The half-equation for chlorine acting as an oxidising agent is: $Cl_2 + 2e^- \rightarrow 2Cl^-$

a) Define the term oxidising agent in terms of electron movement. [1 mark]

b) Indium is a metal that can be oxidised by chlorine.
Write a balanced half-equation for the oxidation of indium metal to form In^{3+} ions. [1 mark]

c) Use your answer to b) and the equation above to form a balanced equation for the reaction of indium with chlorine by combining half-equations. [2 marks]

Redox — relax in a lovely warm bubble bath...

The thing here is to take your time. Questions on redox reactions aren't usually that hard, but they are easy to get wrong. So don't panic, take a nice, deeeeeeeep breath... And always remember your nifty friend the ***oil rig****.*

Periodicity

Periodicity is one of those words you hear a lot in chemistry without ever really knowing what it means. Well it basically means trends that occur (in physical and chemical properties) as you move across the periods. E.g. metal to non-metal is a trend that occurs going left to right in each period... The trends repeat each period.

The **Periodic Table** *arranges Elements by* **Proton Number**

1) The periodic table is arranged into **periods** (rows) and **groups** (columns), by atomic (proton) number.
2) All the elements **within a period** have the same number of **electron shells** (if you don't worry about s and p sub-shells). E.g. the elements in Period 2 have 2 electron shells.
3) All the elements **within a group** have the **same number** of electrons in their **outer shell** — so they have **similar properties**.
4) The **group number** tells you the number of electrons in the outer shell, e.g. Group 1 elements have 1 electron in their outer shell, Group 4 elements have 4 electrons and so on. The **exception** is **Group 0**. Group 0 elements all have full outer shells — that's two electrons for Helium, and eight electrons for all the others.

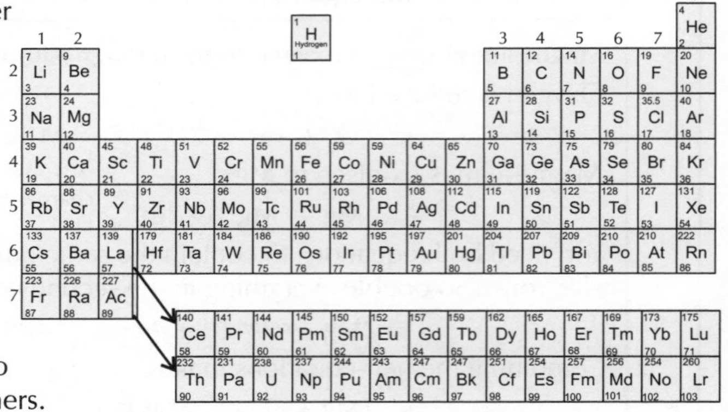

You can use the Periodic Table to work out **Electron Structures**

The periodic table can be split into an **s block**, **d block**, **p block** and **f block** like this: Doing this shows you which sub-shells all the electrons go into.

See page 26 if this sub-shell malarkey doesn't ring a bell.

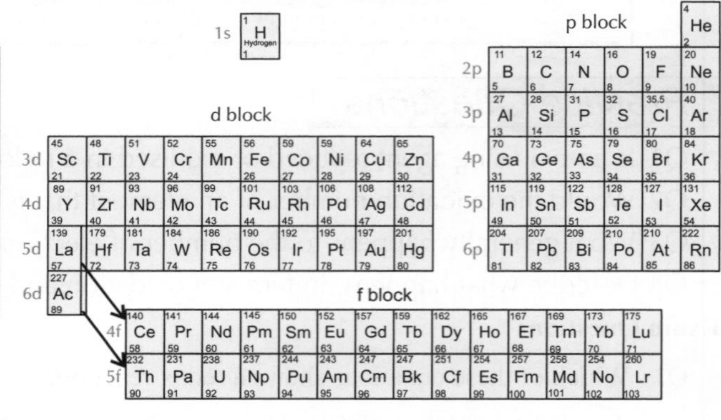

When you've got the periodic table **labelled** with the **shells** and **sub-shells** like the one on the right, it's pretty easy to read off the **electron structure** of any element. Just start at the top and work your way across and down until you get to your element.

Electron structures can also be called electron configurations.

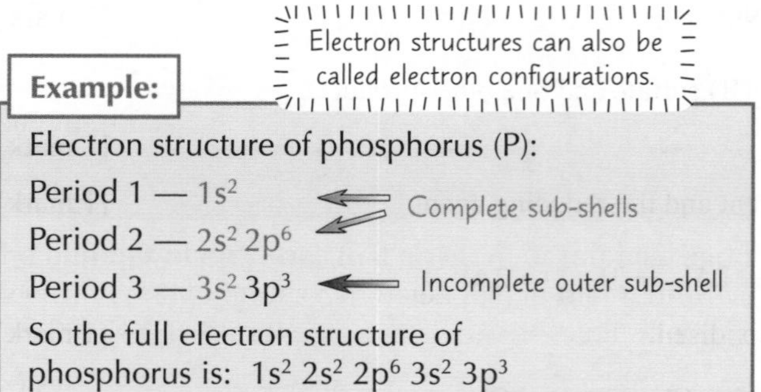

Example:

Electron structure of phosphorus (P):

Period 1 — $1s^2$

Period 2 — $2s^2\,2p^6$

Period 3 — $3s^2\,3p^3$

Complete sub-shells

Incomplete outer sub-shell

So the full electron structure of phosphorus is: $1s^2\,2s^2\,2p^6\,3s^2\,3p^3$

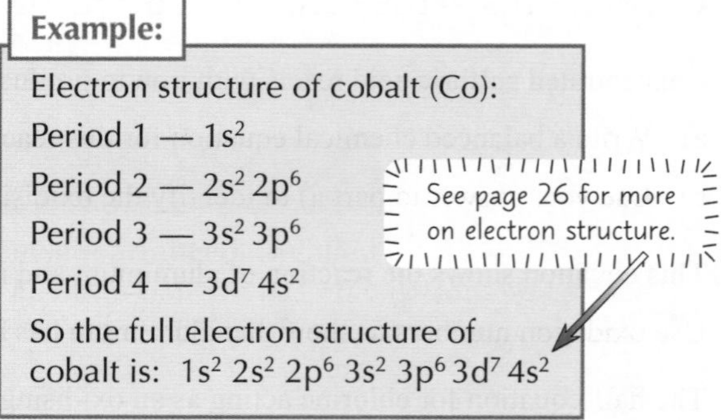

Example:

Electron structure of cobalt (Co):

Period 1 — $1s^2$

Period 2 — $2s^2\,2p^6$

Period 3 — $3s^2\,3p^6$

Period 4 — $3d^7\,4s^2$

See page 26 for more on electron structure.

So the full electron structure of cobalt is: $1s^2\,2s^2\,2p^6\,3s^2\,3p^6\,3d^7\,4s^2$

Atomic Radius **Decreases** *across a Period*

1) As the number of protons increases, the **positive charge** of the nucleus increases. This means electrons are **pulled closer** to the nucleus, making the atomic radius smaller.
2) The extra electrons that the elements gain across a period are added to the **outer energy level** so they don't really provide any extra shielding effect (shielding is mainly provided by the electrons in the inner shells).

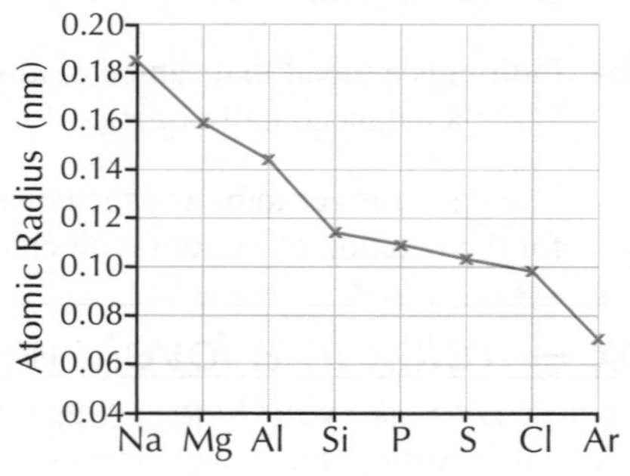

Periodicity

Melting Point is linked to **Bond Strength** and **Structure**

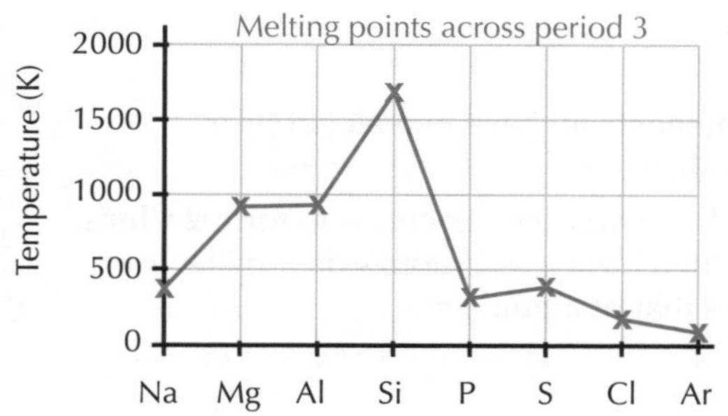

1) Melting points vary across a period as they depend on the **structure** of elements and the **bonding** within them. The graph on the left shows the melting points across **Period 3**.
2) Sodium, magnesium and aluminium are **metals**. Their melting and boiling points **increase** across the period because the **metal-metal bonds** get stronger. The bonds get stronger because the metal ions have an increasing positive charge, an increasing number of delocalised electrons and a decreasing radius.
3) Silicon has a **giant covalent structure — strong covalent bonds** link all its atoms together. **A lot** of energy is needed to break these bonds, so silicon has a **high** melting point.
4) Phosphorus (P_4), sulfur (S_8) and chlorine (Cl_2) are all **molecular substances.** Their melting points depend upon the strength of the **induced dipole-dipole forces** (see page 57) between the molecules. Induced dipole-dipole forces are weak and easily overcome so these elements have **low** melting points.
5) More atoms in a molecule mean stronger induced dipole-dipole forces. Sulfur is the **biggest molecule** (S_8), so it's got a higher melting point than phosphorus or chlorine.
6) Argon has a **very low** melting point because it exists as **individual atoms** (it's monatomic) resulting in **very weak** induced dipole-dipole forces.

Sam is looking hot in the latest periodic trends.

Ionisation Energy Generally **Increases** across a Period

This is because of the **increasing attraction** between the outer shell electrons and the nucleus, due to the number of **protons** increasing (there are a few blips in the trend however — check back to pages 30-31 for more details).

Practice Questions

Q1 Which elements of Period 3 are found in the s block of the periodic table?

Q2 Write down the electron structure of phosphorus.

Q3 Which element in Period 3 has the largest atomic radius?

Q4 Which element in Period 3 has the highest melting point?

Exam Questions

Q1 Explain why the melting point of magnesium is higher than that of sodium. [3 marks]

Q2 This table shows the melting points for the Period 3 elements.

Element	Na	Mg	Al	Si	P	S	Cl	Ar
Melting point / K	371	923	933	1687	317	388	172	84

In terms of structure and bonding explain why:

a) silicon has a high melting point. [2 marks]

b) the melting point of sulfur is higher than phosphorus. [2 marks]

Q3 State and explain the trend in atomic radius across Period 3. [3 marks]

Periodic trends — isn't that just another name for retro chic...

OK, I'll admit it, when it comes to fashion, I'm behind the times. I refuse to stop wearing my favourite pair of neon legwarmers just because they're a tiny bit out of date. The thing is though, every now and then eighties stuff comes back into fashion for a while and suddenly I'm bang on trend. Mind you, that doesn't stop me looking totally ridiculous.

Group 2 — The Alkaline Earth Metals

It would be easy for Group 2 elements to feel slightly inferior to those in Group 1. They're only in the second group, after all. That's why you should try to get to know and like them. They'd really appreciate it, I'm sure.

Group 2 Elements Form 2+ Ions

Element	Atom	Ion
Be	$1s^2 2s^2$	$1s^2$
Mg	$1s^2 2s^2 2p^6 3s^2$	$1s^2 2s^2 2p^6$
Ca	$1s^2 2s^2 2p^6 3s^2 3p^6 4s^2$	$1s^2 2s^2 2p^6 3s^2 3p^6$

Group 2 elements all have two electrons in their outer shell (s^2).

They lose their two outer electrons to form **2+ ions**. Their ions then have every atom's dream electron structure — that of a **noble gas**.

Reactivity Increases Down Group 2

1) As you go down the group, the **ionisation energies** decrease. This is due to the **increasing atomic radius** (because extra electron shells are added as you go down the group), and **shielding effect** (see page 28).
2) When Group 2 elements react they **lose electrons**, forming positive ions (**cations**). The easier it is to lose electrons (i.e. the lower the first and second ionisation energies), the more reactive the element, so **reactivity increases** down the group.

Mr Kelly has one final attempt at explaining electron shielding to his students...

Group 2 Elements React with Water and Oxygen

When Group 2 elements react, they are **oxidised** from a state of **0** to **+2**, forming M^{2+} ions.

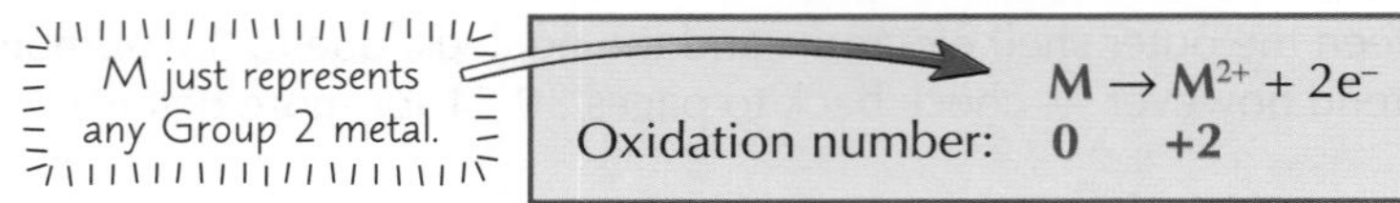

M just represents any Group 2 metal.

Example: $Ca \rightarrow Ca^{2+} + 2e^-$
0 +2

There are a few reactions of Group 2 elements that you need to know...

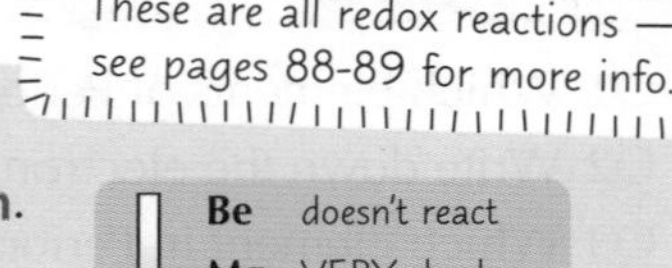

These are all redox reactions — see pages 88-89 for more info.

1 They react with WATER to produce HYDROXIDES.

The Group 2 metals react with water to give a **metal hydroxide** and **hydrogen**.

$$M_{(s)} + 2H_2O_{(l)} \rightarrow M(OH)_{2(aq)} + H_{2(g)}$$

Oxidation number: 0 → +2

E.g. $Ca_{(s)} + 2H_2O_{(l)} \rightarrow Ca(OH)_{2(aq)} + H_{2(g)}$

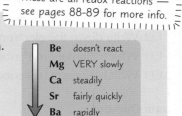

Be	doesn't react
Mg	VERY slowly
Ca	steadily
Sr	fairly quickly
Ba	rapidly

2 They burn in OXYGEN to form OXIDES.

When Group 2 metals burn in oxygen, you get solid white **oxides**.

$$2M_{(s)} + O_{2(g)} \rightarrow 2MO_{(s)}$$

Oxidation number of metal: 0 → +2
Oxidation number of oxygen: 0 → −2

E.g. $2Ca_{(s)} + O_{2(g)} \rightarrow 2CaO_{(s)}$
Ca: 0 → +2; O: 0 → −2

3 They react with DILUTE ACID to produce a SALT and HYDROGEN.

When Group 2 metals react with dilute hydrochloric acid, you get a **metal chloride** and **hydrogen**.

$$M_{(s)} + 2HCl_{(aq)} \rightarrow MCl_{2(aq)} + H_{2(g)}$$

Oxidation number: 0 → +2

E.g. $Ca_{(s)} + 2HCl_{(aq)} \rightarrow CaCl_{2(aq)} + H_{2(g)}$

Like with water, the reactions of Group 2 metals with dilute acid get more vigorous as you go down the group.

Different acids will produce different salts. E.g. if you use dilute sulfuric acid, you'll get a metal sulfate.

Group 2 — The Alkaline Earth Metals

Group 2 Oxides and Hydroxides are *Bases*

The **oxides** and **hydroxides** of Group 2 metals are **bases**. Most of them are **soluble** in water, so are also **alkalis**.

1) The **oxides** of the Group 2 metals react readily with **water** to form **metal hydroxides**, which dissolve. The **hydroxide ions, OH^-**, make these solutions **strongly alkaline** (e.g. pH 12 – 13).
2) Magnesium oxide is an exception — it only reacts slowly and the hydroxide isn't very soluble.
3) The oxides form **more strongly alkaline** solutions as you go down the group, because the hydroxides get more soluble.

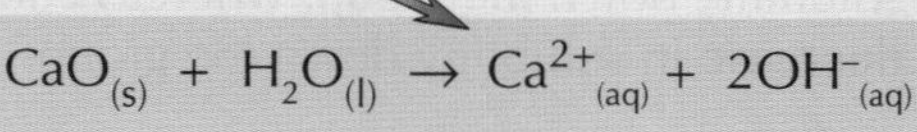

An alkali is a base that's soluble in water.

Because they're **bases**, both the Group 2 oxides and hydroxides will **neutralise** dilute acids, forming solutions of the corresponding salts.

Melting Points Generally *Decrease* Down the Group

1) The Group 2 elements have typical **metallic structures**, with **positive ions** in a **crystal structure** surrounded by **delocalised electrons** from the outer electron shells.
2) Going **down** the group the metal ions get **bigger**. But the number of delocalised electrons per atom doesn't change (it's always 2) and neither does the charge on the ion (it's always +2).
3) The **larger** the ionic radius, the **further away** the delocalised electrons are from the positive nuclei and the **less attraction** they feel. So it takes **less energy** to break the bonds, which means the melting points generally decrease as you go down the group. However, there's a big 'blip' at magnesium, because the crystal structure (the arrangement of the metallic ions) changes.

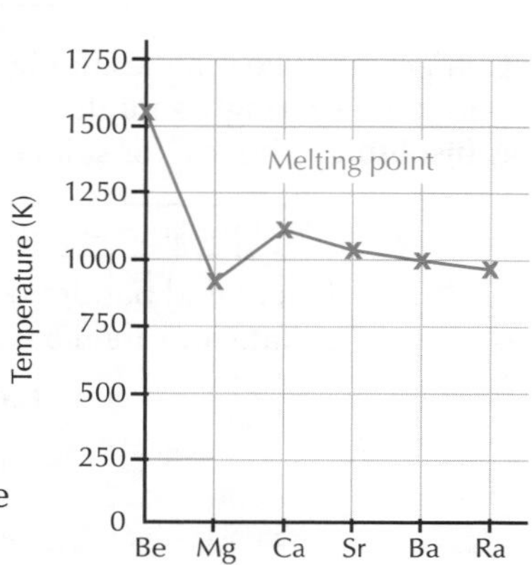

Practice Questions

Q1 Which of the following increases in size down Group 2? A — atomic radius B — first ionisation energy

Q2 Which of these Group 2 metals is the least reactive? A — Mg B — Be C — Sr

Q3 Why does reactivity with water increase down Group 2?

Q4 Why do the melting points of the Group 2 elements decrease down the group?

Exam Questions

Q1 Barium (Ba) can be burned in oxygen.

a) Write an equation for the reaction. [1 mark]

b) Show the change in oxidation state of barium. [1 mark]

c) Describe the pH of the solution formed when the product is added to water. [1 mark]

Q2 The table shows the atomic radii of three elements from Group 2.

Element	Atomic radius (nm)
X	0.105
Y	0.150
Z	0.215

a) Predict which element would react most rapidly with water. [1 mark]

b) Explain your answer. [2 marks]

I'm not gonna make it. You've gotta get me out of here, Doc...

More trends... What is it with Chemistry and trends? Well there are loads more trends to get your teeth into on this page. There's that trend to do with Group 2 reactivity... Oh, and don't forget that melting point trend as well. Those exam questions above will help make sure you've got this Group 2 chemistry nailed. So go on, give them a go.

Uses of the Group 2 Elements

Nice theories are all well and good but theories don't pay the bills. It's all about applications these days. So how can all this knowledge about Group 2 elements be put to good use? Read on to find out...

Solubility Trends in Group 2 Depend on the *Compound Anion*

Generally, compounds of Group 2 elements that contain **singly charged** negative ions (e.g. OH^-) **increase** in solubility down the group, whereas compounds that contain **doubly charged** negative ions (e.g. SO_4^{2-}) **decrease** in solubility down the group.

Group 2 element	hydroxide (OH^-)	sulfate (SO_4^{2-})
magnesium	least soluble	most soluble
calcium	↓	↑
strontium		
barium	most soluble	least soluble

Compounds like magnesium hydroxide, $Mg(OH)_2$, which have **very low** solubilities are said to be **sparingly soluble**. Most sulfates are soluble in water, but **barium sulfate** ($BaSO_4$) is **insoluble**. The test for sulfate ions makes use of this property...

Test for sulfate ions

If acidified barium chloride ($BaCl_2$) is added to a solution containing sulfate ions then a white precipitate of barium sulfate is formed.

$$Ba^{2+}_{(aq)} + SO_4^{2-}{}_{(aq)} \rightarrow BaSO_{4\,(s)}$$

$$\text{E.g.}\quad BaCl_{2(aq)} + FeSO_{4(aq)} \rightarrow BaSO_{4\,(s)} + FeCl_{2(aq)}$$

You need to acidify the solution with hydrochloric acid to get rid of any lurking sulfites or carbonates, which will also produce a white precipitate.

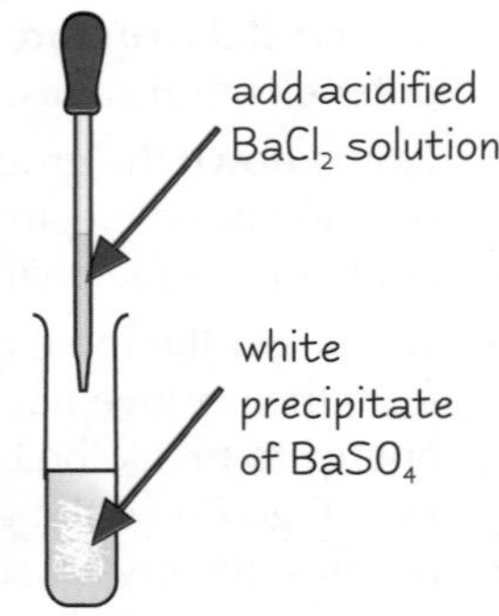

Group 2 Compounds are used to *Neutralise Acidity*

Group 2 elements are known as the **alkaline earth metals**, and many of their common compounds are used for neutralising acids. Here are a couple of common examples:

1) Calcium hydroxide (slaked lime, $Ca(OH)_2$) is used in **agriculture** to neutralise acid soils.

2) Magnesium hydroxide ($Mg(OH)_2$) is used in some indigestion tablets as an **antacid** — this is a substance which neutralises excess stomach acid.

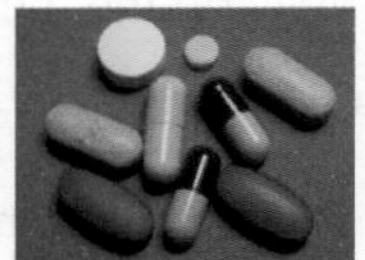

In both cases, the ionic equation for the neutralisation is

$$H^+_{(aq)} + OH^-_{(aq)} \rightarrow H_2O_{(l)}$$

Barium Sulfate is used in *'Barium Meals'*

CHRIS PRIEST / SCIENCE PHOTO LIBRARY

X-rays are great for finding broken bones, but they pass straight through soft tissue — so soft tissues, like the digestive system, don't show up on conventional X-ray pictures.

1) Barium sulfate is **opaque** to X-rays — they won't pass through it. It's used in '**barium meals**' to help diagnose problems with the oesophagus, stomach or intestines.
2) A patient swallows the barium meal, which is a suspension of **barium sulfate**. The barium sulfate **coats** the tissues, making them show up on the X-rays, showing the structure of the organs.

Uses of the Group 2 Elements

Magnesium is used in the Extraction of Titanium

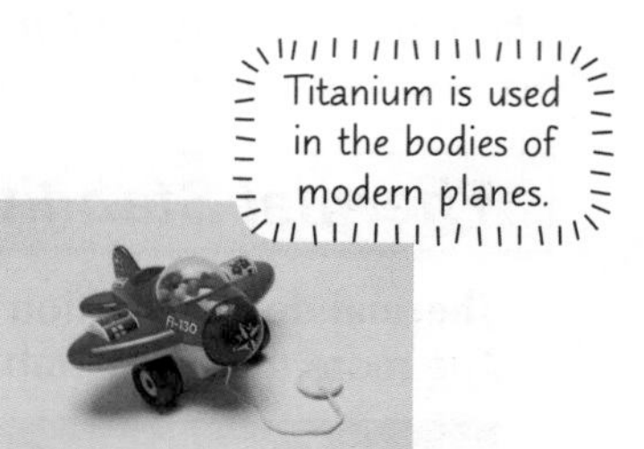

Titanium is used in the bodies of modern planes.

1) Magnesium is used as part of the process of **extracting titanium** from it's ore.
2) The main titanium ore, titanium(IV) oxide (TiO_2) is first converted to **titanium(IV) chloride** ($TiCl_4$) by heating it with carbon in a stream of chlorine gas.
3) The titanium chloride is then purified by fractional distillation, before being **reduced by magnesium** in a furnace at almost 1000 °C.

Calcium Oxide and Calcium Carbonate Remove Sulfur Dioxide

1) Burning fossil fuels to produce electricity also produces **sulfur dioxide**, which pollutes the atmosphere.
2) The acidic sulfur dioxide can be **removed** from **flue gases** by reacting with an alkali — this process is called **wet scrubbing**.
3) Powdered **calcium oxide** (lime, CaO) and **calcium carbonate** (limestone, $CaCO_3$) can both be used for this.
4) A **slurry** is made by **mixing** the calcium oxide or calcium carbonate with **water**. It's then sprayed onto the flue gases. The sulfur dioxide reacts with the alkaline slurry and produces a solid waste product, **calcium sulfite**.

Flue gases are the gases emitted from industrial exhausts and chimneys.

$$CaO_{(s)} + 2H_2O_{(l)} + SO_{2(g)} \rightarrow CaSO_{3(s)} + 2H_2O_{(l)}$$

$$CaCO_{3(s)} + 2H_2O_{(l)} + SO_{2(g)} \rightarrow CaSO_{3(s)} + 2H_2O_{(l)} + CO_{2(g)}$$

Practice Questions

Q1 Which is less soluble, barium sulfate or magnesium sulfate?

Q2 How is the solubility of magnesium hydroxide often described?

Q3 Give a use of calcium hydroxide.

Q4 Which Group 2 element can be used to extract titanium from titanium chloride?

Q5 Write the equation for the removal of sulfur dioxide from flue gases by calcium oxide.

Exam Questions

Q1 Describe how you could use acidified barium chloride solution to distinguish between solutions of zinc chloride and zinc sulfate. Give the expected observations and an appropriate balanced equation including state symbols. [2 marks]

Q2 Choose the Group 2 element, labelled A-D below, which best fits each of the following descriptions.

A magnesium **B** calcium **C** strontium **D** barium

a) Forms hydroxide and sulfate compounds, only one of which is soluble. [1 mark]

b) Forms a hydroxide used to neutralise acidic soils. [1 mark]

c) Forms a very soluble sulfate compound but sparingly soluble hydroxide compound. [1 mark]

Q3 Describe how barium sulfate can be used to diagnose problems with the digestive system. [2 marks]

Wet scrubbing — I thought that's what you did in the shower...

The Group 2 elements and compounds have lots of uses — they're used in agriculture, medicine, for reducing pollution, saving the world... Make sure you know which compound can be used for what though — you don't want to feed limestone to someone who has a problem with their digestive system, things could get horribly clogged up.

Group 1 and 2 Compounds

These pages are about Group 1 and 2 compounds, starting with the thermal stability of their carbonates and nitrates. So — quick, get your vest and long johns on before you topple over — we haven't even started yet.

Thermal Stability of Carbonates and Nitrates Changes Down the Group

Thermal decomposition is when a substance **breaks down** (decomposes) when **heated**. The more thermally stable a substance is, the more heat it will take to break it down.

Thermal stability increases down a group

The carbonate and nitrate ions are **large negative ions** (**anions**) and can be made **unstable** by the presence of a **positively charged ion** (a cation). The cation **polarises** the anion, distorting it. The greater the distortion, the less stable the anion.

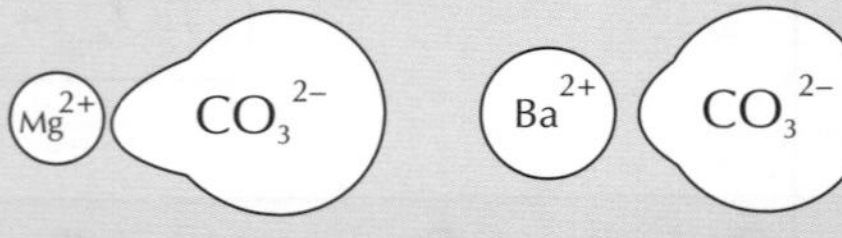

Magnesium ions polarise carbonate ions more than barium ions do, meaning magnesium carbonate is less stable.

Large cations cause **less distortion** than small cations as they have a lower charge density — the charge on the ion is spread out over a larger area. So the further down the group, the larger the cations, the lower the charge density so the less distortion caused and the **more stable** the carbonate/nitrate anion.

Group 2 compounds are less thermally stable than Group 1 compounds

The greater the **charge** on the cation, the greater the **distortion** and the **less stable** the carbonate/nitrate ion becomes. Group 2 cations have a **+2** charge, compared to a **+1** charge for Group 1 cations. So Group 2 carbonates and nitrates are less stable than those of Group 1.

Group 1	Group 2
Group 1 carbonates* are **thermally stable** — you can't heat them enough with a Bunsen to make them decompose (though they do decompose at higher temperatures). *except Li_2CO_3 which decomposes to Li_2O and CO_2 (there's always one...).	Group 2 carbonates decompose to form the **oxide** and **carbon dioxide**. $MCO_{3\,(s)} \rightarrow MO_{(s)} + CO_{2\,(g)}$ e.g. $CaCO_{3\,(s)} \rightarrow CaO_{(s)} + CO_{2\,(g)}$ calcium carbonate → calcium oxide
Group 1 nitrates** decompose to form the **nitrite** and **oxygen**. $2MNO_{3\,(s)} \rightarrow 2MNO_{2\,(s)} + O_{2\,(g)}$ e.g. $2KNO_{3\,(s)} \rightarrow 2KNO_{2\,(s)} + O_{2\,(g)}$ potassium nitrate → potassium nitrite **except $LiNO_3$ which decomposes to form Li_2O, NO_2 and O_2.	Group 2 nitrates decompose to form the **oxide**, **nitrogen dioxide** and **oxygen**. $2M(NO_3)_{2\,(s)} \rightarrow 2MO_{(s)} + 4NO_{2\,(g)} + O_{2\,(g)}$ e.g. $2Ca(NO_3)_{2\,(s)} \rightarrow 2CaO_{(s)} + 4NO_{2\,(g)} + O_{2\,(g)}$ calcium nitrate → calcium oxide, nitrogen dioxide

Here's How to Test the Thermal Stability of Nitrates and Carbonates

How easily nitrates decompose can be tested by measuring...

- how long it takes until a certain amount of **oxygen** is produced (i.e. enough to relight a glowing splint).
- how long it takes until an amount of **brown gas (NO_2)** is produced. This needs to be done in a fume cupboard because NO_2 is **toxic**.

How easily carbonates decompose can be tested by measuring...

- how long it takes for an amount of **carbon dioxide** to be produced. You test for carbon dioxide using lime water — which is a saturated solution of calcium hydroxide. This turns cloudy with carbon dioxide.

You can collect gas using a gas syringe or a test tube upturned in a beaker of water.

Group 1 and 2 Compounds

Group 1 and 2 Compounds Burn with Distinctive **Flame Colours**

...not all of them, but quite a few. For compounds containing the ions below, flame tests can help **identify them**.

Flame colours of Group 1 and 2 metals and their compounds

Li	red		
Na	orange/yellow		
K	lilac	**Ca**	brick-red
Rb	red	**Sr**	crimson
Cs	blue	**Ba**	green

Here's how to do a flame test:

1) Mix a small amount of the compound you're testing with a few drops of **hydrochloric acid**.
2) Heat a piece of **platinum** or **nichrome wire** in a hot Bunsen flame to clean it.
3) Dip the wire into the **compound/acid mixture**. Hold it in a very hot flame and note the **colour** produced.

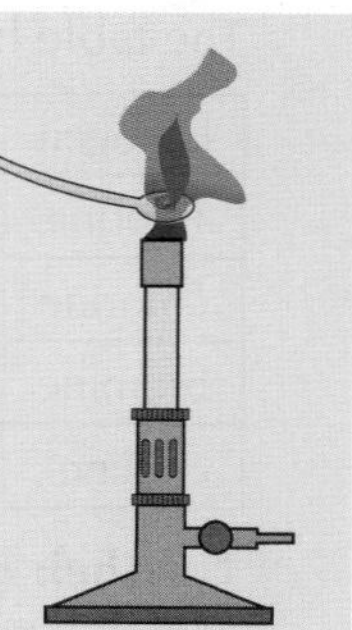

The explanation:

The **energy** absorbed from the flame causes electrons to move to **higher energy levels**. The colours are seen as the electrons fall back down to lower energy levels, releasing energy in the form of **light**. The difference in energy between the higher and lower levels determines the **wavelength** of the light released — which determines the **colour** of the light.

The movement of electrons between energy levels is called electron transition.

Practice Questions

Q1 What is the trend in the thermal stability of the nitrates of Group 1 elements?

Q2 Write a general equation for the thermal decomposition of a Group 2 carbonate. Use M to represent the Group 2 metal.

Q3 Describe two ways that you could test how easily the nitrates of Group 2 decompose.

Q4 What colour flame would you expect a compound containing sodium to burn with?

Exam Questions

Q1 a) When a substance is heated, what changes occur within the atom that give rise to a coloured flame? [2 marks]

b) A compound gives a blue colour in a flame test. What s-block metal ions might this compound contain? [1 mark]

Q2 Barium and calcium are both Group 2 elements. They both form carbonates.

a) Write a balanced equation for the thermal decomposition of calcium carbonate, including state symbols. [2 marks]

b) State whether barium carbonate or calcium carbonate is more thermally stable. Explain your answer. [3 marks]

Q3 a) Write a balanced equation, including state symbols, for the thermal decomposition of sodium nitrate. [1 mark]

b) How could you test for the gas produced in the thermal decomposition? [1 mark]

c) Place the following in order of ease of thermal decomposition (easiest first).

magnesium nitrate **potassium nitrate** **sodium nitrate**

Explain your answer. [3 marks]

All trainee firefighters' worst nightmare — a flame test...

We're deep in the dense jungle of Inorganic Chemistry now. Those carefree days of atomic structure are well behind us. It's now an endurance test and you've just got to keep going. It's tough, but you've got to stay awake and keep learning. That stuff on thermal stability can be particularly hard to get your head around, but I have faith in you, jungle warrior.

Group 7 — The Halogens

The halogens form lovely little diatomic molecules. But don't let their sweet, friendly appearance fool you...

Halogen is used to describe the atom (X) or molecule (X_2). Halide is used to describe the negative ion (X^-).

Halogens are the **Highly Reactive Non-Metals** of Group 7

The table below gives some of the main properties of the first 4 halogens.

Halogen	Formula	Colour	Physical State	Electron configuration of atom	Electronegativity
fluorine	F_2	pale yellow	gas	$1s^2\ 2s^2\ 2p^5$	increases up the group
chlorine	Cl_2	green	gas	$1s^2\ 2s^2\ 2p^6\ 3s^2\ 3p^5$	
bromine	Br_2	red-brown	liquid	$1s^2\ 2s^2\ 2p^6\ 3s^2\ 3p^6\ 3d^{10}\ 4s^2\ 4p^5$	
iodine	I_2	grey	solid	$1s^2\ 2s^2\ 2p^6\ 3s^2\ 3p^6\ 3d^{10}\ 4s^2\ 4p^6\ 4d^{10}\ 5s^2\ 5p^5$	

1) **Their boiling points increase down the group.**
This is due to the increasing strength of the **induced dipole-dipole forces** as the size and relative mass of the molecules increases. This trend is shown in the changes of **physical state** from fluorine (gas) to iodine (solid).
2) **Electronegativity decreases down the group.**
Electronegativity, remember, is the tendency of an atom to **attract** a bonding pair of **electrons**. The halogens are all highly electronegative elements. But larger atoms attract electrons **less** than smaller ones. This is because the electrons are **further** from the nucleus and are **shielded** by more electrons. (See page 28 for more on shielding.)

Halogens **Displace** Less Reactive Halide Ions from Solution

1) Halogen atoms react by **gaining an electron** in their outer shell to form **1–** ions. This means they're **reduced**. As they're reduced, they **oxidise** another substance (it's a redox reaction) — so they're **oxidising agents**. They get **less reactive down the group**, because the atoms become larger. The outer shell is further from the nucleus, so electrons are less strongly attracted to it. So you can also say that the halogens become **less oxidising** down the group.

Halogen	Displacement reaction	Ionic equation
Cl	chlorine (Cl_2) will displace bromide (Br^-) and iodide (I^-)	$Cl_{2(aq)} + 2Br^-_{(aq)} \rightarrow 2Cl^-_{(aq)} + Br_{2(aq)}$ $Cl_{2(aq)} + 2I^-_{(aq)} \rightarrow 2Cl^-_{(aq)} + I_{2(aq)}$
Br	bromine (Br_2) will displace iodide (I^-)	$Br_{2(aq)} + 2I^-_{(aq)} \rightarrow 2Br^-_{(aq)} + I_{2(aq)}$
I	no reaction with F^-, Cl^-, Br^-	

Halogens are more soluble in organic solvents than in water.

2) The **relative oxidising strengths** of the halogens can be seen in their **displacement reactions** with the halide ions. The basic rule is:

> A **halogen** will **displace a halide** from solution if the halide is **below it** in the periodic table.

	Potassium chloride solution $KCl_{(aq)}$ — colourless	Potassium bromide solution $KBr_{(aq)}$ — colourless	Potassium iodide solution $KI_{(aq)}$ — colourless
Add chlorine water $Cl_{2(aq)}$ — colourless	no reaction	orange solution (Br_2) formed	brown solution (I_2) formed
Add bromine water $Br_{2(aq)}$ — orange	no reaction	no reaction	brown solution (I_2) formed
Add iodine solution $I_{2(aq)}$ — brown	no reaction	no reaction	no reaction

3) These displacement reactions can be used to help **identify** which halogen (or halide) is present in a solution.

Chlorine and **Sodium Hydroxide** make **Bleach**

If you mix chlorine gas with cold, dilute, aqueous sodium hydroxide you get **sodium chlorate(I) solution**, $NaClO_{(aq)}$, which just happens to be common household **bleach** (which kills bacteria).

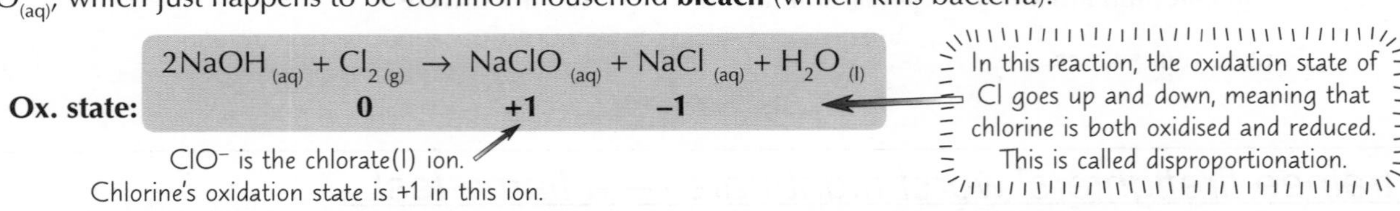

$2NaOH_{(aq)} + Cl_{2(g)} \rightarrow NaClO_{(aq)} + NaCl_{(aq)} + H_2O_{(l)}$
Ox. state: 0 +1 −1
ClO^- is the chlorate(I) ion. Chlorine's oxidation state is +1 in this ion.
In this reaction, the oxidation state of Cl goes up and down, meaning that chlorine is both oxidised and reduced. This is called disproportionation.

> The sodium chlorate(I) solution (bleach) has loads of uses — it's used in **water treatment**, to bleach **paper** and **textiles**... and it's good for **cleaning toilets**, too. Handy...

Group 7 — The Halogens

Chlorine is used to Kill Bacteria in Water

When you mix **chlorine** with **water**, it undergoes **disproportionation**. You end up with a mixture of **chloride ions** and **chlorate(I) ions.**

$$Cl_{2(g)} + H_2O_{(l)} \rightleftharpoons 2H^+_{(aq)} + Cl^-_{(aq)} + ClO^-_{(aq)}$$

Ox. state: Cl: 0 → −1 (in Cl^-) and +1 (in ClO^-)

In sunlight, chlorine can also decompose water to form chloride ions and **oxygen**.

$$Cl_{2(g)} + 2H_2O_{(l)} \rightleftharpoons 4H^+_{(aq)} + 2Cl^-_{(aq)} + O_{2(g)}$$

Chlorate(I) ions **kill bacteria**. So, **adding chlorine** (or a compound containing chlorate(I) ions) to water can make it safe to **drink** or **swim** in. On the downside, chlorine is toxic. It's also very risky to store and transport.

1) In the UK our drinking water is **treated** to make it safe. **Chlorine** is an important part of water treatment:
   - It **kills disease-causing microorganisms**.
   - Some chlorine persists in the water and **prevents reinfection** further down the supply.
   - It prevents the growth of **algae**, eliminating **bad tastes** and **smells**, and **removes discolouration** caused by organic compounds.

2) However, there are risks from using chlorine to treat water:
   - **Chlorine gas** is **very harmful** if it's breathed in — it irritates the **respiratory system**. **Liquid chlorine** on the skin or eyes causes severe **chemical burns**. Accidents involving chlorine could be really serious, or fatal.
   - Water contains a variety of organic compounds, e.g. from the decomposition of plants. Chlorine reacts with these compounds to form **chlorinated hydrocarbons**, e.g. chloromethane (CH_3Cl), and many of these chlorinated hydrocarbons are carcinogenic (cancer-causing). However, this increased cancer risk is small compared to the risks from untreated water — a cholera epidemic, say, could kill thousands of people.

3) We have to weigh up these risks and benefits when making decisions about whether we should add chemicals to drinking water supplies.

Practice Questions

Q1 Place the halogens F, Cl, Br and I in order of increasing: a) boiling point, b) electronegativity.

Q2 What would be seen when chlorine water is added to potassium iodide solution?

Q3 How is common household bleach formed?

Exam Questions

Q1 a) Write an ionic equation for the reaction between iodine solution and sodium astatide (NaAt). [1 mark]

b) For the equation in a), state which substance is oxidised. [1 mark]

Q2 a) Describe and explain the trends in:

i) the boiling points of Group 7 elements as you move down the Periodic Table. [3 marks]

ii) electronegativity of Group 7 elements as you move down the Periodic Table. [3 marks]

b) Which halogen is the most powerful oxidising agent? [1 mark]

Q3 Chlorine is added to the water in public swimming baths in carefully controlled quantities.

a) Write an equation for the reaction of chlorine with water to form chlorate(I) ions. [1 mark]

b) Why is chlorine added to the water in swimming baths, and why must the quantity added be carefully controlled? [2 marks]

Remain seated until the page comes to a halt. Please exit to the right...

The chemistry of fluorine and astatine is hard to study. Fluorine is a toxic gas and astatine is highly radioactive and decays quickly. But, you can predict how they will behave by looking at the trends in the behaviour of the other halogens. Generally, they fit with the trends seen down the other elements in Group 7. Makes life easier doesn't it?

Halide Ions

OK, a quick reminder of the basics first. Halides are compounds with the –1 halogen ion (e.g. Cl^-, Br^-, I^-) like KI, HCl and NaBr. They all end in "-ide" — chloride, bromide, iodide. Got that? Good. Now, you're ready to go in...

The **Reducing Power** of Halides **Increases** Down the Group...

To reduce something, the halide ion needs to lose an electron from its outer shell. How easy this is depends on the **attraction** between the **nucleus** and the outer **electrons**.

As you go down the group, the attraction gets **weaker** because:

1) the ions get bigger, so the electrons are **further** away from the positive nucleus,
2) there are extra inner electron shells, so there's a greater **shielding** effect.

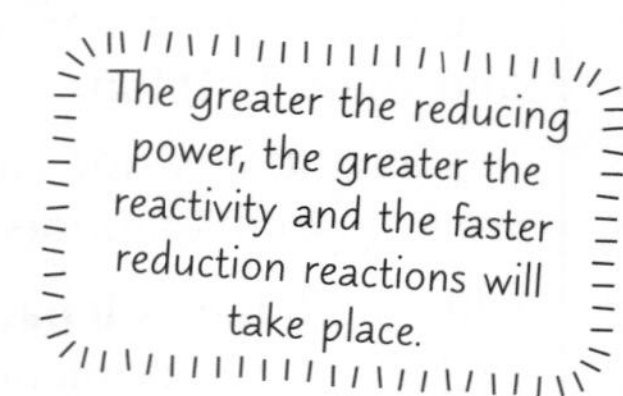

The greater the reducing power, the greater the reactivity and the faster reduction reactions will take place.

So, the further down the group the halide ion is, the easier it loses electrons and the greater its reducing power.

A good example of halogens doing a bit of reduction is the good old halogen / halide displacement reactions (the ones you learned on page 98... yes, those ones). And here come some more examples to learn...

...which Explains their Reactions with **Sulfuric Acid**

All the halides react with concentrated sulfuric acid to give a **hydrogen halide** as a product to start with. But what happens next depends on which halide you've got...

Reaction of NaF or NaCl with H_2SO_4

$$NaF_{(s)} + H_2SO_{4(aq)} \rightarrow NaHSO_{4(s)} + HF_{(g)}$$

$$NaCl_{(s)} + H_2SO_{4(aq)} \rightarrow NaHSO_{4(s)} + HCl_{(g)}$$

1) Hydrogen fluoride (HF) or hydrogen chloride gas (HCl) is formed. You'll see misty fumes as the gas comes into contact with moisture in the air.
2) But HF and HCl aren't strong enough reducing agents to reduce the sulfuric acid, so the reaction stops there.
3) It's not a redox reaction — the oxidation states of the halide and sulfur stay the same (–1 and +6).

Reaction of NaBr with H_2SO_4

$$NaBr_{(s)} + H_2SO_{4(aq)} \rightarrow NaHSO_{4(s)} + HBr_{(g)}$$

$$2HBr_{(aq)} + H_2SO_{4(aq)} \rightarrow Br_{2(g)} + SO_{2(g)} + 2H_2O_{(l)}$$

ox. state of S: +6 → +4 reduction

ox. state of Br: –1 → 0 oxidation

1) The first reaction gives misty fumes of hydrogen bromide gas (HBr).
2) But the HBr is a stronger reducing agent than HCl and reacts with the H_2SO_4 in a redox reaction.
3) The reaction produces choking fumes of SO_2 and orange fumes of Br_2.

Reaction of NaI with H_2SO_4

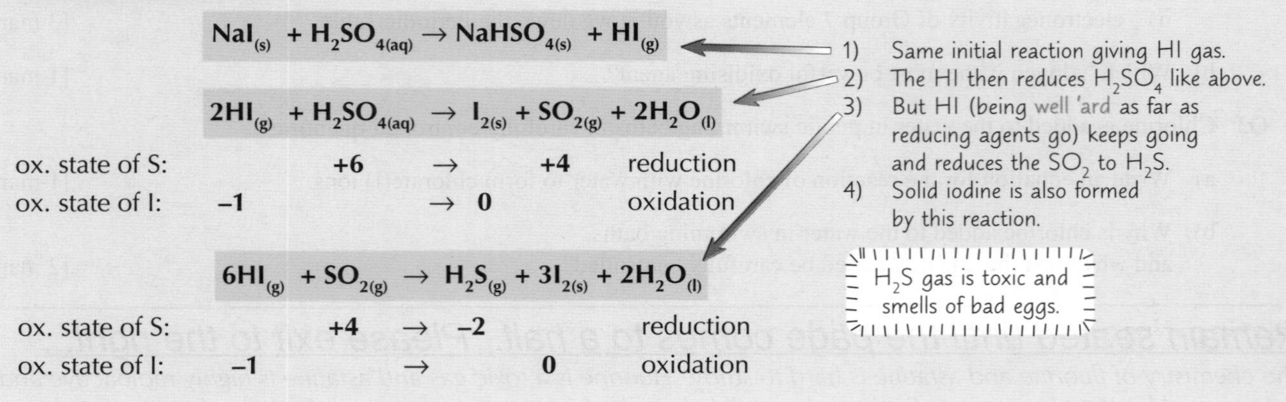

$$NaI_{(s)} + H_2SO_{4(aq)} \rightarrow NaHSO_{4(s)} + HI_{(g)}$$

$$2HI_{(g)} + H_2SO_{4(aq)} \rightarrow I_{2(s)} + SO_{2(g)} + 2H_2O_{(l)}$$

ox. state of S: +6 → +4 reduction

ox. state of I: –1 → 0 oxidation

$$6HI_{(g)} + SO_{2(g)} \rightarrow H_2S_{(g)} + 3I_{2(s)} + 2H_2O_{(l)}$$

ox. state of S: +4 → –2 reduction

ox. state of I: –1 → 0 oxidation

1) Same initial reaction giving HI gas.
2) The HI then reduces H_2SO_4 like above.
3) But HI (being well 'ard as far as reducing agents go) keeps going and reduces the SO_2 to H_2S.
4) Solid iodine is also formed by this reaction.

H_2S gas is toxic and smells of bad eggs.

Halide Ions

Silver Nitrate Solution is used to Test for Halides

The test for halides is dead easy. First you add **dilute nitric acid** to remove ions which might interfere with the test. Then you just add a few drops of **silver nitrate solution** ($AgNO_{3(aq)}$). A **precipitate** is formed (of the silver halide).

$$Ag^{+}_{(aq)} + X^{-}_{(aq)} \rightarrow AgX_{(s)}$$ ...where X is F, Cl, Br or I

1) The **colour** of the precipitate identifies the halide.

SILVER NITRATE TEST FOR HALIDE IONS...		
Fluoride F^-:	no precipitate	
Chloride Cl^-:	white precipitate	forms slowest
Bromide Br^-:	cream precipitate	↓
Iodide I^-:	yellow precipitate	forms fastest

2) Then to be extra sure, you can test your results by adding **ammonia solution**. Each silver halide has a different solubility in ammonia.

SOLUBILITY OF SILVER HALIDE PRECIPITATES IN AMMONIA...		
Chloride Cl^-:	white precipitate, dissolves in dilute $NH_{3(aq)}$	most soluble
Bromide Br^-:	cream precipitate, dissolves in conc. $NH_{3(aq)}$	↑
Iodide I^-:	yellow precipitate, insoluble in conc. $NH_{3(aq)}$	least soluble

Practice Questions

Q1 Give two reasons why a bromide ion is a more powerful reducing agent than a chloride ion.

Q2 Name the gaseous products formed when sodium bromide reacts with concentrated sulfuric acid.

Q3 What is produced when sodium iodide reacts with concentrated sulfuric acid?

Q4 How would you test whether an aqueous solution contained chloride ions?

Exam Questions

Q1 Describe the test you would carry out in order to distinguish between solid samples of sodium chloride and sodium bromide using silver nitrate solution and aqueous ammonia. State your observations. [6 marks]

Q2 The halogen below iodine in Group 7 is astatine (At).

a) Which of the following shows the products that would form when concentrated sulfuric acid is added to a solid sample of sodium astatide.

A $NaHSO_{4(aq)}$, $At_{2(g)}$, $SO_{2(g)}$, $2H_2O_{(l)}$

B $NaHSO_{4(aq)}$, $HAt_{(s)}$, $H_2S_{(g)}$, $2H_2O_{(l)}$

C $NaHSO_{4(aq)}$, $At_{2(s)}$, $H_2S_{(g)}$, $2H_2O_{(l)}$

D $NaHSO_{4(aq)}$, $At_{2(s)}$, $HAt_{(g)}$, $2H_2O_{(l)}$ [1 mark]

b) Predict what would be observed if silver astatide was added to a concentrated ammonia solution. Explain your answer. [2 marks]

Testing times — for the halides and for you...

Chemistry exams. What a bummer, eh... No one ever said it was going to be easy. Not even your teacher would be that cruel. There are plenty more equations on this page to learn. As well as that, make sure you really understand everything... the trend in the reducing power of halides... and the reactions with sulfuric acid...

Hydrogen Halides

I hope you're not fed up with the halogens yet. Still a few more pages about them to go yet. Now it's time for those lovely negative counterparts of the halogens — the halides. And not just any old halides, but hydrogen halides.

Hydrogen Halide = a Halogen + Hydrogen

1) All the halogens have **7 electrons** in their outer electron shells.
2) Hydrogen has **1 electron** in its outer electron shell.
3) Halogens react with hydrogen to form **hydrogen halides**.

Hydrogen Halides can be made using *Ionic Halides*

1) You can make a hydrogen halide by adding a **concentrated acid**, to a solid, **ionic halide**
2) For example, to make **hydrogen chloride** (HCl), add **concentrated phosphoric acid** (H_3PO_4) to **sodium chloride**:

$$NaCl + H_3PO_4 \rightarrow HCl + NaH_2PO_4$$

Ionic equation: $Cl^- + H_3PO_4 \rightarrow HCl + H_2PO_4^-$

3) **All hydrogen halides** can be made this way, using an **ionic halide** and **concentrated phosphoric acid.**
4) Things get more complicated if you try to use **concentrated sulfuric acid** (H_2SO_4) to make hydrogen halides though. Unlike phosphoric acid, sulfuric acid is an **oxidising agent**, so it can get involved in redox reactions.
5) You **can** make **hydrogen chloride** using sulfuric acid:

$$NaCl + H_2SO_4 \rightarrow HCl + NaHSO_4$$

Ionic equation: $Cl^- + H_2SO_4 \rightarrow HCl + HSO_4^-$

6) You **can't** make either **hydrogen bromide** or **hydrogen iodide** using sulfuric acid.
7) When **sodium bromide** or **sodium iodide** react with **sulfuric acid**, the bromide or iodide ions are **oxidised** to make **bromine** or **iodine** gas.
8) This is because iodine and bromine are strong enough **reducing agents** to **reduce** sulfuric acid.
9) When you add **sulfuric acid** to **sodium bromide**, the **bromide ions** are oxidised to **bromine** gas and the **sulfuric acid** is reduced from **sulfuric acid** (oxidation state of S = +6) to **sulfur dioxide** (oxidation state of S = +4).

$$2NaBr + 2H_2SO_4 \rightarrow Na_2SO_4 + Br_2 + SO_2 + H_2O$$

Ionic equation: $H_2SO_4 + 2H^+ + 2Br^- \rightarrow Br_2 + SO_2 + 2H_2O$

10) **Iodine** is such a strong reducing agent that when you add **sulfuric acid** to **sodium iodide** it reduces it all the way from **sulfuric acid** (oxidation state of S = +6) to **hydrogen sulfide** (oxidation state of S = –2).

$$8NaI + 5H_2SO_4 \rightarrow 4Na_2SO_4 + 4I_2 + H_2S + 4H_2O$$

Ionic equation: $H_2SO_4 + 8H^+ + 8I^- \rightarrow 4I_2 + H_2S + 4H_2O$

Hydrogen Fluoride and Hydrogen Chloride are *Stable* when Heated

1) When heated, hydrogen fluoride and hydrogen chloride are **stable**, and won't **split up** into **hydrogen** and **halide ions**.
2) Hydrogen bromide will **split slightly** when heated, and hydrogen iodide even more so.
3) This is because of the **strength** of the **hydrogen-halide bonds**.
4) As you go down Group 7, the **strength** of the bond that the halide forms with hydrogen gets **weaker**.
5) This is because the halogen atoms get **bigger** down the group, meaning the **bonding electrons** are **further away** from the nucleus and **shielded** by more inner electron shells.

Hydrogen Halide	Bond energy (kJ mol^{-1})
H-F	+565
H-Cl	+431
H-Br	+366
H-I	+299

Hydrogen Halides

Hydrogen Halides are **Acidic**

1) Hydrogen chloride, hydrogen bromide and hydrogen iodide all dissolve in water to create **strong acids**. In fact, good old hydrochloric acid is made when hydrogen chloride gas is dissolved in water.
2) When a hydrogen halide is dissolved in water, it **dissociates**. This just means that the molecule **splits apart** to form two ions — in this case a **hydrogen ion** and a **halide ion**:

$HCl_{(aq)} \rightarrow H^+_{(aq)} + Cl^-_{(aq)}$ $HBr_{(aq)} \rightarrow H^+_{(aq)} + Br^-_{(aq)}$ $HI_{(aq)} \rightarrow H^+_{(aq)} + I^-_{(aq)}$

3) It's the hydrogen ions that make the solutions **acidic**
4) Hydrogen fluoride is an exception to the rule — it doesn't fully **dissociate** in water (only a few of the molecules split apart). It's still **acidic**, but it's a **weak acid**.

Hydrogen Halides react with **Ammonia**

1) **Ammonia** (NH_3) is a **base**, so it can **accept a proton** to form the positively charged **ammonium ion** (NH_4^+).
2) The ammonium ion can bond with a negative **halide ion**, to produce an **ammonium halide**:

$HF_{(aq)} + NH_{3(aq)} \rightarrow NH_4F_{(aq)}$ $HBr_{(aq)} + NH_{3(aq)} \rightarrow NH_4Br_{(aq)}$

$HCl_{(aq)} + NH_{3(aq)} \rightarrow NH_4Cl_{(aq)}$ $HI_{(aq)} + NH_{3(aq)} \rightarrow NH_4I_{(aq)}$

Practice Questions

Q1 Write an equation to show how sodium chloride reacts with sulfuric acid.

Q2 Which hydrogen halide is the most thermally stable? Explain why.

Q3 Write an ionic equation to show what happens when hydrogen bromide is dissolved in water.

Q4 What is the product when a hydrogen halide reacts with ammonia?

Exam Questions

Q1 A student wants to make hydrogen iodide using sodium iodide. Which of these reagents should they use?

A hydrochloric acid

B ammonia

C phosphoric acid

D sulfuric acid [1 mark]

Q2 A sample of hydrogen bromide gas is dissolved in water to form an aqueous solution.

a) State what you would see if universal indicator was added to the solution. Explain your answer. [2 marks]

b) If sulfuric acid is added to the solution, the hydrogen bromide ions reduce the sulfuric acid to sulfur dioxide. Write a full, balanced equation for this reaction. [2 marks]

Q3 Potassium iodide and potassium bromide both react with sulfuric acid. Compare the reactions of these two potassium halides with sulfuric acid. You should include suitable chemical equations in your answer. [4 marks]

Hydrogen halides — coming soon to a test tube near you...

There's a lot to remember here so read these pages really thoroughly. It'll help to write out the full and the ionic equations for the reactions of each of the sodium halides with sulfuric acid. The chlorides, bromides and iodides all behave differently, so make sure you don't get them mixed up. Then, power on. Only two pages left in this topic...

Tests for Ions

It is a truth universally acknowledged that chemistry students need to know how to work out which ions are hanging around in a random ionic solution. Here are some tests that will help.*

**OK, I admit it, 'universally acknowledged' is probably a slight exaggeration...*

You Can Use Chemical Tests To Identify Positive Ions

Positive ions (or **cations**) include things like the ions of **Group 1 and 2 metals** and **ammonium ions**.
Here are the **chemical tests** that you need to know to help you identify them:

Use Flame Tests to Identify Ions

Compounds of some **metals** give a characteristic **colour** when heated. This is the idea behind **flame tests**. You saw how to carry them out back on page 97, so look back there if you need a reminder.

On page 97, you also learnt the results of the flame tests of various **Group 1 and 2 metals**, but here's a bonus one.

Copper burns with a **blue-green** flame.

Use Red Litmus Paper and NaOH to Test for Ammonium Ions

1) **Ammonia gas** (NH_3) is alkaline — so you can test for it using a damp piece of **red litmus paper**. (The litmus paper needs to be damp so the ammonia gas can dissolve). If there's ammonia present, the paper will turn **blue**.
2) If you add **hydroxide ions** (OH^-) to a solution containing **ammonium ions** (NH_4^+), they will react to produce **ammonia gas** and water, like this:

$$NH_4^+{}_{(aq)} + OH^-{}_{(aq)} \rightarrow NH_{3(g)} + H_2O_{(l)}$$

3) You can use this reaction to test whether a substance contains **ammonium ions** (NH_4^+). Add some dilute **sodium hydroxide** solution to your mystery substance in a test tube and **gently heat** the mixture. If there's ammonia given off, ammonium ions must be present.

You Can Use Chemical Tests To Identify Negative Ions Too

Negative ions (or **anions**) include things like **halide ions**, **hydroxide ions**, **sulfate ions** and **carbonate ions**.
Here are the **chemical tests** for these ions:

Test for Sulfates with HCl and Barium Chloride

You've already met this test back on page 94, but here's a quick reminder in case you've forgotten.

To identify a **sulfate** ion (SO_4^{2-}), you add a little dilute hydrochloric acid, followed by **barium chloride solution**, $BaCl_{2(aq)}$.

$$Ba^{2+}{}_{(aq)} + SO_4^{2-}{}_{(aq)} \rightarrow BaSO_{4\,(s)}$$

If a **white precipitate** of **barium sulfate** forms, it means the original compound contained a sulfate.

The hydrochloric acid is added to get rid of any traces of carbonate ions before you do the test. (These would also produce a precipitate, so they'd confuse the results.)

Use a pH Indicator to Test for Hydroxides

Hydroxide ions make solutions alkaline. So if you think a solution might contain hydroxide ions, you can use a **pH indicator** to test it. For example:

1) Dip a piece of **red litmus paper** into the solution.
2) If hydroxide ions are present, the paper will turn **blue**.

Tests for Ions

Test for **Halides** with **Silver Nitrate** Solution

To test for **chloride** (Cl^-), **bromide** (Br^-) or **iodide** (I^-) ions, you just add dilute **nitric acid** (HNO_3), followed by **silver nitrate** solution ($AgNO_3$).

A **chloride** gives a **white** precipitate of **silver chloride**.

A **bromide** gives a **cream** precipitate of **silver bromide**.

An **iodide** gives a **yellow** precipitate of **silver iodide**.

There's more info about this test on page 101.

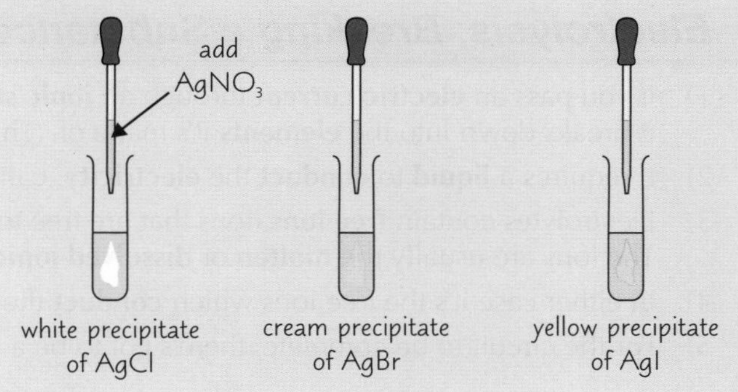

Hydrochloric Acid Can Help Detect **Carbonates**

You can test to see if a solution contains carbonate ions (CO_3^{2-}) by adding an acid. Here's how to do it:

When you add dilute **hydrochloric acid**, a solution containing **carbonate ions** will fizz. This is because the carbonate ions react with the hydrogen ions in the acid to give **carbon dioxide**:

$$CO_3^{2-}{}_{(s)} + 2H^+{}_{(aq)} \rightarrow CO_{2(g)} + H_2O_{(l)}$$

You can test for carbon dioxide using **limewater**. Carbon dioxide **turns limewater cloudy** — just bubble the gas through a test tube of limewater and watch what happens. If the limewater goes cloudy, your solution contains **carbonate ions**.

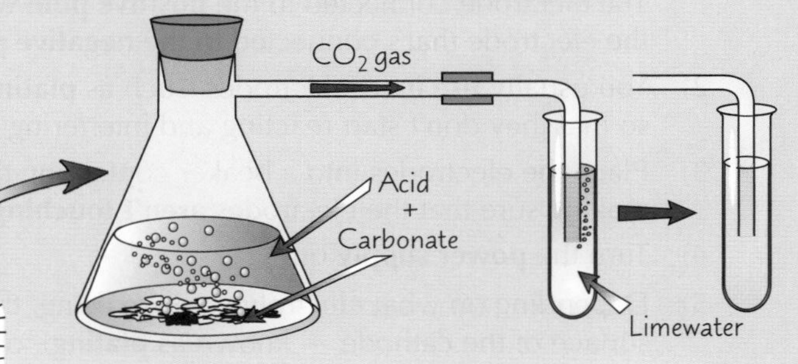

This test also detects hydrogencarbonates — they give off carbon dioxide when they react too.

Practice Questions

Q1 Describe how to carry out a flame test.

Q2 What colour would damp, red litmus paper turn in the presence of ammonia gas?

Q3 Describe how you could test a solution to see if it contained hydroxide ions.

Exam Questions

Q1 A student adds dilute nitric acid and silver nitrate to a solution of an unknown ionic compound. A yellow precipitate forms. Which anion is present in the solution?

A Bromide **B** Carbonate **C** Sulfate **D** Iodide [1 mark]

Q2 A student has a solution of an unknown ionic compound. He performs a flame test on a sample of the solution and notes that the compound burns with a pale green flame. He then reacts another sample of the solution with dilute hydrochloric acid. The reactants fizz and the gas produced turns limewater cloudy. What is the formula of the ionic compound? [2 marks]

Q3 You are given a sample of an ionic compound in solution and asked to confirm that the compound is ammonium sulfate. Describe the tests that you could perform to confirm the identity of the compound. [4 marks]

I've got my ion you...

...and you better have your ion these pages. There are lots of tests to learn and you best not get them all muddled up. Go through each test and make sure you know all the reagents you'd need to do the test, how you'd actually do it, and what a positive result looks like. Then once you know them all, treat yourself with a biscuit — that's a positive result too.

Electrolysis

This chemistry is giving me chills. I'm losing control. The info these pages are supplying — it's electrifying. You better shape up and learn it, cause I need a Chemistry whizz, and my heart is set on yoooooouuuuuuuuuuu... (Oo, oo, oo, honey...)

Electrolysis: Breaking a Substance Down using Electricity

Just the thought of electrolysis made Cathy's hair stand on end.

1) If you pass an **electric current** through an **ionic substance** that's **molten** or in **solution**, it breaks down into the **elements** it's made of. This is called **electrolysis**.
2) It requires a **liquid** to **conduct** the **electricity**, called the **electrolyte**.
3) Electrolytes contain **free ions** (ions that are free to **move about**). The ions are usually the **molten** or **dissolved ionic substance**.
4) In either case it's the free ions which **conduct** the electricity.
5) For the circuit to be complete, there's got to be a **flow of electrons**:

- **Negative ions (anions)** move to the **positive electrode** (the **anode**), and **lose** electrons.
- **Positive ions (cations)** move to the **negative electrode** (the **cathode**), and **gain** electrons.

Electrolysis of an Aqueous Solution

Here's the procedure for carrying out the electrolysis of an aqueous solution:

1) Use wires and clips to connect each **electrode** to the power supply. The electrode connected to the **positive pole** will be the **anode**, and the electrode that's connected to the **negative pole** will be the **cathode**.
2) You usually use **inert** electrodes (such as **platinum** or **carbon** electrodes) so that they don't start reacting and interfering with the electrolysis.
3) Place the electrodes into a beaker containing the **electrolyte**, making sure that the electrodes **aren't touching each other**.
4) Turn the **power supply** on.
5) Depending on what electrolyte you're using, the products will form as **metals** (as a **thin layer** on the surface of the cathode — known as **plating**), or as **gases** (as **bubbles** at the cathode or the anode).

power supply
anode (+ve)
cathode (−ve)
electrolyte

Half-Equations show you what happens at each Electrode

1) Half-equations show the **movement of electrons** during a reaction.
2) In electrolysis you can write **half-equations** to show what's happening at each **electrode**.
3) The half-equation for the **anode** will show **negative ions losing electrons** to form **atoms**. The half-equation for the **cathode** will show **positive ions gaining electrons** to form **atoms**.
4) For example, here are the half-equations for the electrolysis of **molten zinc chloride** ($ZnCl_2$):

Anode: $2Cl^-_{(l)} \rightarrow Cl_{2(g)} + 2e^-$

Cathode: $Zn^{2+}_{(l)} + 2e^- \rightarrow Zn_{(s)}$

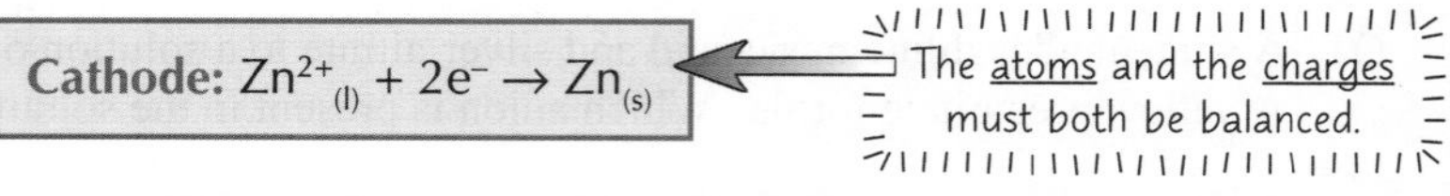

The atoms and the charges must both be balanced.

In Molten Ionic Compounds there's only one source of Ions

It's not too tricky to predict what will happen at the electrodes when you're dealing with a **molten salt**. The only ions that are around are the ones that make up the salt, so the substance will just break up into its **elements**.

Example: Electrolysis is carried out using molten lead bromide ($PbBr_{2(l)}$). Write half-equations to show what will form at each electrode.

Lead ions are positive, so will move to the **cathode** and form **lead**:

$$Pb^{2+}_{(l)} + 2e^- \rightarrow Pb_{(s)}$$

Bromide ions are negative, so will move to the **anode** and form **bromine gas**:

$$2Br^-_{(l)} \rightarrow Br_{2(g)} + 2e^-$$

Electrolysis

Electrolysis of **Aqueous Solutions** is a bit more **Complicated**

1) In **aqueous solutions**, you'll have H^+ and OH^- ions from the **water** as well as the ions from the **ionic compound**.
2) The products formed at each electrode depend on the **reactivity** of the ions, as well as the **concentration** of the salt solution.
3) There are a few **rules** to help you work out what will happen at each electrode:

Cathode

1) If the metal is **less reactive** than **hydrogen** (e.g. silver or copper), then the **metal** will be **formed**.
2) If the metal is **more reactive** than hydrogen (e.g. all **group 1** and **group 2** metals and **aluminium**) **hydrogen gas** will be **formed** (from **hydrogen ions** in the **water**).

Anode

1) If the solution **doesn't** contain a **halide**, **oxygen** will be formed (from **hydroxide ions** in the **water**). Here's the half equation for this reaction: $4OH^-_{(aq)} \rightarrow O_{2(g)} + 2H_2O_{(l)} + 4e^-$
2) If the solution is **concentrated** and contains a **halide**, then the **halogen** will be formed.
3) If the solution contains a halide but is **dilute**, **oxygen** will be formed (from **hydroxide ions** in the **water**).

If you use **metal electrodes** (apart from platinum ones) **metal ions** can also be made at the anode.

For example, in the **purification of copper**, the **anode** is made from **impure copper** and the **cathode** is made from **pure copper**.

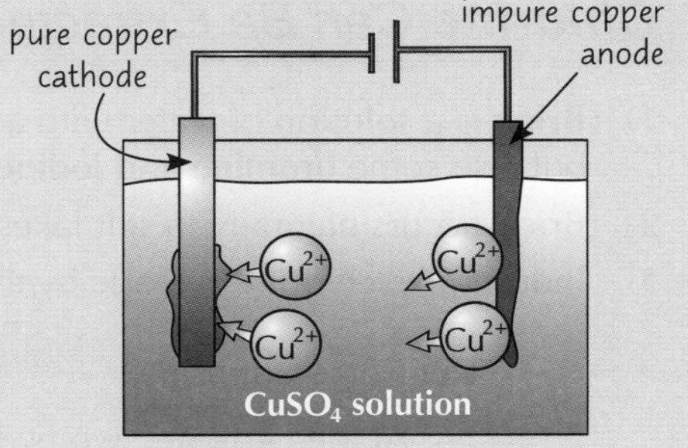

At the **anode**, **copper atoms lose electrons** and become **copper ions**, which enter the solution. These ions are then attracted to the **cathode** where they **gain** electrons to become **copper atoms** again and **plate** the pure copper cathode:

Anode: $Cu_{(s)} \rightarrow Cu^{2+}_{(aq)} + 2e^-$ **Cathode:** $Cu^{2+}_{(aq)} + 2e^- \rightarrow Cu_{(s)}$

The pure cathode **increases** in mass. The impure anode **shrinks**.

Practice Questions

Q1 Why does an ionic substance need to be molten or in solution before you can electrolyse it?

Q2 Describe how you would set up the equipment for the electrolysis of a solution of aqueous copper sulfate.

Q3 Explain what determines the product formed at the cathode when you electrolyse an aqueous solution.

Q4 What is formed at the anode when a concentrated halide solution is electrolysed?

Exam Questions

Q1 Two carbon electrodes are placed into molten copper chloride and the power supply is turned on.

a) What would you see happening at the anode? Explain your answer. [2 marks]

b) What would you see happening at the cathode? Explain your answer. [2 marks]

Q2 A student carries out an electrolysis of a dilute solution of magnesium chloride, $MgCl_{2\,(aq)}$. Write the half-equation for the reaction that occurs at:

a) the cathode. [1 mark]

b) the anode. [1 mark]

Aqueous chemistry problems? I have all of the solutions...

Electrolysis is a bit of a tricky one — just remembering whether it's the cathode or the anode that's the positive electrode is enough to give most people a headache. I just picture a sad, grumpy and generally negative cat, and that seems to help. Don't forget to learn the trick to half-equations too — state symbols, charges and all...

Production of Halogens

Halogens are dead handy and have loads of uses in the chemical industry. I mean, you learnt back on pages 98-99 how useful chlorine is. But now it's time to get to grips with where these fabulous little chemicals come from.

Most Halogens Can Be Extracted by **Electrolysis** of **Halide Solutions**

1) When you **electrolyse** concentrated aqueous solutions containing **halide** ions, the **halogen** element is released at the **anode**.
2) The **halide ions lose electrons** to the electrode and are **oxidised** to atoms, which combine to form **molecules**.

Example: Write half-equations to show what will form at each electrode when a concentrated solution of sodium bromide is electrolysed.

Bromine forms at the anode:

$$2Br^-_{(aq)} \rightarrow 2e^- + Br_{2(aq)}$$

Hydrogen ions (from the water) form hydrogen gas at the cathode:

$$2H^+_{(aq)} + 2e^- \rightarrow H_{2(g)}$$

Halogent

Chlorine Can Be Extracted from **Brine** by **Electrolysis**

1) **Brine** is a solution of water with a high concentration of **salts** — **mainly** sodium chloride, but also some **bromine** and **iodine** salts.
2) Brine occurs naturally in salt lakes or as seawater, or can be made by dissolving **rock salt** in water.
3) Industrially, chlorine is made by the **electrolysis of brine**.

Electrolysis of brine:

1) At the **cathode**, two hydrogen ions accept two electrons to become **one hydrogen molecule**: $2H^+_{(aq)} + 2e^- \rightarrow H_{2(g)}$
2) At the **anode**, two chloride (Cl^-) ions lose their electrons and become **one chlorine molecule**: $2Cl^-_{(aq)} \rightarrow Cl_{2(g)} + 2e^-$
3) The **sodium ions** stay in solution because they're **more reactive** than hydrogen.
4) **Sodium ions** and **hydroxide ions** (from water) are left behind while hydrogen and chlorine are removed, so **sodium hydroxide** (NaOH) is left in the solution.

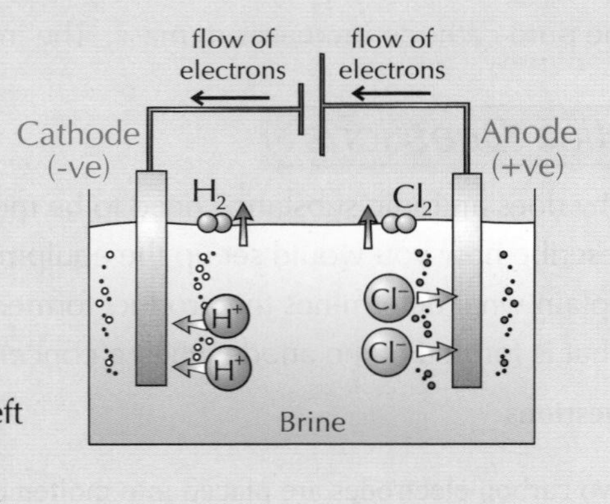

4) The electrodes are made of an **inert** material (e.g. carbon, platinum or titanium).
5) The electrolysis cell is constantly fed with a fresh stream of brine.
6) The **chlorine** is collected as a gas.

The **Sodium Chloride Solution** needs to be **Concentrated**

1) You can only extract **chlorine** from **concentrated sodium chloride** solution.
2) In **dilute** solutions, the chloride ions (Cl^-) **aren't discharged** — they hang on to their electrons. The **OH^-** ions lose electrons instead and the products at the anode are **oxygen** and **water**, not chlorine.

$$4OH^-_{(aq)} \rightarrow 4e^- + 2H_2O_{(l)} + O_{2(g)}$$

Production of Halogens

Bromine and Iodine are Displaced by Chlorine

Bromine and iodine can be extracted from **brine** too, in a displacement reaction (see page 98) using chlorine. The processes for extracting bromine and iodine are very similar.

Bromine

1) **Brine** contains some **bromide ions**.
2) Chlorine is **more reactive** than bromine.
So when you bubble chlorine gas through brine, the chlorine will **displace** the bromine.
3) Here's the equation for this reaction:

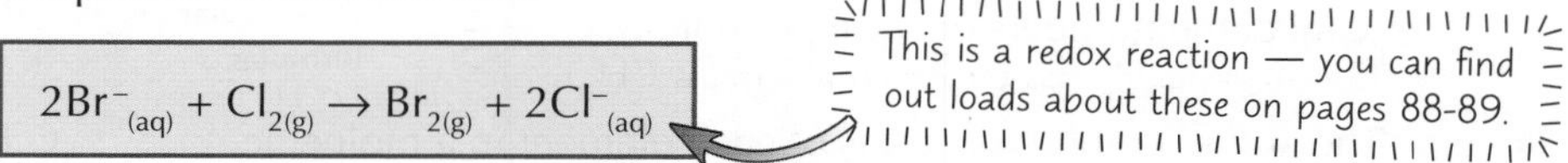
This is a redox reaction — you can find out loads about these on pages 88-89.

$$2Br^-_{(aq)} + Cl_{2(g)} \rightarrow Br_{2(g)} + 2Cl^-_{(aq)}$$

4) The bromine that is produced is then **collected**, **condensed** into a **liquid** and **purified**.

Iodine

1) **Brine** also contains some **iodide ions**.
2) Chlorine is **more reactive** than iodine too. So when you bubble chlorine gas through brine, the chlorine will **displace** the iodine.
3) Here's the equation for this reaction (it's amazingly similar to the bromine equation):

$$2I^-_{(aq)} + Cl_{2(aq)} \rightarrow I_{2(aq)} + 2Cl^-_{(aq)}$$

4) The iodine is **collected**, **purified** and **condensed** into a **grey solid**.

Practice Questions

Q1 What is brine?

Q2 Which electrode does chlorine form at during the electrolysis of brine?

Q3 Describe how bromine is produced from brine.

Exam Question

Q1 Chlorine gas is produced industrially from the electrolysis of sodium chloride solution.

a) Name one natural source of sodium chloride. [1 mark]

b) A student carries out the electrolysis of concentrated sodium chloride solution. Once the electrolysis is complete, they add a few drops of universal indicator to the remaining solution.
What would you expect the student to see? Explain your answer. [2 marks]

c) Another student carries out electrolysis of dilute sodium chloride solution. They also add a few drops of universal indicator to the remaining solution after the electrolysis is complete.
How would their observations differ from those of the student in part b)? Explain your answer. [2 marks]

d) Chlorine gas can be used to displace iodine from brine.
State why chlorine displaces iodine from a solution of iodide ions. [1 mark]

Did you hear the one about sodium, bromine and oxygen? Na Bro...

This page is just full of facts. Chlorine, bromine and iodine can all be extracted from brine — make sure that you don't mix up the process for each one though. Hopefully all the stuff on electrolysis is still fresh in your memory, but look back at p.106-107 for a reminder if you need to. Then it's onto the next topic already. That wasn't too painful was it?

Basic Stuff

This section's all about organic chemistry... carbon compounds, in other words. Read on...

There are Loads of Ways of Representing Organic Compounds

Type of formula	What it shows you	Formula for Butan-1-ol
General formula	An algebraic formula that can describe **any member** of a family of compounds.	$C_nH_{2n+1}OH$ (for all alcohols)
Empirical formula	The **simplest whole number ratio** of atoms of each element in a compound (cancel the numbers down if possible). (So ethane, C_2H_6, has the empirical formula CH_3.)	$C_4H_{10}O$
Molecular formula	The **actual** number of atoms of each element in a molecule.	$C_4H_{10}O$
Structural formula	Shows the arrangement of atoms **carbon by carbon**, with the attached hydrogens and functional groups.	$CH_3CH_2CH_2CH_2OH$
Skeletal formula	Shows the **bonds** of the carbon skeleton **only**, with any functional groups. The hydrogen and carbon atoms aren't shown. This is handy for drawing large complicated structures, like cyclic hydrocarbons.	(zigzag)–OH
Displayed formula	Shows how all the atoms are **arranged**, and all the bonds between them.	H–C(H)(H)–C(H)(H)–C(H)(H)–C(H)(H)–O–H

See page 43 for more on empirical and molecular formulas.

This could also be written as $CH_3(CH_2)_3OH$

Members of Homologous Series Have the Same General Formulas

1) Organic chemistry is more about **groups** of similar chemicals than individual compounds.
2) These groups are called **homologous series**. A homologous series is a bunch of organic compounds that have the same **functional group** and **general formula**. Consecutive members of a homologous series differ by **–CH_2–**.

A functional group is a group of atoms in a molecule responsible for the characteristic reactions of that compound.

Example:

1) The simplest homologous series is the **alkanes**. They're **straight chain** molecules that contain only **carbon** and **hydrogen** atoms. There's a lot more about the alkanes on pages 116-124.
2) The **general formula** for alkanes is C_nH_{2n+2}. So the first alkane in the series is $C_1H_{(2\times1)+2} = CH_4$ (you don't need to write the 1 in C_1), the second is $C_2H_{(2\times2)+2} = C_2H_6$, the seventeenth is $C_{17}H_{(2\times17)+2} = C_{17}H_{36}$, and so on...

3) Here are some of the more common homologous series:

Homologous Series	Prefix or Suffix	Example
alkanes	–ane	propane — $CH_3CH_2CH_3$
branched alkanes	alkyl– (–yl)	methylpropane — $CH_3CH(CH_3)CH_3$
alkenes	–ene	propene — $CH_3CH{=}CH_2$
halogenoalkanes	chloro–/bromo–/iodo–	chloroethane — CH_3CH_2Cl
alcohols	–ol	ethanol — CH_3CH_2OH
aldehydes	–al	ethanal — CH_3CHO
ketones	–one	propanone — CH_3COCH_3
cycloalkanes	cyclo– ... –ane	cyclohexane C_6H_{12}
carboxylic acids	–oic acid	ethanoic acid — CH_3COOH
esters	alkyl– ... –oate	methyl propanoate — $CH_3CH_2COOCH_3$

Basic Stuff

There Are Different **Types** of **Carbon Skeleton**

1) All organic compounds contain a **carbon skeleton**. This can be either **aromatic** or **aliphatic**.
2) **Aromatic** compounds (also called **arenes**) contain a **benzene** ring. You can **draw** benzene rings in two ways:

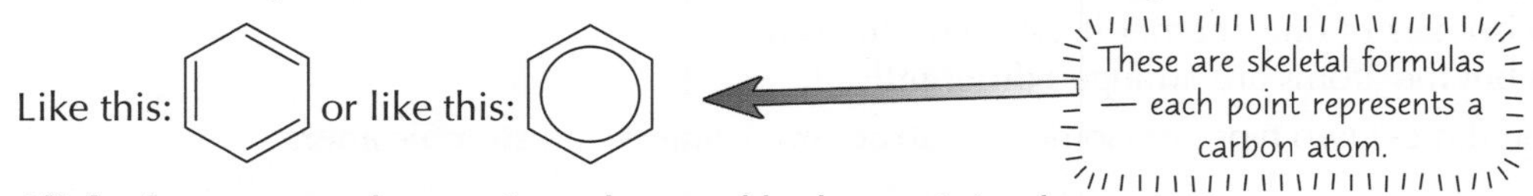

Like this:
or like this:
These are skeletal formulas — each point represents a carbon atom.

3) **Aliphatic** compounds contain carbon and hydrogen joined together in **straight** chains, **branched** chains or **non-aromatic rings**.
4) If an aliphatic compound contains a (non-aromatic) **ring**, then it can be called **alicyclic**.
5) Organic compounds may be saturated or unsaturated. **Saturated** compounds only contain carbon-carbon **single bonds** — like alkanes. **Unsaturated** compounds can have carbon-carbon **double** bonds, **triple** bonds or **aromatic** groups.
6) And finally... an **alkyl group** is a **fragment** of a molecule with general formula C_nH_{2n+1}.

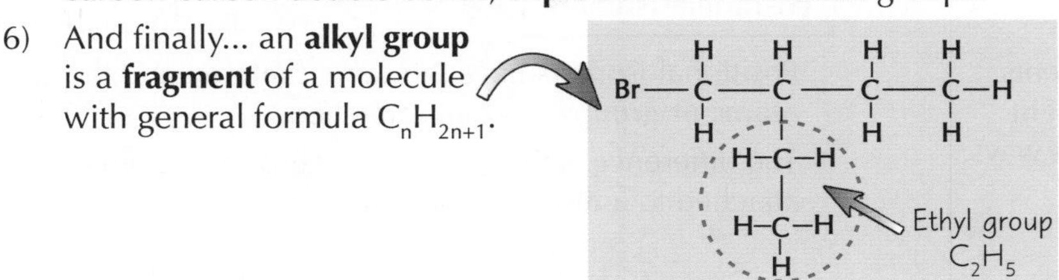

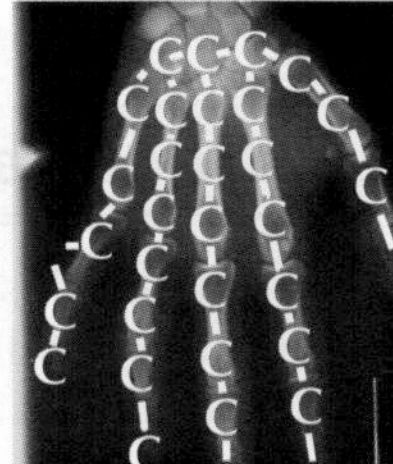

The X-ray revealed a break in Timothy's carbon skeleton.

Nomenclature is a Fancy Word for the **Naming** of Organic Compounds

Organic compounds used to be given whatever names people fancied, but these names led to **confusion** between different countries.

The **IUPAC** system for naming organic compounds was invented as an **international language** for chemistry. It can be used to give any organic compound a **systematic name** using these **rules** of nomenclature...

1) Count the carbon atoms in the **longest continuous chain** — this gives you the stem.

No. of Carbons	**1**	**2**	**3**	**4**	**5**	**6**	**7**	**8**	**9**	**10**
Stem	meth-	eth-	prop-	but-	pent-	hex-	hept-	oct-	non-	dec-

2) The **main functional group** of the molecule usually tells you what **homologous series** the molecule is in, and so gives you the **prefix** or **suffix** — see the table on the previous page.
3) Number the **longest** carbon chain so that the main functional group has the lowest possible number. If there's more than one longest chain, pick the one with the **most side-chains**.
4) Any side-chains or less important functional groups are added as prefixes at the start of the name. Put them in **alphabetical** order, after the **number** of the carbon atom each is attached to.
5) If there's more than one **identical** side-chain or functional group, use **di-** (2), **tri-** (3) or **tetra-** (4) before that part of the name — but ignore this when working out the alphabetical order.

Example: $CH_3CH(CH_3)CH(CH_2CH_3)C(CH_3)_2OH$

1) The longest chain is **5** carbons. So the stem is **pent-**.
2) The main functional group is **-OH** So the name will be based on **'pentanol'**.
3) **Numbering** the longest carbon chain so that -OH has the **lowest** possible number (and you have most side chains) puts -OH on carbon 2, so it's some sort of **pentan-2-ol**.

Longest chain with most side-chains

4) The other side chains are an **ethyl group** on carbon-3, and **methyl groups** on carbon-2 and carbon-4, so the **systematic name** for this molecule is: **3-ethyl-2,4-dimethylpentan-2-ol**.

Isomerism

Isomers are great fun — they're all about putting the same atoms together in different ways to make completely different molecules. It's like playing with plastic building bricks, but it hurts less when you tread on one by accident.

***Isomers** Have the Same **Molecular** Formula*

1) Two molecules are isomers of one another if they have the same **molecular formula** but the atoms are arranged **differently**.
2) On these pages, you'll meet two types of isomers — **structural isomers** and **stereoisomers**.

***Structural Isomers** have different **Structural Arrangements** of Atoms*

In structural isomers the atoms are **connected** in different ways. So they have the **same molecular formula** but different **structural formulas**. There are **three types** of structural isomers:

Chain Isomers

Chain isomers have different arrangements of the **carbon skeleton**. Some are **straight chains** and others **branched** in different ways.

butane　　methylpropane

Positional Isomers

Positional isomers have the **same skeleton** and the **same atoms or groups of atoms** attached.

The difference is that the atom or group of atoms is attached to a **different carbon atom.**

1-chlorobutane　　2-chlorobutane

Functional Group Isomers

Functional group isomers have the same atoms arranged into **different functional groups**.

hex-1-ene　　cyclohexane

***Don't be Fooled** — What Looks Like an Isomer Might **Not** Be*

Beware — sometimes what looks like an isomer, isn't. If you can **switch** between two drawings of a molecule, either by rotating the **C-C single bonds** or rotating the **entire molecule**, then you've drawn the same isomer twice.

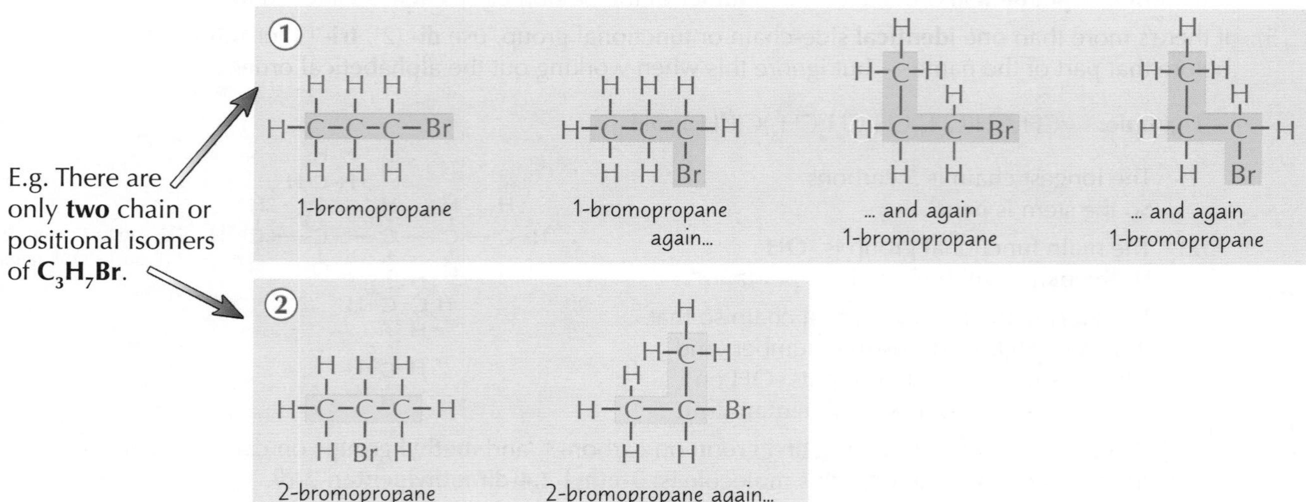

Isomerism

Double Bonds Can't Rotate

1) Carbon atoms in a C=C double bond and the atoms bonded to these carbons all lie in the **same plane** (they're **planar**). Because of the way they're arranged, they're actually said to be **trigonal planar** — the atoms attached to each double-bonded carbon are at the corners of an imaginary equilateral triangle.

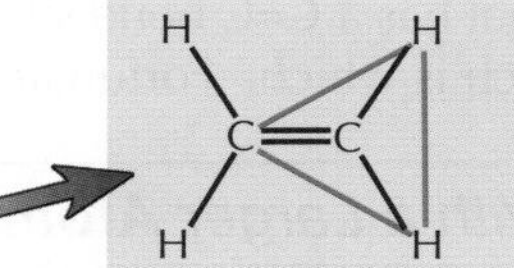

The bond angles in the planar unit are all 120°.

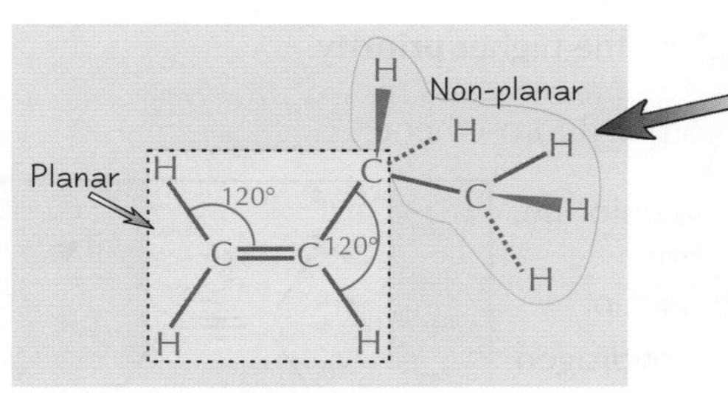

2) Ethene, C_2H_4 (like in the diagram above) is completely planar, but in larger alkenes, only the >C=C< unit is planar.
3) Another important thing about C=C double bonds is that atoms **can't rotate** around them like they can around single bonds (because of the way the p orbitals **overlap** to form a π **bond** — see p.130). In fact, double bonds are fairly **rigid** — they don't bend much either.
4) Even though atoms can't rotate about the **double bond**, things can still rotate about any **single bonds** in the molecule.
5) The **restricted rotation** around the C=C double bond is what causes **alkenes** to form **stereoisomers**.

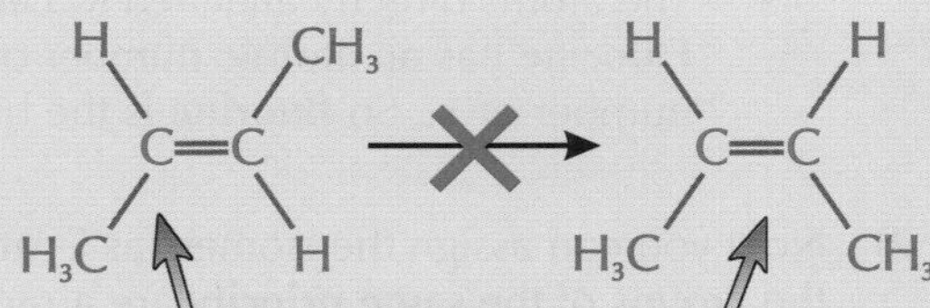

Both these molecules have the structural formula $CH_3CHCHCH_3$. The restricted rotation around the double bond means you can't turn one into the other so they are isomers.

E/Z isomerism is a Type of Stereoisomerism

(You might see E/Z isomerism being called geometric isomerism.)

1) **Stereoisomers** have the same structural formula but a **different arrangement** in space.
(Just bear with me for a moment... that will become clearer, I promise.)
2) Because of the **lack of rotation** around the double bond, some **alkenes** can have stereoisomers.
3) Stereoisomers occur when the two double-bonded carbon atoms each have two **different atoms** or **groups** attached to them.
4) One of these isomers is called the **'E-isomer'** and the other is called the **'Z-isomer'** (hence the name E/Z isomerism).
5) The **Z-isomer** has the same groups either **both above** or **both below** the double bond, whilst the **E-isomer** has the same groups positioned **across** the double bond.

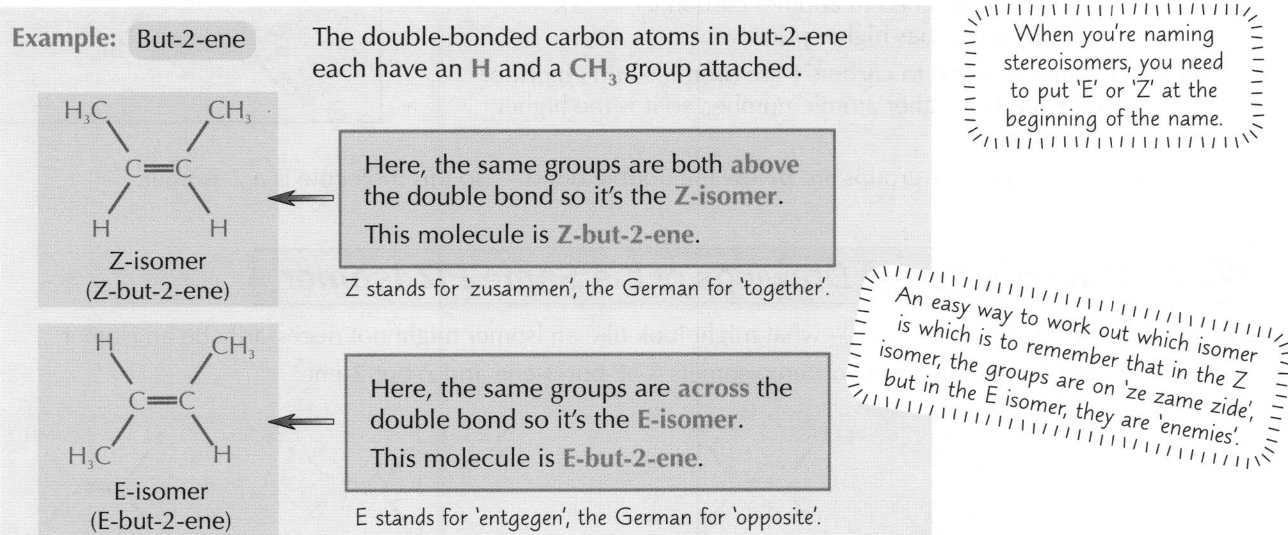

Example: But-2-ene
The double-bonded carbon atoms in but-2-ene each have an H and a CH_3 group attached.
H_3C
CH_3
C=C
H
H
Z-isomer
(Z-but-2-ene)
Here, the same groups are both above the double bond so it's the Z-isomer.
This molecule is Z-but-2-ene.
Z stands for 'zusammen', the German for 'together'.
H
CH_3
C=C
H_3C
H
E-isomer
(E-but-2-ene)
Here, the same groups are across the double bond so it's the E-isomer.
This molecule is E-but-2-ene.
E stands for 'entgegen', the German for 'opposite'.

When you're naming stereoisomers, you need to put 'E' or 'Z' at the beginning of the name.

An easy way to work out which isomer is which is to remember that in the Z isomer, the groups are on 'ze zame zide', but in the E isomer, they are 'enemies'.

Isomerism

The E/Z System Works Even When All the Groups Are Different

A molecule that has a C=C bond surrounded by **four different groups** still has an E- and a Z-isomer — it's just harder to work out which is which. Fortunately, you can solve this problem using the **Cahn-Ingold-Prelog (CIP) priority rules:**

Atoms With a Larger Atomic Number are Given a Higher Priority

1) Look at the atoms **directly bonded** to each of the C=C carbon atoms. The atom with the higher **atomic number** on each carbon is given the higher **priority**.

Example: Here's one of the stereoisomers of 1-bromo-1-chloro-2-fluoro-ethene:

- The atoms directly attached to **carbon-1** are bromine and chlorine. **Bromine** has an atomic number of **35** and **chlorine** has an atomic number of **17**. So **bromine** is the higher priority group.
- The atoms directly attached to **carbon-2** are fluorine and hydrogen. **Fluorine** has an atomic number of **9** and **hydrogen** has an atomic number of **1**. So **fluorine** is the higher priority group.

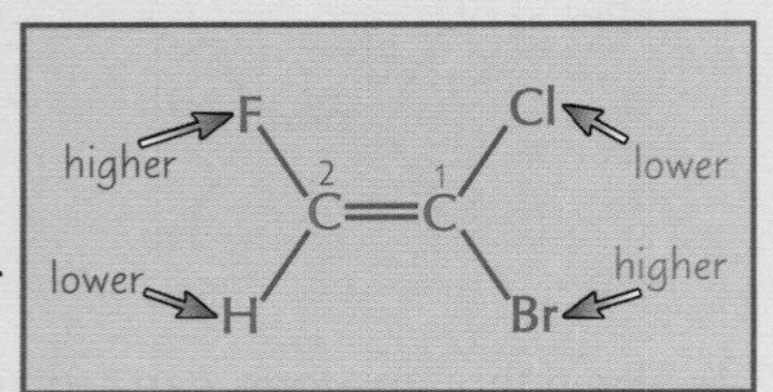

2) Now you can assign the isomers as E- and Z- as before, just by looking at how the groups of the **same priority** are arranged.

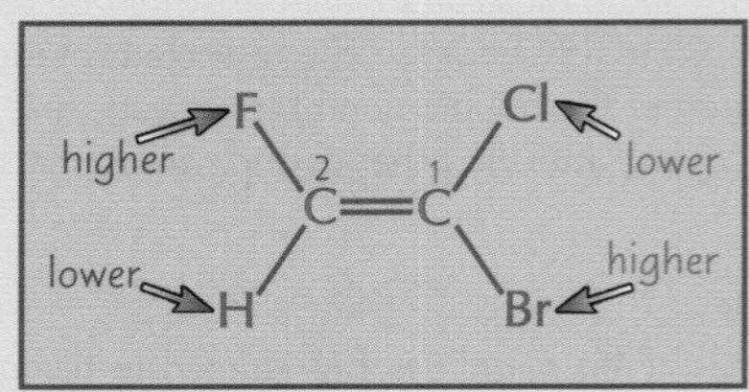

In this stereoisomer of 1-bromo-1-chloro-2-fluoroethene, the **higher priority groups** (bromine and fluorine) are positioned **across** the double bond from one another. So it's the **E-isomer**.

You May Have to Look Further Along the Chain

If the atoms **directly bonded** to the carbon are the **same** then you have to look at the **next** atom in the groups to work out which has the higher priority.

Example: The molecule shown below is a branched alkene. State whether it is an E-isomer or a Z-isomer.

1) The atoms attached to **carbon-2** are both carbons, so you need to go **further along** the chain to work out the priority. The **methyl** carbon is attached to hydrogen (A_r = 1), but the first **ethyl** carbon is attached to another carbon (A_r = 12). So the **ethyl group** has higher priority.
2) The atoms attached to **carbon-1** are bromine and chlorine. **Bromine** has the higher atomic number, so it is the higher priority group.
3) Both higher priority groups are **below** the double bond — so this molecule is a **Z-isomer**.

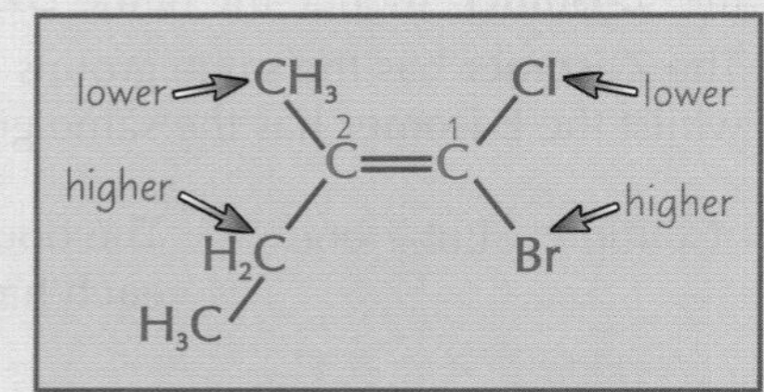

Watch Out for Different Drawings of the Same E/Z Isomer

Watch out with E/Z isomerism too — what might look like an isomer might not necessarily be an isomer...
For example, but-2-ene only has two stereoisomers — E-but-2-ene and Z-but-2-ene:

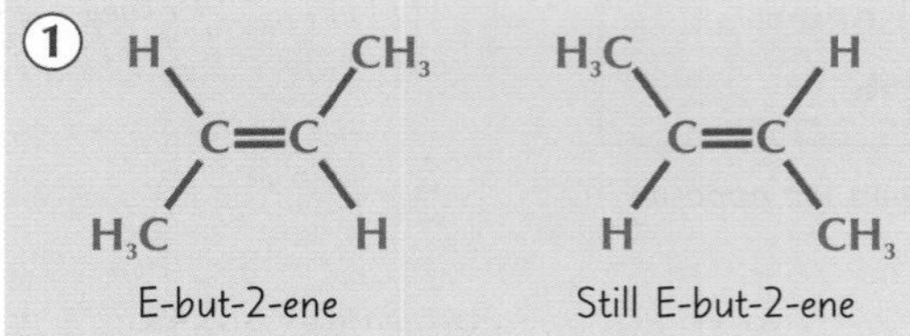

② Z-but-2-ene — Another Z-but-2-ene

Isomerism

E/Z Isomers Can Sometimes Be Called Cis-Trans Isomers

1) If the carbon atoms have at least **one group in common** (like in but-2-ene), then you can call the isomers '**cis**' or '**trans**' (as well as E- or Z-) where...
   - '**cis**' means the same groups are on the **same side** of the double bond,
   - '**trans**' means the same groups are on **opposite sides** of the double bond.

   So E-but-2-ene can be called **trans-but-2-ene**, and Z-but-2-ene can be called **cis-but-2-ene**.

We're talking Latin this time... 'cis' means 'on the same side', while 'trans' means 'across'.

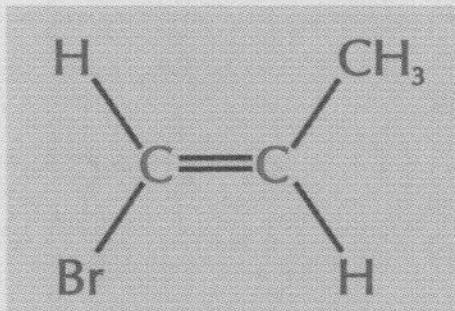

Here's an example:
The **H** atoms are on **opposite** sides of the double bond, so this is **trans-1-bromopropene**.
No problems there.

2) If the carbon atoms both have totally **different** groups attached to them, the cis-trans naming system can't cope.

Here, the **cis/trans** naming system doesn't work because the carbon atoms have **different groups** attached so there's no way of deciding **which isomer** is cis and which isomer is trans.

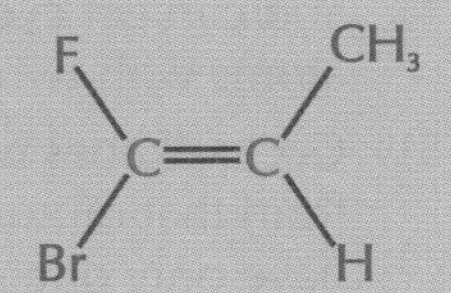

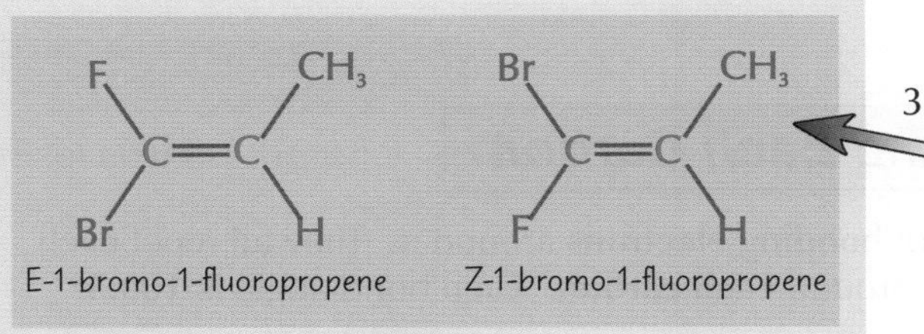

E-1-bromo-1-fluoropropene Z-1-bromo-1-fluoropropene

3) The E/Z system keeps on working though — in the E/Z system, Br has a **higher priority** than F and CH_3 has a higher priority than H, so the names depend on where the Br atom is in relation to the CH_3 group.

Practice Questions

Q1 What are structural isomers?

Q2 Define the term 'stereoisomers'.

Q3 What property of alkenes gives rise to E/Z isomerism?

Q4 Which group would have a higher priority under the CIP priority rules: a bromine atom or an –OH group?

Exam Questions

Q1 There are four halogenoalkanes with the molecular formula C_4H_9Cl.

a) Give the names of all four of these halogenoalkanes. [4 marks]

b) Identify a pair of positional isomers from your answer to part a). [1 mark]

c) Identify a pair of chain isomers from your answer to part a). [1 mark]

Q2 1-bromopropene has the structural formula $CH_3CH=CHBr$.

a) Draw the structure of E-1-bromopropene. [1 mark]

b) Draw the structures of two isomers of 1-bromopropene that do not exhibit E/Z isomerism. [2 marks]

Q3 a) Draw and name the E/Z isomers of pent-2-ene. [2 marks]

b) Explain why alkenes can have E/Z isomers but alkanes cannot. [2 marks]

I just love my new surround-sound stereoisomer...

IMPORTANT FACT: If the two groups connected to one of the double-bonded carbons in an alkene are the same, then it won't have E/Z isomers. So neither propene nor but-1-ene have E/Z isomers. Try drawing them out if you're not sure. And then draw out all the structural isomers of butene. Just to prove you've got this completely sussed.

Alkanes

There's nowt too hard about alkanes. They're all just carbon and hydrogen, hydrogen and carbon, carbon and hydrogen...

Alkanes are **Saturated Hydrocarbons**

1) Alkanes have the **general formula C_nH_{2n+2}**.
2) They only contain **carbon** and **hydrogen** atoms, so they're **hydrocarbons**.
3) Every carbon atom in an alkane has **four single bonds** with other atoms. It's **impossible** for carbon to make more than four bonds, so alkanes are **saturated** (they only contain **single bonds**).

Here are a few examples of alkanes:

If you can't remember how organic compounds are named, have a look back at pages 110 and 111.

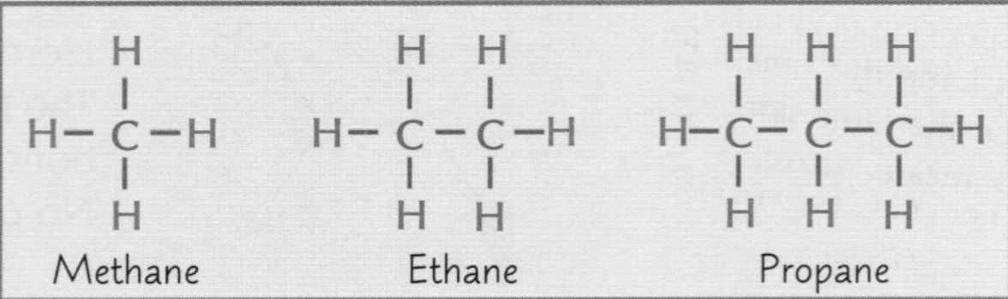

4) You can get **cycloalkanes** too. They have a ring of carbon atoms with two hydrogens attached to each carbon.
5) Cycloalkanes have a **different general formula** from that of normal alkanes (C_nH_{2n}, assuming they have only one ring), but they are still **saturated**.

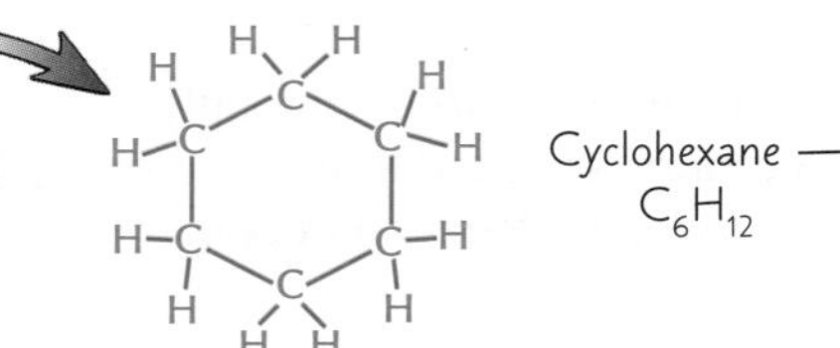

Alkane Molecules are **Tetrahedral** Around **Each Carbon**

In an alkane molecule, each carbon atom has **four pairs** of **bonding electrons** around it. They all repel each other **equally**. So the molecule forms a tetrahedral shape around **each carbon**. Each bond angle is **109.5°**

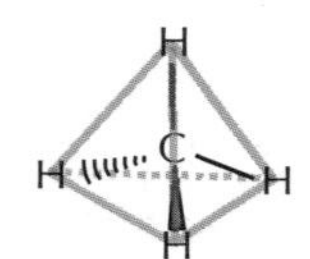

If you draw lines joining up the Hs in CH_4, the shape you get is a **tetrahedron**.

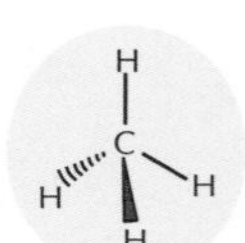

Methane
1 tetrahedral carbon

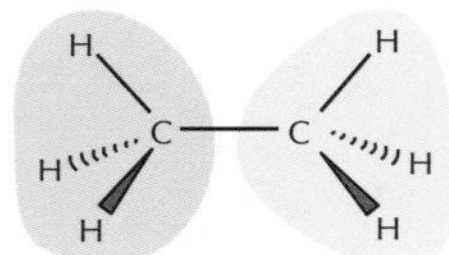

Ethane
2 tetrahedral carbons

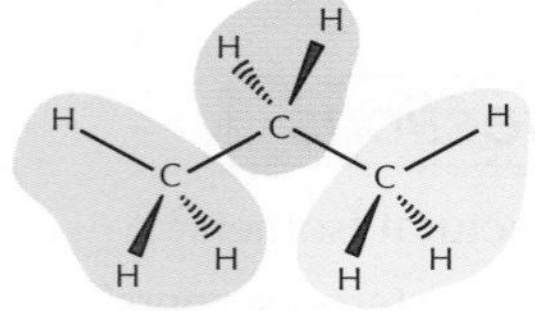

Propane
3 tetrahedral carbons

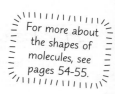

For more about the shapes of molecules, see pages 54-55.

You Can Use **Volumes** to Work Out **Combustion Equations**

Combustion reactions happen between **gases**. All gases at the same temperature and pressure have the same **molar volume**. This means you can use the **ratio** of the **volumes** of gases reacting together to calculate the **molar ratios**, and then work out what **hydrocarbon** is combusting.

There's more on combustion reactions on page 122.

Example: 30 cm³ of hydrocarbon X combusts completely with 240 cm³ oxygen. 150 cm³ carbon dioxide is produced. What is the molecular formula of hydrocarbon X?

- Using the volumes provided, the reaction equation can be written: $30X + 240O_2 \rightarrow 150CO_2 + ?H_2O$.
- This can be simplified by dividing everything by 30: $X + 8O_2 \rightarrow 5CO_2 + nH_2O$.
- 8 moles of oxygen reacts to form 5 moles of carbon dioxide and n moles of water. So any oxygen atoms that don't end up in CO_2 must be in H_2O. This means that $n = (8 \times 2) - (5 \times 2) = 6$.
- This means the combustion equation is: $X + 8O_2 \rightarrow 5CO_2 + 6H_2O$. You can use this to identify X.
- All the carbon atoms from X end up in carbon dioxide molecules, and all the hydrogen atoms from X end up in water, so the number of **carbon** atoms in X is **5** and the number of **hydrogen** atoms in X is **12**.
- The molecular formula of X is C_5H_{12}.

Alkanes

The **Boiling Point** of an Alkane Depends on its **Size** and **Shape**

The smallest alkanes, like methane, are **gases** at room temperature and pressure — they've got very low boiling points. Larger alkanes are **liquids** — they have higher boiling points.

1) Alkanes have **covalent bonds** inside the molecules. **Between** the molecules, there are **induced dipole-dipole** interactions which hold them all together.
2) The **longer** the carbon chain, the **stronger** the induced dipole-dipole interactions. This is because there's **more surface contact** and more electrons to interact.
3) As the molecules get longer, it takes **more energy** to overcome the induced dipole-dipole interactions, and the boiling point **rises**.
4) A **branched-chain** alkane has a **lower** boiling point than its straight-chain isomer. Branched-chain alkanes can't **pack closely** together and they have smaller **molecular surface areas** — so the induced dipole-dipole interactions are reduced.

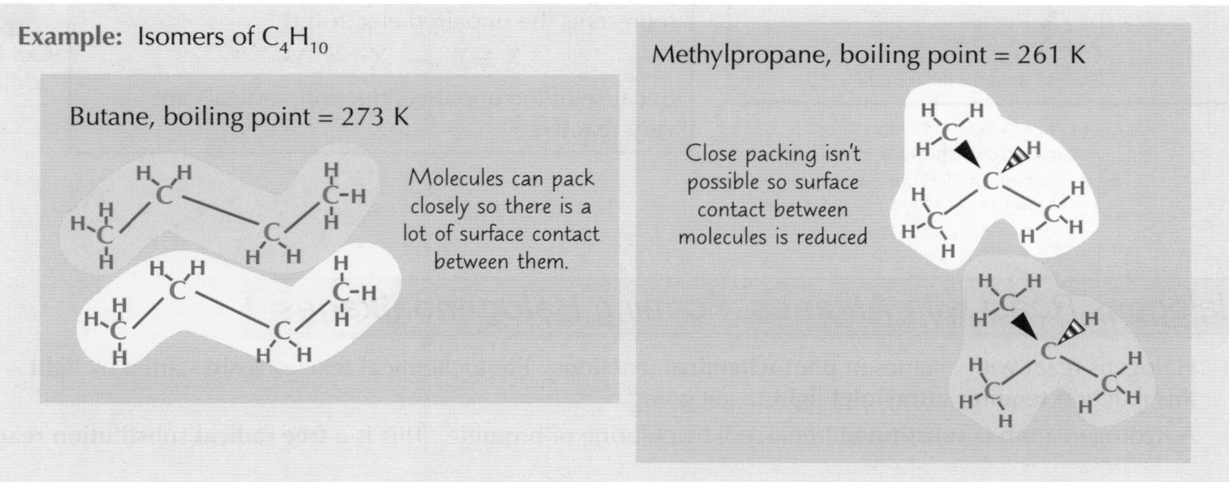

Example: Isomers of C_4H_{10}
Butane, boiling point = 273 K
Molecules can pack closely so there is a lot of surface contact between them.
Methylpropane, boiling point = 261 K
Close packing isn't possible so surface contact between molecules is reduced

Practice Questions

Q1 What is the general formula for alkanes?

Q2 Alkanes are saturated hydrocarbons — explain what the term 'saturated' means.

Q3 What is the H-C-H bond angle in a molecule of methane?

Q4 What kind of intermolecular forces are there between alkane molecules?

Exam Questions

Q1 The alkane ethane is a saturated hydrocarbon.

a) What is a saturated hydrocarbon? [2 marks]

b) i) Draw a diagram of ethane, showing the 3D arrangement of atoms. [1 mark]

ii) What are the bond angles between the hydrogens around each carbon in ethane? [1 mark]

Q2 Nonane is a hydrocarbon with the formula C_9H_{20}.

a) Which would you expect to have a higher boiling point, nonane or 2,2,3,3-tetramethylpentane? Explain your answer. [2 marks]

b) When 25 cm^3 of nonane burns in a limited air supply, the products are carbon monoxide and water. Calculate the volume of carbon monoxide you would expect this reaction to produce. [2 marks]

Tetrahedra — aren't they those monsters from Greek mythology...

Alkanes are the simplest organic compounds you're going to meet, so make the most of them. They're very stable so they don't get up to much. Different alkanes can have different boiling points — even if their molecular formulas are the same. It's all about the strength of the intermolecular forces and how closely the molecules can pack together.

Reactions of Alkanes

Alkanes react with particles that have unpaired electrons (called free radicals). These reactions happen in several steps, and a mechanism breaks reactions down to show you the steps. Watch out, there are a few coming up...

There are **Two Types** of Bond Fission — **Homolytic** and **Heterolytic**

Breaking a covalent bond is called **bond fission**. A single covalent bond is a shared pair of electrons between two atoms. It can break in two ways:

Heterolytic Fission:

In heterolytic fission the bond breaks **unevenly** with one of the bonded atoms receiving **both** electrons from the bonded pair. **Two different** substances are formed — a positively charged **cation** (X^+), and a negatively charged **anion** (Y^-).

$$X{\div}Y \rightarrow X^+ + Y^-$$

('hetero' means 'different')

A curly arrows shows the movement of an electron pair.

Homolytic Fission:

In homolytic fission, the bond breaks evenly and each bonding atom receives **one electron** from the bonded pair. Two electrically uncharged **'radicals'** are formed. Radicals are particles that have an **unpaired electron**. They are shown in mechanisms by a big dot next to the molecular formula (the dot represents the unpaired electron.)

$$X{\div}Y \rightarrow X\bullet + Y\bullet$$

Because of the unpaired electron, radicals are very **reactive**.

Carl loved fission at the weekends.

Halogens React with **Alkanes**, Forming **Halogenoalkanes**

1) Halogens react with alkanes in **photochemical** reactions. Photochemical reactions are started by **light** — this reaction requires **ultraviolet light** to get going.
2) A hydrogen atom is **substituted** (replaced) by chlorine or bromine. This is a **free radical substitution reaction**.

Example: Chlorine and **methane** react with a bit of a bang to form **chloromethane**:

$$CH_4 + Cl_2 \xrightarrow{UV} CH_3Cl + HCl$$

The **reaction mechanism** has three stages:

Initiation reactions — free radicals are produced.

1) Sunlight provides enough energy to break the Cl-Cl bond — this is **photodissociation**.

$$Cl_2 \xrightarrow{UV} 2Cl\bullet$$

2) The bond splits **equally** and each atom gets to keep one electron — **homolytic fission**. The atom becomes a highly reactive **free radical**, Cl•, because of its **unpaired electron**.

Propagation reactions — free radicals are used up and created in a chain reaction.

1) Cl• attacks a **methane** molecule: $Cl\bullet + CH_4 \rightarrow \bullet CH_3 + HCl$
2) The new **methyl free radical**, $\bullet CH_3$, can attack another Cl_2 molecule: $\bullet CH_3 + Cl_2 \rightarrow CH_3Cl + Cl\bullet$
3) The new Cl• can attack **another** CH_4 molecule, and so on, until all the Cl_2 or CH_4 molecules are wiped out.

Termination reactions — free radicals are mopped up.

1) If two free radicals join together, they make a **stable molecule**.
2) There are **heaps** of possible termination reactions. Here are a couple of them to give you the idea:

$$Cl\bullet + \bullet CH_3 \rightarrow CH_3Cl$$
$$\bullet CH_3 + \bullet CH_3 \rightarrow C_2H_6$$

Some products formed will be trace impurities in the final sample.

The reaction between bromine and methane works in exactly the same way.
$$CH_4 + Br_2 \xrightarrow{UV} CH_3Br + HBr$$

Reactions of Alkanes

The Problem is — You End Up With a **Mixture of Products**

1) The big problem with free radical substitution if you're trying to make a **particular product** is that you **don't only get** the product you're after, but a **mixture of products**.
2) For example, if you're trying to make chloromethane and there's **too much chlorine** in the reaction mixture, some of the remaining **hydrogen atoms** on the **chloromethane molecule** will be swapped for chlorine atoms. The propagation reactions happen again, this time to make **dichloromethane**.

$$Cl\bullet + CH_3Cl \rightarrow \bullet CH_2Cl + HCl$$

$$\bullet CH_2Cl + Cl_2 \rightarrow CH_2Cl_2 + Cl\bullet$$

dichloromethane

3) It doesn't stop there. Another substitution reaction can take place to form **trichloromethane**.

$$Cl\bullet + CH_2Cl_2 \rightarrow \bullet CHCl_2 + HCl$$

$$\bullet CHCl_2 + Cl_2 \rightarrow CHCl_3 + Cl\bullet$$

trichloromethane

4) **Tetrachloromethane** (CCl_4) is formed in the last possible substitution. There are no more hydrogens attached to the carbon atom, so the substitution process has to stop.
5) So the end product is a mixture of CH_3Cl, CH_2Cl_2, $CHCl_3$ and CCl_4. This is a nuisance, because you have to **separate** the **chloromethane** from the other three unwanted by-products.
6) The best way of reducing the chance of these by-products forming is to have an **excess of methane**. This means there's a greater chance of a chlorine radical colliding only with a **methane molecule** and not a **chloromethane molecule**.
7) Another problem with free radical substitution is that it can take place at any point along the **carbon chain**. So a mixture of **isomers** can be formed. For example, reacting **propane** with chlorine will produce a mixture of **1-chloropropane** and **2-chloropropane**.

Practice Questions

Q1 What's a free radical?

Q2 What's homolytic fission?

Q3 Write down the chemical equation for the free radical substitution reaction between methane and chlorine.

Q4 Write down three possible products, other than chloromethane, from the photochemical reaction between CH_4 and Cl_2.

Exam Question

Q1 When irradiated with UV light, methane gas will react with bromine to form a mixture of several organic compounds.

a) Name the type of mechanism involved in this reaction. [1 mark]

b) Write an overall equation to show the formation of bromomethane from methane and bromine. [1 mark]

c) Write down the two equations in the propagation step for the formation of CH_3Br. [2 marks]

d) i) Explain why a tiny amount of ethane is found in the product mixture. [1 mark]

ii) Name the mechanistic step that leads to the formation of ethane. [1 mark]

iii) Write the equation for the formation of ethane in this reaction. [1 mark]

e) Name the major product formed when a large excess of bromine reacts with methane in the presence of UV light. [1 mark]

This page is like... totally radical, man...

Mechanisms can be an absolute pain in the bum to learn, but unfortunately reactions are what Chemistry's all about. If you don't like it, you should have taken art — no mechanisms in that, just pretty pictures. Not that mechanisms can't be pretty pictures too... Ah well, there's no going back now. Keep hacking away at it, till you know it all off by heart.

Crude Oil

Crude oil is a big mixture of hydrocarbons. Some parts of the mixture are useful, like the hydrocarbons that make up petrol and diesel, but some aren't. Luckily, it's possible to convert the less useful parts into more usable compounds.

Crude Oil is Mainly Alkanes

1) **Petroleum** is just a fancy word for **crude oil** — the sticky black stuff they get out of the ground with oil wells.
2) Petroleum is a mixture of **hydrocarbons**. It's mostly made up of **alkanes**. They range from **small alkanes**, like pentane, to **massive alkanes** of more than 50 carbons.
3) Crude oil isn't very useful as it is, but you can **separate** it out into useful bits (**fractions**) by **fractional distillation**.

Here's how fractional distillation works — don't try this at home.

1) First, the crude oil is **vaporised** at about 350 °C.
2) The vaporised crude oil goes into a **fractionating column** and rises up through the trays. The largest hydrocarbons don't **vaporise** at all, because their boiling points are too high — they just run to the bottom and form a gooey **residue**.
3) As the crude oil vapour goes up the fractionating column, it gets **cooler**. Because the alkane molecules have different chain lengths, they have different **boiling points**, so each fraction **condenses** at a different temperature. The fractions are **drawn off** at different levels in the column.
4) The hydrocarbons with the **lowest boiling points** don't condense. They're drawn off as **gases** at the top of the column.

You might do fractional distillation in the lab, but if you do you'll use a safer crude oil substitute instead.

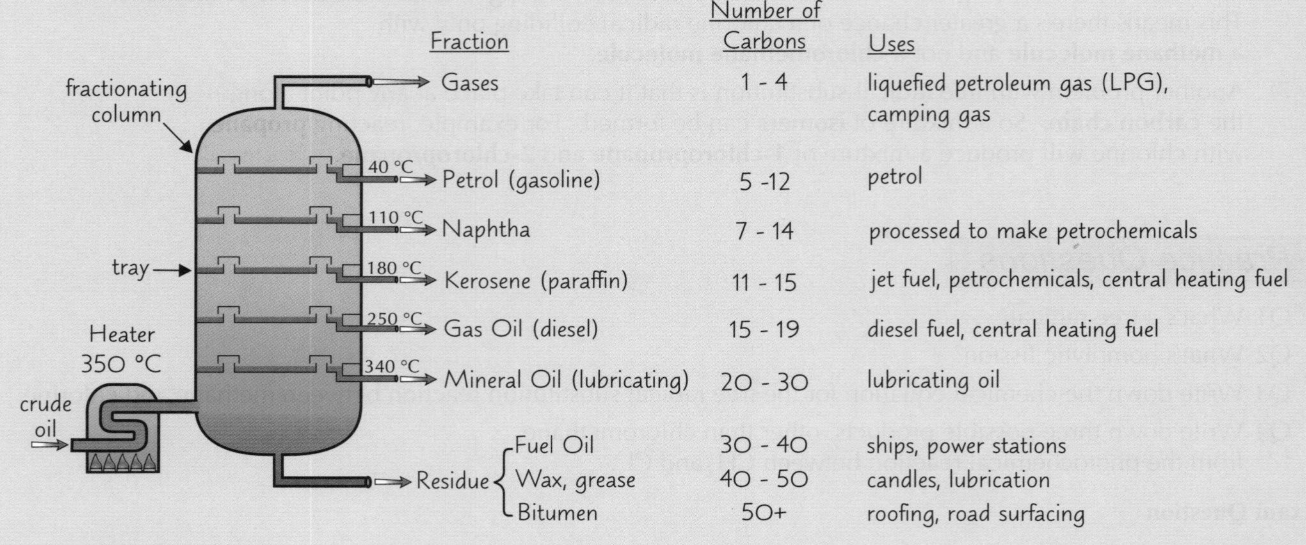

Fraction	Number of Carbons	Uses
Gases	1 - 4	liquefied petroleum gas (LPG), camping gas
Petrol (gasoline)	5 -12	petrol
Naphtha	7 - 14	processed to make petrochemicals
Kerosene (paraffin)	11 - 15	jet fuel, petrochemicals, central heating fuel
Gas Oil (diesel)	15 - 19	diesel fuel, central heating fuel
Mineral Oil (lubricating)	20 - 30	lubricating oil
Residue: Fuel Oil	30 - 40	ships, power stations
Residue: Wax, grease	40 - 50	candles, lubrication
Residue: Bitumen	50+	roofing, road surfacing

Heavy Fractions can be 'Cracked' to Make Smaller Molecules

1) People want loads of the **light** fractions of crude oil, like petrol and naphtha. They don't want so much of the **heavier** stuff like bitumen though. Stuff that's in high demand is much more **valuable** than the stuff that isn't.
2) To meet this demand, the less popular heavier fractions are **cracked**. Cracking is **breaking** long-chain alkanes into **smaller** hydrocarbons (which can include alkenes). It involves breaking the **C–C bonds**.

For example, **decane** could crack like this:

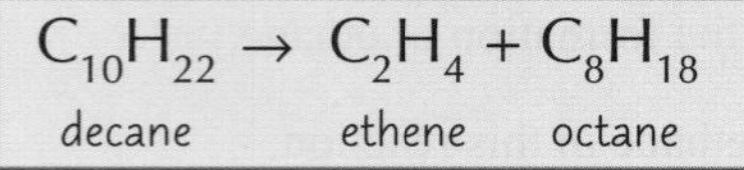

$$C_{10}H_{22} \rightarrow C_2H_4 + C_8H_{18}$$

decane ethene octane

Where the chain breaks is random, so you'll get a different mixture of products every time you crack a hydrocarbon.

Thermal cracking and **catalytic cracking** are two types of cracking:

Thermal Cracking Produces Lots of Alkenes

1) **Thermal cracking** takes place at **high temperature** (up to 1000 °C) and **high pressure** (up to 70 atm).
2) It produces a lot of **alkenes**.
3) These **alkenes** are used to make heaps of valuable products, like **polymers** (plastics). A good example is **poly(ethene)**, which is made from ethene.

Crude Oil

Catalytic Cracking Produces Lots of Aromatic Compounds

1) Catalytic cracking uses something called a **zeolite catalyst** (**hydrated aluminosilicate**), at a **slight pressure** and **high temperature** (about 450 °C).
2) It mostly produces **aromatic** hydrocarbons and **motor fuels.**
3) Using a catalyst **cuts costs**, because the reaction can be done at a **low** pressure and a **lower** temperature. The catalyst also **speeds** up the reaction, saving time (and time is money).

Aromatic compounds contain benzene rings. Benzene rings contain a ring of 6 carbon atoms with delocalised ring of electrons. But don't worry about this too much now. You'll only meet them again if you're doing the A-Level course.

Alkanes can be Reformed into Cycloalkanes and Aromatic Hydrocarbons

1) Most people's cars run on petrol or diesel, both of which contain a mixture of alkanes (as well as other hydrocarbons, impurities and additives).
2) Some of the alkanes in petrol are **straight-chain** alkanes, e.g. hexane — $CH_3CH_2CH_2CH_2CH_2CH_3$.
3) **Knocking** is where alkanes **explode** of their own accord when the fuel/air mixture in the engine is compressed. Straight chain alkanes are the **most likely** hydrocarbons to cause knocking. Adding branched chain and cyclic hydrocarbons to the petrol mixture makes knocking **less likely** to happen, so combustion is more **efficient**.
4) You can convert straight-chain alkanes into branched chain alkanes and cyclic hydrocarbons by **reforming**. This uses a catalyst (e.g. platinum stuck on aluminium oxide).

Hexane can be reformed into cyclohexane and hydrogen gas, which can be reformed into benzene (C_6H_6) and hydrogen gas:

$$\underset{\text{hexane}}{CH_3CH_2CH_2CH_2CH_2CH_3} \xrightarrow{Pt} \underset{\text{cyclohexane} + H_2}{\text{cyclohexane}} \longrightarrow \underset{\text{benzene} + 3H_2}{\text{benzene}}$$

Octane can be reformed into 2,4-dimethylhexane:

$$\underset{\text{octane}}{CH_3CH_2CH_2CH_2CH_2CH_2CH_2CH_3} \xrightarrow{Pt} \underset{\text{2,5-dimethylhexane}}{CH_3CH(CH_3)CH_2CH_2CH(CH_3)CH_3}$$

Practice Questions

Q1 How does fractional distillation work?

Q2 What is cracking?

Q3 Why is reforming used?

Exam Question

Q1 Crude oil is a source of fuels and petrochemicals.
It's vaporised and separated into fractions using fractional distillation.

a) Some heavier fractions are processed using cracking.

i) Explain why cracking is carried out. [2 marks]

ii) Write a possible equation for the cracking of dodecane, $C_{12}H_{26}$. [1 mark]

b) Some hydrocarbons present in petrol are processed using reforming.

i) Name two types of compound that are produced by reforming. [2 marks]

ii) What effect do these compounds have on the petrol's performance? [1 mark]

Crude oil — not the kind of oil you could take home to meet your mother...

This isn't the most exciting topic in the history of the known universe. Although in a galaxy far, far away there may be lots of pages on more boring topics. Imagine a planet where you had to read three pages on crude oil... Yuck... Get fractional distillation and cracking straight in your brain and make sure you know why people bother to do it.

Alkanes and Fuels

Alkanes are absolutely fantastic as fuels. Except for the fact that they produce loads of nasty pollutant gases.

Alkanes** are Useful **Fuels

1) If you burn (**oxidise**) alkanes (and other hydrocarbons) with **plenty of oxygen**, you get **carbon dioxide** and water — it's a **combustion reaction**.

For example, here's the equation for the combustion of propane: $C_3H_{8(g)} + 5O_{2(g)} \rightarrow 3CO_{2(g)} + 4H_2O_{(g)}$

2) This is **complete combustion** — the only products are **water** and **carbon dioxide**. (There's also incomplete combustion, which is really bad — see below.)
3) Alkanes make great **fuels** — burning just a small amount releases a humongous amount **of energy**.
4) They're burnt in power stations, central heating systems and, of course, to power car engines.
5) They do have a downside though — burning alkanes also produces lots of **pollutants**. Handily, that's what the rest of this topic is all about...

Incomplete Combustion** Happens When There's Not Enough **Oxygen

If there's not enough oxygen around, hydrocarbons combust **incompletely**.
This changes the **products** of the reaction and can lead to some nasty side effects.

Carbon Monoxide

- When a hydrocarbon undergoes incomplete combustion, you can get **carbon monoxide** gas instead of, or as well as, carbon dioxide. For example:

$CH_{4(g)} + 1½O_{2(g)} \rightarrow CO_{(g)} + 2H_2O_{(g)}$

$C_8H_{18(g)} + 10½O_{2(g)} \rightarrow 4CO_{2(g)} + 4CO_{(g)} + 9H_2O_{(g)}$

- This is bad news because carbon monoxide gas is **poisonous**. Carbon monoxide molecules bind to the same sites on **haemoglobin molecules** in red blood cells as oxygen molecules. So **oxygen** can't be carried around the body.
- Luckily, carbon monoxide can be removed from exhaust gases by **catalytic converters** on cars.

Carbon

- **Carbon particles** (**soot**) can also be formed by incomplete combustion. For example:

$CH_4 + O_2 \rightarrow C + 2H_2O$

- Soot is thought to cause **breathing problems**. It can also build up in **engines**, meaning they don't work properly.

*Burning Fossil Fuels Contributes to **Global Warming***

1) Burning fossil fuels produces **carbon dioxide**. Carbon dioxide is a **greenhouse gas**.
2) The greenhouse gases in our atmosphere are really good at absorbing **infrared energy** (**heat**). They emit some of the energy they absorb back towards the Earth, keeping it warm. This is called the **greenhouse effect**.
3) Most scientists agree that by **increasing** the amount of carbon dioxide in our atmosphere, we are making the Earth **warmer**.
4) This process is known as **global warming**.

Marjorie loved her new green-house effect.

Alkanes and Fuels

Unburnt Hydrocarbons and *Oxides of Nitrogen* Can Cause *Smog*

1) Engines **don't burn** all of the fuel molecules. Some of them will come out as **unburnt hydrocarbons**.
2) **Oxides of nitrogen** (**NO_x**) are produced when the high **pressure** and **temperature** in a car engine cause the nitrogen and oxygen atoms from the air to react together.
3) Hydrocarbons and nitrogen oxides react in the presence of sunlight to form **ground-level ozone** (O_3), which is a major component of **smog**. **Ground-level ozone** irritates people's eyes, aggravates respiratory problems and even causes lung damage (ozone isn't nice stuff, unless it is high up in the atmosphere as part of the ozone layer).
4) **Catalytic converters** on cars remove unburnt hydrocarbons and oxides of nitrogen from the exhaust.

As if That's Not Bad Enough...Acid Rain is Caused by Sulfur Dioxide

1) Some fossil fuels contain **sulfur**. When they are burnt, the sulfur reacts to form **sulfur dioxide gas** (SO_2).
2) Sulfur dioxide is a bit of a nasty beast. If it gets into the atmosphere, it dissolves in the moisture and is converted into **sulfuric acid**. This is what causes **acid rain**.

The same process occurs when nitrogen oxides escape into the atmosphere — nitric acid is produced.

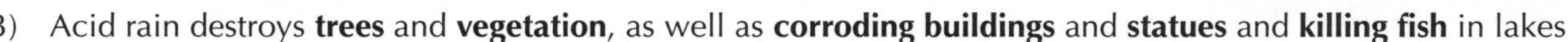

3) Acid rain destroys **trees** and **vegetation**, as well as **corroding buildings** and **statues** and **killing fish** in lakes.

Fortunately, sulfur dioxide can be **removed** from power station flue gases before it gets into the atmosphere. Powdered **calcium carbonate** (limestone) or **calcium oxide** is mixed with water to make an **alkaline slurry**. When the flue gases mix with the alkaline slurry, the **acidic sulfur dioxide** gas reacts with the calcium compounds to form a harmless salt (**calcium sulfate**) — see page 38 for more on this.

Fossil Fuels are *Non-Renewable*

The various kinds of pollution produced by burning these fuels aren't the only problems. They're also becoming more and more scarce as we use more and more of them.

1) The three fossil fuels (**coal**, **oil**, and **natural gas**) are major fuels. They're relatively **easily extracted** and produce a **large amount** of energy when burnt. But, there's a finite amount of them and they're running out.
2) Oil will be the first to go — and as it gets really scarce, it'll become more **expensive**. It's not **sustainable** to keep using fossil fuels willy-nilly.

We Need to be Thinking About Fuels for the Future

1) In the **short term**, it makes sense to be as **economical** with our fuel use as we realistically can — to reduce **pollution** and its effects, and also to **eke out** our decreasing reserves of fossil fuels.
2) But in the **long term**, we're going to have to find more **sustainable** sources of energy. There are various possibilities. None of them is ideal in every way, but each might earn a place in the '**energy mix**' in the future.
3) Developing more sustainable energy sources is a task that will involve all kinds of **scientists** for a long time.

Wind, Solar, and Wave Power

'Renewable' means it won't run out.

1) Examples of renewable fuels include **wind**, **solar**, and **wave** power.
2) As well as being **renewable**, these are also **carbon neutral**, so they don't add **greenhouse gases** (or any other pollution) into the atmosphere.
   However, CO_2 will still be given out during the manufacture of solar panels, wind turbines etc.
3) But there are objections, including:
   - they're not sufficiently **reliable** (it's not always windy or sunny, for example),
   - it takes an **awful lot** of wind turbines, solar panels or wave energy collectors to get even a fraction of the energy currently supplied by fossil fuels.

Biofuels are another type of renewable fuel, made from living matter over a short period of time (see pages 140-141 for more on biofuel).

Alkanes and Fuels

We Could Use More **Hydrogen**

However, oxides of nitrogen (see p. 128) will also be produced if hydrogen is burnt in air at high temperatures.

1) Hydrogen gas can either be **burned** in a modified engine, or used in a **fuel cell**. (A **fuel cell** converts hydrogen and oxygen into **water**, and this chemical process produces **electricity**.) Either way, the big advantage is that **water** is the only waste product.
2) Hydrogen can be obtained from **seawater** — but it takes **energy** to extract it. This is why it's more accurate in some ways to think of hydrogen as an '**energy carrier**' rather than a true '**energy source**'.
3) The method used to extract the hydrogen determines how environmentally friendly the fuel is. If the energy used comes from a **renewable** source, say wind or solar, hydrogen fuel will be pretty much **carbon neutral** (except for the carbon emitted when making the solar panels, wind turbines etc.).
4) There are difficulties in **transporting** and **storing** hydrogen. It's highly **flammable**, and it has to be **liquified** due to the **low energy to volume ratio** of hydrogen gas. It will also mean building a whole new fuel supply **infrastructure** (chemical plants to produce the hydrogen fuel, a network of refuelling stations, pipelines...).

Practice Questions

Q1 Which two compounds are produced when an alkane burns completely?

Q2 Under what conditions does incomplete combustion of a fuel take place?

Q3 Name four pollutants that can be produced when a fuel is burnt. For each pollutant you have named, give one environmental problem that it causes.

Q4 Describe how burning fossil fuels causes acid rain.

Q5 What is meant by a 'renewable' fuel?

Q6 Explain why hydrogen from seawater is more of an 'energy carrier' than a true 'energy source'.

Exam Questions

Q1 Heptane, C_7H_{16}, is an alkane present in some fuels.

a) Write a balanced equation for the complete combustion of heptane. [1 mark]

b) Fuels often contain compounds called oxygenates which are added to ensure that the fuel burns completely.

i) What poisonous compound is produced by incomplete combustion of alkanes like heptane? [1 mark]

ii) Apart from adding oxygenates, how else can this compound be removed from car exhaust gases? [1 mark]

Q2 Burning fossil fuels produces a variety of gaseous pollutants, such as oxides of nitrogen and sulfur dioxide.

a) Explain how oxides of nitrogen are produced in car engines. [2 marks]

b) Explain how sulfur dioxide can be removed from power station flue gases using calcium carbonate. [2 marks]

Q3 a) Describe two disadvantages associated with the continued large-scale use of fossil fuels as an energy source. [2 marks]

b) Describe one advantage and one disadvantage of the following fossil fuel alternatives:

i) wind power [2 marks]

ii) hydrogen [2 marks]

Fuel me once, shame on you; fuel me twice, shame on me...

It's a tricky one. There probably aren't many people who'd be willing to give up energy being 'on tap' like it is here at the moment. And that means that countries everywhere are going to need to make sure they've got reliable supplies of (hopefully clean) energy. So I'm sure you'll be meeting renewable fuels again, and not just in your chemistry exams...

Halogenoalkanes

Don't worry if you see halogenoalkanes called haloalkanes. It's a government conspiracy to confuse you.

Halogenoalkanes are *Alkanes* with *Halogen* Atoms

A **halogenoalkane** is an alkane with at least one **halogen atom** in place of a hydrogen atom.

E.g.

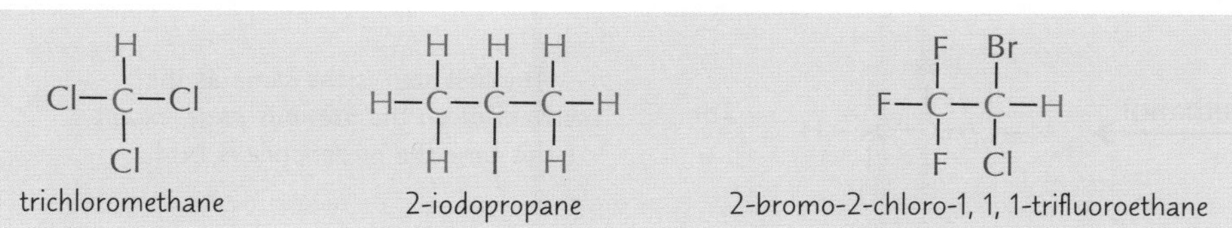

There's more about how to name organic compounds, including halogenoalkanes, on pages 110-111.

The *Carbon–Halogen Bond* in Halogenoalkanes is *Polar*

1) Halogens are much more **electronegative** than carbon, so carbon-halogen bonds are **polar**.
2) The δ+ charge on the carbon makes it prone to attacks from **nucleophiles**.
3) A nucleophile is an **electron-pair donor**.
   It donates an electron pair to somewhere without enough electrons.
4) OH^-, CN^- and NH_3 are all **nucleophiles** that can react with halogenoalkanes.

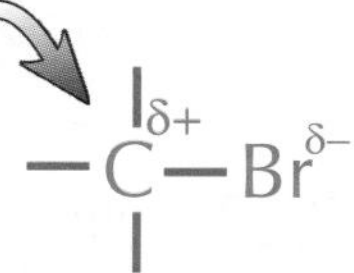

Halogenoalkanes Can Undergo *Nucleophilic Substitution* Reactions

1) A nucleophile can react with a polar molecule by kicking out the functional group and taking its place.
2) This is called a **nucleophilic substitution reaction**. It works like this:

Curly arrows show the movement of electron pairs.

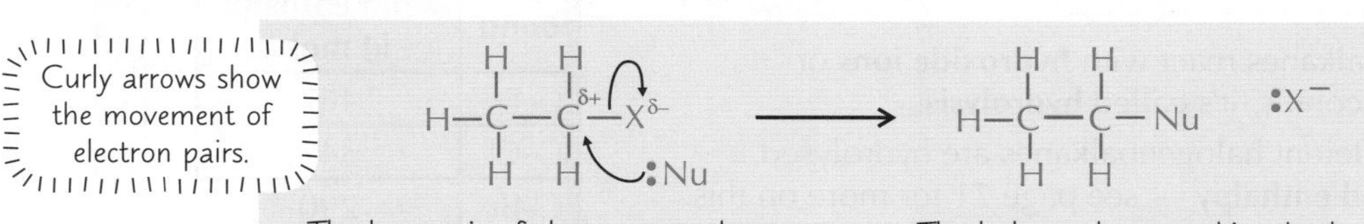

The lone pair of electrons on the nucleophile attacks the δ+ carbon. The C–X bond breaks.

The halogen leaves, taking both electrons with it. A new bond forms between the carbon and the nucleophile.

X stands for one of the halogens (F, Cl, Br or I). **Nu** stands for a nucleophile.

3) The **product** of these reactions depends on what the **nucleophile** is...

Halogenoalkanes React with *Hydroxides* to Form *Alcohols*

For example, bromoethane can react to form ethanol. You have to use **warm aqueous sodium** or **potassium hydroxide** — it's a **nucleophilic substitution reaction**.

This is sometimes called hydrolysis, because exactly the same reaction will happen with water. (Hydrolysis means splitting a molecule apart by reacting it with water.)

Here's how it happens:

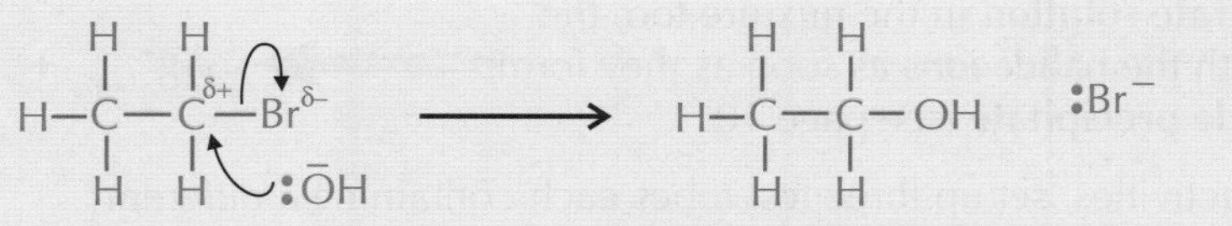

The δ+ carbon attracts a lone pair of electrons from the OH^- ion. The C–Br bond breaks.

The bromine leaves, taking both electrons to become Br^-. A new bond forms between the carbon and the OH^- ion, making an alcohol.

Nitriles Are Formed by Reacting Halogenoalkanes with *Cyanide*

Nitriles have –C≡N groups.

If you **warm** a halogenoalkane with **ethanolic potassium cyanide** (potassium cyanide dissolved in ethanol) you get a **nitrile**. It's yet another **nucleophilic substitution reaction** — the **cyanide ion**, CN^-, is the **nucleophile**.

$$CH_3CH_2^{\delta+}Br^{\delta-} + :\bar{C}\equiv N \xrightarrow[\text{ethanol}]{\text{reflux}} CH_3CH_2CN + :Br^-$$

This follows the same pattern — the lone pair of electrons on the CN^- ion attacks the δ+ carbon, the C–Br bond breaks and the bromine leaves. The carbon chain increases by one.

Halogenoalkanes

Reacting Halogenoalkanes with **Ammonia** Forms **Amines**

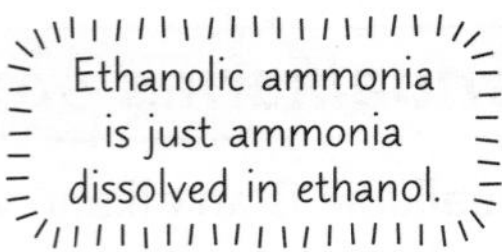
Ethanolic ammonia is just ammonia dissolved in ethanol.

1) If you **warm** a halogenoalkane with excess **ethanolic** ammonia, the **ammonia** swaps places with the **halogen** — yes, it's another one of these **nucleophilic substitution reactions**.

The first step is the same as the mechanism on the previous page, except this time the nucleophile is NH_3.

$$CH_3CH_2Br + NH_3 \xrightarrow{\text{ethanol}} CH_3CH_2NH_3^+ + :Br^-$$

In the second step, an ammonia molecule removes a hydrogen from the NH_3 group, forming an amine and an ammonium ion (NH_4^+).

$$CH_3CH_2NH_3^+ + :NH_3 \rightleftharpoons CH_3CH_2NH_2 + NH_4^+$$

2) The ammonium ion can react with the bromine ion to form ammonium bromide. So the overall reaction looks like this:

$$CH_3CH_2Br + 2NH_3 \xrightarrow{\text{ethanol}} CH_3CH_2NH_2 + NH_4Br$$

3) The **amine group** in the product still has a lone pair of electrons. This means that it can also act as a **nucleophile** — so it may react with halogenoalkane molecules itself, giving a mixture of products.

Iodoalkanes Are *Substituted* the *Fastest*

1) When halogenoalkanes react with **hydroxide ions** or **water** to form alcohols, it's called **hydrolysis**.
2) How quickly different halogenoalkanes are hydrolysed depends on **bond enthalpy** — see page 71 for more on this.
3) **Weaker** carbon-halogen bonds **break** more easily, so they react **faster**.

bond	bond enthalpy kJ mol^{-1}
C–F	467
C–Cl	346
C–Br	290
C–I	228

Faster hydrolysis as bond enthalpy decreases (the bonds are getting weaker).

4) **Iodoalkanes** have the **weakest bonds**, so they hydrolyse the **fastest**.
5) **Fluoroalkanes** have the **strongest bonds**, so they're the **slowest** at hydrolysing.
6) You can **compare the reactivity** of chloroalkanes, bromoalkanes and iodoalkanes by doing an experiment:

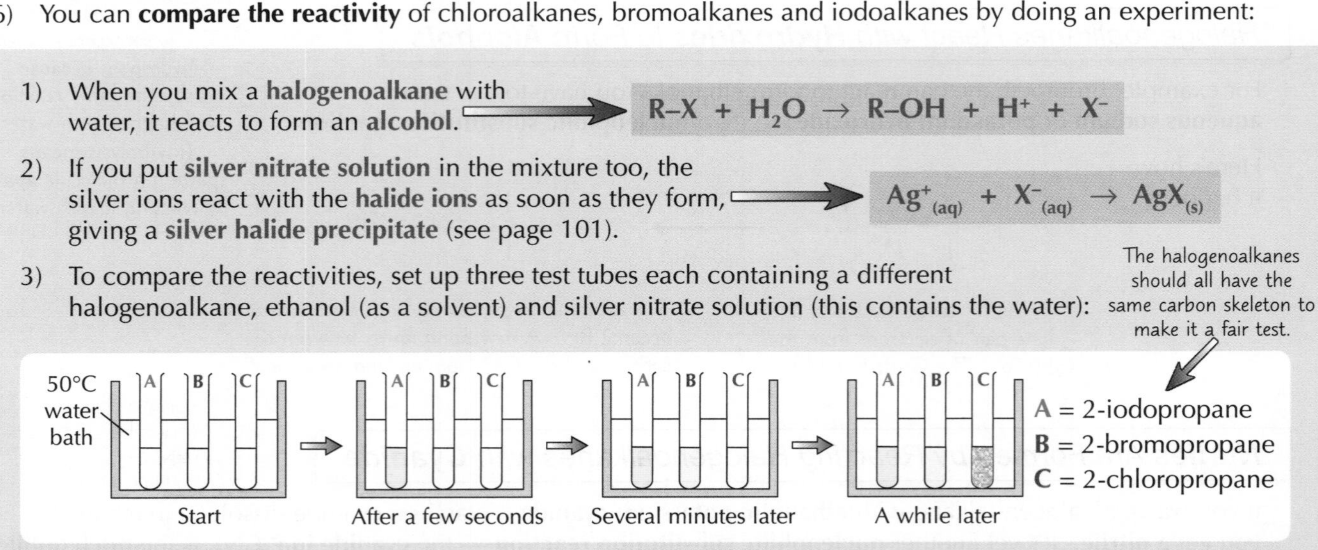

1) When you mix a **halogenoalkane** with water, it reacts to form an **alcohol**. → $R\text{–}X + H_2O \rightarrow R\text{–}OH + H^+ + X^-$
2) If you put **silver nitrate solution** in the mixture too, the silver ions react with the **halide ions** as soon as they form, giving a **silver halide precipitate** (see page 101). → $Ag^+_{(aq)} + X^-_{(aq)} \rightarrow AgX_{(s)}$
3) To compare the reactivities, set up three test tubes each containing a different halogenoalkane, ethanol (as a solvent) and silver nitrate solution (this contains the water):

The halogenoalkanes should all have the same carbon skeleton to make it a fair test.

4) A pale yellow precipitate quickly forms with **2-iodopropane** — so iodoalkanes must be the **most reactive halogenoalkanes**. **Bromoalkanes** react slower than iodoalkanes to form a cream precipitate, and **chloroalkanes** form a white precipitate the slowest of all.

7) You can also use this reaction to compare the rate of hydrolysis, and therefore the reactivities, of **primary**, **secondary** and **tertiary halogenoalkanes** (see next page).

Halogenoalkanes

Halogenoalkanes can be **Primary**, **Secondary** or **Tertiary**

Halogenoalkanes with just **one halogen atom** can be **primary**, **secondary** or **tertiary** halogenoalkanes.

On the **carbon** with the **halogen** attached:

1) A **primary** halogenoalkane has **two hydrogen atoms** and just **one alkyl group**.
2) A **secondary** halogenoalkane has **just one hydrogen atom** and **two alkyl groups**.
3) A **tertiary** halogenoalkane has **no hydrogen atoms** and **three alkyl groups**.

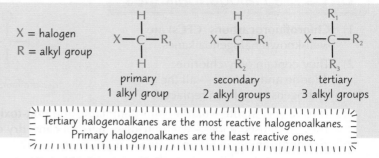

X = halogen
R = alkyl group

$X-CH_2-R_1$	$X-CH(R_2)-R_1$	$X-C(R_1)(R_3)-R_2$
primary 1 alkyl group	secondary 2 alkyl groups	tertiary 3 alkyl groups

Tertiary halogenoalkanes are the most reactive halogenoalkanes. Primary halogenoalkanes are the least reactive ones.

Halogenoalkanes also Undergo **Elimination Reactions**

1) If you warm a halogenoalkane with hydroxide ions dissolved in **ethanol** instead of water, an **elimination reaction** happens, and you end up with an **alkene**.
2) You have to heat the mixture **under reflux** or you'll lose volatile stuff.

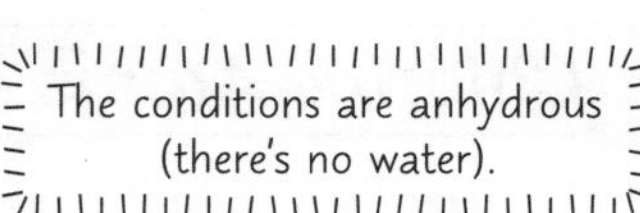
The conditions are anhydrous
(there's no water).

$$H_3C-CHBr^{\delta-}-CH_3 \;(C^{\delta+}) + :OH^- \longrightarrow H_2C=CHCH_3 + H_2O + :Br^-$$

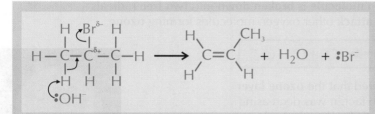

1) OH^- acts as a base and takes a proton, H^+, from the carbon on the left. This makes water.
2) The left carbon now has a spare electron, so it forms a double bond with the middle carbon.
3) To form the double bond, the middle carbon has to let go of the Br, which drops off as a Br^- ion.

3) If you use 2-bromopropane and potassium hydroxide, the equation for the reaction will look like this:

$$CH_3CHBrCH_3 + KOH \xrightarrow[\text{reflux}]{\text{ethanol}} CH_2CHCH_3 + H_2O + KBr$$

4) This is an example of an **elimination reaction**. In an elimination reaction, a **small group** of atoms breaks away from a molecule. This group is **not replaced** by anything else (whereas it would be in a substitution reaction). For example, in the reaction above, H and Br have been eliminated from $CH_3CHBrCH_3$ to leave CH_2CHCH_3.

Practice Questions

Q1 Why are carbon-halogen bonds polar?

Q2 Why does iodoethane react faster than chloroethane with nucleophiles?

Q3 Draw the mechanism for the reaction of bromoethane with potassium hydroxide dissolved in ethanol.

Exam Question

Q1 Three reactions of 2-bromopropane, $CH_3CHBrCH_3$, are shown below.

$$CH_3CHBrCH_3 \xrightarrow{\text{reaction 1}} CH_3CH(OH)CH_3$$
$$CH_3CHBrCH_3 \xrightarrow{\text{reaction 2}} CH_3CH(NH_2)CH_3$$
$$CH_3CHBrCH_3 \xrightarrow{\text{reaction 3}} CH_2{=}CHCH_3$$

a) For each reaction, name the reagent and the solvent used. [6 marks]

b) Under the same conditions, 2-iodopropane was used in reaction 1 in place of 2-bromopropane. What difference (if any) would you expect in the rate of the reaction? Explain your answer. [2 marks]

If you don't read this — you will be eliminated. Resistance is nitrile...

*Another nice mechanism on this page. I don't know about you, but mechanisms are my favourite part of chemistry. Call me mad if you will, but I love those little curly arrows... Hopping about from one place to another, like a little deer hopping through a beautiful, snowy meadow... Before its mother *sniff*... is cruelly shot and... *sniff*...*

Halogenoalkanes and the Environment

Two pages on air pollution coming up, so take a deep breath...
unless you're hanging around somewhere with a lot of air pollution, that is...

CFCs are Halogenoalkanes

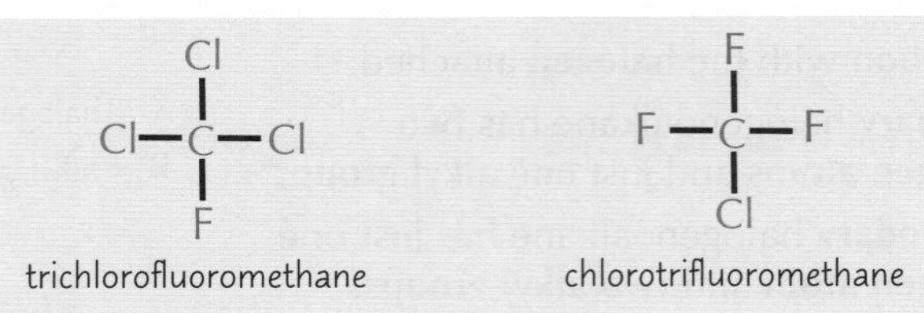

1) **Chlorofluorocarbons** (**CFCs**) are well-known halogenoalkanes.
2) They contain only chlorine, fluorine and carbon — all the hydrogens have been replaced.
3) They're very **stable**, **volatile**, **non-flammable** and **non-toxic**. They were used a lot — e.g. in **fridges**, **aerosol cans**, **dry cleaning**, **air-conditioning** and to make **foamed polymers** — until scientists realised they were destroying the **ozone layer**.

They're stable because of the strength of the carbon-halogen bonds.

Chlorine Atoms are Destroying The Ozone Layer

1) Ozone (O_3) in the upper atmosphere acts as a **chemical sunscreen**. It absorbs a lot of the **ultraviolet radiation** which can cause sunburn or even skin cancer.
2) Ozone's **formed naturally** when an **oxygen molecule** is **broken down** into **two free radicals** by **ultraviolet radiation**. The free radicals **attack** other oxygen molecules forming **ozone**. Just like this:

$$O_2 \xrightarrow{UV} O + O \Longrightarrow O_2 + O \rightarrow O_3$$

3) In the 1970s and 1980s, scientists discovered that the **ozone layer** above **Antarctica** was getting **thinner** — in fact, it was decreasing very rapidly. The ozone layer over the **Arctic** has been found to be thinning too. These 'holes' in the ozone layer are bad because they allow more harmful **UV radiation** to reach the Earth.
4) The 'holes' are formed because **CFCs** in the upper atmosphere absorb UV radiation and split to form **chlorine free radicals**. These free radicals **catalyse** the destruction of ozone — they **destroy ozone molecules** and are then **regenerated** to destroy more ozone. One chlorine atom can destroy 10 000 ozone molecules before it forms a stable compound. Here's what happens:

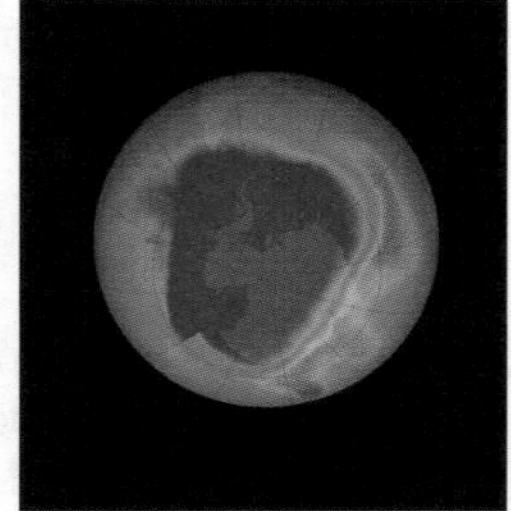
Here's a satellite map showing the 'hole' in the ozone layer over Antarctica. The 'hole' is shown by the blue area.

- **Chlorine free radicals**, Cl•, are formed when the C–Cl bonds in **CFCs** are broken down by **ultraviolet radiation**. E.g. $CF_2Cl_{2(g)} \xrightarrow{UV} \cdot CF_2Cl_{(g)} + Cl\cdot_{(g)}$
- These free radicals are **catalysts**. They react with **ozone** to form an **intermediate** (ClO•) and an oxygen molecule.

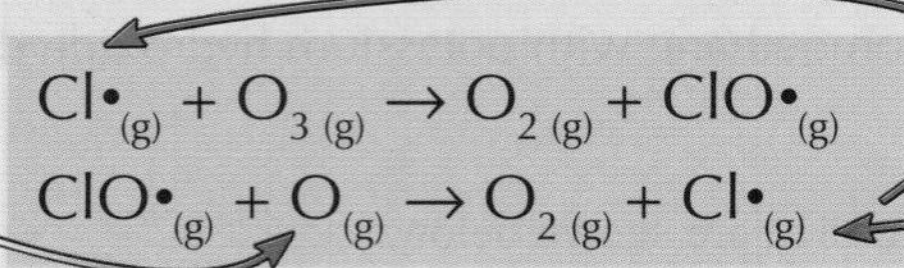

$$Cl\cdot_{(g)} + O_{3\,(g)} \rightarrow O_{2\,(g)} + ClO\cdot_{(g)}$$
$$ClO\cdot_{(g)} + O_{(g)} \rightarrow O_{2\,(g)} + Cl\cdot_{(g)}$$

The O radical comes from the break down of oxygen by ultraviolet radiation.

The chlorine free radical is regenerated. It goes straight on to attack another ozone molecule. It only takes one little chlorine free radical to destroy loads of ozone molecules.

- So the **overall reaction** is... $O_{3\,(g)} + O_{(g)} \rightarrow 2O_{2\,(g)}$ ... and Cl• is the catalyst.

Nitrogen Oxides Can Also Break Ozone Down

1) **NO• free radicals** from **nitrogen oxides** destroy ozone too. Nitrogen oxides are produced by **car and aircraft engines** and **thunderstorms**. NO• free radicals affect ozone in the **same way** as chlorine radicals.
2) The reactions can be represented by these equations, where **R** represents either Cl• or NO•. In both cases, the free radicals act as **catalysts** for the destruction of the ozone.
The overall reaction is: $O_3 + O \rightarrow 2O_2$

$$\mathbf{R} + O_3 \rightarrow \mathbf{RO} + O_2$$
$$\mathbf{RO} + O \rightarrow \mathbf{R} + O_2$$

Formed when UV breaks down O_2.

The harmful radical is regenerated.

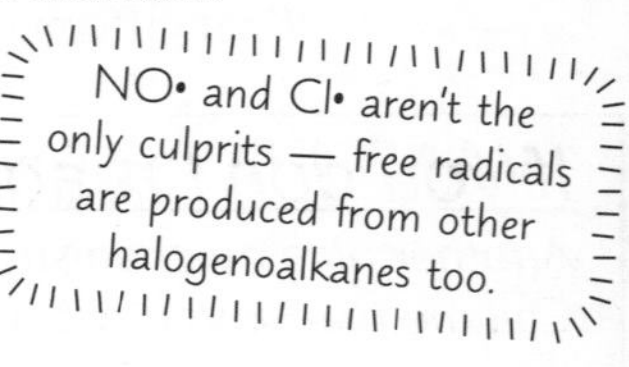

NO• and Cl• aren't the only culprits — free radicals are produced from other halogenoalkanes too.

Halogenoalkanes and the Environment

Chemists Developed **Alternatives** to **CFCs**

1) In the 1970s scientists discovered that CFCs were causing **damage** to the **ozone layer**. The **advantages** of CFCs couldn't outweigh the **environmental problems** they were causing, so they were **banned**.
2) The **Montreal Protocol** of 1989 was an **international treaty** to phase out the use of CFCs and other ozone-destroying halogenoalkanes by the year 2000. There were a few **permitted uses** such as in medical inhalers and in fire extinguishers used in submarines.
3) Scientists supported the treaty, and worked on finding **alternatives** to CFCs.
   - **HCFCs (hydrochlorofluorocarbons)** and **HFCs (hydrofluorocarbons)** are being used as temporary alternatives to CFCs until safer products are developed.
   - **Hydrocarbons** are also used.
   - **HCFCs** are broken down in the atmosphere in 10-20 years. They still damage the ozone layer, but their effect is much smaller than CFCs.
   - **HFCs** are also broken down in the atmosphere. Unlike HCFCs, they **don't** contain **chlorine**, so they don't affect the ozone layer.
   - Unfortunately, **HFCs and HCFCs are greenhouse gases** (see page 122) — they're 1000 times worse than carbon dioxide.
   - Some **hydrocarbons** are being used in fridges but these are greenhouse gases too.
   - Nowadays, most aerosols have been replaced by **pump spray systems** or use **nitrogen** as the propellant. Many industrial fridges and freezers now use **ammonia** as the coolant gas, and **carbon dioxide** is used to make foamed polymers.
4) These substances do have **drawbacks**, but they're currently the **least environmentally damaging** of all the alternatives.
5) The ozone holes **still** form in the spring but are slowly shrinking — so things are looking up.

Practice Questions

Q1 What is a CFC?

Q2 Describe how ozone is beneficial.

Q3 Write equations to show how ozone is formed.

Q4 Write equations to show how ozone is destroyed, using R to represent the radical.

Q5 Name two alternatives to CFCs.

Exam Questions

Q1 Trichlorofluoromethane ($CFCl_3$) is a CFC that was once used widely as an aerosol propellant.

a) What are two useful properties of CFCs? [1 mark]

b) Give equations to show how trichlorofluoromethane catalyses the breakdown of ozone in the upper atmosphere. Your answer should include an equation for the overall reaction. [3 marks]

c) Name another species of free radical responsible for destroying ozone. [1 mark]

Q2 Nitric oxide radicals (NO•) are destructive radicals that can form in the atmosphere. These radicals act as catalysts in the breakdown of ozone. Give equations to show how nitric oxide radicals catalyse the break down of ozone. [2 marks]

WANTED for vandalism — CFCs. Highly volatile, approach with caution...

How scientists found the hole in the ozone layer and used their evidence to instigate government legislation is a great example of How Science Works. The alternatives to CFCs we use now are less stable, so they don't hang around for as long and are less likely to make it to the upper atmosphere. This gives the ozone layer a chance to replenish. Phew.

Alkenes

I'll warn you now — some of this stuff gets a bit heavy — but stick with it, as it's pretty important.

Alkenes are **Unsaturated Hydrocarbons**

1) Alkenes have the **general formula C_nH_{2n}**. They're just made of carbon and hydrogen atoms, so they're **hydrocarbons**.
2) Alkene molecules **all** have at least one **C=C double covalent bond**. Molecules with C=C double bonds are **unsaturated** because they can make more bonds with extra atoms in **addition** reactions.
3) Because there are two pairs of electrons in the C=C double bond, it has a really **high electron density**. This makes alkenes pretty reactive. Here are a few pretty diagrams of **alkenes**:

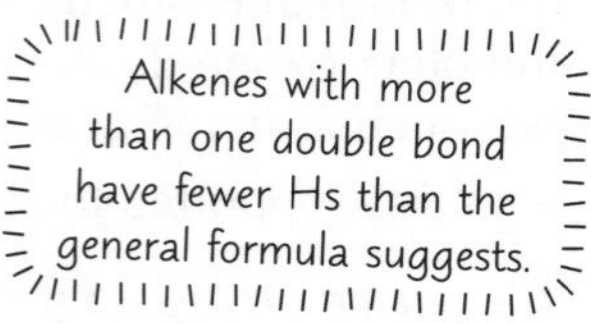

Alkenes with more than one double bond have fewer Hs than the general formula suggests.

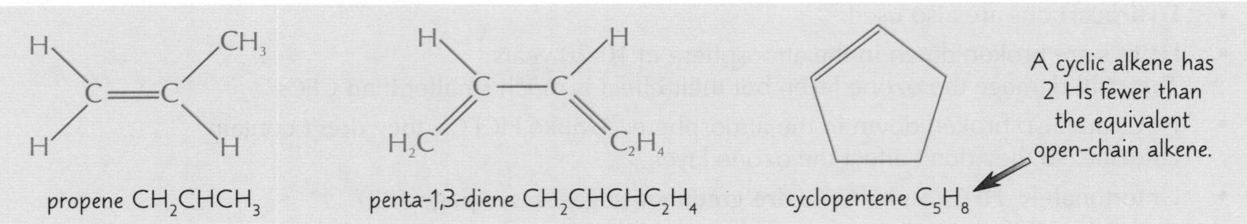

A cyclic alkene has 2 Hs fewer than the equivalent open-chain alkene.
cyclopentene C₅H₈

Bonds in Organic Molecules can be **Sigma** or **Pi Bonds**

Covalent bonds form when **atomic orbitals** from different atoms, each containing a single electron, **overlap**, causing the electrons to become **shared**. A bond forms because the nuclei of the atoms are attracted by **electrostatic attraction** to the bonding electrons. The **way** that atomic orbitals overlap causes different **types** of bond to form.

1) Single covalent bonds in organic molecules are **sigma (σ-) bonds**. A σ-bond is formed when **two orbitals overlap**, in a straight line, in the space between two atoms. This gives the highest possible **electron density** between the two positive nuclei.

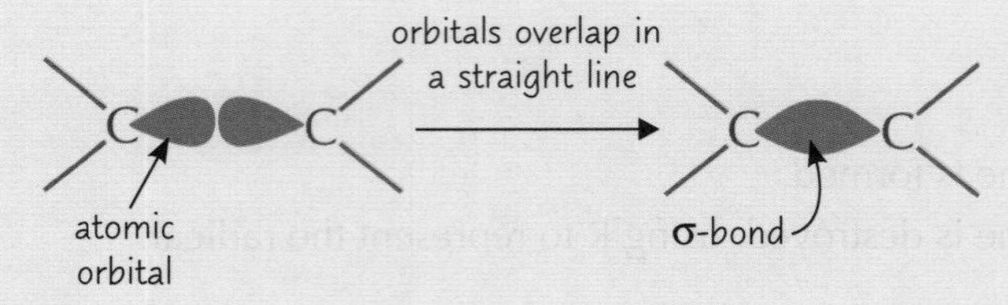

Any type of orbital can form a σ-bond, as long as it points towards the other atom. So you can get σ-bonds made from two s-orbitals, two p-orbitals, one s-orbital and one p-orbital as well as different types of orbitals.

2) The **high electron density** between the nuclei means there is a strong **electrostatic attraction** between the nuclei and the shared pair of electrons. This means that σ-bonds have a high **bond enthalpy** — they're the **strongest** type of covalent bonds.
3) A double bond is made up of a **sigma (σ-) bond** and a **pi (π-) bond**. A **π-bond** is formed when **two lobes** of two orbitals **overlap sideways**. It's got two parts to it — one 'above' and one 'below' the molecular axis. For example, p-orbitals can form π-bonds.
4) In a π-bond, the electron density is **spread out** above and below the nuclei. This causes the **electrostatic attraction** between the nuclei and the shared pair of electrons to be **weaker** in π-bonds than in σ-bonds, so π-bonds have a **relatively low bond enthalpy**.

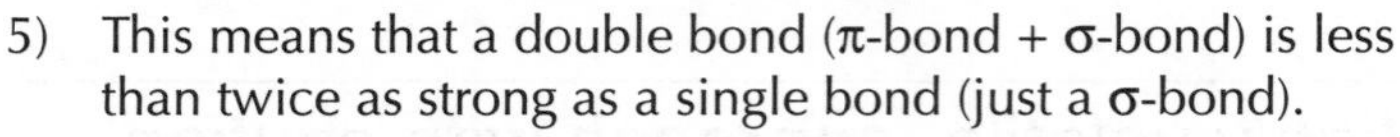

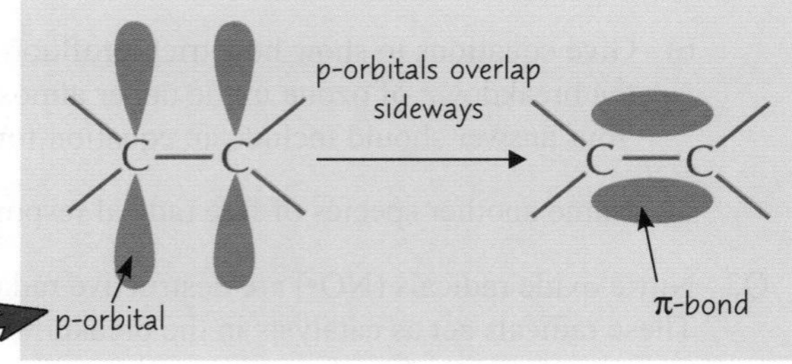

5) This means that a double bond (π-bond + σ-bond) is less than twice as strong as a single bond (just a σ-bond).
6) In alkenes, the **C–C** and **C–H bonds** are all **σ-bonds**. The **C=C bonds** in **alkenes** contain both a σ- and a **π-bond**.

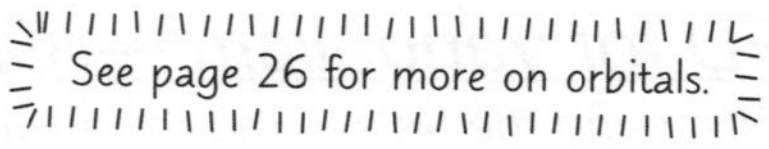
See page 26 for more on orbitals.

Alkenes

Alkenes are Much More Reactive than Alkanes

1) Alkanes only contain C–C and C–H **σ-bonds**, which have a high bond enthalpy and so are difficult to break. The bonds are also **non-polar** so they don't attract **nucleophiles** or **electrophiles**. This means alkanes **don't react** easily.
2) Alkenes are **more reactive** than alkanes because the C=C bond contains both a σ–bond and a π-bond.
3) The C=C double bond contains four electrons so it has a **high electron density** and the **π-bond** also sticks out above and below the rest of the molecule. These two factors mean the **π-bond** is likely to be attacked by **electrophiles** (see page 132). The **low bond enthalpy** of the π-bond also contributes to the reactivity of alkenes.
4) Because the double bond's so **reactive**, alkenes are handy **starting points** for making other organic compounds and for making **petrochemicals**.

Al never went anywhere without Al's cane.

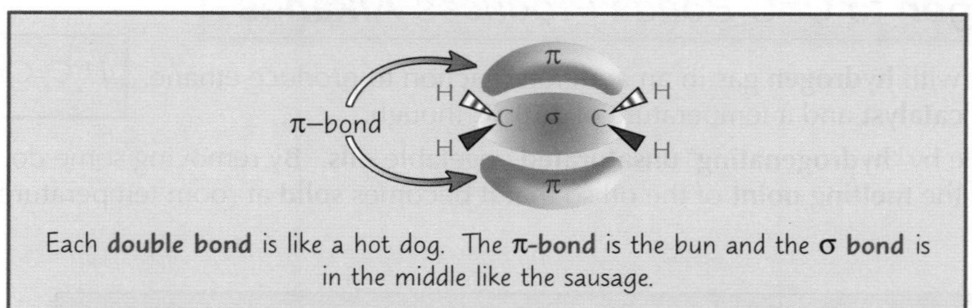

Each **double bond** is like a hot dog. The **π-bond** is the bun and the **σ bond** is in the middle like the sausage.

Practice Questions

Q1 What is the general formula of an alkene?

Q2 Describe how a sigma (σ-) bond forms.

Q3 Describe the arrangement of electrons in a double bond.

Q4 Which is stronger — a sigma bond or a pi bond?

Exam Questions

Q1 Which of the pictures below shows the skeletal formula of an alkene?

A 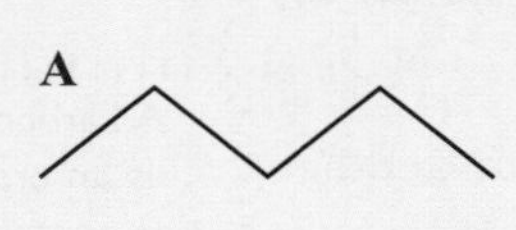

B 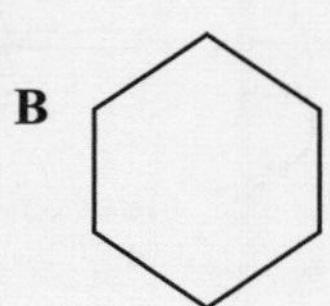

C 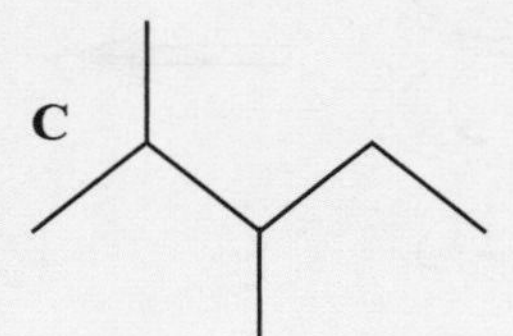

D 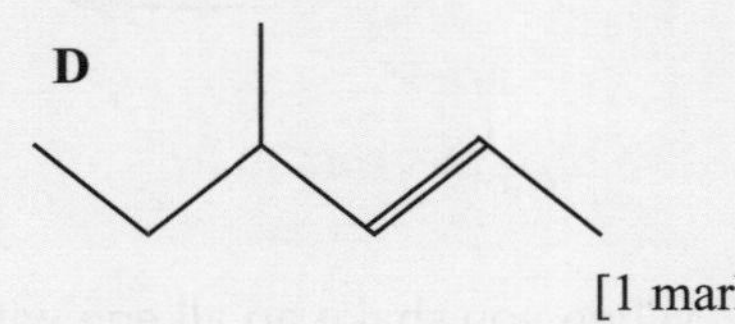

[1 mark]

Q2 Consider the hydrocarbons ethane and ethene.

a) Explain how the type of bonding differs in these two molecules. [2 marks]

b) Explain which of these molecules is more reactive. [2 marks]

Q3 The C=C bond in ethene is made up of two different types of bond.

a) Give one similarity between these bonds. [1 mark]

b) Give one difference between these bonds. [1 mark]

Double, double toil and trouble. Alkene burn and pi bond bubble...

Double bonds are always made up of a σ-bond and a π-bond. So even though π-bonds are weaker than σ-bonds, double bonds will be stronger than single bonds because they have the combined strength of a σ- and a π-bond. Now I hope you've got all this double bond, alkene stuff straight in your head. There's loads more on alkenes comin' up...

More on Alkenes

Now you know all about that reactive double bond, it's time to learn what it gets up to...

Electrophilic Addition Reactions Happen to Alkenes

In an **electrophilic addition** reaction, the alkene **double bond** opens up and atoms are **added** to the carbon atoms.

1) Electrophilic addition reactions happen because the double bond has got plenty of **electrons** and is easily attacked by **electrophiles**.
2) **Electrophiles** are **electron-pair acceptors** — they're usually a bit short of electrons, so they're **attracted** to areas where there are lots of electrons about.
3) Electrophiles include **positively charged ions**, like H^+ and NO_2^+, and **polar molecules** (since the $\delta+$ atom is attracted to places with lots of electrons).

Adding **Hydrogen** to C=C Bonds Produces **Alkanes**

1) Ethene will react with **hydrogen** gas in an addition reaction to produce ethane. It needs a **nickel catalyst** and a temperature of **150 °C** though.
2) **Margarine's** made by '**hydrogenating**' **unsaturated** vegetable **oils**. By removing some double bonds, you **raise** the **melting point** of the oil so that it becomes **solid** at room temperature.

$$H_2C{=}CH_2 + H_2 \xrightarrow[150\,°C]{Ni} CH_3CH_3$$

You can also do this reaction at room temperature with a platinum catalyst.

Halogens React With Alkenes to Form **Dihalogenoalkanes**

1) **Halogens** will react with alkenes to form **dihalogenoalkanes** — the halogens add **across** the **double bond**, and each of the carbon atoms ends up bonded to one halogen atom. It's an **electrophilic addition** reaction.

$$H_2C{=}CH_2 + X_2 \longrightarrow CH_2XCH_2X$$

2) Here's the mechanism — bromine is used as an example, but chlorine and iodine react in the same way.

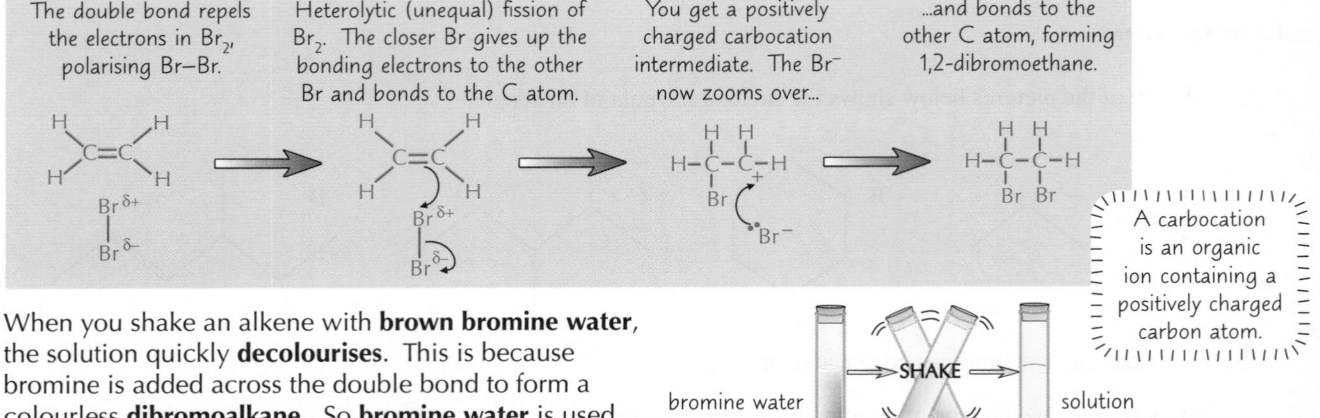

The double bond repels the electrons in Br2, polarising Br–Br.
Heterolytic (unequal) fission of Br2. The closer Br gives up the bonding electrons to the other Br and bonds to the C atom.
You get a positively charged carbocation intermediate. The Br⁻ now zooms over...
...and bonds to the other C atom, forming 1,2-dibromoethane.
bromine water + cyclohexene
SHAKE
solution goes colourless

A carbocation is an organic ion containing a positively charged carbon atom.

3) When you shake an alkene with **brown bromine water**, the solution quickly **decolourises**. This is because bromine is added across the double bond to form a colourless **dibromoalkane**. So **bromine water** is used to test for the presence of **carbon-carbon double bonds**.

Alcohols Can be Made by **Steam Hydration**

1) Alkenes can be **hydrated** by **steam** at 300 °C and a pressure of 60-70 atm. The reaction needs a solid **phosphoric(V) acid catalyst**.
2) The reaction is used to manufacture **ethanol** from **ethene**:

$$H_2C{=}CH_{2\,(g)} + H_2O_{(g)} \underset{\substack{300\,°C \\ 60\text{ atm}}}{\overset{H_3PO_4}{\rightleftharpoons}} CH_3CH_2OH_{(g)}$$

More on Alkenes

Alkenes are **Oxidised** by **Acidified Potassium Manganate(VII)**

1) If you shake an alkene with **acidified potassium manganate(VII)** at room temperature, the **purple** solution is **decolourised**. You've **oxidised** the alkene and made a diol (an alcohol with two -OH groups).
2) For example, here's how **ethene** reacts with acidified potassium manganate(VII):

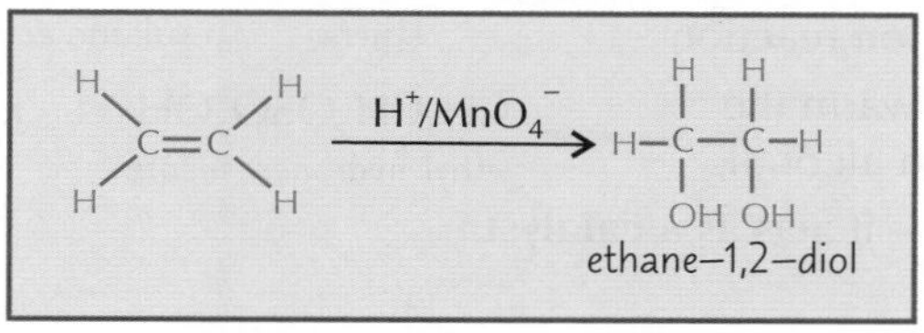

$$H_2C{=}CH_2 \xrightarrow{H^+/MnO_4^-} HOCH_2CH_2OH$$

ethane–1,2–diol

Alkenes also Undergo **Addition** with **Hydrogen Halides**

Alkenes also undergo **addition** reactions with hydrogen halides — to form **halogenoalkanes**.
For example, this is the reaction between **ethene** and HBr:

$$H_2C{=}CH_2 + HBr \longrightarrow CH_2BrCH_3$$

Adding **Hydrogen Halides** to **Unsymmetrical Alkenes** Forms **Two Products**

1) If the hydrogen halide adds to an **unsymmetrical** alkene, there are two possible products.
2) The amount of each product depends on how **stable** the **carbocation** formed in the middle of the reaction is.
3) Carbocations with more **alkyl groups** are more stable because the alkyl groups feed **electrons** towards the positive charge. The **more stable carbocation** is much more likely to form.

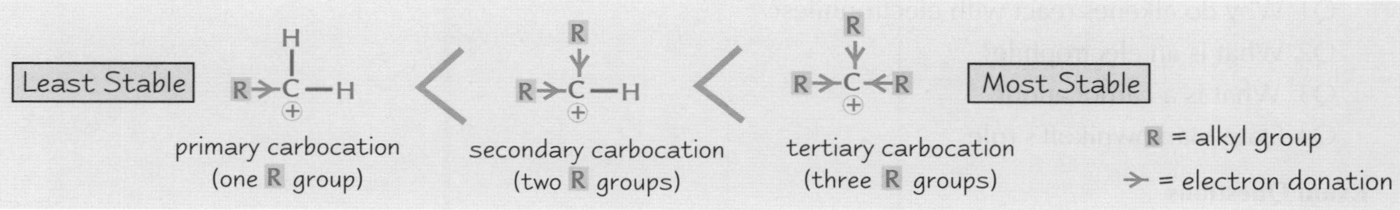

Least Stable — primary carbocation (one R group) < secondary carbocation (two R groups) < tertiary carbocation (three R groups) — Most Stable

R = alkyl group

→ = electron donation

4) Here's how hydrogen bromide reacts with propene:

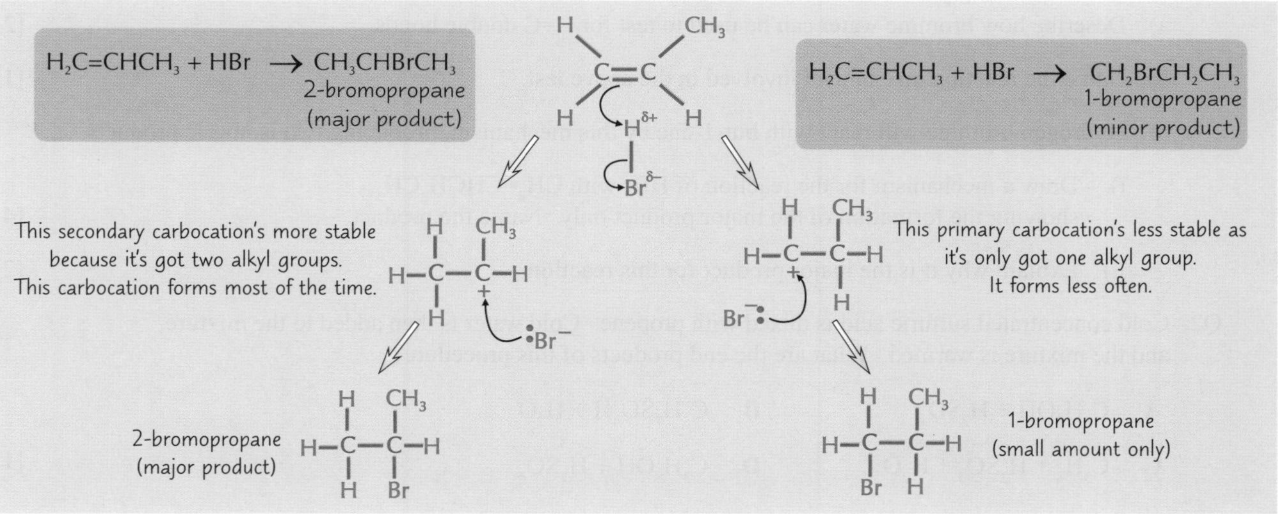

$H_2C{=}CHCH_3 + HBr \rightarrow CH_3CHBrCH_3$ 2-bromopropane (major product)

$H_2C{=}CHCH_3 + HBr \rightarrow CH_2BrCH_2CH_3$ 1-bromopropane (minor product)

This secondary carbocation's more stable because it's got two alkyl groups. This carbocation forms most of the time.

This primary carbocation's less stable as it's only got one alkyl group. It forms less often.

2-bromopropane (major product)

1-bromopropane (small amount only)

5) This can be summed up by **Markownikoff's rule** which says:

> The **major product** from addition of a hydrogen halide (HX) to an unsymmetrical alkene is the one where **hydrogen** adds to the carbon with the **most hydrogens** already attached.

More on Alkenes

Alkenes also Undergo **Electrophilic Addition Reactions** with H_2SO_4

Alkenes will react with **cold concentrated sulfuric acid** to form **alkyl hydrogen sulfates**. You can then convert the alkyl hydrogen sulfates formed into **alcohols** by adding water and warming the reaction mixture. For example:

1) Cold concentrated **sulfuric acid** reacts with an alkene in an **electrophilic addition** reaction.

$$\underset{\text{ethene}}{H_2C{=}CH_2} + \underset{\text{sulfuric acid}}{H_2SO_4} \rightarrow \underset{\text{ethyl hydrogen sulfate}}{CH_3CH_2OSO_2OH}$$

2) If you then add cold **water** and warm the product, it **hydrolyses** to form an alcohol.

$$\underset{\text{ethyl hydrogen sulfate}}{CH_3CH_2OSO_2OH} + H_2O \rightarrow \underset{\text{ethanol}}{CH_3CH_2OH} + H_2SO_4$$

3) The **sulfuric acid** isn't used up — it acts as a **catalyst**.

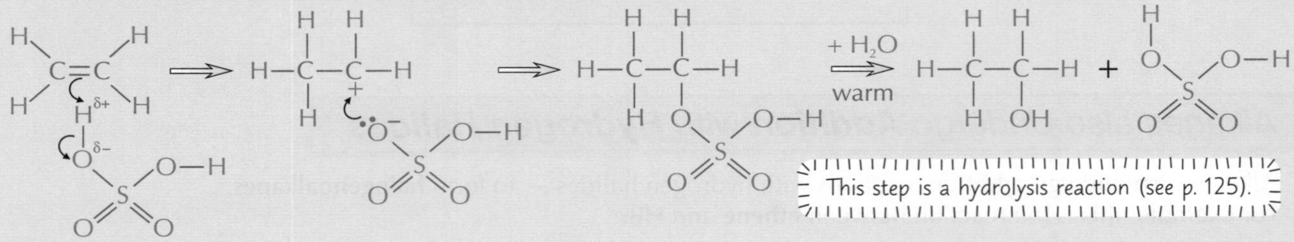

H, H, C=C, H, H, δ+, H, δ−, O, O—H, S, O, O ⟹ H H, H—C—C—H, H, +, O⁻, O—H, S, O, O ⟹ H H, H—C—C—H, H, O, O—H, S, O, O ⟹ (+ H_2O, warm) H H, H—C—C—H, H, OH + H, O, O—H, S, O, O

This step is a hydrolysis reaction (see p. 125).

If you're using this reaction to produce ethanol, then the equation for the overall reaction looks like this:

$$H_2C=CH_2 + H_2O \xrightarrow{H_2SO_4} C_2H_5OH$$

Just as with hydrogen halides on the previous page, if you do this reaction with an **unsymmetrical alkene**, you get a **mixture of products**. The one that's formed via the **most stable** carbocation intermediate will be the **major product**.

Practice Questions

Q1 Why do alkenes react with electrophiles?

Q2 What is an electrophile?

Q3 What is a carbocation?

Q4 State Markownikoff's rule.

Exam Questions

Q1 But-1-ene is an alkene. Alkenes contain at least one C=C double bond.

a) Describe how bromine water can be used to test for C=C double bonds. [2 marks]

b) Name the reaction mechanism involved in the above test. [1 mark]

c) Hydrogen bromide will react with but-1-ene by this mechanism, producing two isomeric products.

i) Draw a mechanism for the reaction of HBr with $CH_2{=}CHCH_2CH_3$, showing the formation of the major product only. Name the product. [4 marks]

ii) Explain why it is the major product for this reaction. [2 marks]

Q2 Cold concentrated sulfuric acid is mixed with propene. Cold water is then added to the mixture, and the mixture is warmed. What are the end products of this procedure?

A $C_3H_7OH + H_2SO_4$ **B** $C_3H_7SO_4H + H_2O$

C $C_3H_8 + H_2SO_4 + H_2O$ **D** $C_3H_8OH + H_2SO_4$ [1 mark]

Got an unsymmetrical alkene? I'd get that looked at...

Wow... these pages really are packed. There's not one, not two, but three mechanisms here. They mightn't be as handy in real life as a tin opener, but you don't need a tin opener to be a Chemistry genius. Get the book shut and scribble them out. Make sure your arrows start at the electron pair and finish exactly where the electrons are going.

Addition Polymers

Polymers are long, stringy molecules made by joining lots of little molecules together. They're made up of one unit repeated over and over and over and over and over and over and over again. Get the idea? Let's get started.

Polymers are Formed from **Monomers**

1) **Polymers** are long chain molecules formed when lots of small molecules, called **monomers**, join together.
2) Polymers can be **natural**, like DNA and proteins, or **synthetic** (man-made), like poly(ethene).
3) People have been using **natural polymers**, like silk, cotton and rubber, for hundreds of years.
4) In the **19th century**, research concentrated on modifying the properties of natural polymers — for example **hardening rubber**, to make it more suitable for machine parts and car tyres.
5) The **20th century** saw the invention and production of **synthetic polymers**, like **nylon** and **Kevlar®**.
6) Scientists are still developing **new polymers**, with new properties, all the time.

Addition Polymers are Formed from **Alkenes**

Alkenes can act as monomers and form polymers because their double bonds can open up and join together to make long chains. These type of polymers are called **addition polymers**.

Addition polymers made from alkenes are called polyalkenes.

Poly(phenylethene) is formed from **phenylethene**.

the double bond opens up

'n' means there are lots of these units

This is what a section of the chain would look like:

phenylethene monomer — poly(phenylethene) polymer — section of poly(phenylethene) polymer

Polyalkene chains are **saturated** molecules (they only contain single bonds in the carbon chain). The main carbon chain of a polyalkene is also **non-polar**. These factors result in addition polymers being very **unreactive**.

The **Properties** of Polyalkenes Depend on Their **Intermolecular Forces**

1) Polyalkene chains are usually **non-polar** — so the chains are only held together by **induced dipole-dipole forces** (see page 57).
2) The **longer** the polymer chains are and the **closer** together they can get, the **stronger** the induced dipole-dipole forces between the chains will be.
3) This means that polyalkenes made up of **long**, **straight chains** tend to be **strong** and **rigid**, while polyalkenes that are made up of **short**, **branched chains** tend to be **weaker** and more **flexible**.

Polymers that contain electronegative atoms (like Cl) can be polar. These polymers will have permanent dipole-dipole forces.

You Can **Modify** The Properties of Polymers Using **Plasticisers**

Adding a **plasticiser** to a polymer makes it more flexible. The plasticiser molecules get **between** the polymer chains and push them apart. This **reduces** the strength of the **intermolecular forces** between the chains — so they can slide around more, making the polymer easy to **bend**.

Poly(chloroethene), PVC is formed from **chloroethene**.

$$n\,H_2C{=}CHCl \longrightarrow \left(-CH_2-CHCl-\right)_n$$

chloroethene monomer — poly(chloroethene) polymer

1) PVC has long, closely packed polymer chains, making it hard but brittle at room temperature. **Rigid PVC** is used to make **drainpipes** and **window frames**.
2) **Plasticised PVC** is much more flexible than rigid PVC. It's used to make **electrical cable insulation, flooring tiles** and **clothing**.

Pretty Polymer.

Addition Polymers

You can Draw the Repeating Unit from a Monomer or Polymer

Polymers are made up of **repeating units** (a bit of molecule that repeats over and over again). The repeating units of addition polymers look very similar to the monomer, but with the double bond opened out.

1) To draw the **repeating unit** of an addition polymer from its **monomer**, first draw the two alkene carbons. Replace the double bond with a single bond. Add a single bond coming out from each of the carbons.
2) Then just fill in the rest of the groups in the same way they surrounded the double bond.

Example: Draw the repeating unit of the polymer formed from ethene, C_2H_4.

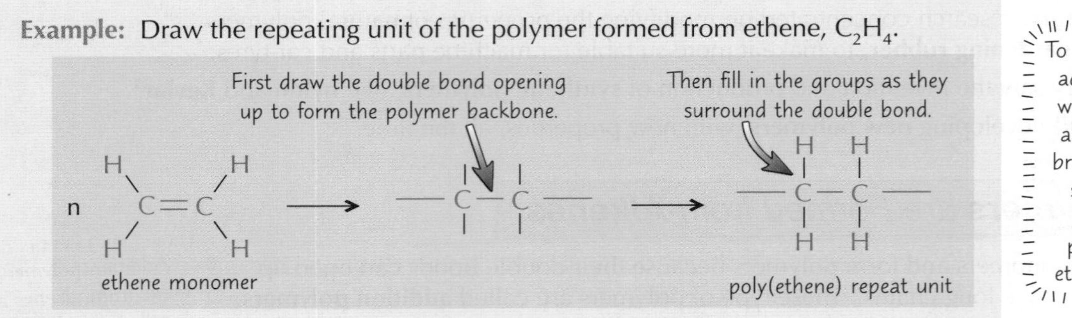

First draw the double bond opening up to form the polymer backbone.
Then fill in the groups as they surround the double bond.
ethene monomer
poly(ethene) repeat unit

To write the name of an addition polymer, you write the name of the alkene monomer, put brackets around it and stick 'poly' in front. For example, the polymer made from ethene is poly(ethene).

3) To draw the **repeating unit** from its **polymer**, you just need to look at the chain and work out which part is repeating. For an addition polymer, the repeating unit should be **two** carbons long (so it looks like the alkene monomer). Once you have the repeating unit, you can easily draw the **monomer** by adding a double bond.

Example: Draw the repeating unit and monomer of the polymer chain Teflon® (poly(tetrafluoroethene)).

section of Teflon® polymer → Teflon® repeat unit → Teflon® monomer

The polymer is only made up of carbon and fluorine atoms, so the repeating unit is just two carbons, surrounded by fluorines.

There are Different Methods for Disposing of Polymers

In the UK over **2 million** tonnes of plastic waste are produced each year. It's important to find ways to get rid of this waste while minimising **environmental damage**. There are various possible approaches...

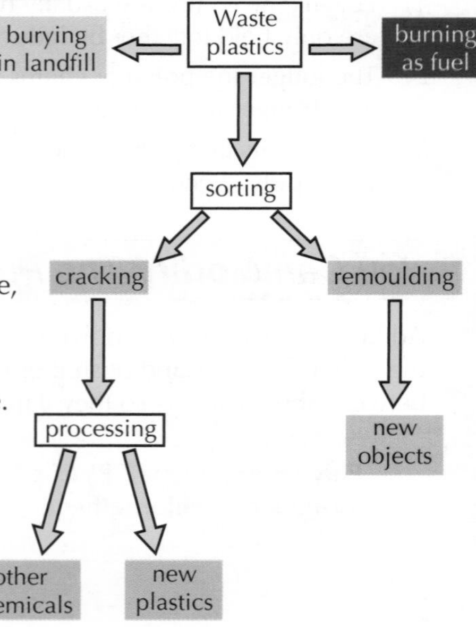

Waste Plastics can be Buried

1) **Landfill** is used to dispose of waste plastics when the plastic is:
   - difficult to separate from other waste,
   - not in sufficient quantities to make separation financially worthwhile,
   - too difficult technically to recycle.
2) But because the **amount of waste** we generate is becoming more and more of a problem, there's a need to **reduce** landfill as much as possible.

Waste Plastics can be Reused

1) Many plastics are made from non-renewable **oil-fractions**, so it makes sense to reuse plastics as much as possible.
2) There's more than one way to reuse plastics. After **sorting** into different types:
   - some plastics (poly(propene), for example) can be **recycled** by **melting** and **remoulding** them,
   - some plastics can be **cracked** into **monomers**, and these can be used as an **organic feedstock** to make more plastics or other chemicals.

Infrared spectroscopy (p. 149) can be used to help sort plastics into different types before they're recycled.

Addition Polymers

Waste Plastics can be **Burned**

1) If recycling isn't possible for whatever reason, waste plastics can be burned — and the heat can be used to generate **electricity**.
2) This process needs to be carefully **controlled** to reduce **toxic** gases. For example, polymers that contain **chlorine** (such as **PVC**) produce **HCl** when they're burned — this has to be removed.
3) Waste gases from the combustion are passed through **scrubbers** which can **neutralise** gases, such as HCl, by allowing them to react with a **base**.
4) Plastics can also be **sorted** before they are burnt to separate out any materials that will produce **toxic gases**.

Chemists Can Work to Make **Polymers Sustainably**

Lots of **chemicals** that are used in the manufacture of polymers are **pretty dangerous**.
The way that a polymer is made should be designed to **minimise** the **impact** on human **health** and the **environment**.
There are a set of principles that chemists follow when they design a **sustainable polymer manufacturing process**:

- Use **reactant** molecules that are as **safe** and **environmentally friendly** as possible.
- Use as few **other materials**, like **solvents**, as possible. If you have to use other chemicals, choose ones that **won't** harm the environment.
- **Renewable raw materials** should be used wherever possible.
- **Energy use** should be kept to a **minimum**. **Catalysts** are often utilised in polymer synthesis to lower energy use.
- Limit the **waste products** made, especially those which are **hazardous** to **human health** or the **environment**.
- Make sure the **lifespan** of the polymer is **appropriate** for its use. If you make a polymer that just keeps breaking, you'll end up having to make loads more than if you create a more enduring polymer.

Scientists can now make **biodegradable** polymers (ones that naturally **decompose**). They decompose pretty quickly in certain conditions because organisms can digest them. Biodegradable polymers can be made from **renewable** raw materials such as **starch** (from maize and other plants), or from **oil fractions** such as the hydrocarbon **isoprene**.

Practice Questions

Q1 What type of polymers do alkenes form?

Q2 Explain why polyalkenes with long, straight chains are stronger than those with short, branched chains.

Q3 Describe three ways in which used polymers such as poly(propene) can be disposed of.

Exam Questions

Q1 The diagram on the right shows a section of the polymer poly(propene).

$$\begin{array}{ccccccccccccc} & H & & H & & H & & H & & H & & H & \\ & | & & | & & | & & | & & | & & | & \\ - & C & - & C & - & C & - & C & - & C & - & C & - \\ & | & & | & & | & & | & & | & & | & \\ & H & & CH_3 & & H & & CH_3 & & H & & CH_3 & \end{array}$$

a) Draw the structure of the monomer that forms this polymer. [1 mark]

b) Draw the structure of the repeating unit of poly(propene). [1 mark]

Q2 The polymer poly(chloroethene) (PVC) is made from chloroethene, shown right.

$$\begin{array}{ccccc} H & & & & H \\ & \diagdown & & \diagup & \\ & C & = & C & \\ & \diagup & & \diagdown & \\ H & & & & Cl \end{array}$$

a) Draw the structure of the repeating unit of poly(chloroethene). [1 mark]

b) Explain how the properties of PVC change when you add a plasticiser. [3 marks]

c) Give two typical uses of plasticised PVC. [2 marks]

Q3 Waste plastics can be disposed of by burning.

a) Describe one advantage of disposing of waste plastics by burning. [1 mark]

b) Describe a disadvantage of burning waste plastic that contains chlorine, and explain how the impact of this disadvantage could be reduced. [2 marks]

Never miss your friends again — form a polymer...

These polymers are really useful — drainpipes, clothing, electrical cable insulation... you couldn't do without them. And someone had to invent them. Just think, you could be the next mad inventor, working for a secret agency...

Alcohols

These two pages could well be enough to put you off alcohols for life...

Alcohols are **Primary**, **Secondary** or **Tertiary**

1) The alcohol homologous series has the **general formula $C_nH_{2n+1}OH$**.
2) An alcohol is **primary**, **secondary** or **tertiary**, depending on which carbon atom the **-OH** group is bonded to.

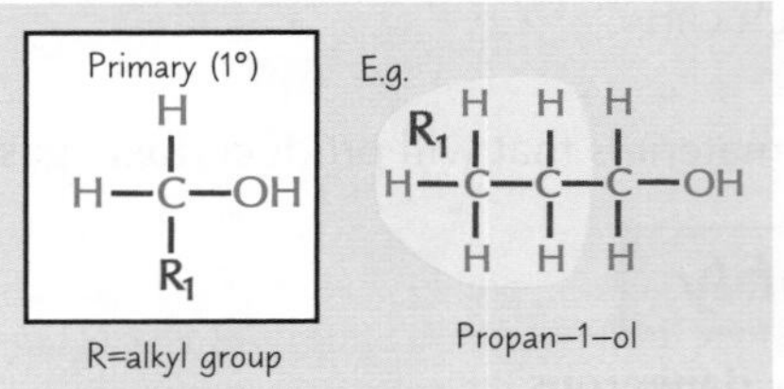

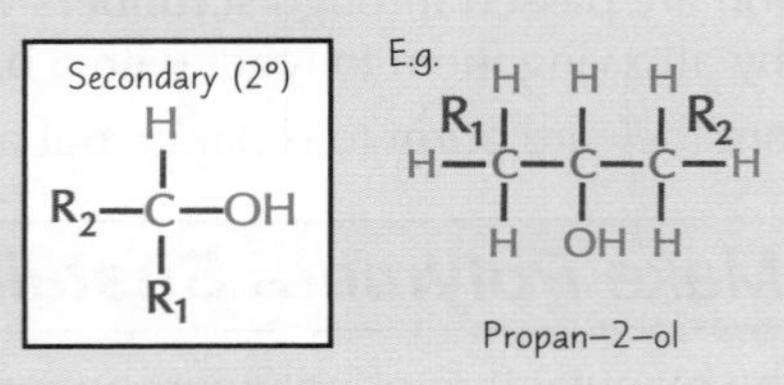

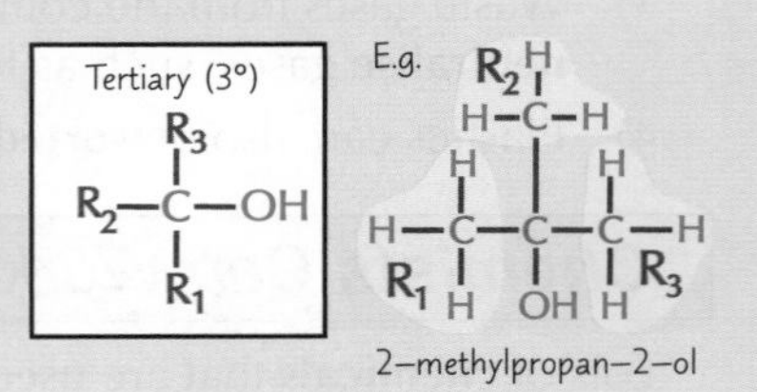

The Hydroxyl Group -OH Can Form **Hydrogen Bonds**

Alcohols are generally **polar molecules** due to the electronegative **hydroxyl group** which pulls the electrons in the C–OH bond **away** from the **carbon atom**.

$$\overset{\delta+}{R_1}-\overset{\delta-}{O}-\overset{\delta+}{H}$$

The electronegative oxygen in the polar hydroxyl group draws electron density away from the hydrogen, giving it a **slightly positive charge**. This positive charge can attract the **lone pairs** on an oxygen from a neighbouring molecule, forming hydrogen bonds (see page 58). This gives alcohols certain properties...

hydrogen bonds

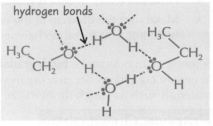

1) When you mix an alcohol with water, hydrogen bonds form between the **-OH** and **H_2O**. If it's a **small** alcohol (e.g. methanol, ethanol or propan-1-ol), hydrogen bonding lets it mix freely with water — it's **soluble** in water.
2) In **larger alcohols**, most of the molecule is a non-polar carbon chain, so there's less attraction for the polar H_2O molecules. This means that as alcohols **increase in size**, their solubility in water **decreases**.
3) Alcohols also form hydrogen bonds with **each other**.
Hydrogen bonding is the **strongest** kind of intermolecular force, so it gives alcohols a relatively **low volatility** (they don't evaporate easily into a gas) compared to non-polar compounds, e.g. alkanes of similar sizes.

-OH can be **Swapped** for a Halogen to Make a **Halogenoalkane**

1) Alcohols will react with compounds containing **halide ions** (such as NaBr) in a **substitution reaction**.
2) The **hydroxyl** (-OH) group is **replaced** by the **halide**, so the alcohol is transformed into a **halogenoalkane**.
3) The reaction also requires an **acid catalyst**, such as H_2SO_4.

Example: To make 2-bromo-2-methylpropane you just need to shake 2-methylpropan-2-ol (a tertiary alcohol) with sodium bromide and concentrated sulfuric acid at room temperature.

$$H_3C-C(CH_3)(OH)-CH_3 + NaBr \longrightarrow H_3C-C(CH_3)(Br)-CH_3 + NaOH$$

alcohol (2-methylpropan-2-ol) → haloalkane (2-bromo-2-methylpropane)

You can also make chloroalkanes if you react an alcohol with hydrochloric acid.

4) If you react an alcohol with phosphorus pentachloride (PCl_5), a chloroalkane is produced. The general equation for this reaction is: $ROH + PCl_5 \rightarrow RCl + HCl + POCl_3$
5) You can make an **iodoalkane** from an **alcohol** by reacting it with **phosphorus triiodide (PI_3)**. **PI_3** is usually made **in situ** (within the reaction mixture) by refluxing the alcohol with 'red phosphorus' and iodine. This is the general equation: $3ROH + PI_3 \rightarrow 3RI + H_3PO_3$

Alcohols

Alcohols React with **Carboxylic Acids** to Form **Esters**

If you heat a **carboxylic acid** with an **alcohol** in the presence of an **acid catalyst**, you get an ester. It's called an **esterification** reaction. Concentrated sulfuric or hydrochloric acid is usually used as the acid catalyst.

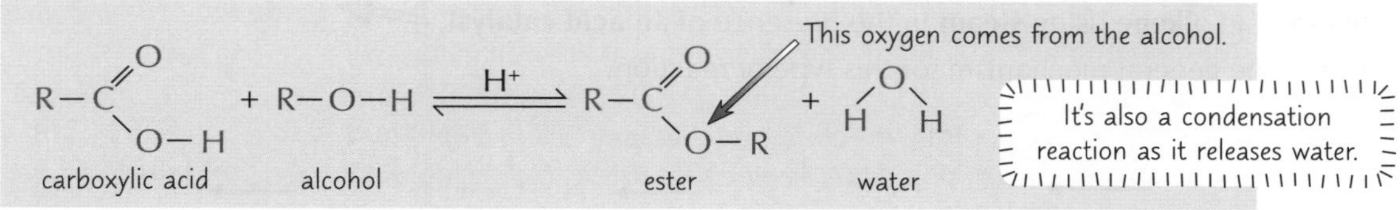

$$\underset{\text{carboxylic acid}}{R-COOH} + \underset{\text{alcohol}}{R-O-H} \xrightleftharpoons{H^+} \underset{\text{ester}}{R-COO-R} + \underset{\text{water}}{H_2O}$$

This oxygen comes from the alcohol.

It's also a condensation reaction as it releases water.

Alcohols Also React with **Acid Anhydrides** to Form **Esters**

If you react an **acid anhydride** with an **alcohol**, you get an ester and a carboxylic acid.

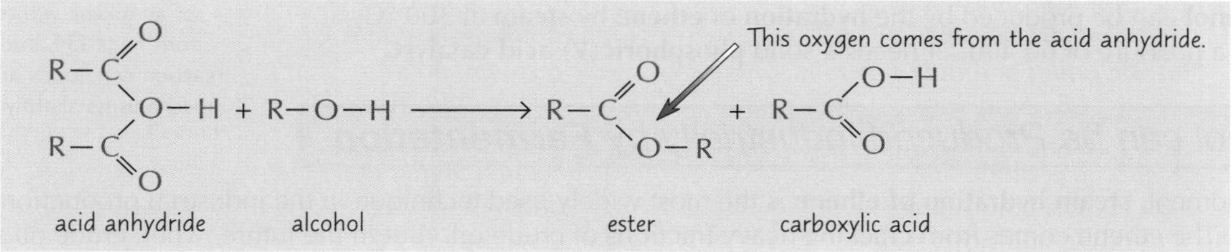

$$\underset{\text{acid anhydride}}{(R-CO)_2O} + \underset{\text{alcohol}}{R-O-H} \longrightarrow \underset{\text{ester}}{R-COO-R} + \underset{\text{carboxylic acid}}{R-COOH}$$

This oxygen comes from the acid anhydride.

Practice Questions

Q1 What is the general formula for an alcohol?

Q2 How do the volatilities of alcohols compare with the volatilities of similarly sized alkanes?

Q3 What products are made when 2-methylpropan-2-ol is mixed with sodium bromide and concentrated sulfuric acid?

Exam Questions

Q1 The formula C_4H_9OH can represent the three alcohols shown below.
Class each alcohol as primary, secondary or tertiary.

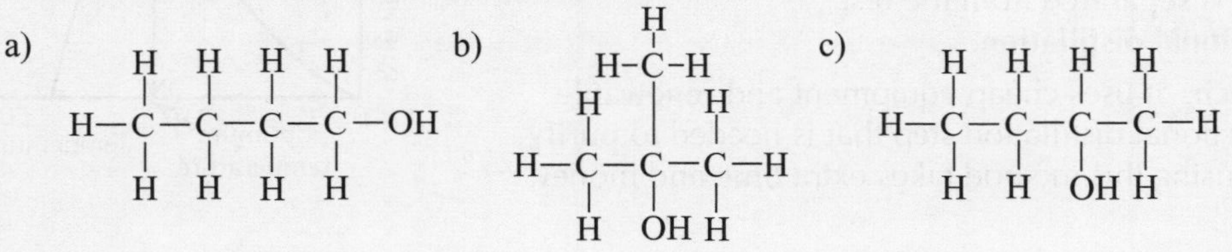

```
a)                          b)        H             c)
     H   H   H   H                  H-C-H                H   H   H   H
     |   |   |   |                H   |   H              |   |   |   |
   H-C---C---C---C-OH             |   |   |            H-C---C---C---C-H
     |   |   |   |              H-C---C---C-H            |   |   |   |
     H   H   H   H                |   |   |              H   H   OH  H
                                  H   OH  H
```

[3 marks]

Q2 a) Draw and name a primary alcohol, a secondary alcohol and a tertiary alcohol, each with the formula $C_5H_{12}O$. [3 marks]

b) Describe how ethanol could be converted into bromoethane [1 mark]

Q3 A student is comparing the properties of ethane (an alkane) and ethanol (an alcohol).

a) The student finds that ethane is insoluble in water, but ethanol is soluble in water.
Explain why ethanol is soluble in water. [2 marks]

b) The student predicts that ethanol will have the higher boiling point of the two molecules.
Do you agree with the student? Explain your answer. [2 marks]

Euuurghh, what a page... I think I need a drink...

Not too much to learn here — a few basic definitions, some fiddly explanations of the properties of alcohols in terms of their polarity and intermolecular bonding, a whole host of ways that alcohols react to make different halogenoalkanes, an esterification reaction... Urgh... It's all getting too much... Think I'm going to faint... THWACK

Ethanol Production

Humans have been making ethanol for thousands of years. We've gotten pretty good at it.

Alcohols are Produced by Hydration of Alkenes

1) The standard industrial method for producing alcohols is to **hydrate** an **alkene** using **steam** in the presence of an **acid catalyst**.

$$C_nH_{2n} + H_2O \underset{}{\overset{H^+}{\rightleftharpoons}} C_nH_{2n+1}OH$$

2) Here's the general mechanism for this type of reaction.

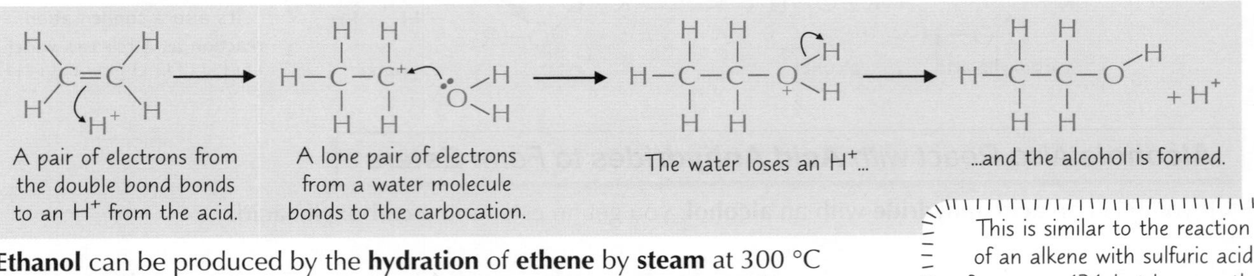

A pair of electrons from the double bond bonds to an H⁺ from the acid.
A lone pair of electrons from a water molecule bonds to the carbocation.
The water loses an H⁺...
...and the alcohol is formed.

3) **Ethanol** can be produced by the **hydration** of **ethene** by **steam** at 300 °C and a pressure of 60 atm. It needs a solid **phosphoric(V) acid catalyst**.

This is similar to the reaction of an alkene with sulfuric acid from page 134, but because the reaction conditions are different the mechanism's slightly different too.

Ethanol can be Produced Industrially by Fermentation

At the moment, **steam hydration of ethene** is the most widely used technique in the industrial production of ethanol. The ethene comes from cracking heavy fractions of crude oil. But in the future, when crude oil supplies start **running out**, petrochemicals like ethene will be expensive — so producing ethanol by **fermentation**, using a renewable raw material like glucose, will become much more important...

Industrial Production of Ethanol by Fermentation of Glucose

1) Fermentation is an **exothermic** process, carried out by **yeast** in **anaerobic conditions** (without oxygen).

$$C_6H_{12}O_{6(aq)} \xrightarrow[\text{yeast}]{30\text{-}40\ °C} 2C_2H_5OH_{(aq)} + 2CO_{2(g)}$$

2) Yeast produces an **enzyme** which converts sugars, such as glucose, into **ethanol** and **carbon dioxide**.
3) The enzyme works at an **optimum** (ideal) temperature of **30-40 °C**. If it's too cold, the reaction is **slow** — if it's too hot, the enzyme is **denatured** (damaged).
4) Once formed, ethanol is **separated** from the rest of the mixture by **fractional distillation**.
5) Fermentation is **low-tech**. It uses cheap equipment and **renewable resources**. But the fractional distillation step that is needed to **purify** the ethanol produced using this method takes extra time and money.

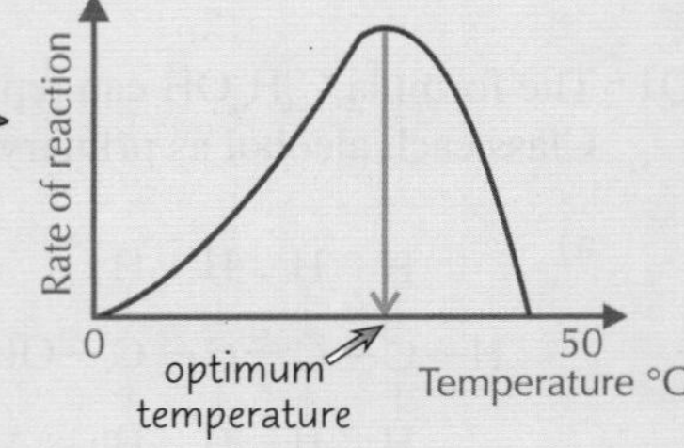

Ethanol is a Biofuel

Ethanol is increasingly being used as a **fuel**, particularly in countries with few oil reserves. For example, in Brazil, **sugars** from sugar cane are **fermented** to produce alcohol, which is added to petrol. Ethanol made in this way is a **biofuel** (and is sometimes called **bioethanol**).

> A biofuel is a fuel that's made from biological material that's recently died.

Biofuels have some advantages over fossil fuels (coal, oil and gas) and some potential drawbacks.

1) Biofuels are **renewable** energy sources. Unlike fossil fuels, biofuels won't run out, so they're more **sustainable**.
2) Biofuels do produce CO_2 when they're burnt, but it's CO_2 that the plants **absorbed** while growing, so **biofuels** are usually still classed as **carbon neutral** (see next page).
3) But one problem with switching from fossil fuels to biofuels in transport is that **petrol car engines** would have to be **modified** to use fuels with high ethanol concentrations.
4) Also, when you use land to grow crops for fuel, that land can't be used to grow **food**. If countries start using land to grow biofuel crops instead of food, they may be unable to feed everyone in the country.

Ethanol Production

Bioethanol Production is **Almost Carbon Neutral**... But **Not Quite**

1) Just like burning the hydrocarbons from fossil fuels, burning ethanol produces **carbon dioxide** (CO_2). Carbon dioxide is a **greenhouse gas** — it contributes to **global warming** (see page 122).
2) But the plants that are grown to produce bioethanol **take in carbon dioxide** from the **atmosphere** when they're growing. As they grow, they take in the same amount of carbon dioxide as burning the bioethanol you produce from them gives out. So it could be argued that burning ethanol as a fuel is **carbon neutral**.

   Here are the **chemical equations** to support that argument...

   Plants take in **carbon dioxide** from the atmosphere to produce **glucose** by **photosynthesis**...

   $$6CO_2 + 6H_2O \rightarrow C_6H_{12}O_6 + 6O_2$$

   6 moles of carbon dioxide are taken from the atmosphere to produce 1 mole of glucose.

   In the **fermentation** process, **glucose** is converted into **ethanol**...

   $$C_6H_{12}O_6 \rightarrow 2C_2H_5OH + 2CO_2$$

   2 moles of carbon dioxide are released into the atmosphere when 1 mole of glucose is converted to 2 moles of ethanol.

   When **ethanol** is **burned**, **carbon dioxide** and water are produced...

   $$2C_2H_5OH_2 + 6O_2 \rightarrow 4CO_2 + 6H_2O$$

   4 moles of carbon dioxide are released into the atmosphere when 2 moles of ethanol are burned completely.

   If you **combine** all three of these equations, you'll find that exactly **6 moles of CO_2** are taken in...
   ...and exactly **6 moles of CO_2** are given out.

3) However, **fossil fuels** will need to be burned to power the machinery used to make **fertilisers** for the crops, **harvest the crops** and **refine and transport** the bioethanol. Burning the fuel to power this machinery produces carbon dioxide. So using bioethanol made by fermentation **isn't completely carbon neutral**.

Practice Questions

Q1 What is the standard method for producing alcohols from alkenes?

Q2 Why should the fermentation of glucose not be carried out at more than 40 °C?

Q3 What is a biofuel?

Q4 Write down one advantage and one disadvantages of replacing fossil fuels with biofuels.

Exam Questions

Q1 Industrially, ethanol can be produced by fermentation of glucose, $C_6H_{12}O_6$.

a) Write a balanced equation for this reaction. [1 mark]

b) State the conditions used for the industrial fermentation of glucose. [3 marks]

c) How is the ethanol separated from the reaction mixture? [1 mark]

Q2 In a classroom debate on the future of fuels, one student states that bioethanol is "carbon neutral". Another student argues that bioethanol is not really a carbon neutral fuel.

a) Explain why bioethanol is sometimes described as a carbon neutral fuel. [1 mark]

b) Explain why bioethanol cannot really be considered a carbon neutral fuel. [2 marks]

Steam hydration or fermentation? Come on, everyone has a favourite...

The hydration reaction here is the opposite of the elimination reaction you'll meet on page 144. Biofuels are a relatively simple idea to get your head round — then it's just a matter of learning about the pros and cons of the hydration and fermentation processes. Then next time you're in a petrol station, stop and think about all your new fuel facts.

Oxidation of Alcohols

Another couple of pages of alcohol reactions. Probably not what you wanted for Christmas...

How Much an Alcohol can be *Oxidised* Depends on its *Structure*

1) The simple way to oxidise alcohols is to burn them. It doesn't take much to set ethanol alight and it burns with a **pale blue flame**. The C–C and C–H bonds are broken as the ethanol is **completely oxidised** to make carbon dioxide and water. This is a **combustion** reaction.

$$C_2H_5OH_{(l)} + 3O_{2(g)} \rightarrow 2CO_{2(g)} + 3H_2O_{(g)}$$

2) You can use the **oxidising agent acidified potassium dichromate(VI)**, $K_2Cr_2O_7$, to **mildly** oxidise alcohols. The **orange** dichromate(VI) ion, $Cr_2O_7^{2-}$, is reduced to the **green** chromium(III) ion, Cr^{3+}. Primary alcohols are oxidised to aldehydes and then to carboxylic acids, secondary alcohols are oxidised to ketones only and tertiary alcohols aren't oxidised at all (unless you burn them).

Learn What *Aldehydes*, *Ketones* and *Carboxylic Acids* are

Aldehydes and **ketones** are **carbonyl** compounds — they have the functional group C=O. Their general formula is $\mathbf{C_nH_{2n}O}$. **Carboxylic acids** have the functional group COOH and have the general formula $\mathbf{C_nH_{2n+1}COOH}$.

ALDEHYDES

1) Have a **hydrogen** and **one alkyl group** attached to the carbonyl carbon atom.
2) Their suffix is **-al**. You don't have to say which carbon the functional group is on — it's always on carbon-1.

propanal
CH_3CH_2CHO

KETONES

1) Have **two alkyl groups** attached to the carbonyl carbon atom.
2) Their suffix is **-one**. For ketones with five or more carbons, you always have to say which carbon the functional group is on.

propanone
CH_3COCH_3

pentan-2-one
$CH_3COC_3H_7$

CARBOXYLIC ACIDS

1) Have a **COOH group** at the end of their carbon chain.
2) Their suffix is **-oic acid**.

propanoic acid
CH_3CH_2COOH

Primary Alcohols will Oxidise to *Aldehydes* and *Carboxylic Acids*

[O] = oxidising agent

$$R{-}CH_2{-}OH + [O] \longrightarrow R{-}CHO + H_2O$$

primary alcohol → aldehyde

then

$$R{-}CHO + [O] \xrightarrow{\text{reflux}} R{-}COOH$$

aldehyde → carboxylic acid

You can control how **far** the alcohol is oxidised by controlling the **reaction conditions**:

1) Gently heating ethanol with potassium dichromate(VI) and sulfuric acid in a test tube produces **ethanal** (an aldehyde). However, it's **tricky** to control the heat and the aldehyde is usually oxidised to form **ethanoic acid**.
2) To get just the **aldehyde**, you need to get it out of the oxidising solution **as soon** as it forms. You do this using **distillation apparatus**, so the aldehyde (which boils at a lower temperature than the alcohol) is distilled off **immediately**.
3) To produce the **carboxylic acid**, the alcohol has to be **vigorously oxidised**. The alcohol is mixed with excess oxidising agent and heated under **reflux**.
4) Heating under reflux means you can increase the **temperature** of an organic reaction without losing **volatile** solvents, reactants or products. Any vaporised compounds cool, condense and drip back into the reaction mixture. So the aldehyde stays in the reaction mixture and is oxidised to carboxylic acid.

Reflux apparatus

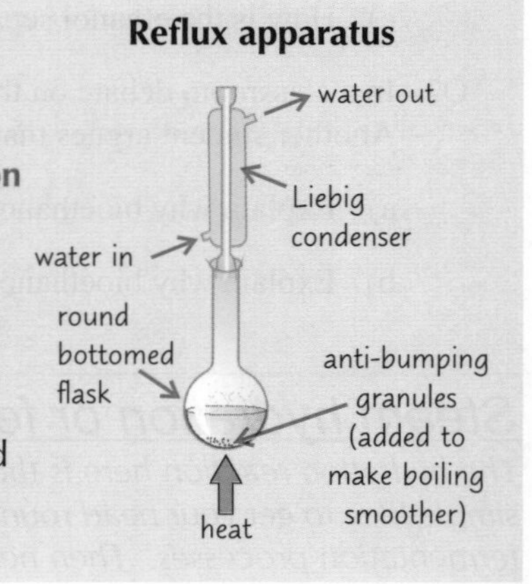

Oxidation of Alcohols

Secondary *Alcohols will Oxidise to* ***Ketones***

$$R_1-\underset{R_2}{\overset{H}{C}}-OH + [O] \xrightarrow{\text{reflux}} (R_1)(R_2)C{=}O + H_2O$$

1) Refluxing a secondary alcohol, e.g. propan-2-ol, with acidified dichromate(VI) will produce a **ketone**.
2) Ketones can't be oxidised easily, so even prolonged refluxing won't produce anything more.

Tertiary *Alcohols* ***can't*** *be Oxidised Easily*

Tertiary alcohols don't react with potassium dichromate(VI) at all — the solution stays orange. The only way to oxidise tertiary alcohols is by **burning** them.

Use Oxidising Agents to ***Distinguish*** *Between* ***Aldehydes*** *and* ***Ketones***

Aldehydes and ketones can be distinguished using **oxidising agents**. Aldehydes are easily oxidised but ketones aren't.

1) **Fehling's solution** and **Benedict's solution** are both deep blue Cu^{2+} complexes, which reduce to brick-red Cu_2O when warmed with an aldehyde, but stay blue with a ketone.
2) **Tollens' reagent** is $[Ag(NH_3)_2]^+$ — it's reduced to **silver** when warmed with an aldehyde, but not with a ketone. The silver will coat the inside of the apparatus to form a **silver mirror**.

There's more details on tests you can use to distinguish between aldehydes and ketones on pages 146-147.

Practice Questions

Q1 What is the colour change when potassium dichromate(VI) is reduced?

Q2 What's the difference between the structure of an aldehyde and a ketone?

Q3 What will acidified potassium dichromate(VI) oxidise secondary alcohols to?

Q4 Describe two tests you can use to distinguish between a sample of an aldehyde and a sample of a ketone.

Exam Question

Q1 A student wanted to produce the aldehyde propanal from propanol, and set up a reflux apparatus using a suitable oxidising agent.

a) i) Suggest an oxidising agent that the student could use. [1 mark]

ii) Draw the displayed formula of propanal. [1 mark]

b) The student tested his product and found that he had not produced propanal.

i) Describe a test for an aldehyde. [1 mark]

ii) What is the student's product? [1 mark]

iii) Write equations to show the two-stage reaction. Use [O] to represent the oxidising agent. [2 marks]

iv) What technique should the student have used to form propanal? [1 mark]

c) The student also tried to oxidise 2-methylpropan-2-ol, unsuccessfully.

i) Draw the skeletal formula for 2-methylpropan-2-ol. [1 mark]

ii) Why is it not possible to oxidise 2-methylpropan-2-ol with an oxidising agent? [1 mark]

I.... I .... just can't do it, R2...

Don't give up now. Only as a fully-trained Chemistry Jedi, with the force as your ally, can you take on the Examiner. If you quit now, if you choose the easy path as Wader did, all the marks you've fought for will be lost. Be strong.

More Reactions of Alcohols

It's like the office Christmas party... The alcohols just keep on coming...

Alcohols can be **Dehydrated** to Form **Alkenes**

1) You can make alkenes by **eliminating** water from **alcohols** in an **elimination reaction**.
2) When an alcohol dehydrates it eliminates **water**.

E.g. **Ethanol** dehydrates to form **ethene**.

$$C_2H_5OH \rightarrow CH_2{=}CH_2 + H_2O$$

> An elimination reaction where water is eliminated is called a dehydration reaction.

Example: There are two methods you can use to dehydrate ethanol to make ethene.

(1) Ethanol vapour is passed over a hot **catalyst** of pumice stone or aluminium oxide, Al_2O_3 — the catalyst provides a **large surface area** for the reaction.

(2) **OR**, you can **reflux** ethanol with **excess** concentrated sulfuric acid at 170 °C. The ethene produced is then collected by displacing water from an upturned measuring cylinder (see page 154 for info on refluxing).

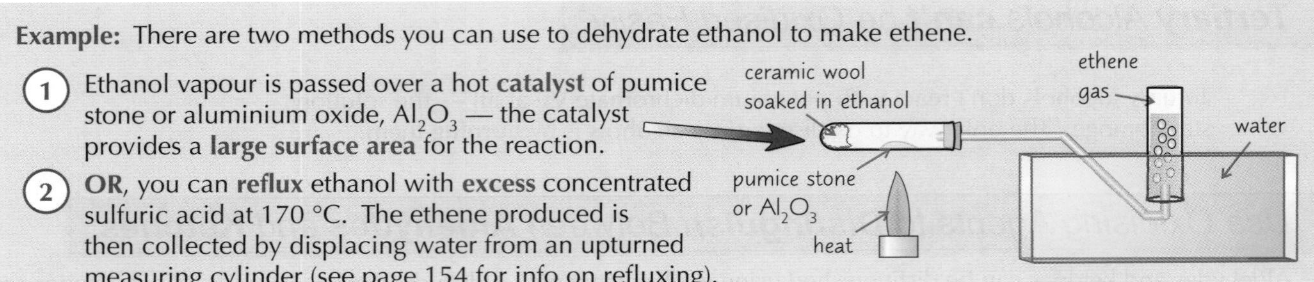

3) The water molecule is made up from the hydroxyl group and a hydrogen atom that was bonded to a carbon atom adjacent to the hydroxyl carbon.
4) This means that often there are **two possible** alkene products from one elimination reaction depending on **which side** of the hydroxyl group the **hydrogen** is **eliminated** from. Also watch out for if any of the alkene products can form **E/Z isomers** (see pages 113-114) — if they can then a mixture of both isomers will form.

Example: When butan-2-ol is heated to 170 °C with concentrated phosphoric acid, it dehydrates to form a mixture of products. Give the names and structures of all the organic compounds in this mixture.

- Elimination can occur between the **hydroxyl group** and the hydrogen either on **carbon-1** or **carbon-3**. This results in **two** possible alkene products — **but-1-ene** and **but-2-ene**.
- In addition, **but-2-ene** can form **E/Z isomers**.
- So there are **3** possible products — but-1-ene, E-but-2-ene and Z-but-2-ene.

Butan-2-ol: $CH_3{-}CH_2{-}CH(OH){-}CH_3$

But-1-ene: $H_3C{-}CH_2(H)C{=}CH_2$

E-But-2-ene: $H(H_3C)C{=}C(CH_3)H$ (trans)

Z-But-2-ene: $H(H_3C)C{=}C(CH_3)H$ (cis)

Practice Questions

Q1 Outline two ways you can form ethene from ethanol.

Q2 Why can the dehydration of alcohols, to form alkenes, result in multiple products?

Exam Question

Q1 When 3-methyl-pentan-3-ol is heated with concentrated sulfuric acid, it reacts to form a mixture of organic products.

a) What is the name of this type of reaction? [1 mark]

b) How many organic compounds will be produced?

A 4 **B** 3 **C** 2 **D** 1 [1 mark]

170 °C + H_2SO_4 and the Sahara desert — no alcohol and very dehydrating...

I promise that's the end of alcohols now. Well... Bad news is there's still one more page that stands between you and completing this topic. It's a pesky page on phenols, which are sort of a bit like alcohols... But still, it's just the one page.

Phenols

Phenols are members of the alcohol family. Don't drink them though — they'd get your insides a bit too clean.

Phenols Have Benzene Rings with **-OH** Groups Attached

Phenol has the formula C_6H_5OH. Other phenols have various groups attached to the benzene ring:

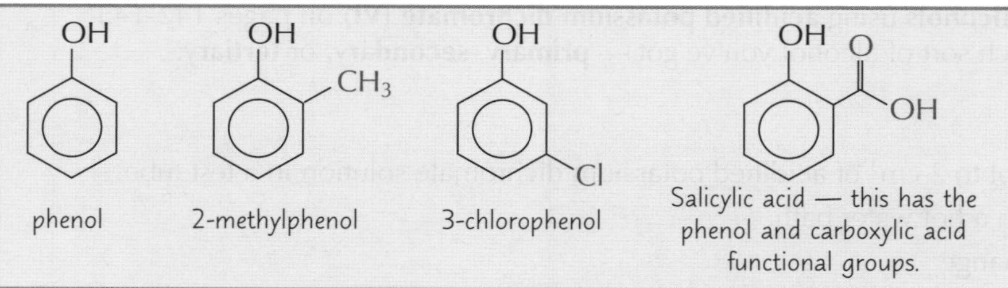

Number the carbons starting from the one with the –OH group.

I see benzene rings everywhere — am I going nuts?

Test for Phenols Using **Iron(III) Chloride** Solution

If you add a phenol to neutral **iron(III) chloride solution** and shake, you get a **purple** solution.

Iron(III) chloride + phenol

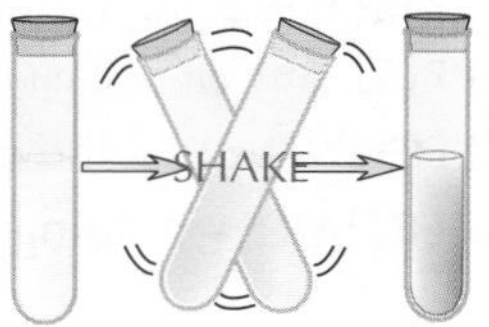

Phenols are **Weak Acids** and **React** with **Strong Alkalis**

1) Phenols dissolve a little bit in water to form a **phenoxide ion** and an H^+ **ion**. So the solution formed is **weakly acidic.**

$$C_6H_5OH \rightleftharpoons C_6H_5O^- + H^+$$

phenoxide ion

2) Phenols react with **alkalis** to produce a **salt** and **water**.
For example, phenol reacts with **sodium hydroxide solution** at room temperature to form **sodium phenoxide** and **water**.
The hydrogen ion on the phenol is removed by the OH^- ion.

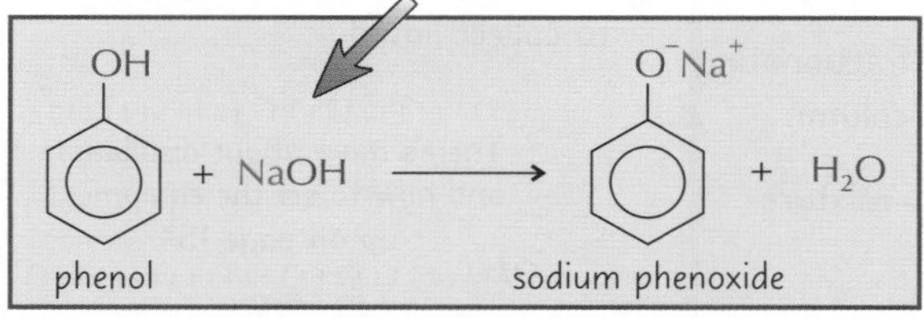

3) Phenols **don't react** with **carbonate** solutions though — sodium carbonate (Na_2CO_3) is not a strong enough base to remove the hydrogen ion from phenol.
4) This is a good way to tell phenols **apart** from **carboxylic acids**, which **react** with alkalis and carbonates (giving off CO_2 gas).

Phenols **React** with **Acid Anhydrides** to Form **Esters**

1) Just like other alcohols, phenols react with **acid anhydrides** to form an **ester** and a **carboxylic acid** (see page 139).
2) Unlike other alcohols, phenols will **not react** with **carboxylic acids** to form an ester (see page 139).
3) This is a good way to test whether a substance is a phenol or a different alcohol.

Practice Questions

Q1 How can you test a compound to see if it is a phenol?

Q2 Are phenols acidic, alkaline or neutral? Explain your answer.

Exam Question

Q1 A student has solutions of phenol, ethanoic acid and salicylic acid (which has a phenol and a carboxylic acid group). Neutral iron(III) chloride solution and sodium carbonate solution are added, separately, to samples of each solution. Complete the table below showing the results of each test. [3 marks]

	phenol	ethanoic acid	salicylic acid
neutral iron(III) chloride solution			
sodium carbonate solution			

Read this page or else — that's a phenol warning...

So, phenols are acids and alcohols that sometimes act a little bit strangely — they don't react with carboxylic acids or carbonates for a start. They're the slightly weird cousins, the black sheep, the odd ones out... Bless their peculiar souls.

Tests for Functional Groups

You met some useful tests for identifying inorganic ions back on pages 104-105. Well, if that wasn't enough to satisfy your budding detective skills, there are also some tests you can carry out to identify a mysterious organic compound.

You Can Test Whether You've Got a Primary, Secondary or Tertiary Alcohol

You've already seen how to **oxidise alcohols** using **acidified potassium dichromate (VI)** on pages 142-143. You can use that reaction to test which sort of alcohol you've got — **primary**, **secondary**, or **tertiary**. Here's what you do:

1) Add 10 drops of the alcohol to 2 cm^3 of acidified potassium dichromate solution in a test tube.
2) Warm the mixture gently in a hot water bath.
3) Then watch for a colour change:

PRIMARY – the **orange** solution slowly turns **green** as an aldehyde forms. (If you carry on heating, the aldehyde will be oxidised further to give a carboxylic acid.)
SECONDARY – the **orange** solution slowly turns **green** as a ketone forms.
TERTIARY – nothing happens — boring, but easy to remember.

The colour change is the orange dichromate(VI) ion ($Cr_2O_7^{2-}$) being reduced to the green chromium(III) ion (Cr^{3+}).

The problem with this test is that it shows the **same result** for **primary** and **secondary alcohols**. To find out which one you started with, you'll have to repeat the experiment and collect some of the **product**:

1) Add excess alcohol to 2 cm^3 of acidified potassium dichromate solution in a round bottomed flask.
2) Set up the flask as part of distillation apparatus (see the picture on the right).
3) Gently heat the flask. The alcohol will be oxidised and the product will be distilled off immediately so you can collect it.

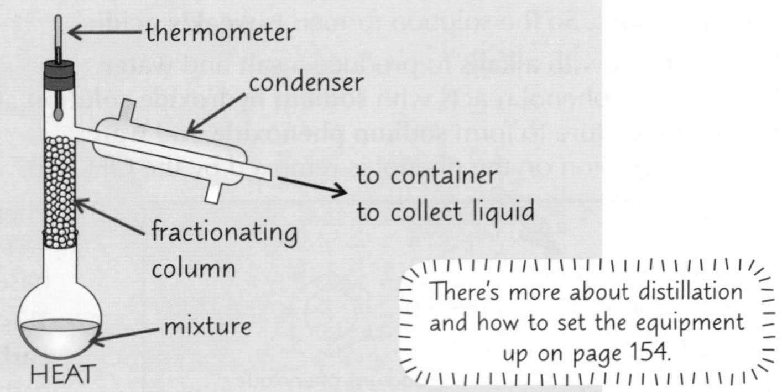

There's more about distillation and how to set the equipment up on page 154.

Once you've collected the product, you'll need to test it to find out if it's an **aldehyde** or a **ketone**. Handily, what's coming up next is how to do just that...

You Can Test Whether You've Got an Aldehyde or a Ketone

There are three main reagents you can use to distinguish between **aldehydes** and **ketones** — Fehling's solution, Benedict's solution and Tollens' reagent.

Fehling's Solution and Benedict's Solution

Fehling's solution and Benedict's solution work in exactly the same way.

1) Add 2 cm^3 of Fehling's or Benedict's solution to a test tube. (Whichever one you use, it should be a clear blue solution.)
2) Add 5 drops of the aldehyde or ketone to the test tube.
3) Put the test tube in a hot water bath to warm it for a few minutes.

ALDEHYDE – the blue solution will give a **brick red precipitate**.
KETONE – nothing happens.

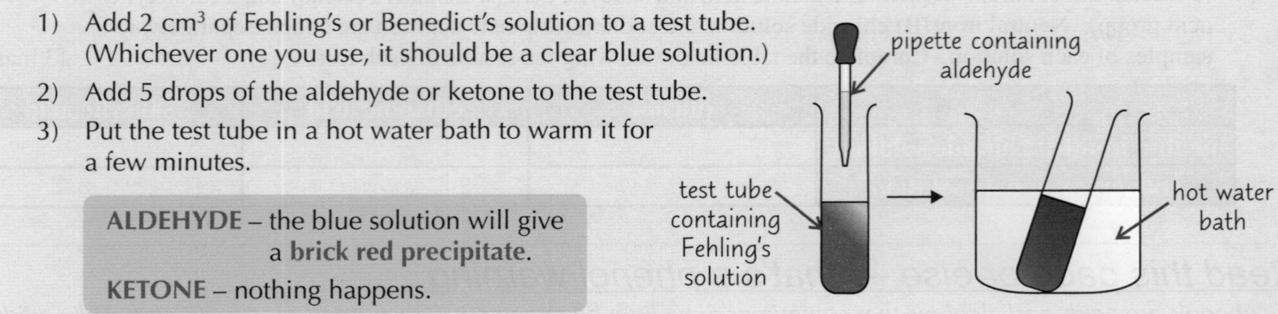

Tests for Functional Groups

Tollens' Reagent

You'd think that two reagents you could use to test for aldehydes and ketones would be enough, but there's one more to go. This one's a bit more tricky, because you have to start by making up the Tollens' reagent yourself.

1) Put 2 cm^3 of 0.10 mol dm^{-3} silver nitrate solution in a test tube.

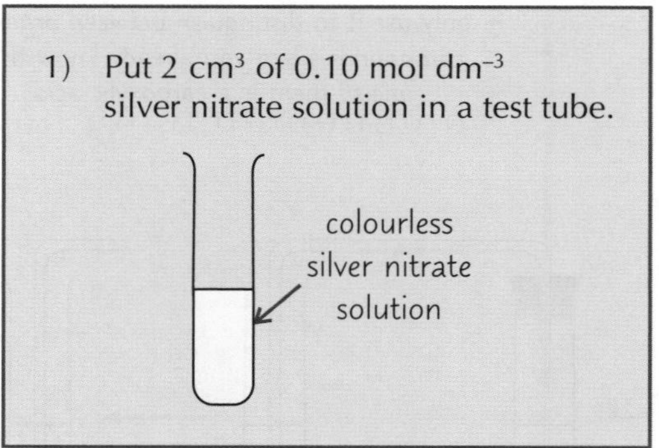

2) Add a few drops of dilute sodium hydroxide solution. A light brown precipitate should form.

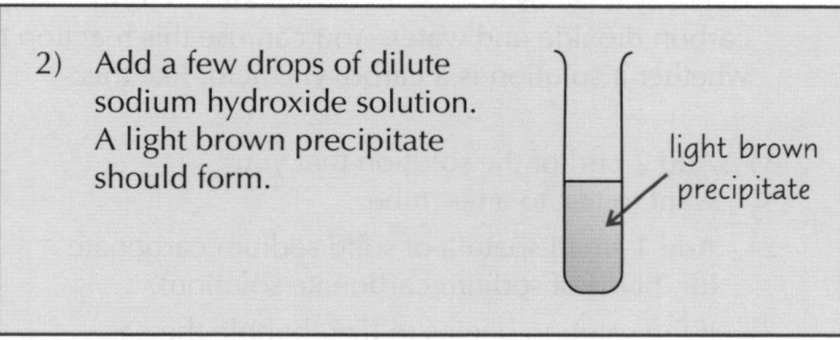

3) Add drops of dilute ammonia solution until the brown precipitate dissolves completely.

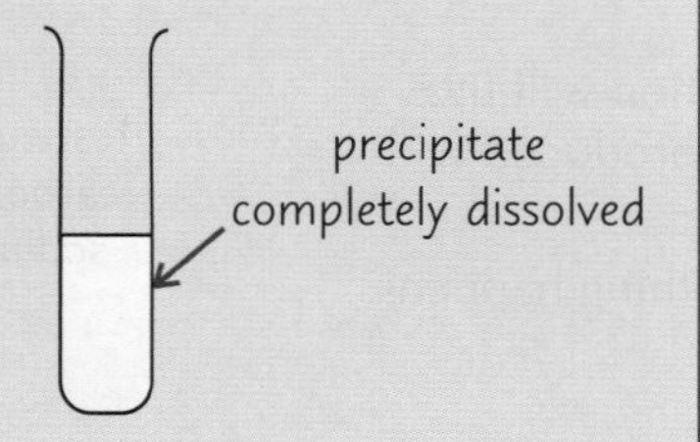

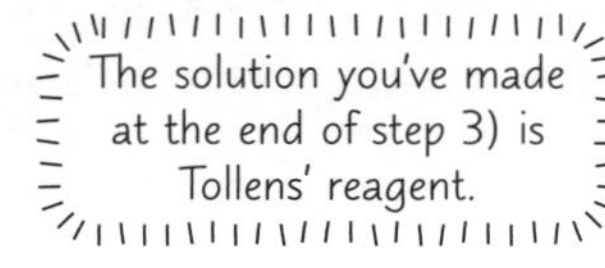

The solution you've made at the end of step 3) is Tollens' reagent.

4) Place the test tube in a hot water bath and add 10 drops of aldehyde or ketone. Wait for a few minutes.

ALDEHYDE – a **silver mirror** (a thin coating of silver) forms on the walls of the test tube.
KETONE – nothing happens.

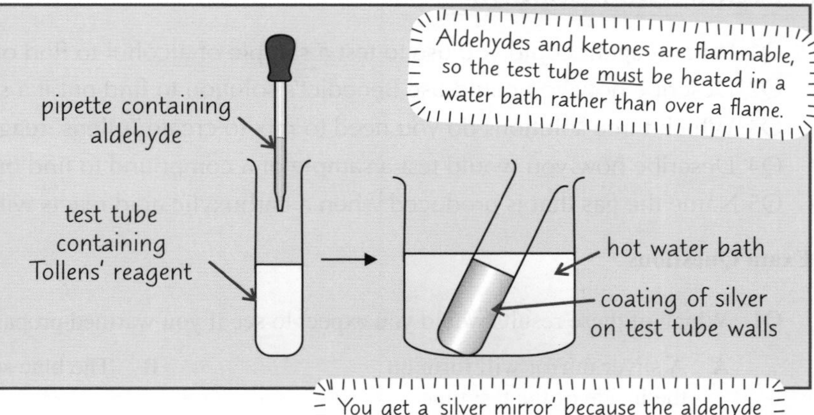

Aldehydes and ketones are flammable, so the test tube must be heated in a water bath rather than over a flame.

You get a 'silver mirror' because the aldehyde reduces the Ag^+ ions to silver atoms.

Use **Bromine Water** to Test for **Alkenes**

Here's another test that you've come across before (on page 132). This one allows you to test a solution to find out if it's an **alkene** — what you're actually testing for is the presence of **double bonds**. Here's what you do:

1) Add 2 cm^3 of the solution that you want to test to a test tube.
2) Add 2 cm^3 of bromine water to the test tube.
3) Shake the test tube.

ALKENE – the solution will decolourise (go from **orange** to **colourless**).
NOT ALKENE – nothing happens.

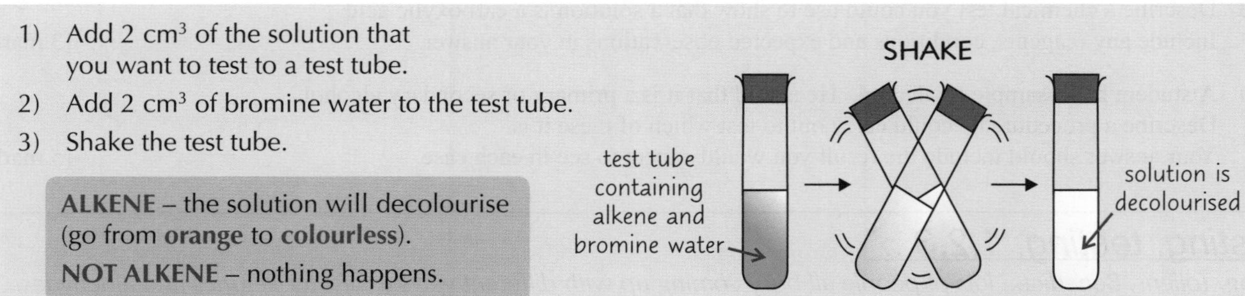

Tests for Functional Groups

Use Sodium Carbonate to Test for Carboxylic Acids

1) There's also a test to work out if something's a **carboxylic acid**. You met carboxylic acids on page 142, so have a look back if you can't remember what they are.
2) Carboxylic acids react with **carbonates** to form a salt, carbon dioxide and water. You can use this reaction to test whether a solution is a carboxylic acid, like this:

Be careful though — this test will give a positive result with any acid, so you can only use it to distinguish between organic compounds when you already know that one of them is a carboxylic acid.

1) Add 2 cm^3 of the solution that you want to test to a test tube.
2) Add 1 small spatula of solid sodium carbonate (or 2 cm^3 of sodium carbonate solution).
3) If the solution begins to fizz, bubble the gas that it produces through some limewater in a second test tube.

CARBOXYLIC ACID – the solution will fizz. The carbon dioxide gas that is produced will turn limewater cloudy.
NOT CARBOXYLIC ACID – nothing happens.

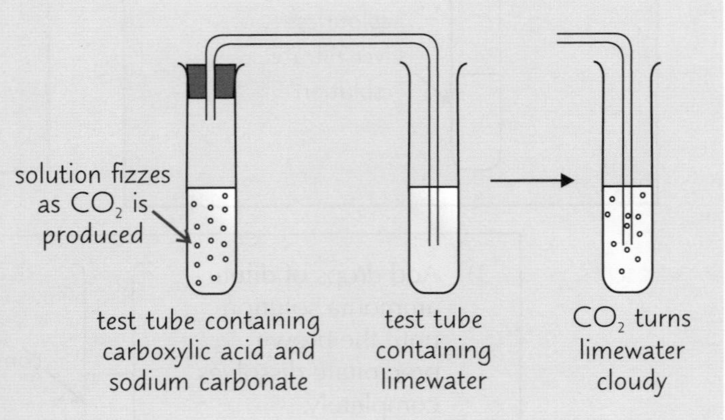

Practice Questions

Q1 What reagent could you use to test a sample of alcohol to find out whether it was a tertiary alcohol?

Q2 Describe how you could use Benedict's solution to find out if a solution was an aldehyde or a ketone.

Q3 Which three solutions do you need to mix to create Tollens' reagent?

Q4 Describe how you would test a sample of a compound to find out if it was an alkane or an alkene.

Q5 Name the gas that is produced when a carboxylic acid reacts with sodium carbonate.

Exam Questions

Q1 Which of these results would you expect to see if you warmed propanone with Fehling's solution?

A A silver mirror will form on the inside of the test tube.
B The blue solution will give a brick red precipitate.
C The orange solution will decolourise.
D Nothing will happen. [1 mark]

Q2 Which of these statements about cyclohexene is correct?

A It produces a brick red precipitate with Fehling's solution.
B It decolourises bromine water.
C It turns limewater cloudy.
D It forms a silver mirror with Tollens' reagent. [1 mark]

Q3 Describe a chemical test you could use to show that a solution is a carboxylic acid. Include any reagents, conditions and expected observations in your answer. [3 marks]

Q4 A student has a sample of alcohol. He is told that it is a primary or secondary alcohol. Describe a procedure he could carry out to test which of these it is. Your answer should include the result you would expect to see in each case. [5 marks]

"Testing, testing, 1,2,3..."

Fehling, Tollens, Benedict... lots of people all busy coming up with different ways to test for ketones and aldehydes. You'd have thought one way would've been enough, and the others could've found something better to do with their time. You know, like finding needles in haystacks, watching paint dry, or figuring out just why a raven is like a writing desk.

Analytical Techniques

If you've got some stuff and don't know what it is, don't taste it. Stick it in an infrared spectrometer or a mass spectrometer instead. You'll wind up with some scary looking graphs. But just learn the basics, and you'll be fine.

Infrared Spectroscopy Helps You Identify Organic Molecules

1) In infrared (IR) spectroscopy, a beam of **IR radiation** is passed through a sample of a chemical.
2) The IR radiation is absorbed by the **covalent bonds** in the molecules, increasing their **vibrational** energy (i.e. they vibrate more).
3) **Bonds between different atoms** absorb **different frequencies** of IR radiation. Bonds in different **places** in a molecule absorb different frequencies too — so the O–H bond in an **alcohol** and the O–H bond in a **carboxylic acid** absorb different frequencies. This table shows what **frequencies** different bonds absorb:

Functional Group	Where it's found	Frequency/ Wavenumber (cm^{-1})
C–H	alkyl groups, alkenes, arenes	2850 – 3100
O–H	alcohols	3200 – 3600
O–H	carboxylic acids	2500 – 3300 (broad)
C=O	aldehydes, ketones, carboxylic acids, esters	1630 – 1820

You don't need to learn this data, but you do need to understand how to use it.

4) An infrared spectrometer produces a **spectrum** that shows you what frequencies of radiation the molecules are absorbing. You can use it to identify the **functional groups** in a molecule:

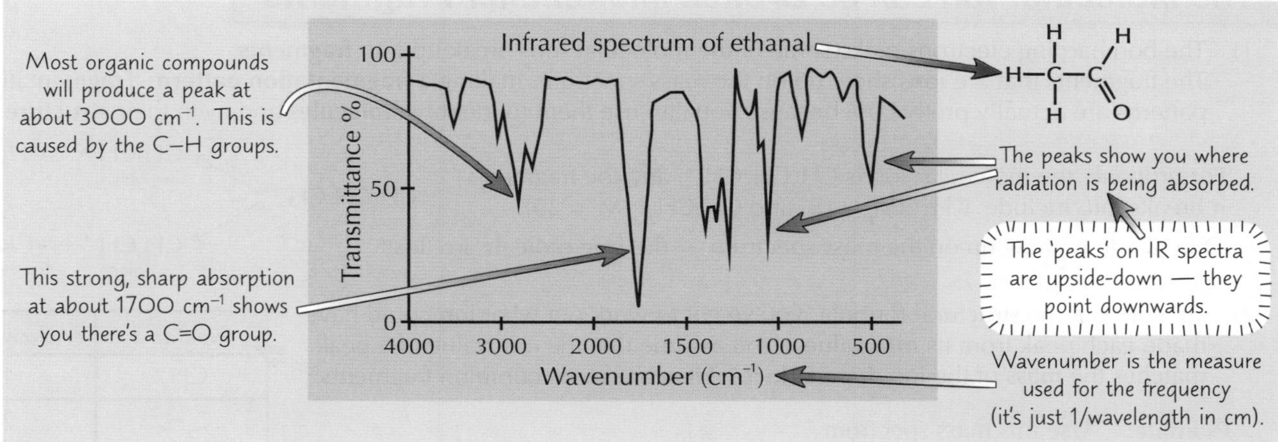
Infrared spectrum of ethanal
Most organic compounds will produce a peak at about 3000 cm⁻¹. This is caused by the C–H groups.
This strong, sharp absorption at about 1700 cm⁻¹ shows you there's a C=O group.
The peaks show you where radiation is being absorbed.
The 'peaks' on IR spectra are upside-down — they point downwards.
Wavenumber is the measure used for the frequency (it's just 1/wavelength in cm).
Transmittance %
100
50
0
4000
3000
2000
1500
1000
500
Wavenumber (cm⁻¹)
H
H
H–C–C
H
O

5) This also means that you can tell if a functional group has **changed** during a reaction. For example, if you **oxidise** an **alcohol** to an **aldehyde** you'll see the O–H absorption **disappear** from the spectrum, and a C=O absorption **appear**. If you then oxidise it further to a **carboxylic acid** an O–H peak at a slightly lower frequency than before will appear, alongside the C=O peak.

There Are Lots of Uses for Infrared Spectroscopy

1) Infrared spectroscopy is used in **breathalysers** to work out if a driver is over the drink-drive limit. The **amount** of **ethanol vapour** in the driver's breath is found by measuring the **intensity** of the peak corresponding to the **C–H bond** in the IR spectrum. It's chosen because it's **not affected** by any **water vapour** in the breath.
2) Infrared spectroscopy is also used to monitor the concentrations of **polluting gases** in the atmosphere. These include **carbon monoxide** (CO) and **nitrogen monoxide** (NO), which are both present in **car emissions**. The intensity of the peaks corresponding to the C≡O or N=O bonds can be studied to monitor their levels.

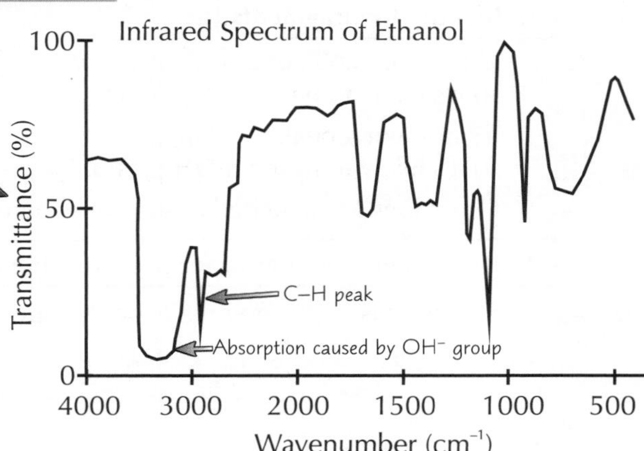
Infrared Spectrum of Ethanol
Transmittance (%)
100
50
0
C–H peak
Absorption caused by OH⁻ group
4000
3000
2000
1500
1000
500
Wavenumber (cm⁻¹)

Analytical Techniques

Mass Spectrometry Can Help to Identify Compounds

1) You saw on pages 22-23 how you can use a mass spectrum to work out the relative atomic mass of an element or the molecular mass of a compound.
2) To find the relative molecular mass of a compound you look at the **molecular ion peak** (the **M peak**). This is the peak with the highest mass/charge ratio (ignoring a small M+1 peak due to the presence of the isotope carbon-13). The mass/charge value of the molecular ion peak is the **molecular mass**.

Assuming the ion has a 1+ charge, which it normally will have.

The *y*-**axis** gives the **abundance of ions**, often as a percentage.

The *x*-**axis** units are given as a '**mass/charge**' ratio.

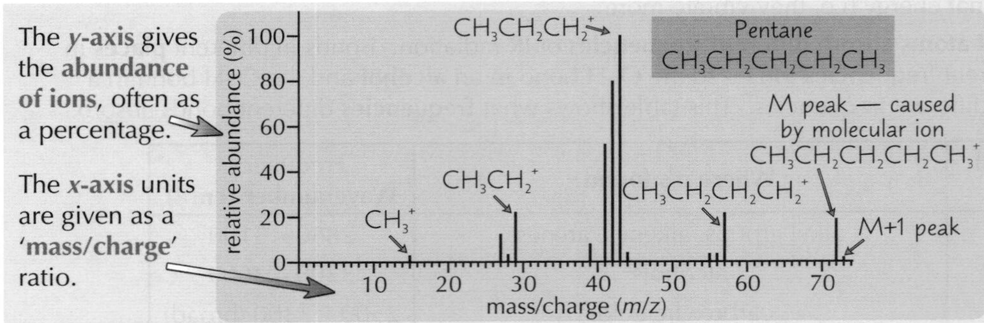

Here's the mass spectrum of pentane. Its M peak is at 72 — so the compound's M_r is 72. For most organic compounds the M peak is the one with the second highest mass/charge ratio. The smaller peak to the right of the M peak is called the M+1 peak — it's caused by the presence of the carbon isotope ^{13}C.

3) You also get **high resolution mass spectrometry**, which gives the *m/z* ratio to lots of **decimal places**. It's used to distinguish between molecules that seem to have the **same** M_r when rounded to the nearest whole number (e.g. propane, $CH_3CH_2CH_3$, and ethanal, CH_3CHO).

The *Molecular Ion* can be *Broken* into *Smaller Fragments*

1) The bombarding electrons make some of the molecular ions break up into **fragments**. The fragments that are ions show up on the mass spectrum, making a **fragmentation pattern**. Fragmentation patterns are actually pretty cool because you can use them to identify **molecules** and even their **structure**.

For propane, the molecular ion is $CH_3CH_2CH_3^+$, and the fragments it breaks into include CH_3^+ (M_r = 15) and $CH_3CH_2^+$ (M_r = 29).

Only the **ions** show up on the mass spectrum — the **free radicals** are 'lost'.

$CH_3CH_2CH_3^+ \rightarrow CH_3CH_2\bullet$ (free radical) $+ CH_3^+$ (ion)

$CH_3CH_2CH_3^+ \rightarrow CH_3CH_2^+$ (ion) $+ \bullet CH_3$ (free radical)

2) To work out the structural formula, you've got to work out what **ion** could have made each peak from its ***m/z* value**. (You assume that the *m/z* value of a peak matches the **mass** of the ion that made it.) Here are some common fragments:

Fragment	Molecular Mass
CH_3^+	15
$C_2H_5^+$	29
$CH_3CH_2CH_2^+$ or $CH_3CHCH_3^+$	43
OH^+	17

Example: Use this mass spectrum to work out the structure of the molecule:

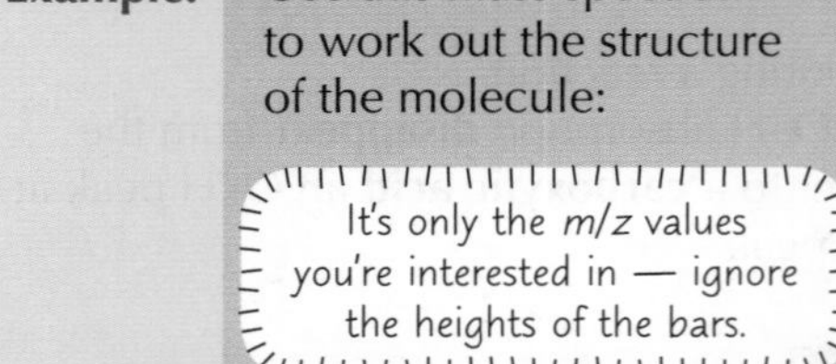

It's only the *m/z* values you're interested in — ignore the heights of the bars.

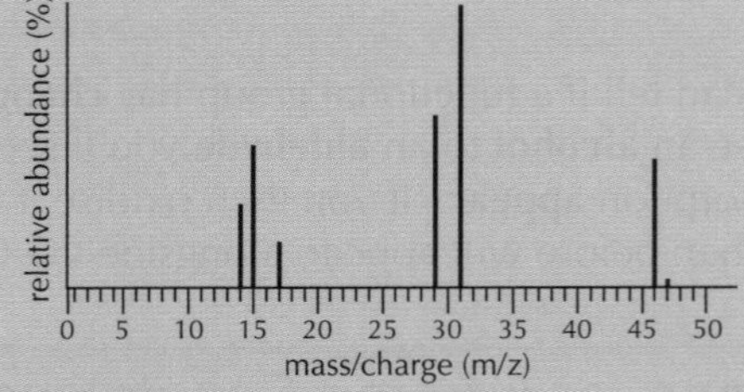

1. Identify the fragments

This molecule's got a peak at 15 *m/z*, so it's likely to have a CH_3 **group**.

It's also got a peak at 17 *m/z*, so it's likely to have an **OH group**.

Other ions are matched to the peaks here:

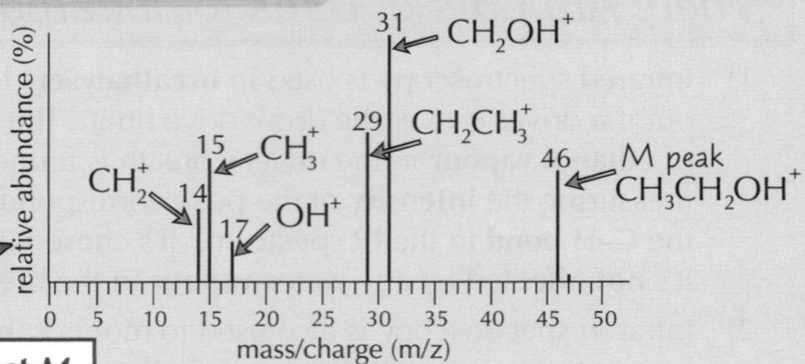

2. Piece them together to form a molecule with the correct M_r

Ethanol has all the fragments on this spectrum.

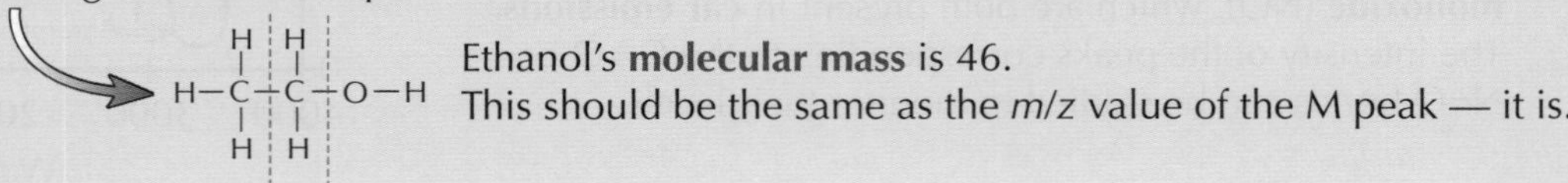

Ethanol's **molecular mass** is 46.
This should be the same as the *m/z* value of the M peak — it is.

Analytical Techniques

*Mass Spectrometry is Used to **Differentiate** Between **Similar Molecules***

1) Even if two **different compounds** contain **the same atoms**, you can still tell them apart with mass spectrometry because they won't produce exactly the same set of fragments.
2) The formulas of **propanal** and **propanone** are shown on the right. They've got the same M_r, but different structures, so they produce some **different fragments**. For example, propanal will have a $\mathbf{C_2H_5}$ fragment but propanone won't.
3) Every compound produces a different mass spectrum — so the spectrum's like a **fingerprint** for the compound. Large computer **databases** of mass spectra can be used to identify a compound from its spectrum.

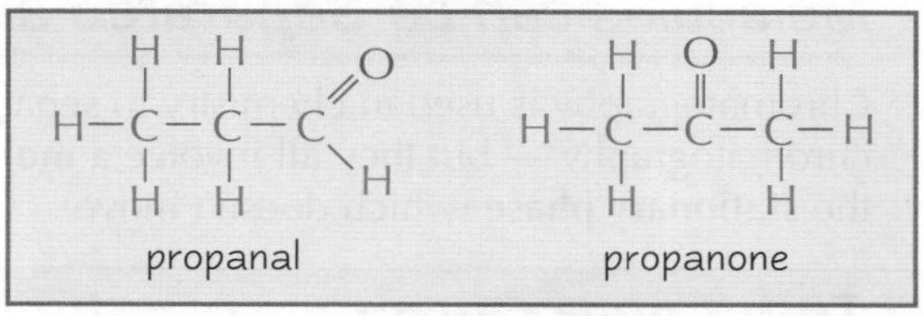

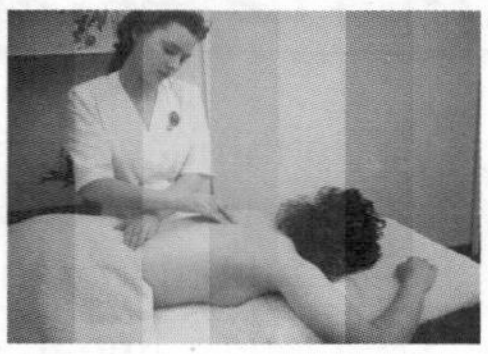
A massage spectrum

*You Can **Combine Techniques** to **Identify** a Compound*

You can identify a compound using data about its **mass or percentage composition**, **IR spectrum** and **mass spectrum**. Here's what you to do:

1) Use the **composition** to work out the **molecular formula** of the compound.
2) Work out what **functional groups** are in the compound from its **infrared spectrum**.
3) Use the **mass spectrum** to work out the **structure** of the molecule.

Have a look at page 43 if you're not sure how to work out a compound's molecular formula from its composition.

Practice Questions

Q1 Which parts of a molecule absorb infrared energy?

Q2 Why do most infrared spectra of organic molecules have a strong, sharp peak at around 3000 cm^{-1}?

Q3 Give two uses of infrared spectroscopy.

Q4 What is the M peak?

Exam Questions

Use the infrared absorption data on p. 149.

Q1 The molecule that produces the IR spectrum shown on the right has composition by mass of: C: 48.64%, H: 8.12%, O: 43.24%.

a) Which functional groups are responsible for peaks A and B? [2 marks]

b) Give the molecular formula and name of this molecule. Explain your answer. [3 marks]

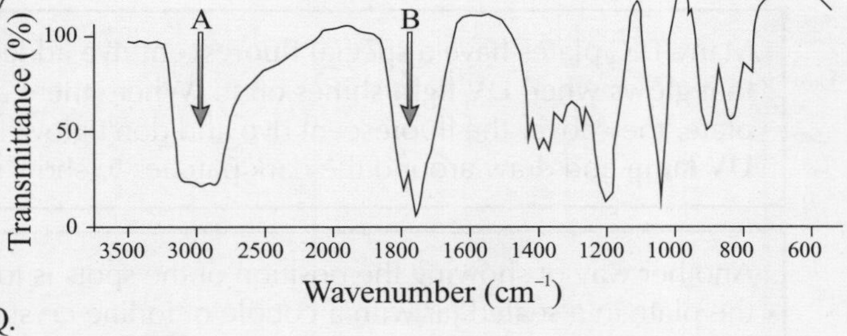

Q2 Below is the mass spectrum of an organic compound, Q.

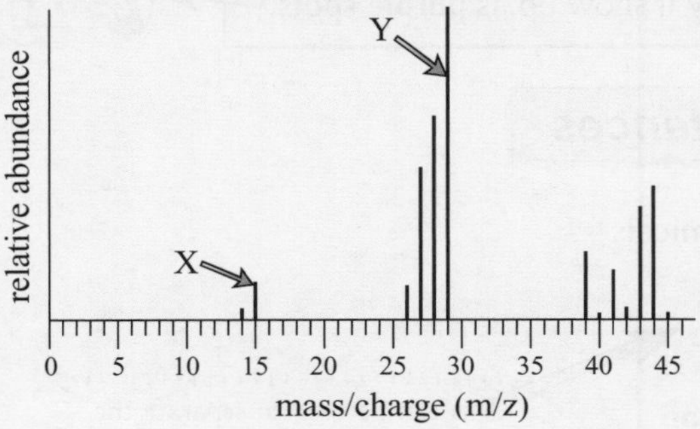

a) What is the M_r of compound Q? [1 mark]

b) What fragments are the peaks marked X and Y most likely to correspond to? [2 marks]

c) Suggest a structure for this compound. [1 mark]

d) Why is it unlikely that this compound is an alcohol? [1 mark]

Use the clues, identify a molecule — mass spectrometry my dear Watson...

Luckily you don't have to remember where any of the infrared peaks are. But you do need to be able to identify them using data given to you in the exams. It's handy if you can learn the molecular masses of the common mass spec fragments, but as a backup you can just work them out from the relative atomic masses of the atoms in each fragment.

Thin Layer Chromatography

I like my chromatography as I like my Marmite®... in a nice thin layer (and maybe accompanied by a crumpet...)

Molecules can be **Separated** and **Identified** Using **Chromatography**

Chromatography is used in chemistry to separate mixtures of molecules. There are many different forms of chromatography — but they all involve a **mobile phase** (a liquid or gas) that moves over a second material called the **stationary phase** (which doesn't move).

Thin Layer Chromatography is a Simple Way of **Separating Mixtures**

1) In thin layer chromatography (TLC), the **stationary phase** is a thin layer of **silica** (**silicon dioxide**) or **alumina** (**aluminium oxide**) fixed to a glass or metal plate.
2) Draw a line **in pencil** near the bottom of the TLC plate (the baseline) and put a small drop of each mixture to be separated on the line.
3) Place the plate in a beaker with a small volume of solvent (this is the **mobile phase**). The solvent level must be **below** the baseline.

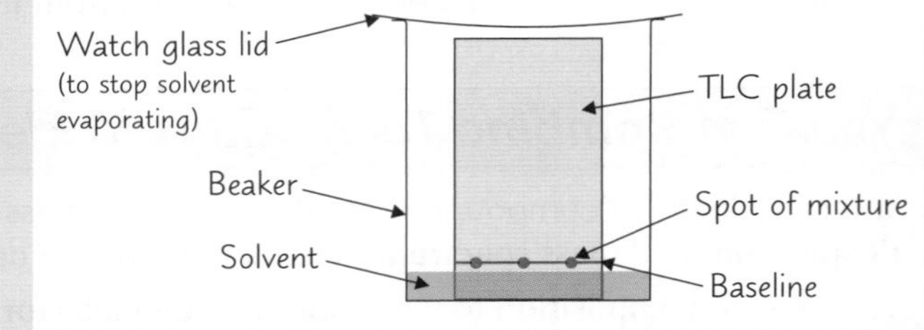

4) Leave the beaker until the solvent has moved almost to the top of the plate. Then remove the plate from the beaker and allow it to dry. Before it's evaporated you should mark how far the solvent travelled up the plate (this line is called the **solvent front**).
5) As it moves up the plate, the solvent will carry the substances in the mixture with it — but some chemicals will be carried **faster** than others and so travel further up the plate. The result is called a **chromatogram**.
6) You can use the **positions of the chemicals** on the chromatogram to identify what the chemicals are.

Colourless Chemicals are Revealed Using **UV Light** or **Iodine**

1) If the chemicals in the mixture are **coloured** (such as the dyes that make up an ink) then you'll see them as a **set of coloured dots** at different heights on the TLC plate...
2) But if there are **colourless chemicals** in the mixture, you need to find a way of making them **visible**. Here are two ways:

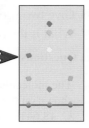

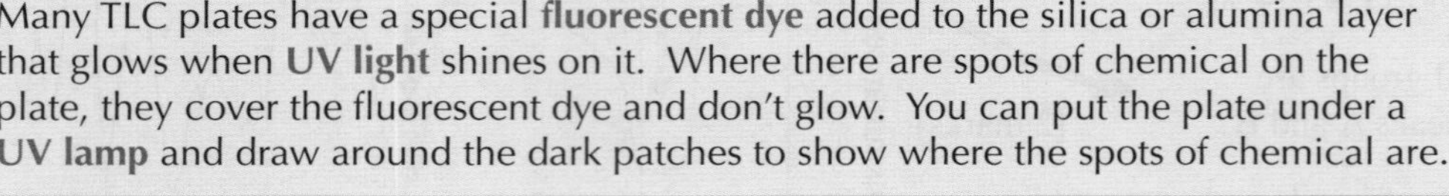
Many TLC plates have a special **fluorescent dye** added to the silica or alumina layer that glows when **UV light** shines on it. Where there are spots of chemical on the plate, they cover the fluorescent dye and don't glow. You can put the plate under a **UV lamp** and draw around the dark patches to show where the spots of chemical are.

Another way of showing the position of the spots is to expose them to **iodine vapour** (leaving the plate in a sealed jar with a couple of iodine crystals does the trick). Iodine vapour is a **locating agent** — it sticks to the chemicals on the plate and they'll show up as **purple spots**.

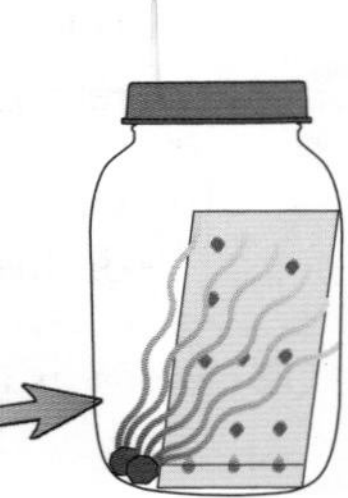

Chromatography can be used to **Purify Substances**

1) The TLC method above separates **very small quantities** of chemicals — ideal for identifying what makes up a mixture.
2) You can also use chromatography to separate **large quantities** of a mixture in an **organic synthesis**.

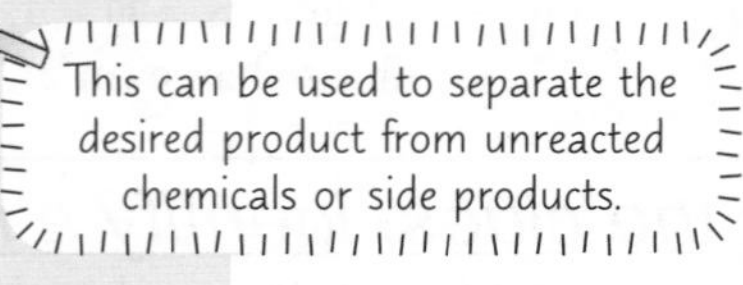

This can be used to separate the desired product from unreacted chemicals or side products.

3) You need larger-scale equipment though, such as a **glass column** (e.g. a burette) packed with silica or alumina (the same **stationary phase** that is used in TLC). You then pour your mixture into the column and run solvent (the **mobile phase**) through it continually.
4) The different chemicals in the mixture move down the column at **different rates**, so they come out at different times, meaning you get pure chemicals.

Thin Layer Chromatography

The **Position** of the Spots on a Plate Can Help to **Identify Substances**

1) If you just want to know **how many** chemicals are present in a mixture, all you have to do is **count the number of spots** that form on the plate.
2) But if you want to find out what each chemical **is**, you can calculate something called an R_f **value**. The formula for this is:

$$R_f = \frac{\text{distance travelled by spot}}{\text{distance travelled by solvent}}$$

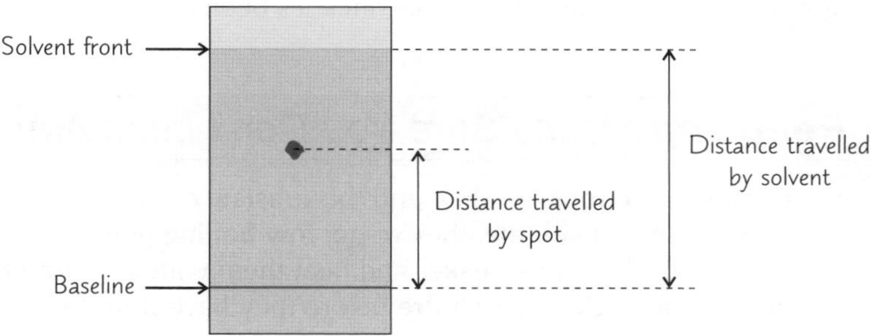

3) R_f values are **always the same** no matter how big the plate is or how far the solvent travels — they're properties of the chemicals in the mixture and so can be used to identify those chemicals.
4) BUT — if the composition of the TLC plate, the solvent, or the temperature change even slightly, you'll get **different** R_f **values**.
5) It's hard to keep the conditions identical. So, if you suspect that a mixture contains, say, chlorophyll, it's best to put a spot of chlorophyll on the baseline of the **same plate** as the mixture and run them both at the **same time**.

Practice Questions

Q1 What are the names of the two phases that are used in all forms of chromatography?

Q2 Give two uses of chromatography.

Q3 What is the formula for calculating R_f values?

Exam Question

Q1 The diagram below shows a chromatogram of four known substances (1 to 4) and two unknowns, labelled X and Y. One of the unknowns is pure and the other is a mixture.

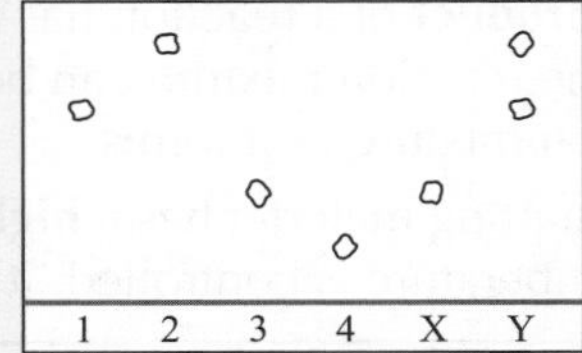

a) State whether each of the different substances is pure or impure. [1 mark]

b) Suggest which of the known substances (1 to 4) are present in the unknown that is a mixture. Explain your answer. [2 marks]

c) The solvent front on the chromatogram was measured at 8 cm from the baseline, and substance 1 travelled 5.6 cm. Calculate the R_f value of substance 1. [1 mark]

d) All the substances on the chromatogram above are colourless. Suggest two methods that could have been used to make these colourless chemicals visible. [2 marks]

Cromer-tography — pictures from my holiday in Norfolk...

Fun fact — 'chromatography' means 'writing with colours' in Greek. Fun, but not particularly useful. Working out R_f values is pretty easy as long as you remember that it's the distance travelled by the spot divided by the distance travelled by the solvent, and not the other way around — think of it as a fraction (and it'll always be less than 1).

Practical Skills

I'm sure learning all this organic chemistry has got you itching to get into the lab and do some experiments. Well, hold your horses and read these pages before you go throwing chemicals around willy-nilly...

Organic Chemistry uses some *Specific Techniques*

There are some **practical techniques** that get used a lot in organic chemistry. They may be used during the **synthesis** of a product, or to **purify** it from unwanted by-products or unreacted reagents once it's been made.

Refluxing Makes Sure You Don't Lose Any *Volatile* Organic Substances

1) **Organic reactions** are **slow** and the substances are usually **flammable** and **volatile** (they've got **low boiling points**). If you stick them in a beaker and heat them with a Bunsen burner they'll **evaporate** or **catch fire** before they have **time to react**.
2) You can **reflux** a reaction to get round this problem.
3) The mixture's **heated in a flask** fitted with a **vertical Liebig condenser** — this continuously boils, evaporates and condenses the vapours and **recycles** them back into the flask, giving them **time to react**.
4) The **heating** is usually **electrical** — hot plates, heating mantles, or electrically controlled water baths are normally used. This **avoids naked flames** that might ignite the compounds.

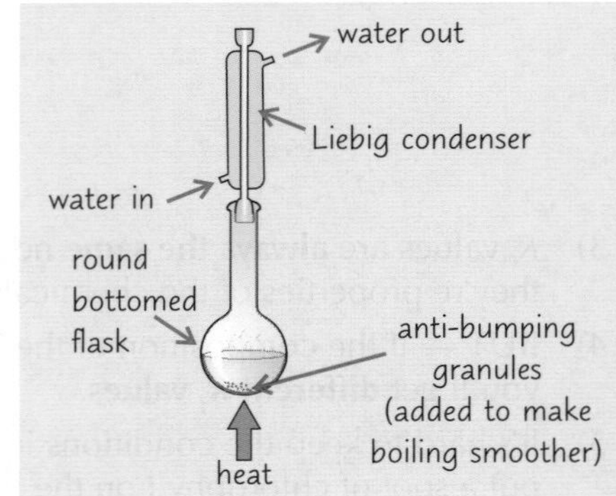

Distillation Separates Substances With Different *Boiling Points*

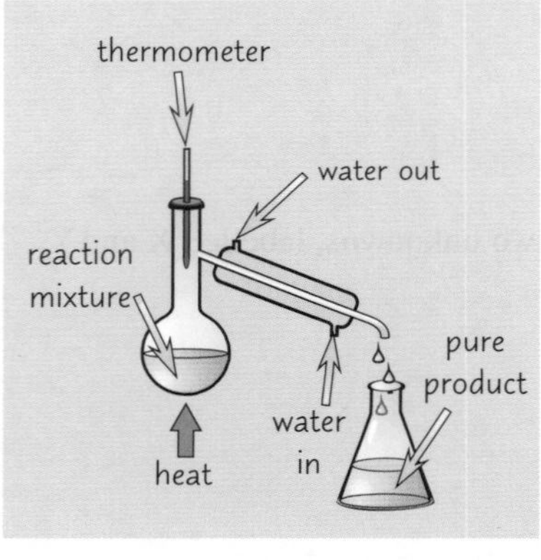

1) Distillation works by **gently heating** a mixture in a distillation apparatus. The substances will evaporate out of the mixture in order of **increasing boiling point**.
2) The thermometer shows the **boiling point** of the substance that is **evaporating** at any given time.
3) If you know the boiling point of your **pure product**, you can use the thermometer to tell you when it's evaporating and therefore when it's condensing.
4) If the **product** of a reaction has a **lower boiling point** than the **starting materials** then the reaction mixture can be **heated** so that the product **evaporates** from the reaction mixture as it forms.
5) If the starting material has a **higher boiling point** than the product, so as long as the temperature is controlled, it won't evaporate out from the reaction mixture.

- Sometimes, a product is formed that will go on to **react further** if it's left in the reaction mixture.
- For example, when you oxidise a **primary alcohol**, it is first oxidised to an **aldehyde** and then oxidised to a **carboxylic acid**. If you want the **aldehyde product**, then you can do your reaction in the **distillation equipment**. The aldehyde product has a **lower boiling point** than the alcohol starting material, so will distil out of the reaction mixture **as soon** as it forms. It is then collected in a separate container.

Volatile Liquids Can be Purified by *Redistillation*

1) If a product and its impurities have **different boiling points**, then redistillation can be used to **separate** them. You just use the same distillation apparatus as shown above, but this time you're heating an **impure product**, instead of the reaction mixture.
2) When the liquid you want **boils** (this is when the thermometer is at the boiling point of the liquid), you place a flask at the open end of the condenser ready to collect your product.
3) When the thermometer shows the temperature is changing, put another flask at the end of the condenser because a **different liquid** is about to be delivered.

Practical Skills

Separation Removes Any **Water Soluble Impurities** From the Product

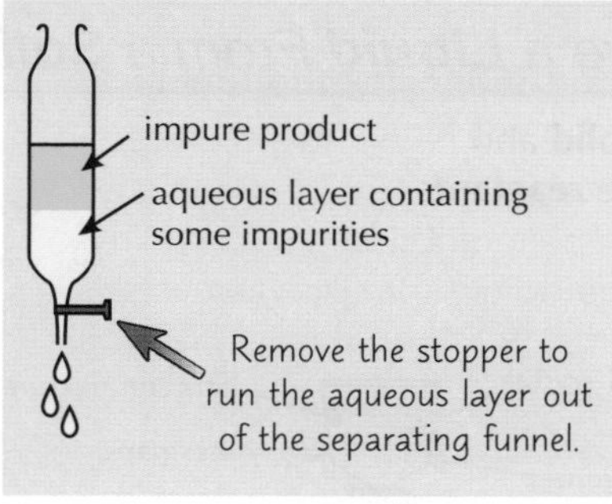
impure product
aqueous layer containing some impurities
Remove the stopper to run the aqueous layer out of the separating funnel.

1) If the product is **insoluble** in water then you can use **separation** to remove any impurities that **do dissolve** in water, such as **salts** or water soluble organic compounds (e.g. alcohols).
2) Once the reaction is completed, the mixture is poured into a **separating funnel**, and **water** is added.
3) The funnel is **shaken** and then allowed to settle. The **organic layer** is **less dense** than the **aqueous layer** so should float on top. Any water soluble impurities should have dissolved in the lower **aqueous layer**. You can then open the stopper on the separating funnel, run off the aqueous layer and collect your product.

- If you use separation to purify a product, the organic layer will end up containing **trace amounts** of **water**, so it has to be **dried**.
- To do this you can add an **anhydrous salt** such as **magnesium sulfate** ($MgSO_4$) or **calcium chloride** ($CaCl_2$). The salt is used as a **drying agent** — it **binds** to any water present to become **hydrated**.
- When you first add the salt to the organic layer it will be **lumpy**. This means you need to add more. You know that all the water has been removed when you can swirl the mixture and it looks like a snow globe.
- You can **filter** the mixture to remove the solid **drying agent**.

Practice Questions

Q1 Draw a labelled diagram to show the apparatus used in a reflux reaction.

Q2 Why might you want to avoid naked flames when performing an experiment with organic substances?

Q3 Name two ways of purifying organic products.

Q4 Name two drying agents.

Exam Question

Q1 a) A student carried out an experiment to make hex-1-ene from hexan-1-ol using the following procedure:

$$\text{HO}\text{-hexyl} \xrightarrow[\text{heat}]{H_3PO_4} \text{hex-1-ene}$$

1) Mix 1 mL hexan-1-ol with concentrated phosphoric acid in a reflux apparatus, and reflux for 30 minutes.
2) Once the mixture has cooled, separate the alkene from any aqueous impurities.
3) Dry the organic layer with anhydrous magnesium sulfate.

i) What is meant by reflux and why is it a technique sometimes used in organic chemistry? [2 marks]

ii) What organic compound is removed in the separating step? [1 mark]

iii) Describe, in detail, how the student would carry out the separation in step 2). [3 marks]

b) In another experiment, the student decides to make 1-hexen-6-ol by carrying out a single dehydration reaction of the diol 1,6-hexanediol.

$$\text{HO}\text{-(CH}_2)_6\text{-OH} \xrightarrow[\text{heat}]{H_3PO_4} \text{CH}_2\text{=CH-(CH}_2)_4\text{-OH}$$

i) If the student follows the procedure in part a), why might he produce a mixture of products? [1 mark]

ii) How could the procedure in part a) be adapted to prevent a mixture of products being formed? [2 marks]

Thought this page couldn't get any drier? Try adding anhydrous $MgSO_4$...

Scientists need to know why they do the things they do — that way they can plan new experiments to make new compounds. Learning the fine details of how experiments are carried out may not be the most interesting thing in the world, but you should get to try out some of these methods in practicals, which is a lot more fun.

More Practical Skills

Don't take your lab coat off or put down your safety specs just yet. There are more practical techniques coming up. Now that you know how to purify an organic liquid, it's time to find out how you would purify an organic solid...

Filtration Under Reduced Pressure is Used to Remove a Liquid From a Solid

Filtration under reduced pressure is normally used when you want to keep the **solid** and discard the **liquid** (filtrate). For example, you can use it to isolate a product if the **reactants** in an organic reaction are **liquids** and the **product** you're after is a **solid**.

1) Place a piece of **filter paper**, slightly smaller than the diameter of the funnel, on the bottom of the Büchner funnel so that it lies flat and covers all the holes.
2) **Wet** the paper with a little solvent, so that it **sticks** to the bottom of the funnel, and doesn't slip around when you pour in your mixture.
3) Turn the **vacuum** on, and then pour your mixture into the funnel. As the flask is under **reduced pressure**, the **liquid** is sucked through the funnel into the flask, leaving the **solid** behind.
4) **Rinse** the solid with a little of the solvent that your mixture was in. This will **wash off** any of the original liquid from the mixture that stayed on your crystals (and also any soluble impurities), leaving you with a **more pure** solid.
5) Disconnect the vacuum line from the side-arm flask and then turn off the vacuum.
6) The solid will be a bit wet from the solvent, so leave it to **dry completely**.

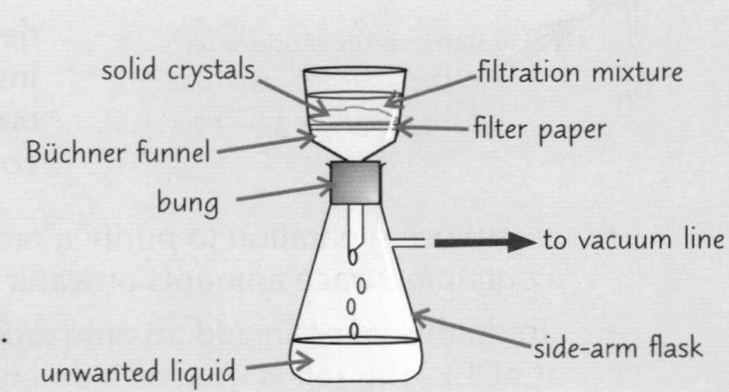

Organic Solids can be Purified by Recrystallisation

If the product of an organic reaction is a solid, then the simplest way of purifying it is a process called **recrystallisation**. First you dissolve your solid in a solvent to make a **saturated** solution. Then you let it cool. As the solution cools, the solubility of the product falls. When it reaches the point where it can't stay in solution, it starts to form crystals. Here's how it's done:

In a saturated solution, the maximum possible amount of solid is dissolved in the solvent.

1) **Very hot solvent** is added to the **impure** solid until it **just** dissolves — it's important not to add too much solvent. This should give a **saturated solution** of the **impure product**.
2) The solution is filtered while it is still hot to remove any insoluble impurities.
3) The solution is left to **cool** down **slowly**. **Crystals** of the **product** form as it cools. The **impurities** stay in solution as they're present in much smaller amounts than the product, so take much longer to crystallise out.
4) The crystals are removed by **filtration** under **reduced pressure** (see above) and **washed** with ice-cold solvent. Then they are dried — leaving you with crystals of your product that are **much purer** than the original solid.

David had no need for recrystallisation — he was pure class.

The Choice of Solvent for Recrystallisation is Very Important

1) When you **recrystallise** a product, you must use an **appropriate solvent** for that particular substance. It will only work if the solid is **very soluble** in the **hot** solvent, but **nearly insoluble** when the solvent is **cold**.
2) If your product **isn't soluble enough** in the hot solvent you **won't** be able to dissolve it all.
3) If your product **is too soluble** in the cold solvent, most of it will **stay in the solution** even after cooling. When you filter it, you'll **lose** most of your product, giving you a very low **yield**.

More Practical Skills

Measuring **Melting Point** is a Good Way to **Determine Purity**

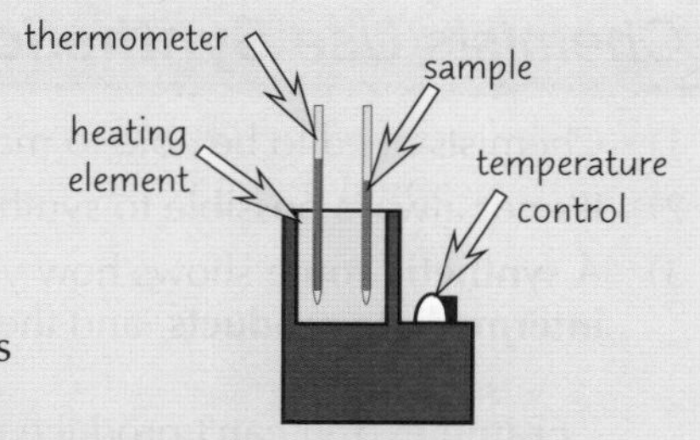

1) You can use **melting point apparatus** to accurately determine the melting point of an **organic solid**.
2) Pack a small sample of the solid into a **glass capillary** and place it inside the **heating element**.
3) **Increase the temperature** until the sample turns from solid to **liquid**.
4) You usually measure a **melting range**, which is the range of temperatures from where the solid **begins to melt** to where it has **melted completely**.
5) You can look up the melting point of a substance in **data books** and compare it to your measurements.
6) **Impurities** in the sample will **lower** the **melting point** and **increase** the **melting range**.

Measuring **Boiling Point** is a Good Way to **Determine Purity**

1) You can measure the purity of an organic, liquid product by looking at its boiling point.
2) If you've got a reasonable volume of liquid, you can determine its boiling point using a **distillation apparatus**, like the one shown on page 154.
3) If you **gently heat** the liquid in the distillation apparatus, until it evaporates, you can read the temperature at which it is distilled, using the thermometer in the top of the apparatus. This temperature is the **boiling point**.
4) You can then look up the boiling point of the substance in **data books** and compare it to your measurement.
5) If the sample contains **impurities**, then your measured boiling point will be **higher** than the recorded value. You may also find your product boils over a range of temperatures, rather than all evaporating at a single temperature.

> Be careful — different organic liquids can have similar boiling points, so you should use other analytical techniques (see Topic 11) to help you determine your product's purity too.

Practice Questions

Q1 What technique could you use to separate an organic solid from liquid impurities?

Q2 When purifying a compound by recrystallisation, why shouldn't you use a cold solvent to dissolve your organic compound?

Q3 Describe a technique you could use to assess the purity of an organic solid.

Q4 Would you expect the boiling point of an impure organic liquid to be higher or lower than for the pure liquid?

Exam Questions

Q1 A scientist refluxes ethyl ethanoate with dilute sodium hydroxide, and obtains impure solid sodium ethanoate.

a) Describe how she could purify this solid by recrystallisation from an appropriate solvent. [3 marks]

b) What would make a solvent appropriate for this recrystallisation process? [1 mark]

c) Describe the melting point range of the impure sodium ethanoate compared to the pure product. [1 mark]

Q2 A student is carrying out an experiment using the apparatus shown on the right. What organic technique is she doing?

A recrystallisation **B** filtration under reduced pressure

C melting point analysis **D** boiling point analysis [1 mark]

Stop! My brain can't hold anymore — it's completely saturated...

Just because the last few pages had 'Practical' in the title doesn't mean you can forget this bit. You can be asked about practical techniques in your exams as well. So before you turn the page, make sure you can tell the difference between a recrystallisation and a filtration, and that you could pick out a Büchner funnel from a glassware identity parade.

Organic Synthesis — Synthetic Routes

There's lots of information on these pages, but you've seen most of it before. It's really just a great big round-up of all the organic reactions you've met in this book. (Maybe not the most exciting thing in the world, but really useful.)

Chemists Use **Synthetic Routes** to Get from One Compound to Another

1) Chemists need to be able to make one compound from another. It's vital for things such as **designing medicines**.
2) It's not always possible to synthesise a desired product from a starting material in **just one** reaction.
3) A **synthetic route** shows how you get from one compound to another. It shows all the **reactions** with the **intermediate products**, and the **reagents** needed for each reaction.

Example: You can't produce **propanone** from **2-bromopropane** via one reaction. Instead you first have to make **propan-2-ol**. The synthetic route is:

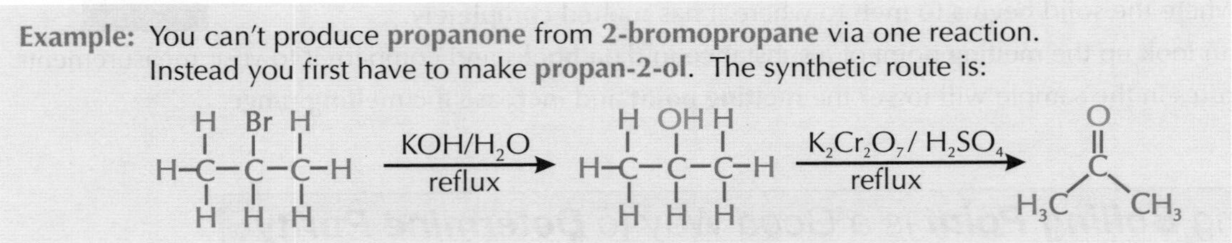

4) Here are all the **organic reactions** you've met so far:

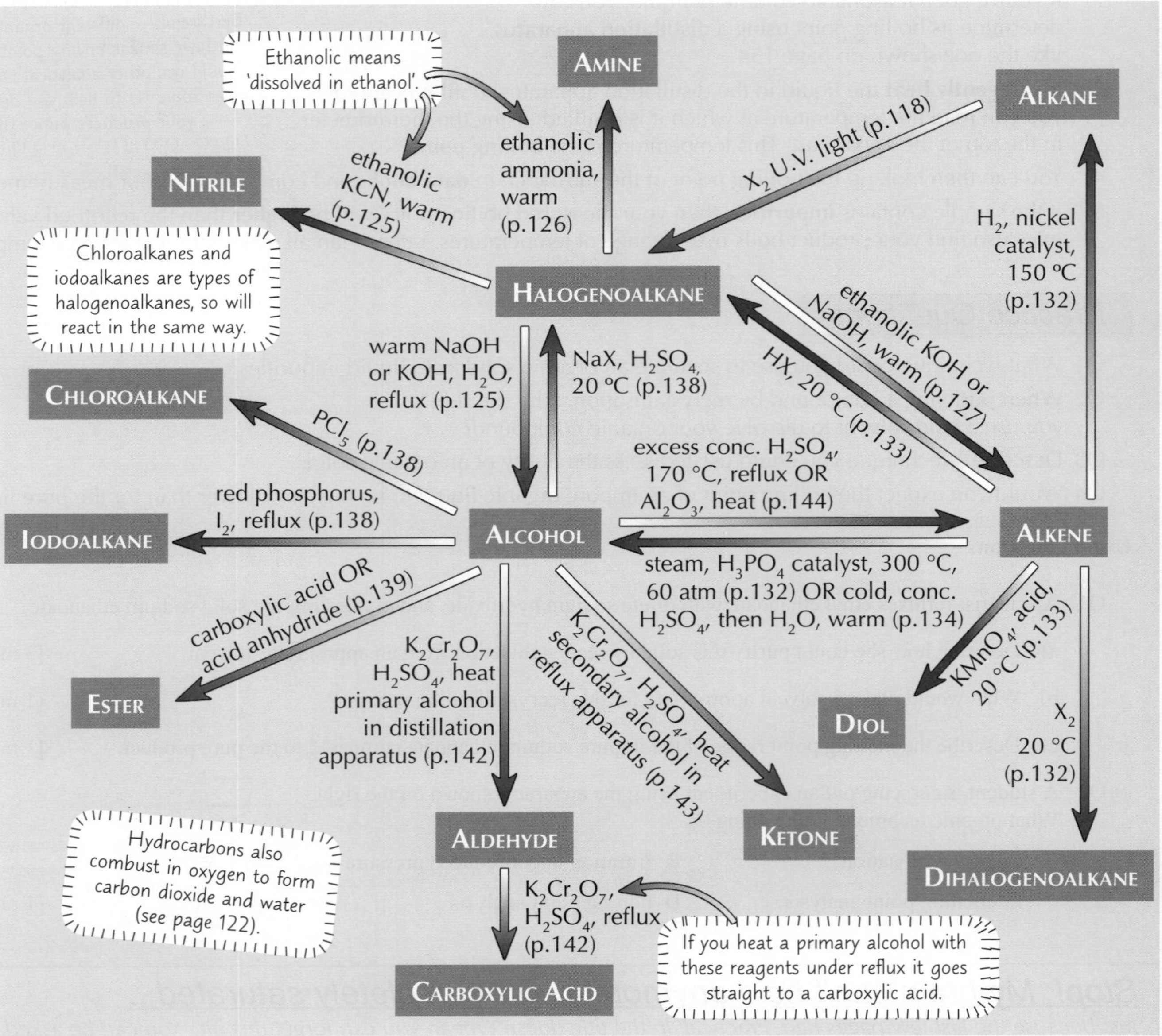

Ethanolic means 'dissolved in ethanol'.

AMINE

ALKANE

NITRILE

ethanolic KCN, warm (p.125)

ethanolic ammonia, warm (p.126)

X_2 U.V. light (p.118)

H_2, nickel catalyst, 150 °C (p.132)

Chloroalkanes and iodoalkanes are types of halogenoalkanes, so will react in the same way.

HALOGENOALKANE

ethanolic KOH or NaOH, warm (p.127)

HX, 20 °C (p.133)

warm NaOH or KOH, H_2O, reflux (p.125)

NaX, H_2SO_4, 20 °C (p.138)

CHLOROALKANE

PCl_5 (p.138)

excess conc. H_2SO_4, 170 °C, reflux OR Al_2O_3, heat (p.144)

red phosphorus, I_2, reflux (p.138)

IODOALKANE

ALCOHOL

ALKENE

steam, H_3PO_4 catalyst, 300 °C, 60 atm (p.132) OR cold, conc. H_2SO_4, then H_2O, warm (p.134)

carboxylic acid OR acid anhydride (p.139)

$K_2Cr_2O_7$, H_2SO_4, heat primary alcohol in distillation apparatus (p.142)

$K_2Cr_2O_7$, H_2SO_4, heat secondary alcohol in reflux apparatus (p.143)

$KMnO_4$, acid, 20 °C (p.133)

ESTER

DIOL

X_2 20 °C (p.132)

Hydrocarbons also combust in oxygen to form carbon dioxide and water (see page 122).

ALDEHYDE

KETONE

DIHALOGENOALKANE

$K_2Cr_2O_7$, H_2SO_4, reflux (p.142)

If you heat a primary alcohol with these reagents under reflux it goes straight to a carboxylic acid.

CARBOXYLIC ACID

Organic Synthesis — Synthetic Routes

Different **Functional Groups** are Involved in Different **Types** of **Reactions**

1) The different **properties** of functional groups influence their **reactivity** — **nucleophiles** don't react with the **electron-rich double bond** in **alkenes**, but they do attack the **δ+ carbon** in **halogenoalkanes**.
2) Here are some of the functional groups you've studied so far and how they'll typically react:

Homologous series	Functional group	Properties	Typical reactions
Alkane	C–C	Non-polar, unreactive	Radical substitution
Alkene	C=C	Non-polar, electron-rich double bond	Electrophilic addition
Alcohol	C–OH	Polar C–OH bond Lone pair on O can act as a nucleophile	Nucleophilic substitution Dehydration/elimination Esterification
Halogenoalkane	C–X	Polar C–X bond	Nucleophilic substitution
Aldehyde/Ketone	C=O	Polar C=O bond	Aldehydes will oxidise
Carboxylic acid	-COOH	Electron deficient carbon centre	Esterification
Acid anhydride	-(CO)O(CO)-	Electron deficient carbon centre	Esterification
Ester	-COOR	Electron deficient carbon centre	—

3) Sometimes a compound will have **more than one** functional group. Make sure you can identify **all** of them.

Make Sure You Give *All* the Information

When planning a synthetic route to make an organic compound, make sure you include:

1) Any **special procedures**, such as refluxing.
2) The **conditions** needed, e.g. high temperature or pressure, or the presence of a catalyst.

Practice Questions

Q1 Why might a chemist want to devise a synthetic route?

Q2 Write a reaction scheme to show how propanone could be formed from 2-bromopropane.

Q3 Name three types of compound that can react to form a halogenoalkane.

Q4 What is the name for the typical reaction of alkenes?

Exam Questions

Q1 The following flowchart shows some of the reactions of 2-methylpropan-1-ol:

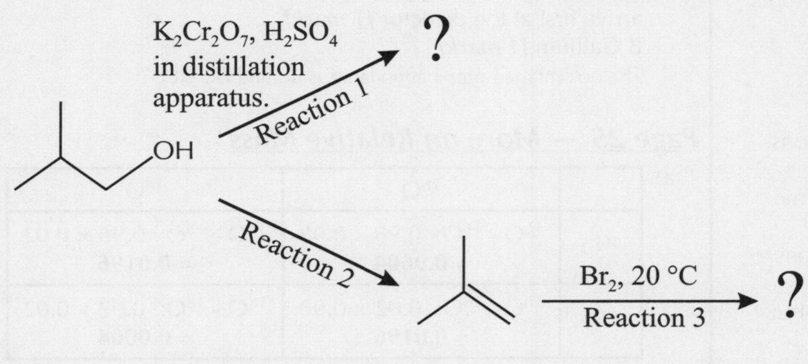

a) Give the skeletal formula of the product of Reaction 1. [1 mark]

b) What are the reagents and conditions needed for Reaction 2? [2 marks]

c) i) Draw the displayed formula of the product of Reaction 3. [1 mark]

ii) What would be observed during the reaction? [1 mark]

Q2 Devise a two step synthetic route for the formation of butanal from but-1-ene. Include all reagents and reaction conditions in your scheme. [3 marks]

Last week I dyed my hair bright pink... I've got synthetic roots...

Woah, there's a lot of information on these pages. But before you go for a well-deserved cuppa, have another look at that big spider diagram on the other page. It links up all the reactions and organic compounds you've met, and it's really useful for planning synthetic routes. So draw it out with all the reagents and conditions. And then have a break.

Answers

Development of Practical Skills

Page 5 — Planning Experiments

1 Using litmus paper is not a particularly accurate method of measuring pH / not very sensitive equipment ***[1 mark]***. It would be better to use a pH meter ***[1 mark]***.

Page 7 — Practical Techniques

1 a) The student measured the level of the liquid from the top of the meniscus, when he should have measured it from the bottom ***[1 mark]***.
b) B ***[1 mark]***.

Page 9 — Presenting Results

1 a) mean volume $= \frac{7.30 + 7.25 + 7.25}{3} = 7.26666...\ \text{cm}^3$
$=$ **0.00727 dm³** or **7.27 × 10⁻³ dm³** (3 s.f.) ***[1 mark]***
b) $0.50 \div 1000 =$ **$0.00050\ \text{mol cm}^{-3}$** or **$5.0 \times 10^{-4}\ \text{mol cm}^{-3}$** ***[1 mark]***

Page 11 — Analysing Results

1 a) 15 °C and 25 °C ***[1 mark]***.
b) Positive correlation ***[1 mark]***.
c) C ***[1 mark]***

Page 13 — Evaluating Experiments

1 a) The volumetric flask reads to the nearest 0.5 cm³, so the uncertainty is ±0.25 cm³.
percentage error $= \frac{\text{uncertainty}}{\text{reading}} \times 100 = \frac{0.25}{25} \times 100 = \mathbf{1.0\ \%}$
[1 mark]
b) E.g. The student should add the thermometer to the citric acid solution and allow it to stabilise before adding the sodium bicarbonate to give an accurate value for the initial temperature ***[1 mark]***. The student should then measure the temperature change until the solution stops reacting to give a valid result for the temperature change of the entire reaction ***[1 mark]***.

Topic 1 — Atomic Structure

Page 15 — The Atom

1 a) Similarity — They've all got the same number of protons/electrons ***[1 mark]***.
Difference — They all have different numbers of neutrons ***[1 mark]***.
b) 1 proton, 1 neutron (2 – 1), 1 electron ***[1 mark]***.
c) $^{3}_{1}H$ ***[1 mark]***

2 a) i) Same number of electrons. $^{32}S^{2-}$ has 16 + 2 = 18 electrons. ^{40}Ar has 18 electrons too ***[1 mark]***.
ii) Same number of protons. Each has 16 protons (the atomic number of S must always be the same) ***[1 mark]***.
iii) Same number of neutrons. ^{40}Ar has 40 – 18 = 22 neutrons. ^{42}Ca has 42 – 20 = 22 neutrons ***[1 mark]***.
b) **A** and **C** ***[1 mark]***. They have the same number of protons but different numbers of neutrons ***[1 mark]***.
It doesn't matter that they have a different number of electrons because they are still the same element.

Page 17 — Atomic Models

1 a) Bohr knew that if an electron was freely orbiting the nucleus it would spiral into it, causing the atom to collapse ***[1 mark]***. His model only allowed electrons to be in fixed shells and not in between them ***[1 mark]***.
b) When an electron moves from one shell to another electromagnetic radiation is emitted or absorbed ***[1 mark]***.
c) The shells of an atom can only hold fixed numbers of electrons ***[1 mark]***. Noble gases have full shells and so do not react ***[1 mark]***. (Alternatively: a full shell of electrons makes an atom stable ***[1 mark]***; noble gases have full shells and do not react because they are stable ***[1 mark]***.)

Page 20 — Atomic Spectra and Nuclear Radiation

1 a) The movement of electrons/an electron ***[1 mark]*** from lower to higher energy levels ***[1 mark]***.
b) Line E (because it is at the highest frequency) ***[1 mark]***.
c) i) It would consist of bright, not dark, lines ***[1 mark]***.
ii) The lines would be at the same frequencies ***[1 mark]***.
d) Because the energy levels get closer together with increasing energy ***[1 mark]***.

2 a) Use $E = h\nu$: $E = (6.63 \times 10^{-34}) \times (5.1 \times 10^{14}) = \mathbf{3.38 \times 10^{-19}\ J}$
[1 mark for correct number, and 1 mark for correct unit]
b) Use $c = \nu\lambda$: $\lambda = \frac{c}{\nu} = \frac{3.00 \times 10^8}{5.10 \times 10^{14}} = \mathbf{5.88 \times 10^{-7}\ m/s}$
[1 mark for correct number, and 1 mark for correct unit]

Page 23 — Relative Mass and the Mass Spectrometer

1 a) First multiply each relative abundance by the relative mass:
120.8 × 63 = 7610.4, 54.0 × 65 = 3510.0
Next add up the products:
7610.4 + 3510.0 = 11 120.4 ***[1 mark]***
Now divide by the total abundance (120.8 + 54.0 = 174.8)
A_r(Cu) = 11 120.4 ÷ 174.8 ≈ **63.6** ***[1 mark]***
You can check your answer by seeing if A_r(Cu) is in between 63 and 65 (the lowest and highest relative isotopic masses).
b) A sample of copper is a mixture of 2 isotopes in different abundances ***[1 mark]***. The average mass of these isotopes isn't a whole number ***[1 mark]***.

2 a) Mass spectrometry ***[1 mark]***
b) You use pretty much the same method here as for question 1 a).
93.11 × 39 = 3631.29, (0.12 × 40) = 4.8, (6.77 × 41) = 277.57
3631.29 + 4.8 + 277.57 = 3913.66 ***[1 mark]***
This time you divide by 100 because they're percentages.
A_r(K) = 3913.66 ÷ 100 = **39.1** (3 s.f.) ***[1 mark]***
Again check your answer's between the lowest and highest relative isotopic masses, 39 and 41. A_r(K) is closer to 39 because most of the sample (93.11%) is made up of this isotope.

3 a) So that they can be accelerated ***[1 mark]*** and detected ***[1 mark]***.
b) Positive ions are accelerated by an electric field ***[1 mark]*** to a constant kinetic energy ***[1 mark]***. Ions with a smaller mass/charge ratio move faster ***[1 mark]***. The faster ions arrive first at the detector ***[1 mark]***.
c) B Gallium ***[1 mark]***.
The percentage isotope abundance is around 60-40.

Page 25 — More on Relative Mass

1 a)

	^{16}O	^{18}O
^{16}O	$^{16}O - ^{16}O$: 0.98 × 0.98 = **0.9604**	$^{16}O - ^{18}O$: 0.98 × 0.02 = **0.0196**
^{18}O	$^{18}O - ^{16}O$: 0.02 × 0.98 = **0.0196**	$^{18}O - ^{18}O$: 0.02 × 0.02 = **0.0004**

[2 marks — 2 marks for a correct abundance for all molecules, 1 mark if three correct abundances]
$^{16}O - ^{18}O$ and $^{18}O - ^{16}O$ are the same, so the relative abundance is 0.0196 + 0.0196 = **0.0392** ***[1 mark]***.

Answers

b) Divide each by 0.0004 to get the simplified relative abundances.

Molecule	M_r	Relative Abundance
$^{16}O-^{16}O$	16 + 16 = **32**	0.9604 ÷ 0.0004 = **2401**
$^{16}O-^{18}O$	16 + 18 = **34**	0.0392 ÷ 0.0004 = **98**
$^{18}O-^{18}O$	18 + 18 = **36**	0.0004 ÷ 0.0004 = **1**

[1 mark for correct relative abundances, 1 mark for correct relative molecular masses]

So the mass spectrum for the sample of O_2 will be:

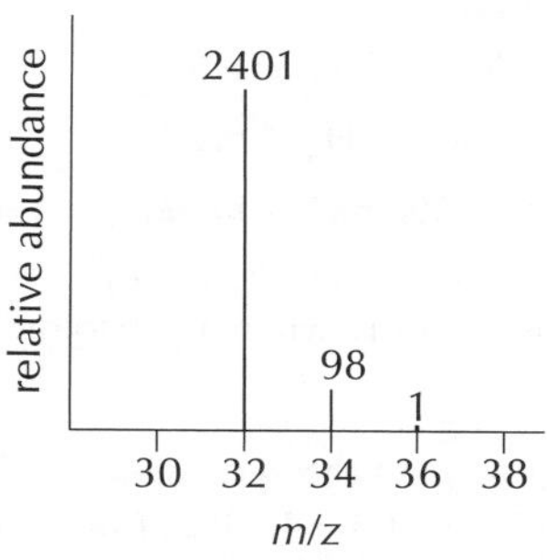

[1 mark for correctly labelled axes, 1 mark for correctly drawn peaks at correct m/z values, with approximately correct heights]

2 a) 100% – 94.20% – 0.012% = **5.788%** ***[1 mark]***

b) 39.1 = ((39 × 94.20) + (40 × 0.012) + (X × 5.788)) ÷ 100 ***[1 mark]***
39.1 = (3674.28 + (X × 5.788)) ÷ 100
3910 – 3674.28 = X × 5.788. So, X = 40.726... = **41** ***[1 mark]***

3 a) 58 ***[1 mark]***

b)

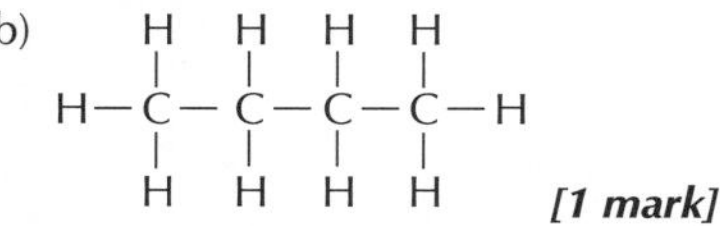

[1 mark]

Page 27 — Electronic Structure

1 a) K atom: $1s^2\ 2s^2\ 2p^6\ 3s^2\ 3p^6\ 4s^1$ ***[1 mark]***
K^+ ion: $1s^2\ 2s^2\ 2p^6\ 3s^2\ 3p^6$ ***[1 mark]***

b) Oxygen atom: **1s** [↑↓] **2s** [↑↓] **2p** [↑↓][↑][↑]

Correct number of electrons in each sub-shell ***[1 mark]***.
Having spin-pairing in one of the p orbitals and parallel spins in the other two p orbitals ***[1 mark]***.
A box filled with 2 arrows is spin pairing — 1 up and 1 down.
If you've put the four p electrons into just 2 orbitals, it's wrong.

2 a) Germanium ($1s^2\ 2s^2\ 2p^6\ 3s^2\ 3p^6\ 3d^{10}\ 4s^2\ 4p^2$) ***[1 mark]***.

b) Ar (atom) ***[1 mark]***, K^+ (positive ion) ***[1 mark]***, Cl^- (negative ion) ***[1 mark]***. You also could have suggested Ca^{2+}, S^{2-} or P^{3-}.

c) $1s^2\ 2s^2\ 2p^6$ ***[1 mark]***

3 a) $1s^2 2s^2 2p^6 3s^2 3p^2$ ***[1 mark]***

b) Two ***[1 mark]***

Page 29 — Ionisation Energy

1 a) $C_{(g)} \rightarrow C^+_{(g)} + e^-$
Correct equation ***[1 mark]***. Both state symbols showing gaseous state ***[1 mark]***.

b) First ionisation energy increases as nuclear charge increases ***[1 mark]***.

c) As the nuclear charge increases there is a stronger force of attraction between the nucleus and the electron ***[1 mark]*** and so more energy is required to remove the electron ***[1 mark]***.

2 a) Group 3 ***[1 mark]***
There are three electrons removed before the first big jump in energy.

b) The electrons are being removed from an increasingly positive ion ***[1 mark]*** so the force of attraction that has to be broken is greater ***[1 mark]***.

c) When an electron is removed from a different shell there is a big increase in the energy required (since that shell is closer to the nucleus) ***[1 mark]***.

d) There are 3 shells ***[1 mark]***.
You can tell there are 3 shells because there are 2 big jumps in energy. There is always one more shell than big jumps.

Page 31 — Trends in First Ionisation Energy

1 a) The shielding from the electrons is the same in these atoms ***[1 mark]*** but there is an increase in the number of protons in the nucleus / nuclear charge ***[1 mark]***. So it takes more energy to remove an electron from the outer shell ***[1 mark]***.

b) i) Boron has the configuration $1s^2\ 2s^2\ 2p^1$ compared to $1s^2\ 2s^2$ for beryllium ***[1 mark]***. The 2p orbital is at a slightly higher energy level than the 2s orbital. The extra distance and partial shielding by the 2s electrons make it easier to remove the outer electron ***[1 mark]***.

ii) Oxygen has the configuration $1s^2\ 2s^2\ 2p^4$ compared to $1s^2\ 2s^2\ 2p^3$ for nitrogen ***[1 mark]***. Electron repulsion in the shared 2p sub-shell in oxygen makes it easier to remove an electron ***[1 mark]***.

2 As you go down Group 2, it takes less energy to remove an electron ***[1 mark]***. This is evidence that the outer electrons are increasingly distant from the nucleus ***[1 mark]*** and additional inner shells of electrons exist to shield the outer shell ***[1 mark]***.

3 a) D ***[1 mark]***

b) Ionisation energy increases across a period ***[1 mark]*** so the Group 0 elements have the highest first ionisation energies of the elements in their period. Ionisation energy decreases down a group ***[1 mark]*** so neon has a higher ionisation energy than krypton.

4 a) A ***[1 mark]***

b) E.g. in sodium, the first electron is removed from the third shell but the second is removed from the second shell ***[1 mark]***. The second shell electron is nearer to the nucleus and experiences less shielding, which means it is much more strongly attracted to the nucleus ***[1 mark]***. In all of the other elements given, the second electron is being removed from the same shell as the first one ***[1 mark]***.

Topic 2 — Amount of Substance

Page 35 — The Mole and Equations

1 M(CH_3COOH) = (2 × 12.0) + (4 × 1.0) + (2 × 16.0) = 60.0 g mol^{-1} ***[1 mark]*** so mass of 0.360 moles = 60.0 × 0.360 = **21.6 g** ***[1 mark]***

2 number of moles = 0.250 × $\frac{60.0}{1000}$ = 0.0150 moles ***[1 mark]***
M_r of H_2SO_4 = (2 × 1.0) + (1 × 32.1) + (4 × 16.0) = 98.1
Mass = 0.0150 × 98.1 = **1.48 g** ***[1 mark]***

3 M_r of C_2H_5Cl = (2 × 12.0) + (5 × 1.0) + (1 × 35.5) = 64.5
Number of moles of C_2H_5Cl = $\frac{258}{64.5}$ = 4.00 moles ***[1 mark]***
From the equation, 1 mole C_2H_5Cl is made from 1 mole C_2H_4, so 4 moles C_2H_5Cl is made from 4 moles C_2H_4 ***[1 mark]***.
M_r of C_2H_4 = (2 × 12.0) + (4 × 1.0) = 28.0
mass of 4 moles C_2H_4 = 4 × 28.0 = **112 g** ***[1 mark]***

4 a) M_r of $CaCO_3$ = 40.1 + 12.0 + (3 × 16.0) = 100.1
Number of moles of $CaCO_3$ = $\frac{15.0}{100.1}$ = 0.150 moles ***[1 mark]***
From the equation, 1 mole $CaCO_3$ produces 1 mole CaO, so 0.150 moles of $CaCO_3$ produces 0.150 moles of CaO ***[1 mark]***
M_r of CaO = 40.1 + 16.0 = 56.1
mass of 0.15 moles of CaO = 56.1 × 0.150 = **8.42 g** ***[1 mark]***

Answers

b) From the equation, 1 mole $CaCO_3$ produces 1 mole CO_2, so 0.150 moles of $CaCO_3$ produces 0.150 moles of CO_2 ***[1 mark]***
$T = 25.0 + 273 = 298$ K and $p = 100 \times 10^3$ Pa ***[1 mark]***
$V = nRT \div p$
Volume of $CO_2 = \frac{0.150 \times 8.31 \times 298}{100 \times 10^3} = 0.00371\ m^3$
$= \mathbf{3.71 \times 10^{-3}\ m^3}$ ***[1 mark]***

5 **$2KI + Pb(NO_3)_2 \rightarrow PbI_2 + 2KNO_3$** ***[1 mark]***
The LHS needs 2 Is, so pop a 2 in front of KI. Then the RHS needs 2 Ks, so put a 2 in front of KNO_3. Once you've done that, everything balances.

Page 37 — Formulas of Ionic Compounds

1 $Sc_2(SO_4)_3$ ***[1 mark]***
Scandium has a charge of +3. Sulfate has a charge of −2. So, for every 2 scandium atoms, you will need three sulfate ions to balance the charge.

2 Na_2O ***[1 mark]***
Sodium is in group 1, so forms ions with a charge of +1.
In compounds, oxygen usually has a charge of −2.

3 a) M of $CaSO_4 = 40.1 + 32.1 + (4 \times 16.0) = 136.2\ g\ mol^{-1}$ ***[1 mark]***
no. moles $= \frac{1.133}{136.2} =$ **0.008319 moles** ***[1 mark]***

b) mass of water = difference in mass between hydrated and anhydrous salt = 1.883 – 1.133 = 0.7500 g ***[1 mark]***
no. moles of water $= \frac{\text{mass}}{\text{molar mass}} = \frac{0.7500}{18.0} = 0.04167$ ***[1 mark]***
X = ratio of no. moles water to no. moles salt $= \frac{0.04167}{0.008319} = 5.009$.
Rounded to nearest whole number, X = **5** ***[1 mark]***

Page 39 — Acids and Bases

1 a) One of: magnesium ($Mg_{(s)}$), magnesium hydroxide ($Mg(OH)_2$), magnesium oxide (MgO) or magnesium carbonate ($MgCO_3$) ***[1 mark]***

b) One of: $Mg + 2HCl \rightarrow MgCl_2 + H_2$,
$Mg(OH)_2 + 2HCl \rightarrow MgCl_2 + 2H_2O$,
$MgO + 2HCl \rightarrow MgCl_2 + H_2O$,
$MgCO_3 + 2HCl \rightarrow MgCl_2 + CO_2 + H_2O$ ***[1 mark]***

2 a) $NaOH_{(aq)} + HNO_{3\,(aq)} \rightarrow H_2O_{(l)} + NaNO_{3\,(aq)}$ ***[1 mark]***

b) neutralisation ***[1 mark]***

Page 42 — Titrations

1 Moles of NaOH $= 0.500 \times \frac{14.6}{1000} = 0.00730$ ***[1 mark]***
From the equation, 1 mole of NaOH neutralises 1 mole of CH_3COOH, so 0.00730 moles NaOH must neutralise 0.00730 moles of CH_3COOH ***[1 mark]***.
Concentration $CH_3COOH = 0.00730 \div \frac{25.4}{1000}$
$= \mathbf{0.287\ mol\ dm^{-3}}$ ***[1 mark]***

2 M_r of $CaCO_3 = 40.1 + 12.0 + (3 \times 16.0) = 100.1$ ***[1 mark]***
Moles of $CaCO_3 = \frac{0.750}{100.1} = 0.00750$ ***[1 mark]***
From the equation, 1 mole $CaCO_3$ reacts with 1 mole H_2SO_4 so, 0.00750 moles of $CaCO_3$ must react with 0.00750 moles of H_2SO_4 ***[1 mark]***.
Volume needed $= \frac{0.00750}{0.250} = \mathbf{0.0300\ dm^3}$ (or $\mathbf{30.0\ cm^3}$) ***[1 mark]***
For titration calculations, you can bet your last clean pair of underwear that you'll need to use this formula: number of moles = conc. × volume (dm^3)

3 a) Titration 3 (42.90 cm^3) is anomalous. It is not concordant with / is significantly different to the other three results ***[1 mark]***.

b) Mean titre $= \frac{45.00 + 45.10 + 44.90}{3} = \mathbf{45.00\ cm^3}$ ***[1 mark]***

c) Moles of NaOH $= 0.400 \times \frac{45.00}{1000} = 0.01800$ ***[1 mark]***
From the equation, 1 mole of NaOH reacts with 1 mole of HNO_3, so 0.01800 moles NaOH must react with 0.01800 moles of HNO_3 ***[1 mark]***.
Moles of $HNO_3 = 0.01800 \div \frac{50.0}{1000} = \mathbf{0.360\ mol\ dm^{-3}}$ ***[1 mark]***

Page 45 — Formulas, Yield and Atom Economy

1 Start by working out how many moles of carbon and hydrogen there would be in 100 g of the hydrocarbon:
Number of moles of C $= \frac{92.3}{12.0} = 7.69$ moles ***[1 mark]***
Number of moles of H $= \frac{7.70}{1.0} = 7.70$ moles ***[1 mark]***
Divide both by 7.69: C: 7.69 ÷ 7.69 = 1. H: 7.70 ÷ 7.69 = 1.00.
So ratio C : H = 1 : 1
Empirical formula = CH ***[1 mark]***
Empirical mass = 12.0 + 1.0 = 13.0
Number of empirical units in molecule $= \frac{78.0}{13.0} = 6$
So the molecular formula = 6 × CH = $\mathbf{C_6H_6}$ ***[1 mark]***

2 a) Moles $PCl_3 = \frac{\text{mass}}{M_r} = \frac{0.275}{137.5} = \mathbf{0.00200\ mol}$ ***[1 mark]***
From the formula, 1 mole of PCl_3 reacts with Cl_2 to form 1 mole of PCl_5, so 0.00200 moles of PCl_3 will react to form 0.00200 moles of PCl_5 ***[1 mark]***.
M_r of $PCl_5 = 31.0 + (5 \times 35.5) = 208.5$
Theoretical yield = 0.00200 × 208.5 = **0.417 g** ***[1 mark]***

b) percentage yield = (0.198 ÷ 0.417) × 100 = **47.5%** ***[1 mark]***

c) 100% ***[1 mark]***. Since the equation shows that this reaction has only one product, its atom economy must be 100% ***[1 mark]***.

Topic 3 — Bonding

Page 47 — Ionic Bonding

1 a) E.g.

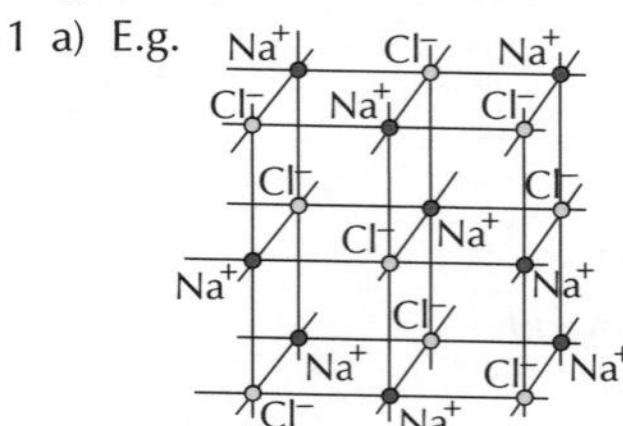

Your diagram should show the following:
- cubic structure with ions at corners ***[1 mark]***
- sodium ions and chloride ions labelled ***[1 mark]***
- alternating sodium ions and chloride ions ***[1 mark]***

b) giant ionic lattice ***[1 mark]***

c) You'd expect it to have a high melting point because the electrostatic attraction between ions ***[1 mark]*** is strong ***[1 mark]*** so a lot of energy is needed to overcome this attraction ***[1 mark]***.

d) You'd expect it to dissolve ***[1 mark]***. Water molecules have a small negative charge at one end, and a small positive charge at the other end. These charges pull the charged ions away from the solid lattice, causing the compound to dissolve ***[1 mark]***.

2 In a solid, ions are held in place by strong ionic bonds ***[1 mark]***. When the solid is heated to melting point, the ions gain enough energy to overcome these forces and move ***[1 mark]***, carrying charge (and so electricity) through the substance ***[1 mark]***.

Page 49 — More on Ionic Bonding

1 Sodium loses one (outer) electron to form Na^+ ***[1 mark]***. Fluorine gains one electron to form F^- ***[1 mark]***. Electrostatic forces of attraction between oppositely charged ions forms an ionic lattice ***[1 mark]***.

2 C ***[1 mark]***

3 a) F^-, Cl^-, Br^-, I^- ***[1 mark]***
All these Group 7 ions have the same charge ***[1 mark]***. As you go down the group the ionic radius increases as the atomic number increases. This is because extra electron shells are added ***[1 mark]***.

Answers

b) Sr^{2+}, Rb^{+}, Cl^{-}, S^{2-} ***[1 mark]***
The ions are isoelectronic, so they all have the same number of electrons but different numbers of protons ***[1 mark]***. As the number of protons decreases, the electrons are attracted to the nucleus less strongly, so the ionic radius increases ***[1 mark]***.

4 a)

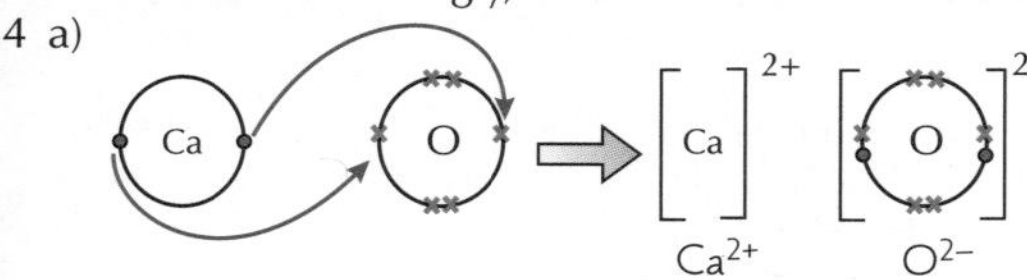

[2 marks — 1 mark for correct electron arrangement, 1 mark for correct charges]

b) Calcium sulfide would have a lower melting point than calcium oxide ***[1 mark]***. Sulfur has one more electron shell than oxygen so would have a larger atomic radius. This means the ions in calcium sulfide can't pack as closely together as the ions in calcium oxide ***[1 mark]***. Ionic bonding gets weaker as the distance between the ions increases, so the ionic bonding in calcium sulfide is weaker than in calcium oxide / less energy is required to break the ionic bonds in calcium sulfide than calcium oxide ***[1 mark]*** (so the ionic melting point is lower).

Page 51 — Covalent Bonding

1 a) The strong electrostatic attraction between a shared pair of electrons and the nuclei of the bonded atoms ***[1 mark]***

b) A single covalent bond only contains one pair of shared electrons. A double covalent bond contains two pairs of shared electrons ***[1 mark]***.

2 a)

H N H
H

[1 mark]

b)

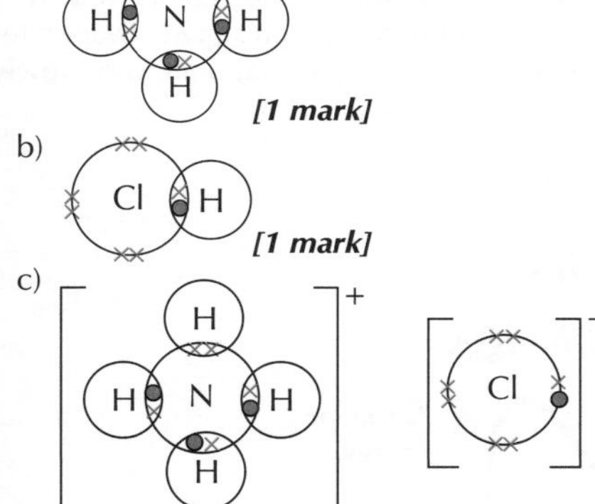

[1 mark]

c)

[1 mark for all bonds shown correctly, 1 mark for correct charges]

3 a) An N–N bond is longer than an N=N bond ***[1 mark]*** as there are four shared electrons in an N=N bond and only two shared electrons in an N–N bond, meaning the electron density between the two nitrogen atoms in the nitrogen double bond is greater than in the nitrogen single bond ***[1 mark]***. This increases the strength of the electrostatic attraction between the positive nuclei and the negative electrons in the N=N bond, making the bond shorter ***[1 mark]***.

b)

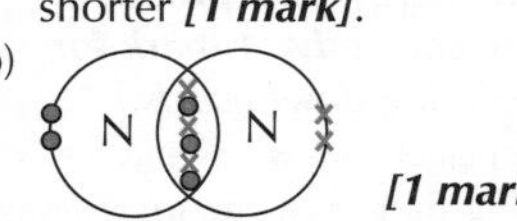

[1 mark]

c) The bond enthalpy of the bond in N_2 would be larger than the bond enthalpy of a nitrogen single bond or a nitrogen double bond ***[1 mark]***. The bond in N_2 is a nitrogen triple bond. There are six shared electrons in this bond, leading to a higher electron density than in N–N or N=N bonds (where there are two and four shared electrons respectively) ***[1 mark]***. This means there's a stronger electrostatic attraction between the two nitrogen nuclei and the bonding electrons, so stronger covalent bonding ***[1 mark]***.

Page 53 — Giant Covalent Structures

1 a) Macromolecular/giant covalent ***[1 mark]***

b) Diamond Graphite

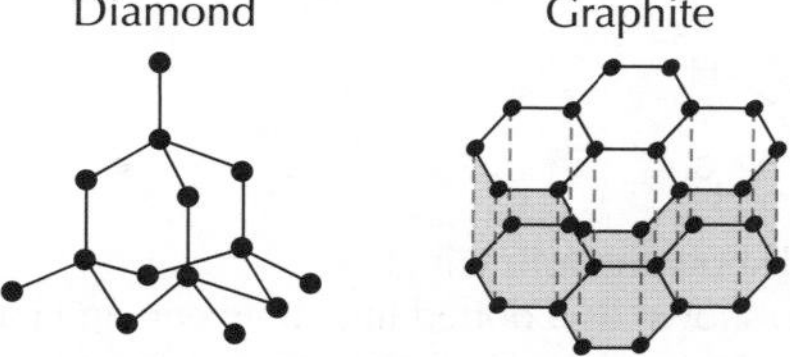

[1 mark for each correctly drawn diagram]

Diamond's a bit awkward to draw without it looking like a load of ballet dancing spiders — just make sure each carbon is connected to four others.

c) Diamond only has electrons in covalent bonds ***[1 mark]***, so is a poor electrical conductor ***[1 mark]***. Graphite has some delocalised electrons which can flow within the sheets ***[1 mark]***, making it an electrical conductor ***[1 mark]***.

2 Graphene is a two dimensional compound, not one dimensional ***[1 mark]***. The delocalised electrons don't weaken the covalent bonds. Instead, they strengthen them, making graphene very strong ***[1 mark]***.

3 Graphite is made up of sheets of hexagons held together by weak induced dipole-dipole forces ***[1 mark]***. These forces are easily broken, meaning the layers can slide over one another ***[1 mark]*** (making graphite a good lubricant).

Page 55 — Shapes of Molecules

1 a) NCl_3:

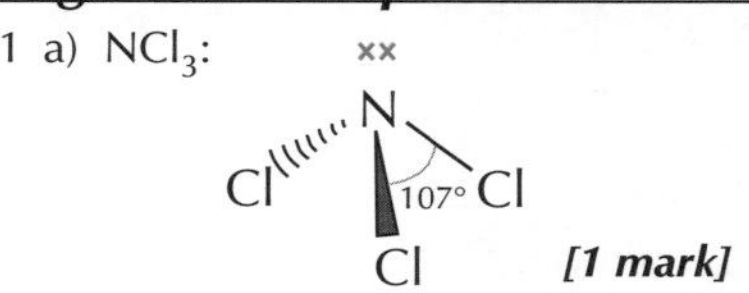

[1 mark]

shape: (trigonal) pyramidal ***[1 mark]***,
bond angle: 107° (accept between 105° and 109°) ***[1 mark]***

b) BCl_3:

Cl Cl
B
120°
Cl

[1 mark]

shape: trigonal planar ***[1 mark]***,
bond angle: 120° exactly ***[1 mark]***

c) BCl_3 has three bonding electron pairs around B which repel each other equally ***[1 mark]***. NCl_3 has three bonding electron pairs and one lone pair ***[1 mark]***. The lone pair repels the bonding pair more strongly than the bonding pairs repel each other ***[1 mark]***.

Page 58 — Polarisation and Intermolecular Forces

1 Decene has a higher boiling point. Decene is a larger molecule than octene, so it has more electrons/a larger surface area ***[1 mark]***. This means that the induced dipole-dipole forces between molecules of decene will be stronger ***[1 mark]***, so it will take more energy to overcome them ***[1 mark]***.

The more energy you need to overcome the intermolecular forces between the molecules, the higher the boiling point of the compound will be.

2 a) The C–Cl bond will be polar, because chlorine has a much higher electronegativity than carbon ***[1 mark]***.

b) The molecule CCl_4 is not polar. Each of the C–Cl bonds in the CCl_4 molecule is polar ***[1 mark]***, but the polar bonds are arranged symmetrically all around the molecule, so the charges cancel out ***[1 mark]***.

Answers

3 a) E.g.

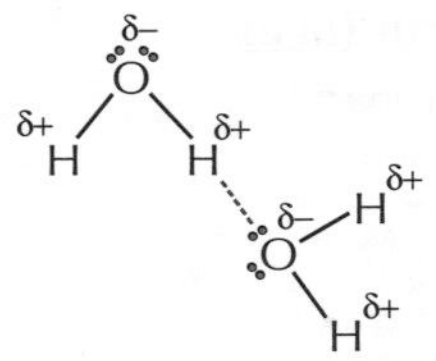

Your diagram should show the following:

- A hydrogen bond, shown as a dotted line, between an H atom on one molecule and an O atom on the other ***[1 mark]***.
- Two lone pairs on each oxygen atom ***[1 mark]***.
- Partial charges on all the atoms ***[1 mark]***.

b) Hydrogen bonding is present in water but not in any of the other group 6 hydrides ***[1 mark]***. Hydrogen bonds are stronger than other intermolecular forces ***[1 mark]***, so more energy is needed to break the intermolecular forces between water molecules than for other group 6 hydride molecules ***[1 mark]***.

Page 61 — Metallic Bonding and Properties of Materials

1 a) E.g.

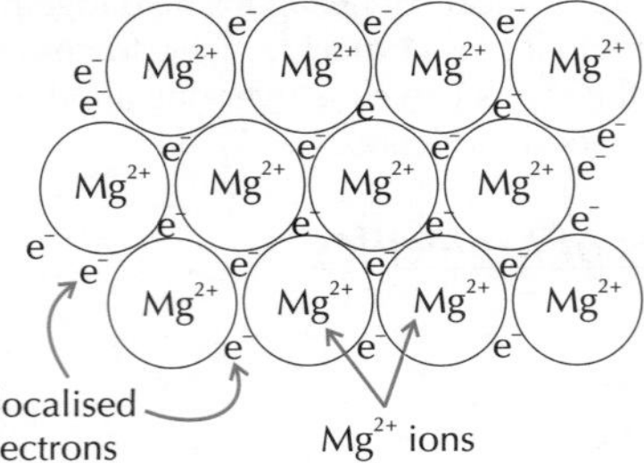

Your diagram should show the following:

- Closely packed Mg^{2+} ions ***[1 mark]***.
- Delocalised electrons ***[1 mark]***.

b) Metals contain delocalised electrons, which can move through the structure to carry a current ***[1 mark]***.

2 A = ionic ***[1 mark]***, B = simple molecular/covalent ***[1 mark]***, C = metallic ***[1 mark]***, D = macromolecular/giant covalent ***[1 mark]***.

3 Iodine is a simple molecular substance ***[1 mark]***. To boil iodine, you only need to break the weak intermolecular forces holding the molecules together, which doesn't need much energy ***[1 mark]***. Graphite is a giant covalent substance ***[1 mark]***. To boil graphite, you need to break the strong covalent bonds between atoms, which needs a lot of energy ***[1 mark]***.

Page 63 — Solubility

1 a) i) Hydrogen bonds ***[1 mark]*** form between the alcohol and water molecules ***[1 mark]***. The (hydrogen) bonds between water molecules are stronger ***[1 mark]*** than bonds that would form between water and the halogenoalkane molecules ***[1 mark]***.

For the last two marks, you could also say that the halogenoalkanes do not contain strong enough dipoles to form hydrogen bonds with water.

ii)

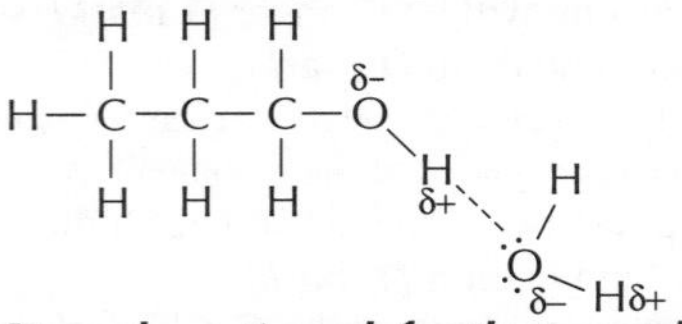

[2 marks — 1 mark for the two substances with relevant δ+ and δ– marked correctly, 1 mark for showing the bond between the hydrogen of the propanol molecule and oxygen of the water molecule]

b) K^+ ions are attracted to the $\delta-$ ends of the water molecules ***[1 mark]*** and I^- ions are attracted to the $\delta+$ ends ***[1 mark]***. This overcomes the ionic bonds in the lattice / The ions are pulled away from the lattice ***[1 mark]***, and surrounded by water molecules ***[1 mark]***, forming hydrated ions:

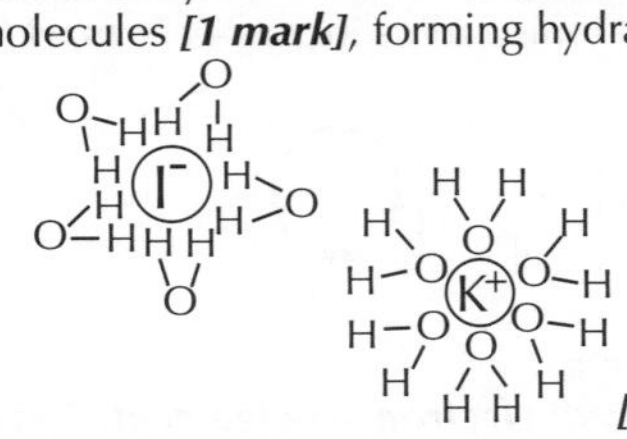

[1 mark]

2 a) Try to dissolve the substance in water ***[1 mark]*** and hexane (or other non-polar solvent) ***[1 mark]***. If X is non-polar, it is likely to dissolve in hexane, but not in water ***[1 mark]***.

Remember 'like dissolves like' — in other words, substances usually dissolve best in solvents that have similar intermolecular forces.

b) X and hexane have induced dipole-dipole forces between their molecules ***[1 mark]*** and form similar bonds with each other ***[1 mark]***. Water has hydrogen bonds ***[1 mark]*** which are much stronger than the bonds it could form with a non-polar compound ***[1 mark]***.

Page 65 — Making Salts

1 D ***[1 mark]***

2 B ***[1 mark]***

3 Titrate some potassium hydroxide with a known volume of sulfuric acid and add some drops of indicator to show when the reaction's finished ***[1 mark]***. Then repeat the titration using the same amount of acid and the exact amount of potassium hydroxide needed to neutralise it, so the salt isn't contaminated with indicator ***[1 mark]***. To get pure potassium sulfate, evaporate some of the water and then leave the rest to evaporate very slowly ***[1 mark]***.

Topic 4 — Energetics

Page 67 — Enthalpy Changes

1

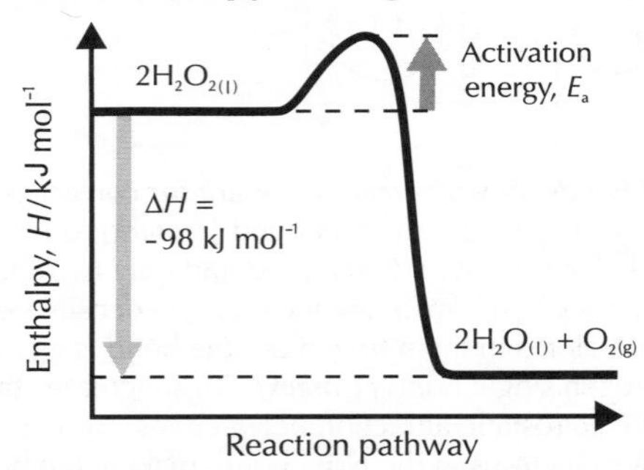

[1 mark for having reactants lower in energy than products. 1 mark for labelling activation energy correctly. 1 mark for labelling ΔH correctly, with arrow pointing downwards.]

For an exothermic reaction, the ΔH arrow points downwards, but for an endothermic reaction it points upwards. The activation energy arrow always points upwards though.

2 a) $CH_3OH_{(l)} + 1\frac{1}{2}O_{2(g)} \rightarrow CO_{2(g)} + 2H_2O_{(l)}$ ***[1 mark]***

Make sure that only 1 mole of CH_3OH is combusted, as it says in the definition for $\Delta_c H^\circ$.

b) $C_{(s)} + 2H_{2(g)} + \frac{1}{2}O_{2(g)} \rightarrow CH_3OH_{(l)}$ ***[1 mark]***

c) Only 1 mole of C_3H_8 should be shown according to the definition of $\Delta_c H^\circ$ ***[1 mark]***.

Answers

3 a) $C_{(s)} + O_{2(g)} \rightarrow CO_{2(g)}$ ***[1 mark]***
b) It has the same value because it is the same reaction ***[1 mark]***.
c) 1 tonne = 1 000 000 g
1 mole of carbon is 12.0 g
so 1 tonne is 1 000 000 ÷ 12.0 = 83 333 moles ***[1 mark]***
1 mole releases 393.5 kJ
so 1 tonne will release 83 333 × 393.5 = **32 800 000 kJ** (3 s.f.) ***[1 mark]***
The final answer is rounded to 3 significant figures because the number with the fewest significant figures in the whole calculation is 12.0.

Page 69 — More on Enthalpy Changes

1 No. of moles of $CuSO_4$ = (0.200 × 50.0) ÷ 1000 = 0.0100 mole ***[1 mark]***
From the equation, 1 mole of $CuSO_4$ reacts with 1 mole of Zn.
So, 0.0100 mole of $CuSO_4$ reacts with 0.0100 mole of Zn ***[1 mark]***.
Heat produced by reaction = $mc\Delta T$
= 50.0 × 4.18 × 2.60 = 543.4 J ***[1 mark]***
0.0100 mole of zinc produces 543.4 J of heat, therefore 1 mole of zinc produces 543.4 ÷ 0.0100 = 54 340 J = 54.340 kJ
So the enthalpy change is **–54.3 kJ mol⁻¹** (3 s.f.) ***[1 mark]***
You need the minus sign because it's exothermic.

2 a) A chemical reaction always involves bond breaking which needs energy / is endothermic and bond making which releases energy / is exothermic ***[1 mark]***. Whether the reaction is exothermic or endothermic depends on whether more energy is used to break bonds or released by forming new bonds over the whole reaction ***[1 mark]***.
b) $q = mc\Delta T$
m = 1.000 kg = 1000 g
no. of moles carbon = mass ÷ M_r = 6.000 ÷ 12.0 = 0.5000 mole ***[1 mark]***
So q = 0.5000 × 393.5 = 196.75 kJ = 196 750 J ***[1 mark]***
So 196 750 = 1000 × 4.18 × ΔT
ΔT = 196 750 ÷ (1000 × 4.18) = **47.1 K** (3 s.f.) ***[1 mark]***

Page 71 — Enthalpy Calculations

1 $\Delta_r H^\circ$ = sum of $\Delta_f H^\circ$(products) – sum of $\Delta_f H^\circ$(reactants) ***[1 mark]***
$\Delta_r H^\circ$ = [0 + (3 × –602)] – [–1676 + 0]
$\Delta_r H^\circ$ = **–130 kJ mol⁻¹** ***[1 mark]***
Don't forget the units. It's a daft way to lose marks.

2 $\Delta_f H^\circ = \Delta_c H^\circ$(glucose) – 2 × $\Delta_c H^\circ$(ethanol) ***[1 mark]***
$\Delta_f H^\circ$ = [–2820] – [(2 × –1367)]
$\Delta_f H^\circ$ = **–86 kJ mol⁻¹** ***[1 mark]***

3 $\Delta_f H^\circ$ = sum of $\Delta_c H^\circ$(reactants) – $\Delta_c H^\circ$(propane) ***[1 mark]***
$\Delta_f H^\circ$ = [(3 × –394) + (4 × –286)] – [–2220]
$\Delta_f H^\circ$ = **–106 kJ mol⁻¹** ***[1 mark]***

4 Total energy required to break bonds = (4 × 435) + (2 × 498) = 2736 kJ
Energy released when bonds form = (2 × 805) + (4 × 464) = 3466 kJ ***[1 mark]***
Net energy change = 2736 + (–3466) = **–730 kJ mol⁻¹** ***[1 mark]***

Page 73 — The Atmosphere

1 a) i) Wavelength in m = 255 × 10⁻⁹ = 2.55 × 10⁻⁷ m.
$$\nu = \frac{c}{\lambda} = \frac{3.00\times10^{8}}{2.55\times10^{-7}} = \mathbf{1.18\times10^{15}\ Hz}$$ ***[1 mark]***
ii) $$E = \frac{hc}{\lambda} = \frac{6.63\times10^{-34}\times3.00\times10^{8}}{2.55\times10^{-7}} = \mathbf{7.80\times10^{-19}\ J}$$ ***[1 mark]***
b) 0.21 ppm ***[1 mark]***

2 $E = h\nu$ = 6.63 × 10⁻³⁴ × 1.80 × 10¹⁵ = **1.19 × 10⁻¹⁸ J** ***[1 mark]***

Topic 5 — Kinetics, Equilibria and Redox Reactions

Page 75 — Reaction Rates

1 Increasing the pressure will increase the rate of reaction ***[1 mark]*** because the molecules will be closer together, so they will collide more frequently and therefore are more likely to react ***[1 mark]***.

2 a) X ***[1 mark]***
The X curve shows the same total number of molecules as the 25 °C curve, but more of them have lower energy.
b) The shape of the curve shows fewer molecules have the required activation energy ***[1 mark]***.

Page 77 — Catalysts

1 a) A ***[1 mark]***
A catalyst only lowers activation energy. It doesn't affect the enthalpy change.
b) The vanadium(V) oxide catalyst is heterogenous because it's in a different physical state to the reactants ***[1 mark]***.

Page 80 — Calculating Reaction Rates

1 a) E.g.

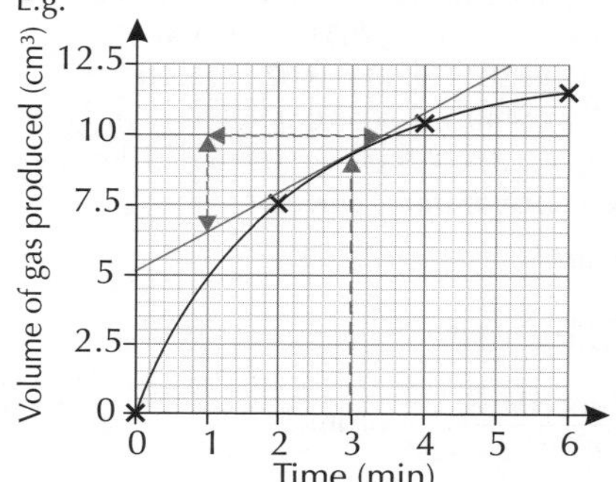

[1 mark for tangent drawn at 3 mins]
rate of reaction = gradient of tangent at 3 mins
gradient = change in y ÷ change in x
e.g. = (10.00 – 6.50) ÷ (3.40 – 1.00)
= **1.46 (± 0.3) cm³ min⁻¹**
[1 mark for answer within margin of error. 1 mark for units.]
Different people will draw slightly different tangents and pick different spots on the tangent so there's a margin of error in this answer.
1.45 (± 0.3) cm³ min⁻¹ means any answer between 1.15 cm³ min⁻¹ and 1.75 cm³ min⁻¹ is worth the mark.
b) E.g. the volume of gas produced could be measured using a gas syringe ***[1 mark]***.
c) One of the reactants is a gas ***[1 mark]***.

Page 83 — Reversible Reactions

1 a) If a reaction at equilibrium is subjected to a change in concentration, pressure or temperature, the position of equilibrium will move to counteract the change ***[1 mark]***.
You could well be asked to give definitions of things like this in an exam, so make sure you learn them — they're relatively easy marks.
b) i) There are the same number of molecules/moles on each side of the equation, so the position of equilibrium will not move ***[1 mark]***.
ii) The reverse reaction is exothermic so the position of equilibrium will shift to the left to increase the temperature ***[1 mark]***.
iii) The position of equilibrium will shift to the right to increase the concentration of nitrogen monoxide ***[1 mark]***.
c) No effect ***[1 mark]***.
Catalysts don't affect the equilibrium position.
They just help the reaction to get there sooner.

Answers

2 a) The forward reaction is exothermic ***[1 mark]***. If you decrease the temperature, the position of equilibrium will move to the right/ the forward reaction will speed up in order to produce heat ***[1 mark]***.

b) i) Increasing pressure increases the yield of ammonia ***[1 mark]***. There are fewer moles of gas on the right hand side of the equation so equilibrium is shifted to the right ***[1 mark]***.

ii) E.g. producing a high pressure is expensive. / The equipment needed to produce a high pressure is expensive. / The cost of producing the extra pressure is greater than the value of the extra yield ***[1 mark]***.

Page 85 — The Equilibrium Constant

1 $K_c = \frac{[H_2][I_2]}{[HI]^2}$ ***[1 mark]***

At equilibrium, $[H_2] = [I_2]$ ***[1 mark]***

$[HI]^2 = \frac{[H_2][I_2]}{K_c} = \frac{0.770 \times 0.770}{0.0200} = 29.6$ ***[1 mark]***

$[HI] = \sqrt{29.6} =$ **5.44 mol dm⁻³** ***[1 mark]***

2 a) i) mass ÷ M_r = 34.5 ÷ [14.0 + (2 × 16.0)] = 34.5 ÷ 46.0 = **0.750 mol** ***[1 mark]***

ii) moles of O_2 = mass ÷ M_r = 7.04 ÷ (2 × 16.0) = **0.220** ***[1 mark]***

moles of NO = 2 × moles of O_2 = 2 × 0.220 = **0.440** ***[1 mark]***

moles of NO_2 = 0.750 – 0.440 = **0.310** ***[1 mark]***

b) Concentration of O_2 = 0.220 ÷ 9.80 = 0.0224 mol dm^{-3}

Concentration of NO = 0.440 ÷ 9.80 = 0.0449 mol dm^{-3}

Concentration of NO_2 = 0.310 ÷ 9.80 = 0.0316 mol dm^{-3}

[1 mark for all three concentrations correct]

$K_c = \frac{[NO]^2[O_2]}{[NO_2]^2}$ ***[1 mark]***

$= \frac{0.0449^2 \times 0.0224}{0.0316^2} = 0.0452$

Units $= \frac{\cancel{[mol\,dm^{-3}]^2}[mol\,dm^{-3}]}{\cancel{[mol\,dm^{-3}]^2}} = mol\,dm^{-3}$

So K_c = **0.0452 mol dm⁻³**

[1 mark for the correct value of K_c, 1 mark for units]

Page 87 — Oxidation Numbers

1 SO_4^{2-} contains sulfur and oxygen so it's a sulfate.
It has an overall charge of –2.
Total charge from the SO_4^{2-} ions = 3 × –2 = –6.
For the overall charge to be 0, the total charge from chromium ions = +6. 6 ÷ 2 = +3.
So the systematic name is **chromium(III) sulfate** ***[1 mark]***.

2 Oxidation number of iron = +2. Charge of nitrate = –1.
You will need a ratio of 1 : 2 of iron : nitrate to make the compound neutral. So the formula is **$Fe(NO_3)_2$** ***[1 mark]***.

3 a) Since lead oxide and sulfuric acid react in a ratio of 1:1, the formula for lead sulfate must be **$PbSO_4$** ***[1 mark]***.

b) i) Oxygen has an oxidation number of –2, so lead must be **+2** ***[1 mark]***.

ii) Sulfate has a charge of –2, so lead must have an oxidation number of **+2** ***[1 mark]***.

Page 89 — Redox Reactions

1 D ***[1 mark]***

2 a) When metals and acids react, they produce hydrogen and a salt.
$Fe_{(s)} + H_2SO_{4(aq)} \rightarrow FeSO_{4(aq)} + H_{2(g)}$ ***[1 mark]***

b) Hydrogen has been reduced from oxidation number +1 to 0.
Hydrogen is the oxidising agent.
Iron has been oxidised from oxidation number 0 to +2.
Iron is the reducing agent ***[1 mark]***.

3 At the start of the reaction, Al has an oxidation number of 0.
In AlI_3, each I ion has an oxidation number of –1. Therefore, Al has an oxidation number of +3 (since (–1 × 3) + 3 = 0).
Al has lost electrons, so it has been oxidised ***[1 mark]***.

4 a) An oxidising agent accepts electrons ***[1 mark]***.

b) $In \rightarrow In^{3+} + 3e^-$ ***[1 mark]***

c) $2In + 3Cl_2 \rightarrow 2InCl_3$ ***[2 marks — 1 mark for correct reactants and products, 1 mark for correct balancing.]***

Topic 6 — Group 2 and Group 7 Elements

Page 91 — Periodicity

1 Magnesium ions have a 2+ charge whereas sodium ions only have a 1+ charge ***[1 mark]***. Magnesium also has more delocalised electrons as sodium ***[1 mark]***. So the metal-metal bonds are stronger in magnesium than in sodium and more energy is needed to break them ***[1 mark]***.

2 a) Si has a giant covalent structure ***[1 mark]*** consisting of very strong covalent bonds ***[1 mark]***.

b) Sulfur (S_8) molecules are larger than phosphorus (P_4) molecules ***[1 mark]***, which results in stronger induced dipole-dipole forces between molecules ***[1 mark]***.

3 The atomic radius decreases across the period from left to right ***[1 mark]***. The number of protons increases, so nuclear charge increases ***[1 mark]***. Electrons are pulled closer to the nucleus ***[1 mark]***.

Page 93 — Group 2 — The Alkaline Earth Metals

1 a) $2Ba_{(s)} + O_{2(g)} \rightarrow 2BaO_{(s)}$ ***[1 mark]***

b) From 0 to +2 ***[1 mark]***

c) Strongly alkaline / pH 12-13 ***[1 mark]***

2 a) Z ***[1 mark]***

b) Z has the largest radius ***[1 mark]*** so it will be furthest down the group / have the smallest ionisation energy ***[1 mark]***.

Page 95 — Uses of the Group 2 Elements

1 Add acidified barium chloride solution to both.
Zinc chloride would not change/no reaction.
Zinc sulfate solution would give a white precipitate ***[1 mark]***.
$BaCl_{2(aq)} + ZnSO_{4(aq)} \rightarrow BaSO_{4(s)} + ZnCl_{2(aq)}$
OR $Ba^{2+}_{(aq)} + SO_4^{2-}{}_{(aq)} \rightarrow BaSO_{4(s)}$ ***[1 mark]***

2 a) D ***[1 mark]***

b) B ***[1 mark]***

c) A ***[1 mark]***

3 Patients can swallow a suspension of barium sulfate which will coat the tissues of the digestive system ***[1 mark]***. This will make them show up on the X-rays so any problems can be diagnosed ***[1 mark]***.

Page 97 — Group 1 and 2 Compounds

1 a) Energy is absorbed and electrons move to higher energy levels. ***[1 mark]*** Energy is released in the form of coloured light when the electrons fall back to the lower levels ***[1 mark]***.

b) caesium ***[1 mark]***

2 a) $CaCO_{3(s)} \rightarrow CaO_{(s)} + CO_{2(g)}$
[1 mark for correct equation, and 1 mark for state symbols]

b) Barium carbonate is more thermally stable ***[1 mark]***. This is because barium is larger than calcium/has a lower charge density than calcium, so it has weaker polarising power ***[1 mark]***. The weaker polarising power of the barium ion causes less distortion of the carbonate ion ***[1 mark]*** (making it more thermally stable).
You'd also get the marks if you used the reverse argument to explain why $CaCO_3$ is less thermally stable.

Answers

3 a) $2NaNO_{3(s)} \rightarrow 2NaNO_{2(s)} + O_{2(g)}$ ***[1 mark]***
b) E.g. O_2 gas relights a glowing splint ***[1 mark]***.
c) magnesium nitrate, sodium nitrate, potassium nitrate ***[1 mark]***
Group 2 nitrates decompose more easily than Group 1 as they have a +2 charge on their cations, compared to the 1+ charge on Group 1 cations. The greater the charge on the cation, the less stable the nitrate anion ***[1 mark]***. The further down the group, the more stable the nitrate as the cations increase in size down the group, and the larger the cation, the less distortion to the nitrate anion ***[1 mark]***.

Page 99 — Group 7 — The Halogens

1 a) $I_2 + 2At^- \rightarrow 2I^- + At_2$ ***[1 mark]***
b) The astatide ***[1 mark]***
2 a) i) Boiling point increases down the group ***[1 mark]*** because the size and relative mass of the molecules increases ***[1 mark]***, so the induced dipole-dipole forces holding the molecules together get stronger ***[1 mark]***.
ii) Electronegativity decreases down the group ***[1 mark]*** because the atoms get larger ***[1 mark]***, and the shielding effect of the inner electrons increases ***[1 mark]***.
b) Fluorine ***[1 mark]***
3 a) $Cl_2 + H_2O \rightarrow 2H^+ + Cl^- + ClO^-$ ***[1 mark]***
b) Chlorine (or the chlorate(I) ions) kill bacteria ***[1 mark]***.
Too much chlorine would be dangerous as it's toxic ***[1 mark]***.

Page 101 — Halide Ions

1 First, separately dissolve each solid in water ***[1 mark]***.
Add dilute nitric acid each solution. Then add a few drops of aqueous $AgNO_3$ ***[1 mark]***. With sodium chloride, the silver nitrate gives white precipitate ***[1 mark]*** which dissolves in dilute ammonia solution ***[1 mark]***. With sodium bromide, the silver nitrate gives cream precipitate ***[1 mark]*** which is only soluble in concentrated ammonia solution ***[1 mark]***.
2 a) C ***[1 mark]***
b) AgAt would not dissolve ***[1 mark]***. E.g. AgI is insoluble in concentrated ammonia solution and the solubility of halides in ammonia solution decreases down the group ***[1 mark]***.
Question 2 is the kind of question that could throw you if you're not really clued up on the facts. If you really know page 100, then in part a) you'll go, "Ah - ha! Reactions of halides with H_2SO_4 — reducing power increases down the group..." If not, you basically won't have a clue. The moral is, it really is just about learning all the facts. Boring, but true.

Page 103 — Hydrogen Halides

1 C ***[1 mark]***
2 a) The solution would turn red/pink ***[1 mark]*** because hydrogen bromide solution is strongly acidic ***[1 mark]***.
b) $2HBr + H_2SO_4 \rightarrow Br_2 + SO_2 + 2H_2O$
[1 mark for all reactants and products correct, 1 mark for equation being correctly balanced]
3 Sodium bromide will reduce sulfuric acid, where the oxidation state of sulfur is +6, to sulfur dioxide, where the oxidation state of sulfur is +4 ***[1 mark]***:
$2NaBr + 2H_2SO_4 \rightarrow Na_2SO_4 + Br_2 + SO_2 + H_2O$ ***[1 mark]***.
Iodide ions are a stronger reducing agent than bromide ions, so will reduce sulfuric acid, where the oxidation state of sulfur is +6, to hydrogen sulfide, where the oxidation state of sulfur is −2 ***[1 mark]***: $8NaI + 5H_2SO_4 \rightarrow 4Na_2SO_4 + 4I_2 + H_2S + 4H_2O$ ***[1 mark]***

Page 105 — Tests for Ions

1 D ***[1 mark]***
2 $BaCO_3$ ***[2 marks — 1 mark for correct cation, 1 mark for correct anion]***
3 Add a few drops of sodium hydroxide to a sample of the solution. Warm the mixture and test any gas that is given off using damp red litmus paper ***[1 mark]***. If the solution contained ammonium ions, the litmus paper will turn blue ***[1 mark]***. Take another sample of the solution and add dilute hydrochloric acid followed by barium chloride solution ***[1 mark]***. If the solution contained sulfate ions, a white precipitate will form ***[1 mark]***.

Topic 7 — Electrolysis

Page 107 — Electrolysis

1 a) At the anode, you would see bubbles of gas appearing ***[1 mark]*** because chloride ions are losing electrons to form chlorine ***[1 mark]***.
b) At the cathode, you would see the electrode being plated ***[1 mark]*** because copper ions are gaining electrons to form copper metal ***[1 mark]***.
2 a) $2H^+_{(aq)} + 2e^- \rightarrow H_{2(g)}$ ***[1 mark]***
b) $4OH^-_{(aq)} \rightarrow O_{2(g)} + H_2O_{(l)} + 4e^-$ ***[1 mark]***

Page 109 — Production of Halogens

1 a) rock salt / sea water / brine ***[1 mark]***
b) The universal indicator would turn the solution blue/purple ***[1 mark]***. The solution would be alkaline, because of the hydroxide ions left in solution ***[1 mark]***.
c) The universal indicator would turn the solution green ***[1 mark]***, because hydrogen ions and hydroxide ions have been discharged, leaving a neutral solution of NaCl ***[1 mark]***.
d) Chlorine is more reactive than iodine ***[1 mark]***.

Topic 8 — Introduction to Organic Chemistry

Page 115 — Isomerism

1 a) 1-chlorobutane, 2-chlorobutane, 1-chloro-2-methylpropane, 2-chloro-2-methylpropane ***[1 mark for each correct isomer]***
b) 1-chloro-2-methylpropane and 2-chloro-2-methylpropane OR 1-chlorobutane and 2-chlorobutane ***[1 mark]***
c) 1-chlorobutane and 1-chloro-2-methylpropane OR 2-chlorobutane and 2-chloro-2-methylpropane ***[1 mark]***
2 a) Br, H / C=C / H, CH_3

E-1-bromopropene ***[1 mark]***

b) H, Br / C=C / H, CH_3 H, CH_2Br / C=C / H, H

2-bromopropene ***[1 mark]*** 3-bromopropene ***[1 mark]***

If one of the C=C carbons has the same two groups attached, then the alkene won't have E/Z isomers.

Answers

3 a) 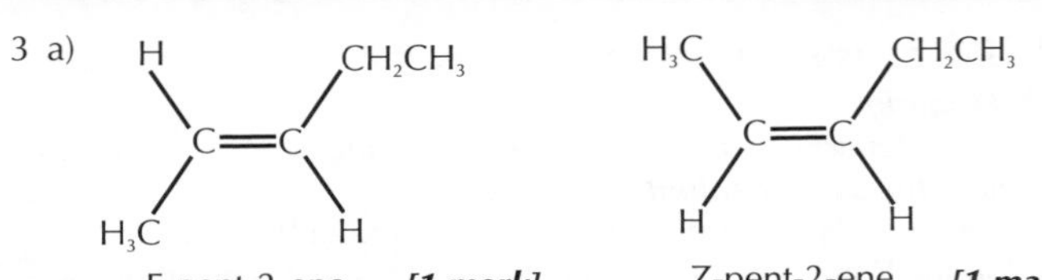

E-pent-2-ene ***[1 mark]*** Z-pent-2-ene ***[1 mark]***

b) E/Z isomers occur because atoms can't rotate about C=C double bonds ***[1 mark]***. Alkenes contain C=C double bonds and alkanes don't, so alkenes can form E/Z isomers and alkanes can't ***[1 mark]***.

Topic 9 — Alkanes and Halogenoalkanes

Page 117 — Alkanes

1 a) One with no double bonds OR all the carbon-carbon bonds are single bonds ***[1 mark]***. It contains only hydrogen and carbon atoms ***[1 mark]***.

b) i) 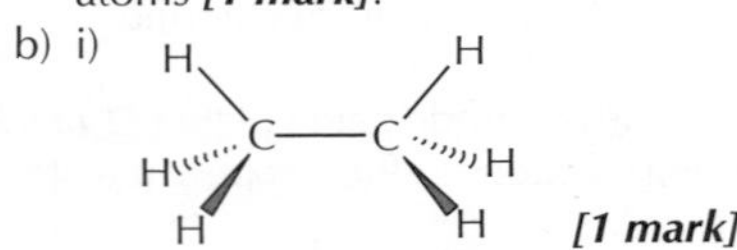

[1 mark]

ii) 109.5° ***[1 mark]***

2 a) Nonane will have a higher boiling point than 2,2,3,3-tetramethylpentane ***[1 mark]*** because the molecules of branched-chain alkanes like 2,2,3,3-tetramethylpentane are less closely packed together than their straight-chain isomers, so they have fewer induced dipole-dipole interactions holding them together ***[1 mark]***.

b) $C_9H_{20} + 9\frac{1}{2}O_2 \rightarrow 9CO + 10H_2O$ ***[1 mark]***
So, $25C_9H_{20} + (25 \times 9\frac{1}{2})O_2 \rightarrow (25 \times 9)CO + (25 \times 10)H_2O$
Volume of CO produced = 25 × 9 = **225 cm³** ***[1 mark]***

Page 119 — Reactions of Alkanes

1 a) Free radical substitution. ***[1 mark]***

b) $CH_4 + Br_2 \xrightarrow{U.V.} CH_3Br + HBr$ ***[1 mark]***

c) $Br\bullet + CH_4 \rightarrow HBr + \bullet CH_3$ ***[1 mark]***
$\bullet CH_3 + Br_2 \rightarrow CH_3Br + Br\bullet$ ***[1 mark]***

d) i) Two methyl radicals bond together to form an ethane molecule. ***[1 mark]***

ii) Termination step ***[1 mark]***

iii) $\bullet CH_3 + \bullet CH_3 \rightarrow CH_3CH_3$ ***[1 mark]***

e) Tetrabromomethane ***[1 mark]***

Page 121 — Crude Oil

1 a) i) E.g. There's greater demand for smaller fractions for things such as motor fuels ***[1 mark]*** / There's greater demand for alkenes to make petrochemicals/polymers ***[1 mark]***.

ii) E.g. $C_{12}H_{26} \rightarrow C_2H_4 + C_{10}H_{22}$ ***[1 mark]***.
There are loads of possible answers — just make sure the C's and H's balance and there's an alkane and an alkene.

b) i) Any two from: Cycloalkanes / arenes/aromatic hydrocarbons / branched alkanes ***[2 marks — 1 mark for each]***

ii) They promote efficient combustion/reduce knocking (autoignition) ***[1 mark]***.

Page 124 — Alkanes and Fuels

1 a) $C_7H_{16} + 11O_2 \rightarrow 7CO_2 + 8H_2O$ ***[1 mark]***

b) i) carbon monoxide ***[1 mark]***

ii) By fitting a catalytic converter ***[1 mark]***.

2 a) The high pressures and temperatures in the engine of a car ***[1 mark]*** cause nitrogen and oxygen from the air to react together ***[1 mark]***.

b) Powdered calcium carbonate is mixed with water to make an alkaline slurry ***[1 mark]***. When the flue gases mix with the alkaline slurry, the acidic sulfur dioxide gas reacts with the calcium carbonate to form a salt/calcium sulfate ***[1 mark]***.

3 a) E.g. Continued use of fossil fuels means increasing amounts of carbon dioxide being emitted, which could lead to problems with climate change ***[1 mark]***. Fossil fuels are also non-renewable, and so they will eventually run out, leading to problems if we do not have alternatives ***[1 mark]***.

b) i) Advantage — e.g. wind power does not emit carbon dioxide into the atmosphere ***[1 mark]*** (although CO_2 will be emitted during the manufacture of wind turbines). Disadvantage — e.g. wind power is not completely reliable ***[1 mark]***.

ii) Advantage — e.g. hydrogen is a 'clean' fuel whose only waste product is water ***[1 mark]***. Disadvantage — e.g. it takes energy to extract hydrogen from seawater ***[1 mark]***.

Page 127 — Halogenoalkanes

1 a) Reaction 1:
Reagent — NaOH/KOH ***[1 mark]***
Solvent — Water/aqueous solution ***[1 mark]***
Reaction 2:
Reagent — Ammonia/NH_3 ***[1 mark]***
Solvent — Ethanol/alcohol ***[1 mark]***
Reaction 3:
Reagent — NaOH/KOH ***[1 mark]***
Solvent — Ethanol/alcohol ***[1 mark]***

b) The reaction would be faster ***[1 mark]*** because the C–I bond is weaker than C–Br/C–I bond enthalpy is lower ***[1 mark]***.

Page 129 — Halogenoalkanes and the Environment

1 a) Any two from: stable/volatile/non-flammable/non-toxic ***[1 mark]***.

b) $CFCl_{3(g)} \xrightarrow{U.V.} \bullet CFCl_{2(g)} + Cl\bullet_{(g)}$ ***[1 mark]***
$Cl\bullet_{(g)} + O_{3(g)} \rightarrow O_{2(g)} + ClO\bullet_{(g)}$ and
$ClO\bullet_{(g)} + O_{(g)} \rightarrow O_{2(g)} + Cl\bullet_{(g)}$ ***[1 mark]***
Overall reaction: $O_{3(g)} + O_{(g)} \rightarrow 2O_{2(g)}$ ***[1 mark]***

c) NO• free radicals ***[1 mark]***

2 $NO\bullet + O_3 \rightarrow NO_2 + O_2$ ***[1 mark]***
$NO_2 + O \rightarrow NO\bullet + O_2$ ***[1 mark]***

Topic 10 — Alkenes and Alcohols

Page 131 — Alkenes

1 D ***[1 mark]***

2 a) Ethane is an alkane, so has a single C–C bond made up of a σ bond ***[1 mark]***. Ethene is an alkene, so has a C=C double bond made up of a σ bond and a π bond ***[1 mark]***.

b) Ethene will be more reactive than ethane because the double bond has a high electron density / the π bond sticks out above and below the plane of the molecule, so it attracts electrophiles ***[1 mark]*** and because the π bond has a low bond enthalpy so is more easily broken than the C–C σ bond in ethane ***[1 mark]***.

3 a) E.g. Both bonds form when two atomic orbitals overlap / when the nuclei of two atoms form electrostatic attractions to a bonding pair of electrons ***[1 mark]***.

b) E.g. σ-bonds form when two atomic orbitals overlap directly between two nuclei, whereas π-bonds form when both lobes of two p-orbitals overlap side-on / in σ-bonds, the electron density lies directly between the two nuclei, whereas in π-bonds, the electron density lies above and below the molecular axis / σ-bonds have a higher bond enthalpy than π-bonds ***[1 mark]***.

Page 134 — More on Alkenes

1 a) Shake the alkene with bromine water ***[1 mark]***. The solution goes from orange to colourless if a double bond is present ***[1 mark]***.

b) Electrophilic addition ***[1 mark]***

Answers

c) i)

```
H         CH2CH3        H  CH2CH3              H  CH2CH3
  \      /              |  |                   |  |
   C=C        ──►   H—C—C—H      ──►      H—C—C—H
  /  δ+ \               |  +                   |  |
H    H    H             H   :Br⁻               H  Br
     |
     Brδ-                                  2-bromobutane
```

[1 mark for each correct curly arrow and 1 mark for the product being correctly named.]

Check that your curly arrows are exactly right, or you'll lose marks. They have to go from exactly where the electrons are from, to where they're going to.

ii) The secondary carbocation OR the carbocation with the most attached alkyl groups ***[1 mark]*** is the most stable intermediate and so is the most likely to form ***[1 mark]***.

2 A ***[1 mark]***

Page 137 — Addition Polymers

1 a)

```
H       H
 \     /
  C=C
 /     \
H       CH3
```
[1 mark]

b)

```
     H   H
     |   |
 —— C — C ——
     |   |
     H   CH3
```
[1 mark]

2 a)

```
     H   H
     |   |
 —— C — C ——
     |   |
     H   Cl
```
[1 mark]

b) When you add a plasticiser, PVC becomes more flexible ***[1 mark]***. This is because the plasticisers get between the polymer chains and push them apart ***[1 mark]***. This reduces the strength of the intermolecular forces between the chains, so they can slide over each other more easily ***[1 mark]***.

c) Any two from: e.g. electrical cable insulation / flooring tiles / clothing ***[1 mark for each]***.

3 a) E.g. Saves on landfill / Energy can be used to generate electricity ***[1 mark]***.

b) E.g. Toxic gases produced ***[1 mark]***. Scrubbers can be used to remove these toxic gases / polymers that might burn to produce toxic gases can be separated out before incineration ***[1 mark]***.

Page 139 — Alcohols

1 a) primary ***[1 mark]***

b) tertiary ***[1 mark]***

c) secondary ***[1 mark]***

2 a) primary: e.g.

```
   H  H  H  H  H
   |  |  |  |  |
H—C—C—C—C—C—OH
   |  |  |  |  |
   H  H  H  H  H
```
pentan-1-ol ***[1 mark]***

secondary: e.g

```
   H  H  H  H   H
   |  |  |  |   |
H—C—C—C—C—C—H
   |  |  |  |   |
   H  H  H  OH H
```
pentan-2-ol ***[1 mark]***

tertiary:

```
          H
          |
        H—C—H
   H  H   |   H
   |  |   |   |
H—C—C—C—C—H
   |  |   |   |
   H  H  OH  H
```
2-methylbutan-2-ol ***[1 mark]***

b) React ethanol with sodium bromide (NaBr) with a concentrated sulfuric acid catalyst ***[1 mark]***.

3 a) Ethanol contains a polar -OH group which is able to form hydrogen bonds with water molecules ***[1 mark]***. Because ethanol is a small alcohol, it can mix freely so is soluble in water ***[1 mark]***.

b) Yes. Ethanol molecules can form hydrogen bonds with each other ***[1 mark]***. Hydrogen bonding is the strongest type of intermolecular force, so it gives alcohols a low volatility compared to non-polar compounds, e.g. alkanes. So, ethanol will have a lower volatility, and therefore boiling point, than ethane ***[1 mark]***.

Page 141 — Ethanol Production

1 a) $C_6H_{12}O_{6(aq)} \rightarrow 2C_2H_5OH_{(aq)} + 2CO_{2(g)}$ ***[1 mark]***

b) In the presence of yeast ***[1 mark]***, at a temperature of between 30 and 40 °C ***[1 mark]***, anaerobic conditions / air/oxygen excluded ***[1 mark]***.

c) Fractional distillation ***[1 mark]***

2 a) E.g. as they grow, the plants used to produce bioethanol take in the same amount of carbon dioxide as burning the fuel you produce from them gives out ***[1 mark]***.

b) E.g. fossil fuels will need to be burned to power the machinery used to make fertilisers for the crops / harvest the crops / refine and transport the bioethanol ***[1 mark]***. Burning the fuel to power this machinery produces carbon dioxide ***[1 mark]***.

Page 143 — Oxidation of Alcohols

1 a) i) Acidified potassium dichromate(VI) ***[1 mark]***

ii)

```
          H
     H    |
 H    \   C=O
  \    C /
   C  /  \
  / \     H
 H   H
```
[1 mark]

b) i) Warm with Fehling's/Benedict's solution: turns from blue to brick-red ***[1 mark]***. OR warm with Tollens' reagent: a silver mirror is produced ***[1 mark]***.

ii) Propanoic acid ***[1 mark]***

iii) $CH_3CH_2CH_2OH + [O] \rightarrow CH_3CH_2CHO + H_2O$ ***[1 mark]***
$CH_3CH_2CHO + [O] \rightarrow CH_3CH_2COOH$ ***[1 mark]***

iv) Distillation ***[1 mark]***

c) i) (skeletal formula) OH ***[1 mark]***

ii) 2-methylpropan-2-ol is a tertiary alcohol ***[1 mark]***.

Page 144 — More Reactions of Alcohols

1 a) Elimination reaction OR dehydration reaction ***[1 mark]***.

b) B ***[1 mark]***

Page 145 — Phenols

1

	phenol	ethanoic acid	salicylic acid
neutral iron(III) chloride solution	purple colour	no colour change	purple colour
sodium carbonate solution	no reaction	gas evolved	gas evolved

[1 mark each for correct results for phenol, ethanoic acid and salicylic acid]

Answers

Topic 11 — Organic Analysis

Page 148 — Tests for Functional Groups

1 D ***[1 mark]***
Propanone is a ketone and so nothing happens when it is warmed with Fehling's solution.

2 B ***[1 mark]***
Cyclohexene is an alkene so it decolourises bromine water.

3 E.g. put a sample of the solution that you want to test in a test tube and add some sodium carbonate ***[1 mark]***. If the solution is a carboxylic acid, the mixture will fizz ***[1 mark]***. If you collect the gas produced and bubble it through limewater, the limewater should turn cloudy ***[1 mark]***.

4 E.g. add excess alcohol to acidified potassium dichromate solution ***[1 mark]*** in a round bottomed flask. Set up the flask as part of distillation apparatus, gently heat it and collect the product ***[1 mark]***. Place some Fehling's solution/Benedict's solution/ Tollens' reagent in a test tube and add a few drops of the product ***[1 mark]***. Put the test tube in a hot water bath to warm it for a few minutes ***[1 mark]***. If the blue solution gives a brick red precipitate/if a silver mirror forms on the inside of the tube, the alcohol was a primary alcohol. If there is no change, the alcohol was a secondary alcohol ***[1 mark for a correct observation that matches the reagent used]***.

Page 151 — Analytical Techniques

1 a) A: O–H group in a carboxylic acid ***[1 mark]***.
B: C=O as in an aldehyde, ketone, carboxylic acid or ester ***[1 mark]***.

b) From the percentage composition data, the ratio of elements in the compound, C:H:O is 3:6:2 ***[1 mark]*** so the empirical formula is $C_3H_6O_2$ ***[1 mark]***. The spectrum suggests that the compound is a carboxylic acid, so it must be propanoic acid (CH_3CH_2COOH) ***[1 mark]***.
If you're not sure how you'd go about finding the empirical formula of a compound from its percentage composition, have a read of page 43 and have a go at the exam questions there.

2 a) 44 ***[1 mark]***

b) X has a mass of 15. It is probably a methyl group/CH_3^+ ***[1 mark]***.
Y has a mass of 29. It is probably an ethyl group/$C_2H_5^+$ ***[1 mark]***.

c)

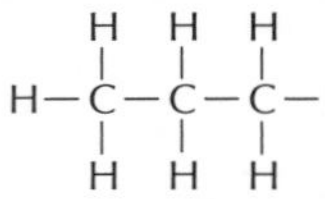

```
   H  H  H
   |  |  |
H—C—C—C—H
   |  |  |
   H  H  H
```

[1 mark]

d) If the compound was an alcohol, you would expect a peak with *m/z* ratio of 17, caused by the OH fragment ***[1 mark]***.

Page 153 — Thin Layer Chromatography

1 a) Substances 1, 2, 3, 4 and X are pure. Substance Y is impure ***[1 mark]***.

b) 1 and 2 ***[1 mark]*** since the spots present in mixture Y are at the same height (and so would have the same R_f values) as 1 and 2 ***[1 mark]***.

c) R_f = spot distance ÷ solvent distance
= 5.6 ÷ 8 = **0.7** ***[1 mark]***
There are no units as it's a ratio.

d) A fluorescent dye could have been added to the TLC plate and then a UV light shone on it to reveal the spots ***[1 mark]***. Or the spots could have been exposed to iodine vapour ***[1 mark]***.

Topic 12 — Organic Synthesis

Page 155 — Practical Skills

1 a) i) Reflux is continuous boiling/evaporation and condensation ***[1 mark]***. It's done to prevent loss of volatile liquids while heating ***[1 mark]***.

ii) Unreacted hexan-1-ol ***[1 mark]***

iii) Pour the reaction mixture into a separating funnel and add water ***[1 mark]***. Shake the funnel and allow the layers to settle. The lower layer is the denser aqueous layer and contains water soluble impurities ***[1 mark]***. This can be run off, so only the organic layer, containing the product and other organic impurities, remains ***[1 mark]***.

b) i) The alkene product may dehydrate again to form a diene ***[1 mark]***.

ii) Carry out the experiment in a distillation apparatus ***[1 mark]*** so the singly dehydrated product is removed immediately from the reaction mixture and doesn't react a second time ***[1 mark]***.

Page 157 — More Practical Skills

1 a) Dissolve the solid product in a minimal amount of hot solvent ***[1 mark]***. Leave the saturated solution to cool slowly and filter to remove the crystals of pure product ***[1 mark]***. Wash the crystals in cold solvent, and then dry them ***[1 mark]***.

b) An appropriate solvent would be one which sodium ethanoate is very soluble in when it's hot and nearly insoluble in when it's cold ***[1 mark]***.

c) The melting point range of the impure product is lower and broader than that of the pure product ***[1 mark]***.

2 B ***[1 mark]***

Page 159 — Organic Synthesis — Synthetic Routes

1 a)

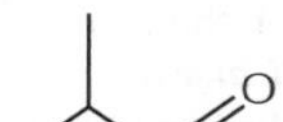

O

[1 mark]

b) E.g. Excess concentrated sulfuric acid (H_2SO_4) ***[1 mark]***, 170 °C, reflux ***[1 mark]***.

c) i)

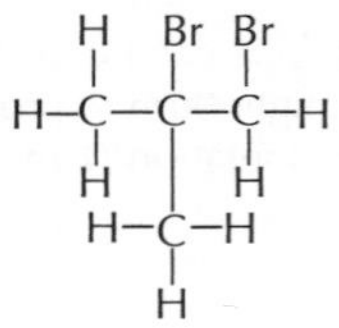

```
   H  Br Br
   |  |  |
H—C—C—C—H
   |  |  |
   H  |  H
   H—C—H
      |
      H
```

[1 mark]

ii) The mixture would turn from orange/brown to colourless ***[1 mark]***.

2

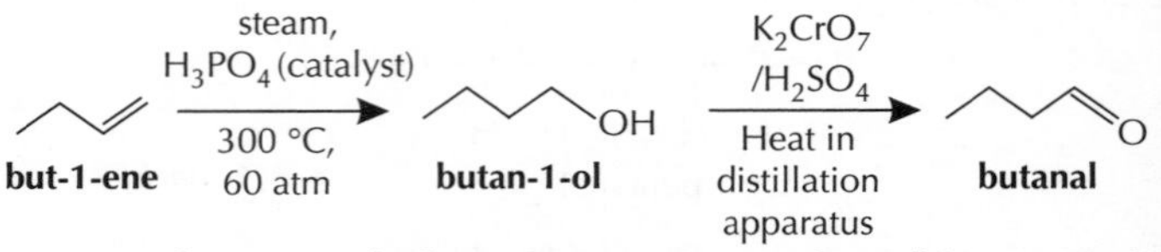

but-1-ene —(steam, H_3PO_4 (catalyst), 300 °C, 60 atm)→ **butan-1-ol** (OH) —(K_2CrO_7 /H_2SO_4, Heat in distillation apparatus)→ **butanal** (O)

[3 marks — 2 marks for correct reagents and conditions, 1 mark for intermediate butan-1-ol product.]

Index

Index

Index

The Periodic Table

Relative Atomic Mass →
Atomic number →

(1)	(2)											(3)	(4)	(5)	(6)	(7)	(0)
							1.0 H Hydrogen 1										4.0 He Helium 2
6.9 Li Lithium 3	9.0 Be Beryllium 4											10.8 B Boron 5	12.0 C Carbon 6	14.0 N Nitrogen 7	16.0 O Oxygen 8	19.0 F Fluorine 9	20.2 Ne Neon 10
23.0 Na Sodium 11	24.3 Mg Magnesium 12											27.0 Al Aluminium 13	28.1 Si Silicon 14	31.0 P Phosphorus 15	32.1 S Sulfur 16	35.5 Cl Chlorine 17	39.9 Ar Argon 18
39.1 K Potassium 19	40.1 Ca Calcium 20	45.0 Sc Scandium 21	47.9 Ti Titanium 22	50.9 V Vanadium 23	52.0 Cr Chromium 24	54.9 Mn Manganese 25	55.8 Fe Iron 26	58.9 Co Cobalt 27	58.7 Ni Nickel 28	63.5 Cu Copper 29	65.4 Zn Zinc 30	69.7 Ga Gallium 31	72.6 Ge Germanium 32	74.9 As Arsenic 33	79.0 Se Selenium 34	79.9 Br Bromine 35	83.8 Kr Krypton 36
85.5 Rb Rubidium 37	87.6 Sr Strontium 38	88.9 Y Yttrium 39	91.2 Zr Zirconium 40	92.9 Nb Niobium 41	95.9 Mo Molybdenum 42	98 Tc Technetium 43	101.1 Ru Ruthenium 44	102.9 Rh Rhodium 45	106.4 Pd Palladium 46	107.9 Ag Silver 47	112.4 Cd Cadmium 48	114.8 In Indium 49	118.7 Sn Tin 50	121.8 Sb Antimony 51	127.6 Te Tellurium 52	126.9 I Iodine 53	131.3 Xe Xenon 54
132.9 Cs Caesium 55	137.3 Ba Barium 56	138.9 La Lanthanum 57	178.5 Hf Hafnium 72	180.9 Ta Tantalum 73	183.9 W Tungsten 74	186.2 Re Rhenium 75	190.2 Os Osmium 76	192.2 Ir Iridium 77	195.1 Pt Platinum 78	197.0 Au Gold 79	200.6 Hg Mercury 80	204.4 Tl Thallium 81	207.2 Pb Lead 82	209.0 Bi Bismuth 83	209 Po Polonium 84	210 At Astatine 85	222 Rn Radon 86
223 Fr Francium 87	226.0 Ra Radium 88	Ac Actinium 89	Rf Rutherfordium 104	Db Dubnium 105	Sg Seaborgium 106	Bh Bohrium 107	Hs Hassium 108	Mt Meitnerium 109	Ds Darmstadtium 110	Rg Roentgenium 111	Cn Copernicum 112		Fl Flerovium 114		Lv Livermorium 116		

The Lanthanides	140.1 Ce Cerium 58	140.9 Pr Praseodymium 59	144.2 Nd Neodymium 60	144.9 Pm Promethium 61	150.4 Sm Samarium 62	152.0 Eu Europium 63	157.2 Gd Gadolinium 64	158.9 Tb Terbium 65	162.5 Dy Dysprosium 66	164.9 Ho Holmium 67	167.3 Er Erbium 68	168.9 Tm Thulium 69	173.0 Yb Ytterbium 70	175.0 Lu Lutetium 71
The Actinides	232.0 Th Thorium 90	Pa Protactinium 91	238.1 U Uranium 92	Np Neptunium 93	Pu Plutonium 94	Am Americium 95	Cm Curium 96	Bk Berkelium 97	Cf Californium 98	Es Einsteinium 99	Fm Fermium 100	Md Mendelevium 101	No Nobelium 102	Lr Lawrencium 103